THE COMPENDIUM OF NUÄR ORIGIN, CULTURE, AND MORAL EVALUATION

2ND EDITION

J. TAB CHAROA

The publisher wishes to acknowledge and thank Dr. Douglas H. Johnson for his invaluable help and support for Africa World Books and its mission ofpreserving and promoting African cultural and literary traditions and history. Dr. Johnson and fellow historians have been instrumental in ensuring that African people remain connected to their past and their identity. Africa World Books is proud to carry on this mission.

ISBN: 9780645819519

Cover design, typesetting and layout: Africa World Books
Unit 3, 57 Frobisher St, Osborne Park, WA 6017
P.O. Box 1106 Osborne Park, WA 6916

DEDICATION

This book entitled "The Compendium of Nuär Origins, Culture, and Moral Evaluation" is dedicated to my dear sister Cuol Charoa. May he continue bless my sister and her children.

TABLE OF CONTENTS

ACKNOWLEDGEMENTS

Primarily, I would like to express my gratitude and thanks to His Eminence Cardinal Stephen Ameyu, the Archbishop of the Catholic Archdiocese of Juba for accepting for the second time to write an imprimatur (approval) for the publication of my book. I thank him sincerely for his willingness and readiness to offer this service. May almighty God accompany him and protect him in the pastoral episcopate in the Archdiocese of Juba.

Furthermore, I would like to express my sincere gratitude to Rev. Professor Guido Oliana for having accepted to write a foreword for my book entitled "Compendium of Nuär Origin, Culture, and Moral Evaluation." I do acknowledge that it is not the first time I asked him to write a foreword for my book. I appreciate his readiness and willingness and I ask God the Father to grant him protection and good health.

From the depth of my heart, I would like to give a vote of thanks and gratitude to the most Rev. Sr. Felicita Humwara Bortel, Sacred Heart Sister (SHS), for her constant encouragement and prayer for me. She persistently challenged me to continue writing more books as a means to serve the people of God both locally and in the world at large. May her constant prayer for me, provide me with good health as I continue with a desire to write books as one way of serving the people of God in our region and beyond. May almighty God give her good health and protection as she continues serving the people of God in her Congregation of the Sacred Heart Sisters.

My humble appreciation and thanks go to Mr Elijah Paulino and Rev. Sr. Dr Janet Kiden from the Congregation of Sisters of the Blessed Virgin Mary, for their acceptance to proofread my book. I appreciate their readiness and willingness and I pray that God may bless each of them while serving at the Catholic University of South Sudan. May God give them good health and wisdom.

My gratitude also goes to Mr Micheal Thilyaŋ, the full-time catechist of the Catholic Diocese of Malakal who entirely cooperates with me in every aspect about valuable information such as the ones of Thi̱a̱ŋ and Laak Nuar migration and reasons for their migration needed for the completion of this book. May God bless him and his family. Furthermore, I would like to express my gratitude and thanks to Mr. Thomas Gatluak who was able to connect me with Mr. Tai Yuo̱l Nyamar Gaaŋ/Tai Yuo̱l Nyamar Gaaŋ.

Furthermore, I would like to thank both Mr. Stephen Duɔth Dɛŋ and Madam Mary Nyaye̱e̱ni̱ Manyäl, the Mother of a twin by the name Nyaruɔ̱t Gatwär, whom I celebrated her puɔ̱th/chose for ritual purification at home, St. Stephen Center Magatëën. Both Mr. Stephen Duɔth Dɛŋ and Madam Mary Nyaye̱e̱ni̱ Manyäl, have provided me with credible information about the Nuär ritual ceremony about twins. The ritual ceremony under chapter ten, article II, about twins, is an interview, which I made with Mr. Stephen Duɔth Dɛ̈ɛ̈ŋ. This is because he who is a twin, went through the steps that I have documented therein when his twin sister by name Nyaböth Dɛ̈ɛ̈ŋ was married to a man called Henry Koaŋ Maliɛth. I pray that God may give him protection and bless his family.

Deep down sincerely, I would like to express my appreciation and gratitude to Mr. Martin Rick Kör who lectured me for five hours about the meaning of Earth-Master/Kuär Muɔ̱ɔ̱n/Leopard Skin. Through his lecture, I have learned many things about the true meaning of Earth-Master/Kuär Muɔ̱ɔ̱n/Leopard Skin such as the origin, the consecration, and the installation of a person to this Holy office. I believe that his information such as the one of Ji̱käny West is reliable because Mr. Martin Rick Kör himself is a Kuär Muɔ̱ɔ̱n/ Earth-Master/ Leopard Skin. May almighty God bless him and bless his entire family.

Furthermore, with great respect and humility, I would also like to express my deepest gratitude to Mr. Peter Lök Char who was able to lecture me on the meaning of Wud Ɣɔ̱ɔ̱k/ Guän Puɔ̱da/Cow-Master. Mr. Peter himself is a Wud Ɣɔ̱ɔ̱k/Guän Puɔ̱da/Cow-Master. His information is reliable because he used to accompany his father when he went on a spiritual mission. He used to carry the instruments for a mission. He said that sometimes, his father used to delegate him to perform spiritual services as a Wud Ɣɔ̱ɔ̱k/Guän Puɔ̱da/ Cow-Master. Hence, apart from his father and himself, he mentioned another man by the name Mr. John Nyaŋ Diɛd Baadɛŋ as a prominent Guän Puɔ̱da/Cow-Master among the Bul Nuär.

Regarding the reliable information, I got from Ji̱käny East; I would like to express my sincere gratitude and appreciation to Mr. Tai Yuo̱l Nyamar Gaaŋ/Tai Yuo̱l Nyamar Gaaŋ for his deep knowledge about myths, and reason for Ji̱käny migration to the Eastern White Nile, led Latjɔ̱r Duäc (Diŋyian). In this regard, I consider him a living encyclopedia among Ji̱käny East. He belongs to a clan call Ciëŋ Nyacuɔl, Ji̱gɔal Gaaŋ (Ciëŋ Wuaŋ). May God bless him and his family too.

My gratitude and appreciation also go to Mr. James Lam from Gaatwär Nuär. He lectured me about Gaatwär Nuär migration to the Eastern White Nile for five hours and a half. He is a Catholic Catechist at the Parish of Ascension, Ayo̱t. Actually; he is stationed at Mogok/ Moy Go̱w. For example, when I used to hear about Buok Kapiɛl, Puɔ̱l Bɔyian, Nuär Mɛr, and Dɛŋ Le̱e̱ka̱, I thought, they were legends, but through my interview with him, my illusion was clarified.

I sincerely appreciate and thank Mr. John Mut Lual from Lɔu Nuär. The reliable information, that I documented about the Lɔu Nuär migration and the reason for going to the Eastern White Nile, was the result of his lecture to me as I engaged him to answer certain specific questions. Mr. John Mut Lual belongs to Pathai Payam but his Boma is Pulchuol, where his own family is. May God give him good health and protection including his own family.

My utmost gratitude to Honourable Kwong Danhier Gatluak who enabled me to have contact with Mr. Michael Gatlɔɔth Kän, at Protection of Civilian (POC-Juba). From the depth of my heart, I appreciate Mr. Michael Gatlɔɔth Kän, for his cooperation that allowed me to have access to reliable information about Nyuɔŋ Nuär migration from Adɔk to their present territory. May God give him good health and bless his family.

Finally, I would like to appreciate and thank Mr. James Köŋ Jäny who was able to provide me with credible information about the role (function) of guan bööthni/kuär muɔn/ earth-master (leopard skin) or crow/jakɔk. May God give him protection and good health.

FOREWORD

This is the second edition, reviewed and enlarged, of Fr. James Tab Charoa's volume Nuär Origin, Culture, and Moral Evaluation, whose first edition was published in 2020. This means that Nuär people and others have appreciated the book as well. In this second edition, the title carries the word Compendium to indicate that only some elements about the history and culture of the Nuär people have been considered in this present volume. This highlights the riches and multiple dimensions of this extraordinary ethnic group of South Sudan.

For the first edition, Fr. Dr. George Jangara Modi wrote the foreword at the time, he was a lecturer of philosophy at Saint Paul's Major Seminary of Juba (Munuki). I agree with one of his statements: "The originality of this work [...] lies in the author bringing in a new taste of personal experience as a "son of the land." He has revealed what the prominent anthropologists who lived among the Nuär for several years could not discover by themselves. The book digs deeper into understanding concepts about the Nuär and their origins. It clarifies the previous ambiguities through conceptual analysis of terminologies. The author has thus contributed to the

African cause in general and to the Nuär people in particular. This is a must-read book for all the Nuär people and anybody who wants to have a glimpse of the African lifestyle."

In my contribution to this new foreword, I would like to highlight four main aspects of the work: 1) the motivations of the author to write the book; 2) the method of Fr. James Tab in his approach; 3) the patristic background in discovering and valuing the cultural values of culture and religions as an inspiration for assessing also Nuär's culture; 4) the magisterial support of this positive patristic assessment in Vatican Council II and the recent teaching of Popes as well.

Fr. Charoa intends to help his people not to lose their memory of their origin and cultural values. "I do not want my people to forget their origin and culture." Thus, the book depicts a comprehensible passion in what he writes.

The method of Fr. Tab relies on two main sources: his personal experience of the culture of his people, being the "son of the land," as he defines himself, and the professional writings of anthropologists, who spent several years among the Nuär to study and understand the intriguing history and cultural values of this ethnic group of South Sudan. As the volume indicates, Tab assesses personally some of the statements of anthropologists, in particular of H. Johnson and Evans-Pritchard. At times, he criticizes their judgments as not being correct. The author analyses critically the object of his approach resorting to philosophical, anthropological, biblical, theological, and moral considerations.

Philosophically. He recalls first the Pre-socratic Parmenides in his view of the immutability of reality and Heraclitus in his opposite view of the permanent change of reality. This is to underline that any culture undergoes a process of change in its understanding of values, and yet, at the same time, it is immutable and permanent in affirming other basic values about morals. This implies that the one who wants to study a culture should not be satisfied with a spirit of archaeological conservationism, but ought to have a dynamic perception of things in their positive evolution. A culture is not a collection of items for a museum, but something alive that evolves while remaining faithful to some permanent traits of the identity of one particular ethnic group. Continuity and discontinuity should characterize the study of a culture.

Anthropologically. Fr. Tab also brings the view of sophist Protagoras in his statement that "man is the measure of all things" to underline the anthropological aspect of any culture, which serves man and not vice-versa, man serving a fixed culture. This dynamic vision of culture is and should be an important factor never to be forgotten if one wants to respect and value culture as something alive and serving the common good of its people in the change of time. Therefore, missionaries (African and non-African) who want to evangelize the Nuär must learn deeply the language, history, and culture, if they intend to promote an effective evangelization.

Fr. Tab values the Nuär's myths and dancing. The myths answered essential human questions: where people come from, what is their meanings of life, and where is their final destination. Nuär's dances, important channels of tradition, are celebrations of life that help people assimilate and live their cultural values. This calls for a meaningful process of inculturation. Of course, these cultural values should undergo a "serious evaluation" and a radical purification or even transformation, if they are contrary to the Gospel.

The appreciation of Nuär culture and its purification and

enrichment should integrate and promote basic Christian ethical principles of respect for human dignity, option for the poor and the vulnerable, spirit of solidarity and subsidiarity, participation in the promotion of the common good, respect for people's rights, sense of responsibility, and the constructive role of the government. However, Fr. Charoa does not stop at mere anthropological considerations in assessing his culture, but, as a Christian theologian, enlightens it with a biblical, moral, and magisterial reflection, to make sure that the cultural values should be compatible with the Gospel.

Biblically. Biblical references are shown in particular when Fr. Tab deals with the attributes of God-Koth. Koth means to "blow." In Gen 2:7 God the creator is said to blow his breath in human nostrils the breath of life, so that they become living beings. God has also qualified as a tutor in his absolute freedom to govern the world without interference from anyone. This is seen in the light of Is 9:5-6 where God is proclaimed as a wonderful counsellor, God-hero, and eternal Father. God is indeed the creator (cääk) who created all things imprinting in them his image (cf. Gen 1:27). God (täh) made the world out of preexisting matter. He is the creator and protector of what he created. In trying to promote Nuär cultural values, Fr. Charoa recalls the meaning full words of Jesus, who stated that he has not come to abolish the law (cultural values), but to fulfil it (cf. Mt 5;17-18).

In the Nuär view of creation, we find an intriguing possibility of a comparative study of their vision, which is similar to the philosophical understanding of the creation of the ancient Greeks (creation out of a pre-existing matter), about the Christian vision of creation ex nihilo (creation from nothing). The idea of God being a protector of his creation could be seen in the Christian light of Providence or as St. Augustine states as creatio continua (continual creation).

Patristically. The positive approach to cultural values was felt as a necessity by the Fathers of the Church, who intended to facilitate the acceptance of Christianity by the intellectuals of their time.

The martyr Justine speaks of the "seeds of the Word" (the pre-existing logos) inseminated in non-Christian cultures and religions in such a way that the non-Christian people, who lived according to the inspirations of the Word, could be called Christians. Justine states: "We have been taught that Christ is the firstborn of God and we have declared him above all to be the Word in whom the whole human race has participated. Those who lived with the Word are Christians even if they were held to be atheists like Socrates, Heraclitus, and such as these among the Greeks."[1] The theologian Karl Rahner based on this view his theology of the "anonymous Christians."

Clement of Alexandria speaks of the presence of "scintillations" of the Logos in non-Christian cultures and religions. "The Greeks, having received certain scintillations of the divine Word, having given forth some utterances of truth, they indeed bore witness that the force of truth is not hidden [...]." Clement compares the function of Greek philosophy to the Law of Moses. Just as the Law was school-master, a paidagogos, for the Hebrews to lead them to Christ, so was philosophy for the Hellenic mind. "Philosophy [...] was a preparation, paving the way for him, who is perfected in Christ."[2] *Irenaeus* says: "The Word of God has never ceased

---

1 Cf. Justine, *Apology* I, 46.

2 Clement of Alexandria, *Stromata* 1, 5, in ANF, 305.

to be present to the human race.[3] *Hilary*, commenting on *Jn* 1:19 says: "The rays of the Word are ready to shine whenever the windows of the soul are opened".[4]

Augustine states: "Christian religion did exist among the ancients, nor was it absent at the beginning of the human race, until the coming of Christ in the flesh when the true religion which had already existed began to be called Christian [...]."[5] Again: "At all times and in all places from the origin of humankind those who believe in him, who came to know him in whatever manner, and who led godly and righteous life, undoubtedly became saved through him [...]."[6]

The Fathers, however, also see the negative aspects of non-Christian religions and religious philosophies. According to Origen and St. Augustine, philosophers often discover partial truths, but in their pride, they begin to worship the work of their intellect. Thus, in their way, they also became idolaters.[7] Hence, a twofold relationship of Christianity to other religions and religious philosophies needs to be fostered. Christianity must assess critically and at the same time respect other religions and religious philosophies. Christianity has to expose its errors but uphold and integrate its truths. Through proper critical study and discernment, I feel that the approach of the Church Fathers could be properly applied to Nuär's cultural and religious values. That is what Fr. Tab does in assessing his culture.

---

3 Cf. Irenaeus, *Against Heresies*, 3,16,1.

4 Hilary, *On Psalm* CXVIII, 12, 5.

5 Augustine, *Retractationes* 1, 13, 3, in CSEL 36:58-59.

6 Augustine, *Epistola* 102, 2, 12, in CSEL 34, 54ff.

7 Cf. Origen, *Hom. on Lev.* 7,6; *Hom. in Jesu Nave* 7,1; Augustine, *City of God* 8,11.

Magisterially. Vatican Council II was inspired by this approach of the Fathers of the Church in some passages of its documents. Nostra Aetate (Declaration on the relation of the Church to non-Christian religions), n. 2 encourages Christians to foster "dialogue and collaborations with the followers of other religions carried out with prudence and love and in witness to the Christian faith and life." Christians are invited to "recognize, preserve, and promote the good things, spiritual and moral, as well as socio-cultural values found among these men." *Lumen Gentium* (Dogmatic Constitution on the Church), n. 16 asserts: "Whatever good or truth is found amongst them is looked upon the Church as a preparation for the Gospel." *Ad Gentes* (Decree on the Mission Activity of the Church), n. 9 attests: "Whatever good is found to be sown in the hearts and minds of men, or the rites and cultures peculiar to various peoples, not only is lost, but is healed, uplifted, and perfected for the glory of God, the shame of the demon, and the bliss of men."

The journey of inculturation is an ongoing challenge for the Church in Africa. It implies a deep knowledge of the culture to both appreciate it and criticize it if some aspects are not compatible with the Gospel. The inculturation of the Gospel, as John Paul II states in Redemptoris Missio (Encyclical Letter The Mission of the Church, 1990), is today "particularly urgent", but it is a lengthy process. It does not require a "purely external adaptation." It consists of "a profound, all-embracing", and "a difficult process, for it must in no way compromise the distinctiveness and integrity of Christian faith." The Church transmits Christian values to various cultures, "at the same time taking the good elements that already exist in them and renewing them from within" (principle of incarnation).

In this way, "the universal Church herself is enriched with forms of expression and values in the various sectors of Christian life, such as evangelization, worship, theology and charitable works. She comes to know and express better the mystery of Christ. [...] The process of inculturation is a slow journey that should accompany the whole of missionary life,"[8] to express the enrichment of a particular culture with universal values (principle of Catholicity). According to the Exhortation, The Church in Africa (Ecclesia in Africa, 1995) John Paul II highlights that inculturation is "an urgent priority in the life of the particular Churches, for a firm rooting of the Gospel in Africa". It is defined as "a requirement for evangelization", "a path towards full evangelization", and "one of the greatest challenges for the Church" in Africa.[9]

In his Exhortation Commitment of Africa (Africae Munus, 2011), Pope Benedict XVI deals with the topic of inculturation underlining three basic dimensions, which should serve as methodological guidelines to creatively inspire a true process of inculturation.[10] 1) There is a need for deep study and rigorous discernment of African cultural values. Discernment always implies clarification, distinction, purification, and selection. 2) There is a need to highlight the Holy Spirit as the true agent of inculturation. This helps to

8 John Paul II, Encyclical Letter *The Mission of the Church* (*Redemptoris Missio*) (7 December 1990), Nairobi: Paulines Publications Africa 1995, n. 52.

9 John Paul II, Post-synodal Apostolic Exhortation *The Church in Africa* (*Ecclesia in Africa*) (4 September 1995), Nairobi: Paulines Publications Africa 1995, n. 59.

10 Benedict XVI, Post-synodal Apostolic Exhortation *Africa's Commitment* (*Africae Munus*), Nairobi: Paulines Publications Africa 2011, nn. 36-38.

understand that inculturation is not an artificial construct. It is a matter of conjugating properly the principle of incarnation with the principle of catholicity (universality). 3) There is a need to underline the courageous and creative imagination of various cultural forms to detect and appreciate the deep-rooted human longings of African culture in the dynamic perspective of their true and final fulfilment in Jesus Christ. This can be applied also to Nuär culture.

Against the background of the patristic, Vatican Council II, and magisterial awareness of the "seminar verbi" which has surfaced, the approach of Fr. James Tab is in order. It responds critically and constructively to the invitations of Vatican II and the recent teaching of the Magisterium.

By Rev. Prof. Guido Oliana

PREFACE

When I wrote my first book about the Nuär entitled "The Nuär Origin, Culture, and Moral Evaluation" published by Rafiki for Printing and Publishing, I said that I was prompted by Sr. Elena Balatti CMS. After I reflected upon many issues with regard to Nuär origin, culture, and moral evaluation, I discovered that my first book about the Nuär did not capture every dimension of their own lives. Furthermore, I have realized that what we call "culture" is not a simple issue if it has to reflect and represent the philosophy of human life. In this sense, one must be tempted to say that "culture is a mystery" which requires unfolding hidden mysteries, if one would like to know it in depth.

When I was writing my first book about the Nuär, I collected different books, written by different renowned anthropologists about the Nuär such as Evans-Pritchard, P. P. Howell, and Douglas H. Johnson. Those who read those books might wrongly conclude that those anthropologists have written everything about the Nuär. However, what they wrote may only cover 20% of the Nuär origin, and culture. In my first book, I offered some critiques about those books written by active observers called anthropologists.

Earlier, I have mentioned that culture is a mystery that requires the discovery of unfolding hidden mysteries. In this regard, I have discovered many things about the Nuär people, which were covered neither by my first book nor by anthropologists who wrote about them. Therefore, due to the fresh unfolding hidden information about the Nuär people, I decided to reflect on a suitable title for my book which will be the second edition. The decision to change the title from the original title of the previous book came because of realizing that the second edition has captured 95% of all the unfolding hidden information about Nuär people. However, I did not change completely, the title of my first book; rather, I have added something new to it such as the term "compendium."

However, to access reliable information about the Nuär origin, and culture, I chose to interview various persons who have deep knowledge about the Nuär origin, and culture. I interviewed those individual persons whom I consider as living encyclopedias and treasurers of Nuär origin, and culture. They lectured me instead of me lecturing them. For example, the interview of each person can go from four to five hours without stopping. From there, I have learned that when writing about the origin and culture of indigenous people, it is not enough to read books but rather, the indigenous people should become books for us. Therefore, due to their insights regarding detailed information about the Nuär origin, and culture that I have received from them, the term 'compendium, fits for the title of my book of this second edition.

Furthermore, the term compendium is described as a collection of concise but detailed information about a particular subject, especially in a book or other publication. In this sense, I believe that the second edition of my book will be an invaluable compendium of useful information about the Nuär origin, culture, and moral evaluation. Furthermore, a compendium is a compilation of knowledge about a particular subject. Compendia is plural and compendial is an adjective. Therefore, this collection of knowledge plays a vital role in protecting public health. In this sense, it is my conviction that this book entitled "Compendium of Nuär Origin, Culture, and Moral Evaluation" will preserve and protect Nuär culture from fading away.

I believe that this book will be of great help to young people who are born in megacities and towns. This is because every human person ought to live by past, present, and, future. In this regard, any dichotomy between those tenses will create a dramatic vacuum. In this sense, it is very important for every human person to know his/her historic origin, and culture, and to be able to evaluate his/her cultural values.

I assume the responsibility to write this book because I consider myself the grandson of Gɛ̈ɛ̈k. Being a descendant of Ŋɔ̱r (Thi̱a̱ŋ) Gɛkä; I decided to write this book as an elder descendant son of Ŋɔ̱r (Thi̱a̱ŋ) Gɛkä. First, I believe that when my paternal brothers, the descendants of Di̱näy (Lɔu Nuär) read it, they will say, 'Our elder brother has offered us an excellent service.'

Second, when the descendants of the last born of Gɛ̈ɛ̈k that is, Bul Cöl Gɛ̱ɛ̱k, (Gaat Bol Gɛkä read it, they will also say, our elder brother has done a par excellent job. Third, when Ji̱käy west and Ji̱käy east read it, they will say, if Gɛ̈ɛ̈k were not to cut the gourd to remove our Great Grandfather/ Ki̱i̱r Kak Kër) from it, we were going to miss this marvellous work. Fourth, when Gaatwär and Ɣa̱a̱k Nuär read it, they say, that if we were to remain in heaven, we were not going to have this Nuär cultural heritage. Fifth, how wonderful, it will be for my nephews, Laak, Le̱e̱k, including Ji̱käny Nuär when they read it, they will say, Bravo, our Uncle, for the nice work. Sixth, when Dɔk and Nyuɔŋ Nuär, the sons of Guɛk Gaw read it, they say, our paternal brother has provided us with an amazing cultural heritage.

It is my pleasure to dedicate my private time to writing this book to preserve Nuär cultural heritage, which consists of the past, present, and future. This is because I do not want my people to forget their origin and culture. I am aware that not every single cultural value can be compatible with the Gospel's values. No human culture is perfect. However, we are in a world of constant change, but there are certain issues, which do not change.

In my first book, I referred to various sources about permanent change which appears in the following paragraphs as I said, to avoid any fragmentation of knowledge and myopic outlook of changes in certain cultural values of Nuär in the past, we ought to refer to natural laws and principles of immutability and change. However, we ought to remind ourselves that natural law, principles of immutability, and change, do have their historical controversies.

It is believed that past, present, and future are governed by natural law with its characteristics of universality, immutability, and Indispensability. In this sense, the concept of natural law as immutable was asserted by the Pythagorean doctrine of unchanging mathematical relationships as the essence of reality. The Eleatic principle states that nature obeys laws of permanent being and that the laws of physics, biology, and chemistry are fixed and permanent. For example, note that the Greek word for physics means unchanging nature. These propositions were analysed critically by the Sophists. They enquired whether such unchanging laws of nature could be accepted as the basis for laws governing man.

According to the Second Vatican Council, "Beneath all changes there ar,e many realities which do not change and which have their ultimate foundation in Christ, who is the same today, yesterday and forever."[11] These realities remain permanently and historically not like the characteristics of man and his world. Within the concept of immutability and changeability, Zeller concurs with Parmenides who "Saw, however, the deception of the sense in the apparent physical world becoming and passing away, and recognized the unchangeable being behind it."[12]

In his philosophical, work "On Nature": Parmenides of Elea differs from Sophists concerning his doctrine of "truth." He reaffirms that truth can never be known through sense perception. According to Parmenides, the truth can only be known through pure reason, which he called (logos-word). Contrary to Protagoras of Abdera and Heraclitus who asserted the theory of relativism of "truth" Parmenides on the other hand, taught that change itself is impossible, coming into existence and ceasing to exist are both impossible. He considers the theory of change as an illusion, that is, to believe in untrue things as true. He said, for example, that the future and past do not exist because what exists must be "permanent." According to him, only 'present' is possible.

---

11 Second Vatican Council, Pastoral Constitution on the Church in the Modern World, *Gaudium et Spes*, No. 5, AAS58, 1965.

12 Edward Zeller, *Outline of the History of Greek Philosophy*, New York, The Worl Publishing Company, 1795, pp. 61-62.

On the other hand, while Parmenides emphasizes the principle of immutability, Heraclitus believes and upholds the doctrine of the theory of relativism (changeability). It is argued that the human race has passed from a rather static concept of reality to some more dynamic and evolutionary ones. According to E. Zeller and Heraclitus:

> *Something is involved in incessant change and is subject to new modifications. Everything flows and nothing is permanent: one can never step twice into the same river. We are and we are not; everything passes into something else and thus seems to be something that assumes different shapes and passes through most varied states: "From everything One is made and from One everything.*[13]

Another leading philosopher among the Sophists at the top of the list was called Protagoras of Abdera (C. 481-411 B.C.). He is not to be confused with Pythagoras of Samos, who founded the Pythagorean Order. Protagoras of Abdera was the most influential leader of Sophists. He based his entire philosophy on the theory of relativity of truth, expressed in the famous statement "Man is the measure of all things, of that they are, that they are, and of that they are not, they are not"[14] or, quoted from the obligatory special referent material for all the testimonies and fragments from the works of pre-Socrates referred to as ' DK 80 BI': "Man is the measure of all things–things which exist insofar as they exist, and

---

13 Edward Zeller, *Outline of the History of Greek Philosophy*, New York, The Worl Publishing Company, 1795, pp. 61-62.

14 Ibid, p. 26.

things which do not exist insofar as they do not exist."[15] Thus, Protagoras of Abdera was the first sophist to formulate the theory of relativism (subjectivism)

This doctrine of the theory of relativism had an enduring impact on the history of philosophy down to our contemporary times. It is argued that not only did Protagoras of Abdera proclaim the relativity of truth (that what is true for you is true only for you and what is true for me is only true only for me). Consequently, even the theory of relativism of morals (that right and wrong are matters of personal opinion or choice). In addition, as a most remarkable corollary, Protagoras of Abdera derived from this principle the doctrine of equal rights for all humankind, including women and slaves. In this philosophical theory of relativism, Protagoras of Abdera asserts that there is no absolute truth or absolute knowledge, about knowledge, as such, depending on the perspective of the individual. What an individual holds as existing or not existing depends on the person.

After we have exhausted the controversial issues of natural law, the principles of immutability, and the theory of relativism, the contemporary Nuär communities should understand that some of their customs and cultural values might permit change. Only those, which are compatible with the Gospel's values; ought to be maintained. However, some cultural values require serious evaluation. In this sense, every

---

15 Diels-Kranz, DK 80 BI, the initials DK stands for Diels-Kranz, the authors of *Die Fragmente der Vorsokratiker*, Ist ed. 1903; 6th ed., 3. Vol., Berlin, 1951-52. This work continues to be obligatory reference material for all the testimonies and fragments from works of the pre-Socrates period. The first number refers to the chapter. The numbering of chapters follows the order of the different philosophers studied in the work. The letter tells you whether the citation refers to an indirect testimony (A) or to a fragment (B). The number following the letter tells you the order in which the citation is found.

Nuär man or woman ought to know that human customs and cultural values are not all permanent. Some permit change within the customs that include cultural values but not morals. Consequently, human customs and cultural values require serious evaluation to make sure that some excellent values based on virtues keep lasting validity.

The book consists of eleven chapters. The first two chapters discuss various theories of Nuär origin both in the Western and in the Eastern White Nile. In chapter one, all the Nuär clans are mentioned. Koch County is presented as a cradle of Nuär origin specifically, at Jiath li̲i̲c (Ŋɔ̱ɔ̱b li̲i̲c). Koch County is referred to as the "Centre of the House." This is because there are three major clans in the north and the colonizers disturbed three major clans in the south of Koch County. These clans, the British Administration had led to what was called the Nuär settlement. Finally, Taŋ Kuany Kuunär was presented in the last part of chapter one.

More detailed information is given to the Nuär of Eastern White Nile. Some of those theories of Nuär's origin are very dramatic. However, about the discovery of myths of Nuär origin, one must acknowledge that they are not scientific evidence, but rather reflect the deepest desire of human beings to know his/her origin. I ought to point out that anthropologists, who wrote about the Nuär origin, wrongly concluded that every Nuär man and woman trace his/her to Ŋɔ̱ɔb Tree at Koch County, specifically at a village called li̲i̲c.

In this second revision of the edition of my book, it is proven that three major Nuär clans do not trace their origin to Ŋɔ̱ɔb Tree at Koch County. For example, Gaatwär and Ɣa̲a̲k Nuär claimed that they came down from heaven while both Ji̲käny West and Ji̲käny East, claimed that their Great

Grandfather Kiir Kak Kër was removed from the gourd by Gɛ̈ɛ̈k Gaw Raan Kuoth.

Furthermore, we must point out that those myths, try to answer very essential questions such as first, where do we come from? Second, what are we doing here and now (the purpose of our existence)? Third, from here, where are we going? The myths may seem to be stupid; nevertheless, every human person must trace his/her origin through the myths.

The Nuär migration to the Eastern White Nile was described in detail. Each group gave an account of their migration. Outstanding figures were mentioned as leaders of migration. The Nuär migration to the eastern White Nile was not an easy task. During migration, there appeared many brutal dictators.

Chapter three discusses God's attributes, spirits, some mysterious powers, and some traditional powers that tempter with true belief in God, while chapters four and five present three Major Prophets of Nuär such as Ŋundeŋ Böŋ (Ŋundeŋ Can) from eastern Nuär, Kuolaŋ Kët and his daughter Nyaruac Kuolaŋ from western Nuär. Chapters six, seven, eight, and nine discuss Nuär marriage from a broader perspective from different viewpoints by different anthropologists. While chapters six, seven, and eight, present an untrue union between a man and a woman, chapter nine presents the true union between them.

Chapter ten discusses very important issues such as the Nuär customary laws and other ritual ceremonial rites from various articles. About inculturation, these articles are very important for both missionaries and local clergy, including other pastoral agents. Chapter eleven recommends the way forward about Nuär cultural values that are compatible with

Gospel Values. The book in general, could be helpful for missionaries working among the Nuär specifically in areas of marriage and religion.

One of the main problems this book can tackle as far as evangelization is concerned, is that missionaries always overlook the beauty of the local cultures they evangelize. Normally, the missionaries have a superficial view towards any culture of people they evangelize. This happens probably because of a lack of engagement in studying the culture or a lack of good materials and sources from which the details of the local culture of local people can be studied. This book about the Nuär origin, culture, and moral evaluation, elucidates any missionary evangelizing in the Nuär area who wants to know the Nuär culture in depth. This is because; this work will help the missionary to go deep into the Nuär culture as it describes the center of Nuär moral norms of marriage.

From the pastoral perspective, the reader of this book will benefit from two things: first, he/she will appreciate the beauty of the Nuär culture and the details this book provides. As far as evangelization is concerned, this appreciation will help him/her to enter into the culture with respect, removing the shoes of prejudice as Moses was told by God to remove his shoes because the land on which he was standing was a holy ground (Ex 3: 5). Similarly, a missionary who reads this book must recognize the holiness and work of God in the Nuär culture before he/she embarks in his/her pastoral activities for evangelization.

He/she will be enriched with more knowledge, which will facilitate his/her pastoral work among the Nuär people. Through this knowledge, the missionary or any reader will come to know the strong sense of morality in Nuär culture.

He will be able to see the similarities and dissimilarities between the Nuär cultures and Christian values of marriage.

What qualifies this book to include everything about Nuär life such as their origin, religion, God, marriage, and culture? The justification is found in the descriptions of culture. By descriptions, culture is defined as "The customary beliefs, social edge to succeeding generations."[16] It is further explicated as the customary beliefs, social forms, and material traits of a racial, religious, or social group; also, the characteristic features of everyday existence (as diversions or a way of life) shared by people in a place or time. Culture is described as the set of shared attitudes, goals, and practices that characterize an institution or an organization. In addition, it is also explained as the set of values, conventions, or social practices associated with a particular field, activity, or social characteristics.

In addition, if inculturation, the dialogue between the Gospel and local cultural values is to be achieved, then, every Christian person should excavate every aspect of his/her cultural values to the surface. This seems to be my intention in writing this book. However, when we talk of dialogue between the Gospel and local culture, certain terms are to be pointed out such as inculturation, enculturation and acculturation.

One need not confuse the term inculturation with both enculturation and acculturation. There is a need to make a distinction between enculturation and acculturation. Enculturation is described as the process by which people learn the dynamics of their surrounding culture and acquire

16 *Merriam-Webster's Collegiate Dictionary*, Eleventh Edition, Massachusetts: Merriam-Webster, Incorporated, 2003, p, 304. s

values and norms appropriate or necessary. Furthermore, enculturation is referred to the process of learning our own (native) culture, whereas, acculturation is the process of learning and adopting host cultural norms, values, and beliefs. Again, enculturation is the first step in cultural familiarization, while acculturation comes along after and is the second step in this process.

Another peculiarity of this book is the recommendation on the moral dimension of Nuär cultural values, which is not a typical anthropological approach. Anthropologists do not pass judgment on the customs and cultural values of the local people. Nevertheless, the book presents both anthropological and moral approaches. This is because; moral theology uses information from other fields of science to pass its verdict when and where it is necessary.

This is the characteristic and authority of ethics and moral theology. I wrote this book not as an active observer of the customs and cultural values of the Nuär people. Rather, I wrote it as the true son of the soil of Nuär with moral authority due to my specialization in sacred moral theology. My moral authority is that I use the anthropological information about the life of my people to tell them what they ought to do and what they ought not to do in their customs and cultural values.

Finally, it is unfortunate that we were unable to get either the photo of prophet Ŋundɛŋ or the one of his son Guɛk Ŋundɛ̈ŋ. The two photos on the cover page of the book are the photos of two men from eastern Nuär sent from the British Museum in London. The tall man was called Gang Wan Waŋ. His mother was called Nyachuol who committed suicide after she heard a rumour that her son was killed during the battle between Anyuak and Nuär, which later on, became untrue. The other short man was called Yo̱y Bi̱ni Kuɛ̈k, a cousin to Gang Wan Waŋ. Both men lived during the British colonial period. The role of their photos is to draw readers' attention to Nuär culture.

CHAPTER ONE

THE NUÄR ORIGIN, RESISTANCE, AND SETTLEMENT

Introduction

Chapter one discusses the conceptual analysis of terminologies such as Nuër and ciën as an irrelevance to traditional burial, the matrix of the term Nuër and term Nuär as an exclusion of non-Nuär. In addition, it explains the following terms ran-human beings, death-people, the similarities between Nuär and other tribes, and the various opinions of Nuär topography and ecology. Furthermore, the chapter discusses different theories about Nuär origins such as H. Johnson's version of Nuär origin, Evans-Pritchard's version of Nuär origin, the contemporary Nuär's version of their origin, and the genealogical version of the ancestral line tree

In addition, the chapter presents mythological and genealogical origins of major Nuär Clans such as the origin of J̲ikäny ciëŋ and J̲ikäny dɔar, the mythological origin of

Gaatwär Nuär, Nnuɔŋ and Dɔk Nuär, Gɛ̈ɛ̈k clans, the origin of Laak and Leek Nuär, and the origin of Thi̲a̲ŋ Nuär. Finally, it discusses the causes of Nuär resistance and settlement and, the causes of a series of strenuous military operations in addition, it offers critiques on anthropologists.

1. Conceptual Analysis of Terminologies

The assumption of names of many tribes in the African continent by anthropologists has created both irrelevance and disturbance. Unfortunately, some tribes in our continent have attributed names that do not belong to them at all or even in their language, which means evil. It is further unfortunate that such names which were attributed to some tribes by anthropologists and colonizers have become their true names today even in the official documents.

Thanks to the sense of negritute (black consciousness), any tribe that is given a wrong name, ought to make people aware of their true name otherwise. For example, when a name is given to someone, it carries with it the concept of dignity and identity of that person. Should you call me by the wrong name, I will not respond to you. Even the Sacred Scripture says God gave all living creatures to Adam to subdue and name them (Cf. Gen: 2:18-20, 2:20). For example, calling someone's name indicates perfect communication and respect due to that person. What kind of person is that can eat the fruit of a tree, which he/she does not know, in a forest? Here and now, the emphasis is to name each tribe by their true name. This emphasis leads us to the discussion of the terms "nuër" and 'ciën' in the Nuär language.

1.1 Irrelevance of Nuër & Ciën to Traditional Burial

The 'Nuär' are today called 'Nuër, however, the word 'more nu' which is supposed to be written 'nuër' has a bad connotation in the Nuär language. In addition, it is neither to be confused with the term 'ciën.' According to Nuär, the two words 'Nuer and ciën mean different things altogether. Unfortunately, our respectful anthropologist E. Evans-Pritchard used them in his writing about the Nuär religion as if they have no difference. Due to this confusion, the example below will illustrate clearly the meaning of nuër. The pronoun he/she will be used for the sake of formality otherwise; the example below demonstrates a fight between men.

Let us see from the following illustrations about the term nuër (nuer)-fearing ruining one's life. For example, if two people disagree or quarrel over a thing, which leads to fighting in which one of them, kills another. The term 'nuër'-fearing ruining one's life will apply to the murderer in the first place. In this sense, the Nuär believe that the murderer has become automatically hostile to God and his creatures including earthly products. He/she has lost his/her relationship with God and with everything in creation. Consequently, the murderer ought not to taste any earthly products created by God because of nuër-fearing ruining his/her own life. In this case, it seems as if everything in the ecosystem were a toxin to the murderer.

This is because the Nuär believe that the blood of the victim person has become part of every product of creation that fights back in the form of nuër-fearing ruining one's life. In this sense, every product of creation declares the murderer unclean and unfit to taste the earthly products.

His/her conscience ought to abide by this declaration otherwise should he/she act contrary, he/she will die as a result of nuër-fearing ruining one's life.

This automatic sanction brought by God through earthly products upon the murderer permits no dispute. Consequently, the murderer will realize that he/she is in trouble with God, creation, and the relatives of the victim. Should he/she try to taste any product of creation, he/she will nuër-fearing ruining one's life.

The Nuär do believe that there is a critical situation of the standoff between the murderer and God including his earthly products. Consequently, the murderer is forced to fast and starve by God and his earthly products.

However, to resolve this dilemma of nuër-fearing ruining one's life, the Nuär believe that among them, there are clans who are called-priests-kua̱r muɔ̱ɔ̱n-Earth Masts. The priest-kuär muɔ̱ɔ̱n-Earth Master is believed to have the authority to restore the relationship between the murderer and the earthly products. Such authority is exercised only by a male priest-kuär muɔ̱ɔ̱n-Earth Mast among the Nuär people. He is not called 'leopard skin' as E. Evans-Pritchard claimed but he wears leopard skin when exercising his authority. Sometimes, he can perform these moral and spiritual duties without wearing leopard skin.

Therefore, the function to be performed by the Earth-Master-kuär muɔɔn upon the murderer as a ritual purification is called 'bi̱e̱r'-the act of cutting the skin of the upper part of the wrist of a murderer for his blood to pour down. As he/she poured the blood of the innocent person on the ground, also, part of his/her blood ought to be poured on the ground as a dispensation from nuër-fearing ruining one's life.

According to J. Pui Yak, "The purification ritual is often conducted to avoid the eventual death of the killer, for it is believed, that once the killer drinks water or eats any food before the performance of the ritual, he will be afflicted by a phenomenon called nueer [nuër] which meanɛ haunting". [17] As we mentioned earlier, the Earth Master who would kill a cow or a goat as a primary step in the ritual and then proceed to sill the blood of the killer by cutting the upper part of his wrist performs the system of bier. After the first two rituals are conducted, the Earth Master will then finally, take some water and put them in the mouth of the killer to drink and the killer will be allowed to drink or eat normally.

This is considered a sign of reconciliation between the murderer, God, and earthly products. After this process of ritual purification is done by the priest-Kuär muɔ̱ɔ̱n-Earth-Master, the murderer is allowed to eat earthly products without nuër-fearing ruining one's life. Here, the lifting of the sanction of the murderer by the priest-Kuär muɔ̱ɔ̱n-Earth-Master from nuër-fearing ruining one's life is limited to him alone. It is not extended to the family of the murderer and the family of the deceased person.

However, the term 'nuër'-fearing ruining one's life is extended to the family of the deceased person and the family of the murderer in different ways. The Nuär believe that both families cannot eat earthly products without nuër-fearing ruining their lives. For example, the degree of nuër-fearing ruining their lives is because they cannot eat together or share the same liɛr pi̱ny-the same cup of water. The Nuär will say that the family of the murderer and the family of the

17 Jameɛ Pui YakYiel, *The Nuer Culture*, Rak Media for Printing, Juba, 2021, P.51.

deceased have ‘cɔ̲a̲k’-bone, kiɛ ‘tɛr’-enmity, kiɛ thöŋ-fatal. These terms explain how difficult it is for the two families not to eat together or share the same liɛr pi̲ny-the same cup of water because of nuër-fearing ruining their lives.

The Nuär believed that the blood of the victim had set a boundary between the two families. Thus, the enmity between the two families is characterized by the following terms such as cɔ̲a̲k’-bone, kiɛ ‘tɛr’-enmity, kiɛ thöŋ-fatal as we have above-mentioned. These terms maintain the word ‘nuër-fearing ruining their lives between both families. Furthermore, the Nuär believe that even when the settlement of the cut-compensation of the deceased person is done, these terms such as cɔ̲a̲k’-bone, kiɛ ‘tɛr’-enmity, kiɛ thöŋ-fatal will still exist to maintain nuër.

In the meantime, the relatives of the deceased will adopt different techniques of revenge, which the Nuär call bi̲e̲m-hunt. However, the Nuär differentiate between hunting and bi̲e̲m. According to them, ka̲a̲k-hunting is for animals, while bi̲e̲m, and is a technique to be used to kill anyone of the relatives of the murderer or murderer himself. Here, two things are clear that is, bi̲e̲m-aiming to kill any of the relatives of the murderer or murderer himself, and not to eat with them exist.

The Nuär believe that even when the settlement of the cut compensation of the deceased person is done, cows do not substitute the value of the human person. Worse, those cows that the family of the deceased received from the family of the murderer, as cut compensation for their loved one, remind them of cɔ̲a̲k’-bone, kiɛ ‘tɛr’-enmity, kiɛ thöŋ-fatal. The presence of those cows adds more to happiness in the family of the deceased person. The cut compensation only removes bi̲e̲m-technique to be used to kill anyone of the relatives of the murderer or murderer himself. After the cut compensation, there ought, no need from the family of the deceased to kill anyone of the relatives of the murderer or murderer himself. Nevertheless, cɔa̱k'-bone, kiɛ 'tɛr'-enmity, kiɛ thöŋ-fatal will continue to exist between the two families.

The worst part is that when the family of the deceased marries his wife with those cows of cut compensation first child will be called tɛr-enmity if he is a boy, if she is a girl, she will be called nyatɛ̈r-girl of enmity. In this sense, the name will remind them about the murder of their father. Such a name will always make that child grow with a revengeful mentality against the murderer or anyone of his/her relatives. Unfortunately, the terms such as cɔa̱k'-bone, kiɛ 'tɛr'-enmity, and kiɛ thöŋ-fatal will always make the relationships of the two families fragile. For example, any little dispute, can reactive violence between them due to cɔa̱k'-bone, kiɛ 'tɛr'-enmity, kiɛ thöŋ-fatal.

The Nuär know that such relationships between them can never be brought to normality. Even marriage between the two families is not permissible due to cɔa̱k'-bone, kiɛ 'tɛr'-enmity, kiɛ thöŋ-fatal. In this case, even the priest-Kuär muɔ̱ɔ̱n-Earth-Master has no spiritual power to restore their relationships. This is due to the complexity of the term nuër-fearing ruining their lives. Furthermore, the expectation of nuër-fearing ruining their lives does not come directly from participation in the killing of the deceased person. They can eat earthly products without nuër-fearing ruining their lives as long as they do not eat and share the same cup of water. In this regard, the priest-Kuär muɔ̱ɔ̱n-Earth-Master has no spiritual power to eradicate nuër-fearing ruining the lives of the two families.

The relationships between the two families ought to have no remedy, only the standoff with lasting enmity. However, in other incidents in which an accidental killing occurred among the relatives which can have a lasting enmity, the relatives will opt for something which the Nuär called to̱o̱l cɔ̱a̱k-breaking of bone. Here, to̱o̱l cɔ̱a̱k-breaking of bone is a reconciliatory tool used to bring the relationships of the relatives to their normality by eradicating cɔ̱a̱k'-bone, kiɛ 'tɛr'-enmity, kiɛ thöŋ-fatal.

This is done to avoid more harm to the families. The priest-Kuär muɔ̱ɔ̱n-Earth Master plays a greater role in this process of reconciliation and forgiveness within these families. For example, a bull will be tied down in the middle of the relatives or families. Each senior elder of the family (relatives) will pray in turn, moving around the bull and holding a spear while everyone sits down and listens. The prayers are spiritually rich, they a centered on reconciliation and forgiveness.

Finally, the priest-Kuär muɔ̱ɔ̱n-Earth Master will be asked to spear the bull. He will asperse the relatives (families) with the blood of the victim as a sign of reconciliation and forgiveness. The priest-Kuär muɔ̱ɔ̱n-Earth Master will warn every member of the family not to recall the incidence of cɔ̱a̱k'-bone, kiɛ 'tɛr'-enmity, kiɛ thöŋ-fatal. Consequently, the relatives will eat the sacrificial meat together as a sign of restoration of the relationships among them.

Another word, that requires conceptual analysis, is called 'ciën'-expectation of blood revenge misfortune. Every true Nuär man or woman knows the difference between the two terms that is, nuër-fearing ruining one's life referred to the murderer, nuër-fearing ruining their lives for the two families, and ciën-expectation of blood revenge misfortune. These differences are clear and distinct.

What is in the mind of Nuär when they use the term 'ciën'? The Nuär believe that ran ɛ yaŋ Koth-means human being is a cow of God. This is due to the fact; that they love cows more than anything else does. In the First Edition, we pointed out some essential elements the Nuär attaches to cows. Therefore, according to Nuär, as a cow is everything to them, the human being is everything to God. Even in the book of Genesis, humankind is the summit of creation.

However, when the Nuär say that ran ɛ yaŋ Koth-human being is a cow of God, they have the deepest belief that ran ɛ dɔ̱a̱r Koth-human being is an innocent of God. Therefore, based on those beliefs such as, ran ɛ yaŋ Human being is a cow of God and ran ɛ dɔ̱a̱r Koth- the human being is an innocent of God, no person can kill another without 'ciën'-expectation of blood revenge misfortune. In this sense, the Nuär will say, cuo ran näk baaŋ-do not kill a human being without justified reason such as in the case of self-defence. Or cuo naath näk baaŋ-do not kill people without justified reason due to ciën'-expectation of blood revenge misfortune.

The Nuär believe that ciën'-expectation of blood revenge misfortune is imminent for a person who kills another person without any justified reason or who kills people without any justified reason. Their conscience is very clear in this regard. The Nuär will say that the blood of the innocent life will fight back upon the murderer in a form of ciën'-expectation of blood revenge misfortune. Should any misfortunate happen upon the murderer, or to his relatives, they will say, ca ciɛn-expectation of blood revenge misfortune. The spellings change due to irregularities.

The Nuär drew this belief through their own practical experiences. They have witnessed that someone who killed another person or who killed persons without any justified reason must experience ciën'-blood revenge as a misfortune. Consequently, the majority of them believe in ciën'-blood revenge. However, this belief is not limited to Nuär, but also, to other tribes in the continent. For example, there is a common belief that 'when you do evil, great evil will come back to you.'

Based on conceptual analysis of the terms, nuër-fearing ruining one's life and ciɛn-expectation of blood revenge misfortune we have made, now, we can see whether our active observer and outstanding anthropologist E. Evans-Pritchard correctly used these words. E. Evans-Pritchard lived among the Nuär and wrote many books about them. In his discussion about the concepts of soul and ghost, he said, "We can perhaps best start this discussion by considering what happens at death when man disintegrates into his three parts, ring-ri̲ŋ-flesh, yeah-[yiëë], and ti̲i̲y-breath or life, and tie-[ti̲i̲y], intellect or soul."[18]

According to Evans-Pritchard, when the burial is completed, the master of ceremonies of the dead man's family dips a handful of wild rice in water and asperses the grave-diggers with it. He added that they then go to the nearest stream to wash themselves. They may not drink water before they have been aspersed and have washed lest they die of the consequences (nuer).

Before we make any contrary view about the usage of the term 'number-nuër by E. Evans-Pritchard, we ought to agree

18 E.E. Evans-Pritchard, *Nuër Religion,* New York: Oxford University Press, 1956, p.144.

with him on Nuär anthropological understanding of man that consists of three components, ri̲ŋ-flesh, yiëë-breath, and ti̲i̲y-soul or intellect. These three components, according to Nuär, are what constitutes the human person. However, they further believe that other creatures share with them ri̲ŋ-flesh, and yiëë-breath-life but fall short of ti̲i̲y soul. In this sense, other creatures do not possess ti̲i̲y-soul and intellect as a human being does. They only have ri̲ŋ-flesh, yiëë-breath.

According to Nuär, ti̲i̲y means three things. Firstly, it means soul, secondly, it means sperm-de̲e̲dh and thirdly, it means heart. However, one needs to know to differentiate them from the context which in they are used. The Nuär believe that when someone dies, it is the ti̲i̲y-soul that goes back to God. This is because human life is a gift from God through ti̲i̲y-sperm and ovum as 'sacred sexual' ratios distributed equally to both males and females for procreation.

In this sense, ti̲i̲y-soul and sperm are a central focus of Nuär's anthropological understanding of the human person. Consequently, their concept of the resurrection centres upon ti̲i̲y-soul. However, sometimes, this concept of the living dead remains a mystery. The Nuär anthropological understanding of the human person consists of three components above-mentioned. They further point to the term 'lua̲n'-dignity of the human person. For example, the Nuär will say 'ŋu ca lua̲n dɛ guath' that means, the respect due to his/her dignity as a human person is disregarded. In short, he/she ceases to be respected which might be due to various reasons.

However, to further our understanding of those three components observed by Evans-Pritchard among the Nuär. According to Nuär, no presence of human life without ri̲ŋ-flesh, yiëë-breath, and ti̲i̲y- soul or intellect. In this regard,

Evans-Pritchard's observation was correct. However, we ought to analyze four things about Nuär traditional burial: firstly, there is a role master of ceremonies of the dead man's family who dips a handful of wild rice into the water. Secondly, asperses (springle) the gravediggers with it, and thirdly, gravediggers go to the nearest stream to wash themselves, fourthly, they may not drink before they have been aspersed and have washed lest they die of the consequences of nueer).

We ought to make this analysis with regards to Nuär traditional burial not only to critique Evans-Pritchard's observation but also, to see whether what we say to ourselves sometimes is true or not. For example, we do hear people say "Africans live as Christians and die as pagans." Therefore, according to the observations above-mentioned, the role of the master of ceremonies (the role of the senior elder of the family) of the deceased during the burial is not to participate in the digging of the grave. The gravediggers are supposed to be Wudni̲ tä ci̲ cuol-means senior members of the families. Since death is considered the most fearful thing in life, women, unmarried persons, and children are not allowed to participate in digging the grave. Wudni̲ tä ci̲ cuol-means senior members of the family who have experienced in life.

The role of the senior elder of the families at the grave is the mediation between the living and the jɔɔk-living dead. However, he has specific roles to play such as dipping a handful of wild rice into the water and, secondly, asperses the gravediggers with it. Firstly, the meaning of dipping a handful of wild rice into the water means bringing the seed back to life. For example, no seed can germinate without water. Furthermore, dipping wild rice in water symbolizes the t̲i̲i̲y-soul of the loved one to live.

Secondly, to asperse the gravediggers symbolizes two things, first, that the deceased person still lives among the members of the family, and second that the number of families will multiply despite the death of their dear one. Thirdly, going to the nearest stream to wash symbolizes a gesture of goodbye to the deceased person. Fourthly, that they may not drink before they have been aspersed and have washed lest they die of the consequences of nueer), means that they cannot drink any water before saying good-bye to their dear by washing themselves.

This last one has nothing to do with nueer (nuër) as Evans-Pritchard claimed. Neither nuër-fearing ruining one's life nor ciën-expectation of blood revenge misfortune. These terms nuër-fearing ruining one's life and ciën-expectation of blood revenge misfortune are related to killing as we have discussed earlier. Consequently, they have nothing to do with the ritual burial of our dear one as Evans-Pritchard falsely believed.

However, the two concepts of nuër-fearing ruining one's life and ciën-expectation of blood revenge misfortune are closely related to the incidence of the two sons of Adam, Cain and Abel. The Sacred Scripture asserts that..."Cain attacked his brother Abel and killed him. Then the Lord asked Cain, where is your brother Abel? He answered, I do not know. Am I my brother's keeper? God said: What have you done? Your brother's blood cries out to me from the ground!" (Gen 4:8-10).

The statement, which says that your brother's blood cries out to me from the ground, is very close to the concepts of both nuër-fearing ruining one's life and ciën-expectation of blood revenge misfortune. The expression, which states that your brother's blood cries out to me from the ground, demonstrates that God was not happy and consequently, even everything on the ground, was not happy with Cain. The killing of the innocent person ɛ yaŋ Koth-means a human being is a cow of God and requires ciën-expectation of blood revenge misfortunate.

How can the concept of aspersing the gravediggers with wild rice in Nuär traditional burial dialogue with the gospel of life? For example, Jesus says "Amen, amen, I say to you unless a grain of wheat falls to the ground and dies, it remains just a grain of wheat; but if dies, it produces much fruit" (Jn 12: 24). If the asperse with wild rice in Nuär traditional burial symbolizes hope for the multiplications of family despite the loss of their dear one, how can this concept be connected with God's promise to Abraham? In acting according to God's demand, "I will bless you and make your descendants as countless as the stars of the sky and the sands of the seashore; your descendants will take possession of the gates of their enemies, and in your descendants, all the nations of the earth will find blessings, because you obeyed my commands" (Gen 22: 17-18).

1.2 Matrix of the Term 'Nuër'

According to Merriam-Webster's Collegiate Dictionary, the word matrix means something within or from which something else originates, develops, or takes form. Historically, we are all aware that the African continent went through dramatic which have affected the life of the indigenous people. First, the coming of the Arabs in the North and then the coming of the British as colonizers in the continent including the influence of two religions. Christianity and Islam are factors that affected all areas of life of the indigenous people.

No doubt that the matrix of the term 'nuër' can be traced back to the consequence of the interactions between the Nuär people with Arabs in the North and the colonialists, specifically the British, who by then colonized Sudan. Both groups by then were incapable of articulating and writing the word "Nuär" as it was pronounced to them by the Nuär themselves. The British colonizers, since they interacted first with the Arabs in the North, wrote the word 'Nuër', which was supposed to be written 'Nuär', based on how the Arabs had pronounced it to them.

In all the official documents in the North, there is no difference between the way the word 'Nuër' is pronounced in Arabic and the English language. Consequently, the way it was pronounced, has affected the way it is written. For example, other mistakes of wrong names were applied to 'Collo' an ethnic group who are today unfortunately 'Shilluk', and to the Anyuak who are unfortunately today called "Anuak.' In South Sudan and elsewhere in our continent, there are cases whereby wrong names were attributed to many tribes and unfortunately, have become their true names. Therefore, it depends on some contemporary tribes of South Sudan who found themselves victims of those wrong names to raise their complaints to the High Court of South Sudan through their lawyers. Otherwise, they will remain with names irrelevant to them say nothing about them at all, or mean something different in their language.

It is unfortunate, that the so-called anthropologists who claim to write about the concrete life of the indigenous people by inserting themselves amid the local people were unable to re-assert and to truly articulate and stipulate the true name of tribes of the indigenous people. Therefore, contemporary anthropologists, the so-called active 'observers', should begin to learn and to write perfectly the language of the indigenous people to arrive at a true understanding of their languages and the true names of each tribe.

The above-mentioned wrong attribution of names to some tribes in the continent does not disqualify the enormous efforts, which different anthropologists have made by putting down into writing indigenous cultures. Many anthropological works such as the pioneering study of the famous British social anthropologist E.E. Evans Pritchard, "The Nuär of South Sudan", have become one of anthropology's classic case studies.

No doubt, the life of primitive man, as he is generally called, has attracted many anthropologists, the so-called active observers who are well-known in the field of anthropology. Among the well-known anthropologists who spent a good part of their lives among the Nuär were the already mentioned: Prof. Edward Evans Pritchard who has written books: The Nuër: A Description of the Modes of Livelihood and Political Institutions of a Nilotic People (1940), and Kinship and Marriage among the Nuër (1951) and Nuär Religion (1956).

Dr. Howell, who has written on Nuär (Nuër) law, combines anthropological training with administrative experience. Prof. Edward Evans Pritchard who wrote the foreword of the book of Dr. Howell states that..."combination very necessary if the principles [Nuär law], which can only be revealed by anthropological research, are to be presented in the form most useful to Officers of the Administration." We need to add Douglas H. Johnson who wrote his book on the Nuär entitled Nuër Prophets: A History of Prophets from the Upper Nile in the

Nineteenth and Twentieth Centuries, New York, Clarendon Press, 1994.

Contemporary anthropologists are making great efforts to write correctly the language of the indigenous people. An example is Sharon E. Hutchinson who wrote a book on Nuär entitled Nuër Dilemmas: Coping with Money, War, and the State, London, University Press, 1996, which has impressed me so much. In her book, she was able to write some Nuär expressions in the Nuär language. Active observers may not do the job well to become part of the concrete situation of the indigenous people but they are far better at "incarnating" in the life of primitive people.

1.3 The Term 'Nuär'-The Exclusion of Non-Nuär

If the word 'Nuër' fear ruining one's life in the Nuär language, what about the term 'Nuär' for the Nuär themselves? With absolute certainty, the Nuär call themselves 'Nuär' and not nuër. The term Nuär applies to those who can trace their origins back to 'däär ciëŋ'-the centre of the specifically in Jagɛi Nuär at present-day known as Koch-County Li̱i̱c under a ŋɔ̱b tree as we have above-mentioned. In that ŋɔ̱b tree, every Nuär claims his/her origin.

When the Nuär uses the word Nuär, they exclude others who are not Nuär. For example, when a Nuär man says ' I am a Nuär', it is like saying 'I am an English man, or I am an Italian man, or I am a Japanese. For the Nuär, the term 'Nuär carries with it the concept of nations-döör. According to them, anyone who is a foreigner is called a 'juɔ̱r'-foreigner.

1.4 The Term 'Ran-Human Being

Previously, we discussed and asserted that at death, man disintegrates into his three ri̲ŋ, flesh, yiëë-breath, and ti̲i̲y-intellect or soul. The Nuär uses the word 'ran' always in singular form. Usually, when Nuär uses the word 'ran', it simply means a human being who is made up of three components that are ri̲ŋ-flesh, yiëë-breath and ti̲i̲y, soul or intellect as we have discussed in the context of ciën-fearing revenge misfortune. According to Nuär, these three components apply to every human person whether that person is a Nuär or a juɔ̲r-foreigner. They believe that a human being regardless of his/her religion, nationality, culture, social status, poverty, handicap, infancy, adolescence, adult, and old, he/she still a human being.

Furthermore, the word 'ran' is used for a human being to distinguish him/her from other creatures. According to Nuär, other lower creatures have only two components such as ri̲ŋ-flesh, yiëë-breath. They believe that other creatures do not have ti̲i̲y-soul or intellect. Consequently, belief in Jɔɔk-living dead always refers to the specific part of the human person called ti̲i̲y-soul or intellect. When a Nuär man or a woman says to you, 'you have no ti̲i̲y-soul or intellect, he/she simply compares you to an animal which has only two components such as ri̲ŋ-flesh, yiëë-breath or in short, you have not heart.

The word 'ran' is a noun and it refers to every human being as we have above-mentioned above. When it is used as an adjective, its spellings change. For example, the Nuär can say ram mi lual-a red person, ram mi bor-a white person, and ram mi ca̲a̲r-a black person. However, when the Nuär expresses a sense of superiority, they will address each other as 'gat ram mä raan'-son of the human being in a singular form.

When they use that expression, they exclude the rest who are non-Nuär, the foreigners-juur. My father was using another expression such as 'gat lorä-son of the meaning or purpose. My stepbrother Köŋ Charoa who used to imitate my father's expression always calls me 'gat lorä-son, meaning son of purpose. When the Nuär uses those expressions, they feel a sense of pride and enjoy the taste of their language. According to P.P. Howell, their extraordinary vitality, expressed in a peculiar vivacity of speech, in physical courage and endurance, their arrogance and democratic outlook coupled with a most engaging sense of humour, make them outstanding among the peoples of Sudan.

1.5 The Term Naath-People

Another word similar to the word 'ran' is the word 'naath'. It is always used in plural form. The word naath in Nuär does have the same meaning as the Arabic word 'naath' but this is by coincidence. Evans-Pritchard and P.P. Howell who met Nuär experienced the taste of their language. According to them, "The Nuër called themselves Naath, which simply means 'people.' For example, the Nuär can say 'kɔn nɛy tin Naath 'we are the real People.' ...An expression which is sufficiently descriptive of their purpose and reveals their arrogant belief in their superiority over other human beings."

Sometimes, they can call themselves 'gaat nɛni̲ tin Naath' sons of the People. Both Evans-Pritchard and P.P. Howell affirm that by other tribes, they are often spoken of as Nuër, and to be explicit to the arrogant stranger, they will sometimes, say 'kon Nuëri', [kɔn Nuäri], 'we are the Nuër [Nuär]. Here, we find the exclusion of others in Nuär's three tunes.

For example, when they refer to themselves as Nuär, they exclude others when they call themselves 'kɔn nɛy tin Naath, and finally, when they say 'kɔn Nuäri.'

1.6 Similarities Between Nuär and Other Tribes

In a wider context, the Nuär are part of Negroid peoples who formerly occupied the Nile Valley as far as the north, and as far as the southern border of Egypt. In South Sudan however, Negroes of the tall slender race known as the Nilotic, have withstood Arab encroachments to the present day. The Nuär are among the categories of Nilotic people such as Anuak (Anyuak), Dinka (Jieng), and Collo (Shilluk).

The categories of Nilote peoples including Nuär developed a full-fledged pastoral economy and pressed southward at the expense of the earlier Cushitic and Bantu immigrants, giving rise to such tribes as the Acholi, Alur, Bari, and Lango of northern Uganda and the Luo and Nandi of Kenya. Furthermore, according to K. Bichiok and R. Kor, the Nuär has descended from the Nilotic people of South Sudan in Africa. They are tall and dark people; they are the second largest Nilotic people of the ethnic group of South Sudan.

The Nuär tribe is about 430,000 in the Nile Valley in Southern Sudan and has a typical Nilotic culture. It has been asserted that they are primarily both pastoralists and agriculturalists in their economic systems. The Nuär subsist on a diet of milk, butter, and fresh blood drawn from their cattle, however, they supplement this fare with maize and pearl millet grown by subsidiary agricultural activities in different geographical territories.

According to P.P. Howell, the Nuär culturally are near to

Dinka, and their two different languages have close affinities. He argues that they are of the same stock, but it remains a mystery why the Nuär should have emerged as a separate people with comparative suddenness about the beginning of the nineteenth century. They have driven the Dinka (Jieng) out of so much of their territory, seized so many of their wives and cattle, and absorbed whole sections of Dinka into their society.

1.7 Various Opinions on Nuär Topography and Ecology

The settlement pattern reflects the division of the year into well-defined wet and dry seasons. It is argued, "During the rainy season, the Nuär inhabit permanent villages of between sixty and a hundred inhabitants each, located on knolls or ridges and composed of circular huts with thatched roofs and walls of wattle and daub." [19] During the dry season, the Nuär migrate with their flocks and occupy temporary cattle camps near water holes.

According to P.P. Howell, "The Nuër country is set in the savannah and marshland of the Southern Sudan between latitudes 10° N. and 7° N. and with a seasonal rainfall between 800 and 1,000 mm. He further states that it is a special topographical and climatic feature which accounts for the present mode of life of the people."[20] The total area of Nuärland in

---

19 George P. MurDock, Arthur Tuden and Peter B. Hammond, "African Negro Art; Anthropology; Archaeology; Egypt: Ancient Civilization" *in the Collier's Encyclodpedia, Vol.I. of Twenty-Four Volumes, New York: (1995), pp. 260-270.*

20 P.P. Howell, *A Manuel of NuërLaw*, p.9. Average are: Malakal, 818 mm.; Fangak, 1136 mm.; Bentiu, 797 mm; Ler, 902 mm.; Abwong, 744.; mm.; Akobo, mm 925 mm.; Shambe, 819 mm. Fangak is exceptional, possibly owing to the heavy bush and Acacia forest in that region.

South Sudan is approximately 32,000 square miles. It has a population of about 350,000; however, the density of the population is low. According to P.P. Howell, some areas, however, are more densely populated than others not due to various reasons.

According to the geographical and administrative divisions since independence in 2011, the Nuär land occupies the east of Bahr el-Jebel to Zaraf, Pibor, and the Sobat valley for about 64,750 square kilometres. K. Bichiok and R. Kor assert, "The Nuär population is composed of two groups known as Geah and Haak and they are represented as sons of man (Ran)." The Geah groups: Bul, Leek, Lak, Jagɛi, Thiaŋ, Lou and Jikäny. The Haak groups Gaawar, Dɔk, and Nyuɔŋ/Dor. The Jikäny Kiir people Gaajak, Gaajiok, and Gaaguaŋ. Administratively, they are distributed into the four following Districts such as Western Nile Bitim (Bentiu), Central Fangak, and Eastern Nile consisting of Nuär of Akobo and Nasir.

In his observation of seasonal periods, P. Howell asserts that during the rainy season, roughly from May until November, but varying from one year to another. The people occupy higher ground better drained and comparatively free from flood. It is believed that this higher ground, where they build their permanent villages and cattle-byres, and have their cultivations, is limited and widely distributed. In some areas, it is concentrated in narrow ridges, usually running parallel to the main channels of the rivers, and in others, it is dispersed in isolated outcrops. P. Howell affirms that such natural features have their effects on the size of communities, and communications. Therefore, on political and social structure, producing local variation of detail is difficult.

1.8 Different Theories of Nuär Origin

The Nuär like other tribes in Africa have their mythological theories of their origin. Based on information gathered and written about Nuär by anthropologists, there is a conclusive general conviction of their origin. As we shall discuss later, all the anthropologists who investigated the Nuär mythological origin, concluded that all the Nuär of Western Nile, of Central Fangak, and Eastern Nile that is, Nasir and Akobo, do claim their mythological origin back to their ancestral homeland in central Western Nuär called 'däär Ciëŋ.' They trace their origin to a specific tree called "Ŋɔ̱ɔ̱b" in Nuär language, which is located at Ko̱c County.

It is called däär Ciëŋ because Jagɛi Nuär is at the centre of Western Nuär. In the north of Jagɛi Nuär, you have Jikäny, Leek, and Bul Chol Gɛ̱ɛ̱k and in the south of Jagɛi Nuär, you have Dok, Ha̱a̱k, and Nyuɔŋ. Therefore, in these seven major clans, Jagɛ Nuär is at the centre, and even within Jagɛi Nuär itself, the tree called 'Ŋɔ̱ɔ̱b'not tamarind tree is at the centre. This tree exists in "Ko̱ch County in a village called li̱c. According to Nuär, it is known by the famous name 'Thar Jiath Li̱i̱c-under the tree of li̱ic. Based on this mythological conviction, the Nuär would never allow others to tell them where they came from but rather would like to tell them where they came from about their origin.

Furthermore, about the mythological origin of Nuär, there are first six identified theories of periods in Nuär history started at the beginning of the nineteenth century as follows: First, the period before their movement eastwards, about which little is known, but when they must have been fewer in numbers and more closely united as a people. According to P. Howell, what was then a tribe would, in numbers, be approximately similar to a tribal segment today. Tribal boundaries were less defined. Second, the period of initial invasion when they moved eastwards in waves, which began with cattle, raids and ended in permanent occupation.

P. Howell asserts this period is recounted in traditions relatively fresh in the minds of the Nuër and not yet merged into tribal mythology. Third, the period of numerical expansion by natural processes and by the absorption of huge numbers of Dinka and therefore much of Dinka culture. This period was characterized by the facility with which Dinka elements were incorporated into Nuär society without remarkable frictions. According to P.P. Howell, it is probable that at this time the Nuär lost much of their former cohesion, particularly as they were almost simultaneously subjected to the disrupting effects of slave raids from the north. The

Fourth, at any rate, the third period seems to have been followed almost immediately by a period of disharmony, suspicion, internal strife, and political fission. Fifth period, as the pressure from the North increased, a return to a semblance of cohesion was necessary. There emerged the great Nuär leaders or 'Prophets' who arose as symbols of tribal resistance to foreign aggression represented first in the Dervish forces who attempted to establish slaving centres in Nuär land and finally by the forces of the Khartoum government.

The sixth period, states that in the years, that followed, the administration was limited to an attempt to hold the Nuär from their attacks on the Dinka, to prevent fighting among themselves, and to the collection of taxes. According to P.P. Howell, naturally, enough the Nuär resented this, particularly the collection of tribute in cattle and prevention of cattle raids, and despite the outstanding efforts of individual administrators such as Struvè, Stigand, and Jackson, the attempt to establish ordered administration was only partially successful.

1.8.1 H. Johnson's Version on Nuär Origin

According to H. Johnson, the focal point for the Nuär in their settlement in the east was a tamarind tree (koat) at the village of Koat-Liec-[Koch-Liic). All the Nuär as the historical homeland considered that Tree. It is located to the west of Bahr el-Jebel. It is believed that "All Nuër groups, except the Jikäny, claim to have originated beneath that tree. H. Johnson mistakenly believed that was burned (sic) down about 1918, but the site is still sacred. It is still the focus of sacrificial activity on behalf of all Nuër. It is argued that the tree is a communal symbol of communities that consist of past, present, and future. According to H. Johnson "In a sense, trees 'create' communities by gathering people under them and consequently, it represents the community in many myths throughout the region."[21]

Furthermore, the tamarind tree as the origin where the life of all Nuär began, symbolizes social and genealogical incorporation. As such, the tree figures in most cases Nuär myths. It is believed that in their most generalized concept, these myths, account for the appearance of the Nuär, the Dinka, and other peoples with whom the Nuär have met. Specifically, the relationship between Nuär descent groups, or

---

21 Douglas H. Johnson, *Nuër Prophets, A History of Prophecy from the Upper Nile in the Nineteenth and Twentieth Centuries,* New York, Oxford University Press, 1994, p. 45.

clans. According to H. Johnson, the Nuär clans claim descent from the two brothers such as Geak-Gaw and Haak, either directly or by incorporation. It is believed that the Jagɛi of the west and the Jinäc of the Lou, are represented as direct descendants of Geak.

The ancestors of many other clans, however, appear independently, either falling directly from the tree or the sky near it and joining one or other of the two broad divisions of the Nuär by adoption or marriage into the family of one of the two brothers. The founding ancestors of the Jimɛm lineage of earth-masters-kuaa̱r muɔɔn (and the two main Gaawar clans, the Jakär and Gaatwaror Gaawär), were all brought in and attached to the original community surrounding the tree. It is argued that the foreigners who were incorporated into the Nuär lineage system thus appear to be a long-established practice, for example, pre-dating the nineteenth-century east expansion.

Such belief that all the Nuär originated from the same tree in the western Nile affects even the way the dead are buried both in the west and in the east. Evans-Pritchard affirms, "I have believed that in western Nuërland a man is buried facing east and a woman facing west, but in the eastern Nuërland both sexes are buried facing west. He asserts, "Nuër have told me this is because the eastern Nuër originally came from the west and that in western Nuërland, their ancestors were created; but, as seen, they also associate the passage from birth to death with the movement of the sun across the sky."[22]

The connections between the western, and eastern Nuär, affect even the present generations. For example, the desire to see the place where Nuär ancestors originated for the people of Lajɔr Duäc (Lajɔr Dingyian), the so-called 'Jikany dɔar',

22 E.E. Evans-Pritchard, *Nuër Religion*, p. 145.

is so great. It is a nostalgia. In 2007, a prominent politician a member of the parliament by the name Peter Charleman Chawach Rabaŋ flew by airplane from Khartoum to Unity State-Bitim-Bentiu to attend a certain function of celebration. During his visit to his ancestral land, he went to Ko̱ch-Li̱ch on January 11, 2007. He attended a prayer in which a yellow ox was prepared to be sacrificed to the ancestors in the place of Tamarind Tree at Ko̱ch-Lich, the place in which all Nuär claim their origin.

According to Peter Charleman Shawach Rabaŋ, when the elders finished the prayers-pal, "they asked him to spear the yellow ox, which he did with great joy."[23] Furthermore, on January 12, 2007, he went to Guet, the original place of Lajɔr Duäc (Lajɔr Diŋyiɛ̈n) before he could leave for the eastern Nile. C. Rabaaŋ himself offered the grey ox as a sacrifice to the ancestors, specifically in the presumable place of the tomb of the wife of Lajɔr Duäc (Lajɔr Diiŋyiɛ̈n).

About my testimony, on December 17, 2020-January 9, 2021, I went to langkien (Nyi̱rol) to the territory of Gabaal to celebrate Christmas with a Catholic community under the request of the Parish Priest Rev. Fr. Dirping Chan. Gabaal consists of two sections: La̱a̱ŋ and Yɔal Bäŋ BAL (Cieŋ Nyar Kuac). I arrived in the morning. The parishioners at the airport warmly welcomed me. When we arrived at the Catholic Chapel, we all went inside headed by the Parish Priest. I was asked to say a word of prayer. Finally, I briefly introduced myself to the faithful. When they heard that I came from the West, they became very enthusiastic and eager to hear more about my particular clan.

23 Interview with prominent politician who was a member of the parliament by name Char Chawich Rabang, Juba- at POCs, May 18, 2019.

In the evening, a good number of catechists and a legion of marry plus some men came to greet me. After a brief period of introduction, I was asked, which clan are you from in western Nuär? I replied I am from Jagɛi Nuär. They all responded, so you are from Däär ciëŋ gueth ëë caak kɛ kɔn dial thi̱n thar jiath li̱i̱c that means, you are from the centre of the house where we were all created under Li̱i̱c tree. Furthermore, one person asked me if I could tell him about my specific clan in western Nuär. I said, I am from rɛ̈ëŋ yian. Immediately, he pointed out some men between those sitting around, saying, so and so are from rɛ̈ëŋ yian.

During my stay with Gabal for some days, I came to realize that there is no single person in eastern Nuär who cannot trace his/her origin back to western Nuärland. It was amazing to see that each of them can trace his/her origin back even to a small ancestral clan in the western Nuär homeland. Based on this personal experience, I can conclude that those from central and eastern Nuär, are from various clans of western Nuär.

1.8.2 Evans-Pritchard's Version on Nuär Origin

Some anthropologists who are considered 'to have been active observers among the Nuär' have approached the historical account of Nuär origin from different perspectives. Their records on Nuär origin proved beyond no doubt and pointed to the Jagɛi area of western Nuärland, specifically the county called Koch-li̱ch which the Nuär refer to as the 'Centre of the House.'

Evans-Pritchard asserts that the Nuär can hardly be said to have a creation myth, though our authorities record fragmentary accounts of the creation of men, parts of which I have myself heard. He states these accounts state that men were created in the Jagɛi country of western Nuërland at a certain tamarind tree, at the foot of which offerings and, according to Mr. Jackson; sacrifices were sometimes made until it was destroyed by fire in 1918. Evans-Pritchard believed that many details in the versions given by Mr Jackson and Captain Fergusson are foreign, either Dinka or, in Mr. Jackson's account, Shilluk (Collo) and in Captain Fergusson's account possibly even Atuɔt or Mundari. I regard Father Crazzolara's version as the closest to Nuär tradition. In this version, the tamarind tree called Liic was itself the mother of men who, according to one account, emerged from a hole at its foot or, according to another account, dropped off its branches like ripe fruits.

God, creative Spirit, is the final Nuär explanation of everything, which exists in the universe. According to Nuär, he made heavens, the earth, and the waters on the earth, and the beasts and birds and reptiles and fish, and he is the author of custom and tradition. According to Nuär, God instituted marriage and prohibitions based on each category of species. He provided them with faculties and qualities for both males and females according to their categories for their continuity. If the institution of marriage and its prohibitions are abused, he provides norms, which frustrate those abuses. For example, sex should be between males and females of the same nature.

1.9 The Contemporary Nuär's Version of Their Origin

According to contemporary Nuär, the version of their origin requires a new assessment of recent counties established by the South Sudan government after the independence in 2011. This new assessment does not ignore the four major areas of Nuärland such as Bitim-Bentiu, Fangak, Akobo, and Nasir but rather, it helps to give a holistic outlook on contemporary Nuär communities. Therefore, below are general descriptions of contemporary Nuär according to their states and counties.

First, Western Nuär/ Bitim (Bentiu): All Jikäny are from Jiok Kiir (Gaatjiook). Thiang Kiir and Kun Kiir, Jiok Kiir whose mother was called Duany. Thiang Kiir or Mathiaang (Gaatjaak), whose mother was called Nyakuini. Kun Kiir (Gaatguang), whose mother was called Nyaboora Targɛi.

Second, Guit County: Inhabited by the Jikäny kuec ciëŋ community in the eastern Bentiu. Other groups of the Jikäny community in the eastern Nuär in western Ethiopia are called (Jikäny dɔar). Third, Mayɔm County: Inhabited by Bulchöl Geah. Kuac and Gok communities are in the western part of the state. Fourth, Rupkɔtni County: inhabited by the Leek community in the northern Bentiu. Fifth, Koch County: Inhabited by the Jagɛi community in central Bentiu. Sixth, Mayiandit County: Inhabited by Haak Bikol-Kuoth community in the far southwestern part of the state. They are also known as Gaat bikol-kuoth. Seventh, Lɛɛr County: Inhabited by the Dɔk community in the southern part of the state. Eighth, Paynyi̱jiar County: Inhabited by the Nyuong (Nyuɔŋ) community in the far southern part of the state.

Ninth, Fangak County: is inhabited by Thiang, Laak, and, Tenth, Ayod County: is inhabited by Gaatwaar. Lou Nuär: eleventh, Urӧӧr County: inhabited by Dak kä diɔ̱ɔ̱k that is, Yo̱l Da̱k kɛ Bo̱r Da̱k kɛ Jack Da̱k (Ciëŋ Dak). Twelveth, Langkein County: inhabited by Baal. (Gaatbaal). Thirteenth, Akobo County: inhabited by Mor and Go̱n (Gaat Nyabiel)

Nuär/Jikany: The Nuär/Gaatwär I am talking about belongs to Nuär/Fangak. They consist of two large families such as the Baarand the Nyaŋ. The Baar live between Wau (not Wau of Bahr-el-Ghazal) and Kuac Dɛŋ. The Nyaŋ live between Mogok and Pagil. These are considered original Gaatwär. With time, Nuär of other groups or even people belonging to other tribes and places came to live with them. They are called Gaatwär migrants or aggregated. According to their social standard, they divide themselves into two classes, the Jicieng Nuärä (=those living in villages, normally take care of cows) and the Ji̱rɛ̈ɛ̈k Nuärä (those living in towns, the educated or the developed ones).

1.9.1 Genealogical Version of Ancestral Line Tree

The Nuär do have various myths of their origin and they all believe to have originated from one place as we have mentioned earlier. Like Israelites, apart from being decanted from the Ŋɔ̱ɔ̱b tree, the Nuär also trace their origin through their ancestors (genealogy). By tracing their origin according to each family's ancestors (genealogy) which always ends up with a totem. In this regard, one gets the diverse versions of Nuär origins. For example, it was a common practice when parents sit around the fire in the evening with their children, they ask each to count his/her grandfathers/grandmothers from both sides of the parents. Each child is taught to know his/her ancestors because the Nuär believe that knowing the genealogies of one's ancestors, leads to the core myth of their origin.

However, unfortunately, counting the number of the ancestors does not automatically lead to the Ŋɔ̱ɔ̱b tree at

Koch-Li̠i̠c Jagɛi Nuär but rather to some totems. This seems to be the common belief about the myths of their origin for the majority of them. When we speak of the myth of the origin of certain tribes such as Nuär, it will be inappropriate to associate it with a precise date and year. This should be considered as both a mystery and beyond scientific evidence because mythological origin, attempts to explain the origin of the beginning of life.

In my interview with contemporary Nuär girls and one boy at the Protection of Civilians (POC) site in Unity-Bentiu-Rubkona I interviewed: 1. Elizabeth Nyaboth able to count her: Matik Gatluak, Balkam, Duop, Kan Yiok Kaŋ, Elaŋ Kuan, Thiey Roal, Kuɔ̱ŋ Lek. 2. Veronica Nyajima: Peter Makuei, Buor Kiacg, Khor Tejok, Luɔ̱m Thon, Kiir Baŋ, Nyathaak Dak, Rial Kiir. 3. Mr. Kɔ̱a̱ak grandfathers: Gatley, Liee Wäl, Rɛ̈ɛth Koc, Luth Guɛ̈ɛ̈, Toto Dɔany, Kok Bi̠li̠w, Ŋɛc Nyɛtha̠a̠k Da̠k, Rialkier Penyier Puychaw, Caaw.

1.10 Myths and Genealogical Origins of Major Nuär Clans

Considering themselves as nations-döör, when the word 'Nuär is used by them, it is applied to four major areas of Nuär land occupied by them. When they say to themselves, 'kɔn Nuäri̠ Da̠ŋ ŋuan-We are four Nuär, they refer namely to first, Bentiu (Bentim) Unity State in the Western Nile which consists of seven major clans such as Jikany Cieŋ, Bul, Leek, Dɔk, Haak, Jagɛy, and Nyuɔŋ.

Second, the Nuär of Central Fangak: which consists of Major clans such as Thi̠a̠ŋ (kɛ̱ɛ̱k gɛKä-elder son of Gɛk), Laak, and Gaatwäär. Third, the Nuär of Akobo-(Wa̠a̠d-Buordiid)),

Lou Nuär which consists of five clans such as Dak kä di<u>ɔɔ</u>k-three major clans of Dak such as Y<u>oo</u>l Dak Clan, B<u>oo</u>r Dak Clan, Jak Dak Clan, G<u>o</u>n (Gabaal) and Mor. Fourth, the Nuär of Nasir: Eastern Jikany: Jikäny which consists of major clans such as Gaajiok, Gaaguaŋ, and Gaajaak with their small segments or subdivisions. Consequently, all these segments, do call themselves 'Nuär' and not 'Nuër.'

1.10.1 J<u>i</u>käny Ciëŋ and J<u>i</u>käny Dɔar

According to the mythological narrative of J<u>i</u>käny West, K<u>ii</u>r Kak Kër was believed to be the Great Grandfather of J<u>i</u>käny K<u>ii</u>r. It was believed that Gɛ̈ɛ̈k Gaw cut him out from the gourd of a Dinka (Jieŋ) man called Yuel Kuot. Furthermore, the myth said that the wife of Yuel reported to her husband "when her infant cries, I heard another voice of a child crying also at our farm." Consequently, Yuel and his wife decided to come to the place of the gourd at the farm and found the gourd.

Then, when I tried to pick out the gourd, it was very strong like a stone/päm. Consequently, they came back home with his wife. Yuel decided to go to Gɛ̈ɛ̈k Gaw and reported to him that there was a child inside the gourd on my farm. However, I tried to carry it but I was unable to do so. When Gɛ̈ɛ̈k heard this, he told Yuel to go back home and he promised him that he would come to his house. At midnight, Gɛ̈ɛ̈k prayed to God, asking him to give him the power to resolve the problem reported to him by Yuel Kuot.

In the following morning, he took three oxen to the house of Yuel Kuot. When he arrived, he asked Yuel and his wife to provoke the child to cry. When the child was provoked, it cried and the child inside the gourd cried at the farm. Then, Gɛ̈ɛ̈k went back home and brought three oxen for scarification. He returned to the house of Yuel. Upon his arrival, he killed one ox at the periphery of the kraal of the byre/wi̱c na̱l luak. Then, he came to the rie̱k shrine and killed another ox. Finally, he went to the farm where the child was inside the gourd and killed a third ox in the presence of Yuel and his wife. Consequently, he cut the gourd and removed the child from it. Therefore, the name Ki̱i̱r/kie̱r derived from the sacrificial beasts, which Gɛ̈ɛ̈k offered to God.

1.10.1.1 Ritual Purification After His Birth

Gɛ̈ɛ̈k commanded Yuel and his wife to take the child to the river to be washed. After they washed the child, unfortunately, blood was bleeding from his eyes. Gɛ̈ɛ̈k named Ki̱i̱r Kak Kër because he was given three ritual sacrifices/kɛ ɣöö ca kiir kɛ thiaŋ dä diɔ̱k). Ki̱i̱r was taken by the wife of Yuel Kuot and suckled him with her child. He grew up in their house until he was initiated into manhood.

1.10.1.2 Ki̱i̱r's Miracle, Profession & Origin of Thi̱a̱ŋ

However, when Ki̱i̱r had reached the age of puberty, he was unable to look at people because his eyes were very red (wizard). One time, he wizard antelope and it became dormant. Consequently, he has castrated it. However, Ki̱i̱r beat it with a stick and the antelope got well again.

After Ki̱i̱r was initiated, he became a blacksmith/cui la bël at the house of Yuel Kuot. One day, something happened to him after he married a girl. The myth said that the antelope, which he castrated, came to the house where they were. When the people tried to kill it, Kiir prevented the people not to kill it. The antelope asked the people "Where is Kiir Kak Kër? The people replied he was inside the byre.

Then, the antelope said, "Let him come out." When Kiir came out, the antelope asked him, "Why did you castrate me? Kiir kept quiet, but the antelope, said to him, "When you give birth to a child, his name will always be called Thiaŋ as my remembrance because I will not give birth due to castration you imposed on me. Later on, his wife gave birth to a baby boy but unfortunately, the mother died. Consequently, the child was named Thiaŋ. After the death of his first wife, Kiir married a second wife who bore him a son called Kun Kiir/ Jaak Kiir but she also died.

1.10.1.3 Kiir Migration to Gɛ̈ɛ̈k Territory

After the death of his two wives, the two families of in-laws decided to chase Kiir away from their territory. Then, the myth said that he took refuge in the territory of Gɛ̈ɛ̈k who removed him from the gourd. While he was on his way to the territory of Gɛ̈ɛ̈k, he arrived at the bank of the river. However, he could not cross the river due to a lack rowing boat. Then, he called bäär/dëëb rɛy/fishermen who were on the other side of the river to bring him a boat, because his life was in danger from his in-laws.

However, when the fishermen arrived, they asked him to come to the boat, however, he did not look at them but rather, turned his face downward. They asked him "Why do you look downward? He replied I am a wizard (my eyes are very red) that is why I cannot look at you. The fishermen said to him unless you are Ki̱i̱r Kak Kër. He answered, yes, I am. Then, he looked at them and consequently, they took some water and sprinkled his eyes with water. Then, he was told, "From today onward, your wizard is over/pɛɛth du cɛ thuɔ̱k. They told him, that only Mut Wiu/ a mysterious power will remain you.

Consequently, they rowed him to the other side of the river of the territory of Gɛ̈ɛ̈k Gaw. When Ki̱i̱r arrived at the territory of Gɛ̈ɛ̈k, he found out that he had already died. He only got his grandchildren. Afterwards, the family of Yuel Kuot brought his two sons to him. Then, the three sons of Lɛ̈k Bol that is, Lou Lɛ̈k, Bul Lɛ̈k, and Yo̱t Lɛ̈k, decided to give Ki̱i̱r their sister name Duany Lɛk (Gɛkä) Bol who was unfortunately paralyzed.

Then Duany said to her brothers "My brothers you know that I am paralyzed and yet you gave me to a dog whose origin cannot be traced". Her brothers answered, "You have no other husband accept Ki̱i̱r." Finally, Duany accepted him. She bore him a baby boy. Then, her brothers asked her, "Did you give birth"? Then, Duany answered, "Yes." Her brothers asked her again "Is it a dog or a human being? She replied, it is like a human being. Her brothers told her your son will be called "Jo̱k/dog due to what you said last time.

1.10.1.4 The Origin of J̱ikäny & Their Genealogy

After the birth of Jo̱k, his brothers-in-law asked Ki̱i̱r, to repair their fishing spears and other spears. Then, he asked his brothers-in-law "What will you give me." They promised him a calf. Then, he repaired their fishing spears and other spears. After a month, he asked his brothers-in-law to give him his promised calf. However, they were able to give it to him on time. Then, Ki̱i̱r kept on asking them every morning and evening of the day. Finally, they gave him his loan. Sometimes, when his sons visit their uncles, they used to call "the children of the man of no compromise/ meaning Ji̱käny/ Jiäka̱ny." Finally, Ki̱i̱r died.

After the death of Ki̱i̱r, Thiaŋ was asked by the three wives of his uncle to inherit Duany Lɛ̈k. Then, Duany gave birth to Nyaŋ Ki̱i̱r who was the last-born and grandfather of Gaatguak. The list of Ki̱i̱r is as follows: 1. Mathia̱ŋ Ki̱i̱r, the grandfather of Thi̱a̱ŋ (the myth said that Ki̱i̱r gave his spear to Thi̱a̱ŋ) 2. Kun Ki̱i̱r/Jaak Ki̱i̱r, the father of Gaatjaak, 3. Jo̱k Ki̱i̱r, the father of Gaatjo̱k, and lastly, Nyaŋ Ki̱i̱r.

1.10.1.5 The Myth of Ki̱i̱r's Birth According to Ji̱käny East

According to Ji̱käny East, Ki̱i̱r was a son of Nyabaar, the daughter of King Nyihe of Bäär). The myth said that someone impregnated Nyabaar; however, her grandmother was afraid to inform the King. Nevertheless, she continued to pray to God fearing that if the king discovers, he will kill his granddaughter because he was a very brutal King. Nevertheless, when the King realized that his granddaughter was pregnant, he called the granddaughter. He said to her, this girl is pregnant. However, the grandmother denied it. She claimed that the girl was only sick. The king accepted it with doubt in his mind.

Furthermore, the myth said that some months later, the girl delivered a gourd with a placenta in the presence of some women including her grandmother. Then, King Nyihe was called to see by himself the miracle that had happened. When he came, he saw exactly the gourd, which was delivered, by his granddaughter and the placenta. Then, he decided to take the gourd to the river nearby and put it on the water. After that, he sacrificed a goat to God.

Furthermore, the myth said that the gourd was carried away by currents/waves along the river. When the gourd arrived at the territory of Dink/Jieŋ, they tried to put it out from the river but they could not. Consequently, they left it. It was said that the gourd continued to flow through the river until it arrived at the territory of Gɛ̈ɛ̈k while his Sons were taking shower in the river. However, when they saw the gourd floating towards them, they were amazed at the gigantic gourd. Consequently, they ran towards it to pull it to the dry land. They said to themselves, we should cut it into two. They pulled it out from the river, however, when they were about to cut it, unfortunately, they saw the blood coming out of the gourd.

Then, they ran home and informed their father Gɛ̈ɛ̈k. He asked them, what has happened? They responded; we saw a gigantic gourd in the river floating as it was carried by the waves. We pulled it out from the river but we tried to cut it, and the blood was coming out of it. Then, Gɛ̈ɛ̈k went with his children to the riverside while commanded them to bring his spear. When they arrived, he tried to cut it but the gourd was bleeding with blood and also it was very hard. He prinks it with the tip of his spear, unfortunately, the tip of his spear gets broken inside the gourd. Then, Gɛ̈ɛ̈k called a grandfather of Ngok/Ŋɔk Dinka named Ngok who was known for having a big spear for killing animals.

When Ngok/Ŋɔk arrived, Gɛ̈ɛ̈k first commanded him to remove the wooden stick of his spear and to use the spear to cut the gourd into two. Then, Ngok/Ŋɔk cut it, the gourd divided itself into halves. The right part contained a human being and the left one, contained certain items such as leopard skin/thɔ̲a̲n, dëëth, the tip of the spear which got broken inside the gourd, stone/päm. Then, Gɛ̈ɛ̈k said to Ki̲i̲r, it is good that you are a human being, then, we must talk because God has created me before you.

When Ki̲i̲r began to talk, then, Gɛ̈ɛ̈k commanded his children to bring two cows to be sacrificed to him. When the two cows were brought, Gɛ̈ɛ̈k sacrified them to Ki̲i̲r. He asked him to go with him to the cattle camp but Ki̲i̲r said to him, go first and prepare a shelter/hut for me, which Gɛ̈ɛ̈k did as he was told. When evening hour came, Ki̲i̲r came and entered a room with its door open towards the homeless.

Then, Ki̲i̲r he told the people that he did not need food. Furthermore, he gave conditions to Gɛ̈ɛ̈k that he should only be seen by the elderly people including Geek When Gɛ̈ɛ̈k came to see him in the evening, he found him to be a blacksmith/bël. However, Gɛ̈ɛ̈k told Ki̲i̲r to marry a wife. He married two wives with cows of Gɛ̈ɛ̈k. His wives were Nyaborä Targek and Nyakuini̲. Unfortunately, Ki̲i̲r killed his two wives with his wizard eyes/kɛ pɛɛth dɛ. They left him two children, Thi̲äŋ Ki̲i̲r and Kun Ki̲i̲r.

Finally, Gɛ̈ɛ̈k gave him his daughter Duany Gɛkä without payment of cows. They gave birth only to one child by the name of Jo̱k and then, Ki̱i̱r died. Then, Mathi̱a̱ŋ/Thi̱äŋ inherited the wife of his father by name Duany Gɛkä who bore a son by the name Nyaŋ Ki̱i̱r. After the death of Ki̱i̱r, his son Nyaŋki̱i̱r asked his grandfather Gɛ̈ɛ̈k to distribute the items that were rolled in the leopard skin when his father was removed out from the gourd. The items that were found on the left half of the gourd were the following: first, leopard skin, second, the broken part of the spear of Gɛ̈ɛ̈k, third, the stone/päm and fourth, dëëth/irons.

As for distributions of those items, Gɛ̈ɛ̈k took the leopard skin, he gave to Mathi̱a̱ŋ/Thi̱äŋ, the broken part of the spear, he gave the stone/päm to Nyaŋ Ki̱i̱r to sharpen his spear with it, and fourth, he divided the irons/dëëth between Kun Ki̱i̱r Kak Kër and Jök. For example, Nyaŋ Ki̱i̱r Nuär are brave they can fight Gaajök and Gaajak and defeat them.

1.11 Various Myths of Gaatwär Nuär Origin

Various myths are concerning the origin of Gaatwär Nuär. However, although one can see that these variations nevertheless there is a convergent. The variations of their mythological origin are due to the complexities of their myths. These myths portray the depth of their belief. The similarities and the commonalities are very amazing. The detailed information enhance the richness of their origin.

1.11.1 First Version

According to the version of Gaatwäär Nuär on their origin, Ka̱r and Wa̱a̱r who descended from heaven were their ancestors. This myth further says that Wa̱a̱r has a semi-divine origin. The Gaatwäär Nuär believed that previously, the people of the earth used to travel frequently to visit the people of heaven since the dwellers of heaven were in constant communication with those of the earth. However, according to their myth of creation, Ka̱r and Wa̱a̱r were heavenly beings. The ground was so dear to Ka̱r (or Jaka̱a̱r) that he frequently descended to it via the rope that connected the sky to the tamarind tree, where God had first created people in Koch County. Ka̱r and his brother Lök (jalök) one day decided to follow Wa̱a̱r to see for themselves where he was heading.

Wa̱a̱r descended using the rope and sat on a tamarind tree branch as he waited for his brother's arrival. When a woman spotted him as she and her dog were gathering firewood, she informed Ka̱r who was in the hamlet of the situation. Consequently, he went to his brother and invited him to leave the tree to accompany him to the settlement place. Unfortunately, Wa̱a̱r rejected the invitation.

Then Ka̱r went to the house, he killed an ox and roasted the meat knowing how Wa̱a̱r likes the roasted meat. Fortunately, the aroma of grilled pork caught Wär and finally, he was unable to refuse the invitation. He descended from the tree and sat down at his brother's beautiful table. While Wa̱a̱r was trying to go back to paradise (heaven), he realized the rope was unfortunately cut. Ka̱r intentionally cut the rope to stay on the planet with his brother Lök (Jalök). Another version said that Wär Ɣa̱a̱k Koth came from heaven when his sister

Ka̱a̱r Ɣa̱a̱k Kuoth made a trick to burn a slice of meat. After she roasted the meat, Wär smelled it, he immediately came down from heaven.

1.11.2 Second Version

However, other Nuär also narrate this mythological origin from different angles. They said that during a severe storm, Waar had fallen from the sky as a result. He was discovered on the ground by a dog already wounded. The legend further asserts that Lök (Jalök) was the owner of the dog. The dog was pursuing Kuei's wife as she searched for firewood. Kuei's wife, who also took care of him, brought Wa̱a̱r home. Then a disagreement over Wa̱a̱r emerged between Kuei and Lök. Lök said Wa̱a̱r should join his family since it was his dog that discovered him.

However, according to Kuei, Wa̱a̱r should stay with his family, asserting that it was his wife who took care of him. During that argument, Ka̱r stepped up and said that Wa̱a̱r was his brother. Currently, Ka̱r was the brother of Lök and the son of Ha̱a̱k. Wa̱a̱r became a member of the Ha̱a̱k's family in this manner. After getting married to Nyabak Do̱o̱r, Wa̱a̱r had five children, whose names were Yian (also spelt Riak), Keer (Can), Padang (Jamuo̱k), The̱p, and Tur. Gatwäär is the name of Wa̱a̱r's son. Buok is the son of Käpɛ̈l, Ge̱ŋ, Jaak, Rɔ̱th, Tur, and Wa̱r.

1.11.1.3 Third Verion

The Cier and Padaŋ of western Nuär, believe that once there was someone by the name Wa̱a̱r who used to live on land while Thiliɛy used to live underwater. It was said that Thiliɛy used to beat his drum under the water and Wa̱a̱r used to hear the sound of his drum. Furthermore, Wäa̱r used to beat his drum while living on the land. The legend said that Wa̱a̱r took the initiative to go to a river and asked Thiliɛy who are you living underwater? Further, Wa̱a̱r said to him, come out because I want to see if you are a human. Then, Thiliɛy came out with his small drum. Wa̱a̱r asked him, why do you live underwater while you are a human? Then, Thiliɛy answered him, I am staying underwater with Nyiwär/a kind of fish which Gaatwär do not eat because they consider it as their god.

Finally, Wa̱a̱r invited Thiliɛy to go with him inside a room. Then, they sat down, and Wa̱a̱r showed Thiliɛy his small drum. Fortunately, they discovered that their drums were similar to each other. Then, they decided to make an agreement. However, Wa̱a̱r said to Thiliɛy, we cannot make an agreement between us, because there is another human being called Ba̱r (originated from Dinka Jieŋ). Then, they both went to him and finally, found him. After they met at home, they made an agreement with regard to the division of their roles which we shall discuss later on in chapter three.

1.13 Nuɔŋ and Dɔk Nuär

According to the mythological origin of Nuär Nyuɔŋ, it is said that they descended from Guɛ̈k Ga̱w. They are the paternal brothers of Dɔk Nuär. Therefore, both Nyuɔŋ and Dɔk Nuär descended from the same father, by name Guɛ̈k Gaw. The myth said that Guɛ̈k and Gɛ̈ɛ̈k were brothers; their father is called Ga̱w Raan Kuoth.

Furthermore, it is said that it was Gatluak Nyääk who led the migration from Dɔk territory to the present territory that Nyuɔŋ Nuär have settled. Furthermore, after Nyuɔŋ left their own territory at Adɔk, Gatluak Nyääk who led the migration, divided them into two areas such as Do̱o̱r and Nyuɔŋ. Consequently, they call themselves, Nyuɔŋ Gatluak Nyääk up to date.

1.13.1 Children of Nyuɔŋ Nuär

It is said that Nyuɔŋ has six children such as first, Leek, second, Liath, third, Mök, fourth, Lua̱c, fifth, Gaattiɛl and sixth, Tha̱a̱k. His children were five children; however, Tha̱ak came after a different version and consequently, joined Nyuɔŋ's children. According to this version, Tha̱a̱k was found among the deer. However, when they took the cattle for grazing, they saw the boy among the deer, living with them. One day Nyuɔŋ's sons made a plan to capture him. They hide near the pool where the deer and the boy used to come to drink water. Immediately, they caught him and brought him home.

When they arrived home, the boy remained with Liath. However, he was given to Leek to stay with him. Sometimes, Tha̱a̱k do perform some mysterious works. For example, whenever they took cattle for grazing, he always pulled the tuft of grass (Thuc) and the water came out from it, and finally, the cattle would drink. People realized that he had a small power. They asked themselves, how do Tha̱a̱k get water at a place, where there is no river, just by pulling out the tuft of grass (Thuc)?

1.14 Gɛ̈ɛ̈k Clans

According to this traditional line tree, the Lɔu-Nuär are children of Na̱i Gɛkä (Di̱näy Gɛkä) from Koch County (Li̱ic County). The Lɔu-Nuär simply became known as Lɔu. It is stated that while the family of Gɛ̈ɛ̈k was multiplying in number, consequently, the land became smaller. Sometimes, internal disagreements started to occur rising to the level of conflict. Other reasons were related to power struggles among the leaders, which led the individual groups to migrate in search of better living conditions.

The term Nuär is an adjective that was historically formed by the ancient ancestors through rites, while the name 'Lɔu' is a nickname relating to the colour of a bull, which indicates grey. However, according to the myths, Na̱i Gɛkä (Denäy Gɛkä) was physically weaker at birth than his twin brother Diit. As a result, he was given the moniker Näi-Näi, which later changed to Na̱i, and his children were given the names Di̱näy (or Ji̱näy). Bäny, Yien, Nyaŋ, and their sisters Nyabiɛl and Paduai were Na̱i's children. Bäny Ji̱näy (Di̱näy) grew rapidly in number, multiplied, and surpassed the number of the rest of his brethren. However, in the interim, he had three sons by his wife Nyagön, Dak, Baal, and Rɛɛt, and their descendants came to be known as Gon. Baal (Gabaal) occupied Nyirol County, while Yien and Rɛɛt resided in Urör County.

1.14.1 Other Children of Nyamor

The two sisters of Nyaŋ, (also known as Galiɛk), are Nyabiɛl and Paduai. These three formed the clan of Mor Nuär living in Akobo County at present. As opposed to her sister Paduai, who had a son named Bol, Nyabiɛl had two boys that are, Mac and Jɔk. The community grew larger which consequently, led to Jɔk's independence, which became known as a Jɔak-Jɔak community. Consequently, Uncle Nyaŋ (Galik) and his cousin Bol, joined the older brother Mac, and as a result, the three groups formed Jimaac.

On the one hand, the J̱inäy (Ḏinäy) children from Nyagön and Nyamor, grew closer to each another, and on the other hand, they had a bull with a grey tint that they named Lɔu. A yellow bull named Rɛ̈ɛ̈ŋ-yian that had some white on the bottom belonged to the Bäny children. When the two bulls fight (Lɔu and Rɛ̈ɛ̈ŋ-yian), this occasionally becomes a source of joy and sociable entertainment for the two communities of Lɔu and Bäny. It is said the J̱inäy (Ḏinäy) family was split into two factions, each of which supported one of the two bulls above-mentioned.

Additionally, according to reliable sources about this legend, the Rɛ̈ɛ̈ŋ-yian bull used to triumph over the Lɔu bull. However, the Lɔu bull finally, defeated the Rɛ̈ɛ̈ŋ-yian. The Bäny children who were the supporters of Rɛ̈ɛ̈ŋ-yian bull became irritated out of superiority and pride. As a result, they lost control of their fury, which, unfortunately, led to the attack of Lɔu Bull supporters who were children of J̱inäy (Ḏinäy). The two supporters of the two bulls fought each other.

This was because the Lɔu supporters could no longer tolerate the Rɛ̈ɛ̈ŋ-yian supporters' intimidation. On the hand other, due to the fighting, Bäny's children so (A) J̱inäy (Ḏinäy), replaced by the name Lɔu and on the other hand, (b) the name Bäny was replaced by the Rɛ̈ɛ̈ŋ-yian. Therefore, to avoid further conflict between the families, Lɔu decided to migrate to a new location in the eastern White Nile.

1.15 The Origin of Laak and Leek Nuär

Ju̱eny Däre̱l was a man who probably came from the Dinka (Jieŋ) area as claimed by Nuär. They believed that he got lost in the bush and was consequently, found by a daughter of Gɛ̈ɛ̈k by the name Kɛ̈ɛ̈r Gɛkä. She brought him to her father's house. Ju̱eny remained in the family of Gɛ̈ɛ̈k for some time. After they got used to each other, they began to fall in love with each other. Finally, Kɛ̈ɛ̈r ended up by conceiving a child. Kɛ̈ɛ̈r informed Ju̱eny that she was pregnant. Fearing to face the consequence from the sons of Gɛ̈ɛ̈k that is, from Ŋɔ̱r (Thiaŋ) and Denäy, they both decided to escape away. According to Nuär culture, to impregnate a girl before marriage is considered a great loss and offence for the family. They believe that marriage involves many steps between two families leading to the payment of bride-wealth.

It was said that while they were in hiding, Ju̱eny built a raft by joining bundles of herbs for their accommodation. Consequently, they lived in a swamp place, which sometimes got dry according to the season. Meanwhile, the brothers of Kɛ̈ɛ̈r, Ŋɔ̱r (Thiaŋ), and Denäy Gɛɛkä, were searching for them, however, they could not find them. To sustain their lives in that lonely swamp place, during the day, Ju̱eny used to go fishing and Kɛ̈ɛ̈r used to gather lilies to cook bulbs. The narrative asserts that they survived in such a terrible situation for a few months until Kɛ̈ɛ̈r gave birth to her first-born son whom they named Leek, referring to their memorial experience.

After some time, Jue̱ny went to search for firewood in a bush. However, in the process, he became too thirsty. He hopelessly sat under a tree to rest and think about what to do next. Suddenly, he saw a lizard coming down from a tree heading towards a prairie. Jue̱ny said to himself, that lizards could not live far away from a place where there is no water. He thought he could find water by following it. When he followed it, Jue̱ny discovered a location of a pond hidden in the grass. Consequently, he drank plenty of water. Finally, he went back home and carried his firewood. The narrative said that when Jue̱ny arrived home, he found out that his wife who was pregnant, had given birth to a second son, whom they named Laak (Laak means lily).

After that, they both decided to return home to Gɛ̈ɛ̈k's family. When they reached home, the two sons of Gɛ̈ɛ̈k, Ŋɔ̱r (Tiaŋ or Böth) Denäy had wanted to kill Jue̱ny, but their father rebuked and warned them not to kill the husband of their sister. Based on this narrative, the Nuär believe that Le̱e̱k and Laak were part of the group called Rel because they were children of a certain Jue̱ny Da̱re̱l, and Kɛ̈ɛ̈r was their mother. Consequently, Le̱e̱k and Laak became nephews to Ŋɔ̱r (Thiaŋ or Böth) and Denäy, sons of Gɛ̈ɛ̈k. The sons of Gɛ̈ɛ̈k became their uncles. This is the reason why Ŋɔ̱r (Thiaŋ) are not to be called Laak.

However, from what we learned from the narrative of the birth of Laak and Le̱e̱k, we can conclude that Laak's family became fishermen until this day. Thus, they inherited this profession from their father Jue̱ny Da̱re̱l who used to fish in swamp places. Even the family name of Laak is associated with lilies, which is due to the fact their father used to sleep in swamp places, and today, Laak is living on an Island full of fish in the area of Fangak. They are professional fishermen who mostly supply other Nuär with dry fish including the western Nuär.

1.16 The Origin of Thi̱a̱ŋ Nuär

According to a reliable source, Nyanawe̱l Ber who was from Aweil of Dinka. The source said she was married to Gɛ̈ɛ̈k. five sons and one daughter of Gɛ̈ɛ̈k and Nyanwe̱l Be̱r after they came out of the tree, were blessed with six children, five boys, and one girl, and they were the following: first, Ŋɔ̱r (Thi̱a̱ŋ), second, Böth (Nai), (Lɔu), third, Dit, (Jidiɛt) Rɛ̈ɛ̈ŋ-Yian, fourth, Bol, (Bul), fifth, Bör and sixth, their only sister called Kɛ̈ɛ̈r who later gave birth to two boys, Laak and Le̱e̱k. Seventh, it is said that La̱ŋ Gɛkä, whose mother was called Ko̱r Bi̱juɛt, whom the Nuär claimed to be a beast (Lɛt).

Ŋɔ̱r: Kɛ̈ɛ̈r, Bol, Nai̱ (Denäy), and Diit Gɛkä, who were twin brothers. Ba̱ŋ, Riak, and Lek, Ŋɔ̱r Gɛkä were the names of the three sons of Thi̱a̱ŋ. While Nyaŋ and Yɔak Ba̱ŋ were the offspring of Ba̱ŋ Ŋɔ̱r. It is stated that the people of Marɛ̈ɛ̈ŋ (Mareang) belong to the Thi̱a̱ŋ tribe. Furthermore, it is believed that they descended from Ŋɔ̱r, the first-born son of Gɛ̈ɛ̈k, who was nicknamed Thi̱a̱ŋ. Furthermore, this myth of the origin of Thi̱a̱ŋ claimed that Ŋɔ̱r was the son of Gɛ̈ɛ̈k Gaw Raan Kuoth. It is said that Thi̱a̱ŋ passed through Waath Di̱e̱ŋ to the Eastern White Nile.

Thi̱a̱ŋ (also known as Ŋɔ̱r) Gɛ̈ɛ̈kä was one of the Nuär sub-clans that originated from the Western White Nile. When a certain man named Jue̱ny Däre̱l impregnated his sister Kɛ̈ɛ̈r Gɛkä, consequently, Jue̱ny paid to Gɛ̈ɛ̈k a brown ox. Nevertheless, Thi̱a̱ŋ still wanted to murder Jue̱ny who had impregnated his sister. When his father realized that his son was not happy with Jue̱ny and wanted to kill him, he handed him the ox that was paid to him by his son-in-law. However, more detailed information about this incidence of pregnancy of Kɛ̈ɛ̈r Gɛkä by Jue̱ny will be discussed in the context of Laak Nuär migration.

1.16.1 The Role of Mutbak (The Holy Lance)

The fabled relic of the Holy Lance of Gɛ̈ɛ̈k is called "Mutbak Thia̱a̱ŋ" (the Holy Spear of Gɛ̈ɛ̈k). When Gɛ̈ɛ̈k realized that his children had increased in number and the possibility of intermarriage among them was imminent, he employed the Mutbak (Holy Spear for ritual purification) to rid his children of incest. Mutbak-means ca rual bak-no incest. To exempt them from incest, he sacrificed a brown-white cow (Yaŋ mä Jaak). Finally, Gɛ̈ɛ̈k brought a sausage tree nut and split it in half with his large lance. After he had done that, he advised all his children not to consume any milk or meat from Jaak.

This ritual purification took place in Koch Li̱ic "the Center of the House" where Ŋɔ̱ɔ̱b Li̱ey is located. After that ritual purification, Gɛ̈ɛ̈k decided to give his Holy Lance to his first-born son Ŋɔ̱r (Thia̱ŋ). When Thia̱ŋ Nuär decided to leave for the Eastern White Nile, they took with them the Holy Lance. Up to today, the "Holy Lance" is kept by a sub-clan of Thia̱ŋ Nuär called Riak, in an area called Tööc in Central Fangak, at a village called Pathiay at the house of a certain called Jok Ruac.

The Thia̱ŋ Nuär believed that Mutbak is the part of living community. For example, if one would like to marry a girl (nyakuɔŋ) from Thia̱ŋ Nuär, he must pay Mutbak a cow otherwise. Furthermore, according to Thi̱a̱ŋ Nuär, Mutbak reminds them of their origin back to Koch Li̱i̱c County, as grandsons of the elder son of Gɛ̈ɛ̈k, in the Western White Nile. They further believe that Mutbak is a symbol of their unity that has a lasting living memory. Prophet Ŋundeŋ said in one of his songs… "Wiu köör kämni̱ ɣä raan, Bi̱ Wiu pɛn piny jɛn ɛ mut thiaŋdam-Wiu of war give me a person, Wiu will fall down He is our Thi̱a̱ŋ spear…"[24]

1.17 The Causes of Nuär Resistance and Settlement

The Nuär like any other tribes in South Sudan or Sudan by then, went through touch periods of colonization. The 'World Supper Power' like the British colonied Sudan for many years. This period of foreign invaders led to resistance because the concept of the term "World Supper Power' had no meaning among some local indigenous Africans. For example, the Nuär who egalitarian society cannot adore a white based on his/her colour, superiority, and military power including well trained army like the British colonizers.

According to them, all men are equal, whether black or white or brown all deserve equal treatment and equal dignity. Contrary to this conviction, the Nuär can test it with manhood because they believe that every human person can die through killing regardless of his/her superiority, colour, religion, etc. Therefore, below is the famous recap of Nuär resistance, which led to the assassination of Captain Fergusson and the consequent settlement.

For example, in 1928, first, there was a constant raid on

---

24 J. Tab Charoa, *The Nuär Origin, Culture, and Moral Evaluation,* p. 217.

neighbouring tribes by Nuär and the lack of internal security reached its climax. Second, according to P.P. Howell, Captain Fergusson who was nicknamed Wɔrkuei by Nuär was assassinated. He was a district commissioner in Western Nuär. Third, the Lou Nuär led by Gwek Ŋundɛŋ had been showing open defiance for some time. Third, in that same year, Gaawar Nuär led by Dual Diu descended on the Dinka of Bor District and attacked the government post at Duk Faiwil.

About the assassination of Captain Fergusson who was nicknamed Wɔrkuei, was a medical doctor. As a British administrator, he was at Nyuɔŋ Nuär in a specific area called Paynyi̱jiar (Ganyliɛl) in western Nuär. As a medical doctor, his translator always accompanied Captain Fergusson from Dinka of Yirol by the name of Athor Bey, the father of the former minister of Finance, Mr Deng Athor Bey. Captain Fergusson (Wɔrkuie) in his speech declared that he could treat people with hernia-thiɛt. Unfortunately, according to John Nhial, M.r Athor Bey translated to the Nuär the speech of Captain Fergusson (Wɔrkuie) by stating that "if there are two initiated sons from one father-mä tɛ Wud mi̱ tee gaat rɛw tä ca ga̱a̱r,), Captain Fergusson (Wɔrkuie), said, he would castrate one ba dho̱l kɛl kuir, and if there were five initiated sons, he would castrate three"[25] kä mä kɛ gaat dheec, ba dɔ̱ɔ̱k kuir.

Captain Fergusson delivered this enlightenment speech about the treatment of hernia to the Nyuɔŋ Nuär community at Lake Jor (Paynyi̱jiar-Ganyliɛl). When the Nyuɔŋ Nuär heard that Captain Fergusson was going to castrate their sons according to the number of initiates from each father,

25 Interview with Mr. John Nhial, Catechist for the Catholic Church, fron Nyuɔŋ Nuär at POCs Juba, as from May 29, 2019.

they said to themselves 'We have never heard this kind of practice in our life.' Consequently, two men by the names, of Gatkëk Jiëk and Cuɔl Wɛŋ, decided to assassinate Captain Fergusson (Wɔrkuei). As a result, they assassinated him due to the wrong translation from the English language to the Nuär language by Author Bey. According to J. Nhial, the body of Fergusson (Wɔrkuie) was buried in a tomb at Kɔt and it is still there to this day bearing a cross on it.

As a result, the British Administration to search and arrest Gatkëk Jiëk and Cuɔl Wɛŋ commissioned a man by the name of Wuɔ̱n Kuoth, the father of Malual Wun. He was able to capture and arrest them in Gaawär Nuär. Finally, handed them to the British Administration. Consequently, both were condemned to be hanged upon the tree called 'kuel" at Lake Jor (Paynyi̱jiar) where they killed Captain Fergusson (Wɔrkuie) in Nyuɔŋ Nuär. Kuel in Nuär language means something that leopard-skin or earth-master uses to identify the dispute between two people. For example, leopard-skin or earth-master asks each person to jump over it to identify the guilty person between the two. Should any guilty person between the two pretend to jump over it to deny his/her guilt, something bad will happen to him/her instantly.

As to the reason why the Nuär said to themselves 'We have never heard this kind of practice in our life, this does not mean that they know nothing at all about castration. They know the real meaning of castration because they used to castrate a male calf to become an ox. However, they are aware that ox does not produce due to the result of castration. Therefore, according to them, castration cannot be applied to the human person, because it will make someone impotent and consequently, terminate human life. Based on this conviction, Gatkëk Jiëk and Cuɔl Wɛŋ took it upon themselves to assassinate Captain Fergusson fearing that they would finish because of castration. In this regard, resistance against the British colonizers was a priority and legitimate. Whether this resistance was done with local tools such as spears, or with clubs, that does not matter.

About the assassination of Captain Fergusson, which was unfortunate, however, it would be unwise to throw blame to Mr. Athor Bey for making a wrong translation. Everyone should know that it was due to a lack of medical and biological terms such as people healing with 'hernia' and 'castrating testicles.' Nobody should think that his level of education could allow him to know the differences between healing hernia and castration. In this incident, one could guess that Mr. Athor Bey was trying his level best to save the situation.

1.17.1 Causes of Series of Strenuous Military Operations

The unfortunate catastrophes we discussed above such as the assassination of Captain Fergusson, the constant raids on neighbouring tribes by Nuär, Lou Nuär led by Gwek Ŋundɛŋ had shown open defiance, Gaawar Nuär led by Dual Diu descended on the Dinka of Bor District and attacked the government post at Duk Faiwil.

Another unfortunate thing happened to Fr. Pty Payan. He was a Catholic priest from Mill Hill Congregation who worked in St. Mary Parish of Yɔanyaŋ (Rubkɔni̱) Bentiu with his colleagues. The father was invited by his friend by the name Valentino Gai Neen at Yɔanyaŋ to go with him to Mayɔm for a family visit after he returned from Rome.

After they arrived in Mayɔm, they happened to attend an occasion of a wedding ceremony at Wudube which belongs to Ciëŋ Paraŋ. While they stood there as spectators, a certain man by the name of Wuor Kuɔn from Ciëŋ Nyawäär admired the bald head of the father, and intentionally beat him. Consequently, the Nuär Ciëŋ Nyawäär were forced by the British Administrator to pay 270 cows as compensation through Monytuil Wicja̱ŋ, the head chief of Bul.

These and other things unfortunate things, which happened, had led the British Administrators to launch a series of strenuous military operations against the Nuär, both in Western Nuär Bentiu (Bitium), Central Nuär, Fangak and Eastern Nuär Nasir and Akobo.

According to P.P. Howell, the "Reprisals followed and took the form of a series of strenuous military operations which were known as the Nuär Settlement." Whatever the moral verdict, the Nuär learned their lesson and came to heed. A period of pacification followed, through just and sympathetic methods of such men as Captain H. A. Romilly, Captain A. H. Alban, and Mr. H.G. Wedderburn-Maxwell, the feelings of fear and suspicion, which were natural enough in the circumstances, were quickly eradicated. According to P.P. Howell, these men laid the foundations of a sound administrative system to follow. He concludes that "From an excessively arrogant, not co-operative and suspicious people, the Nuär rapidly became what they are now: still proud, still intensely democratic with a fine spirit of independence, but essentially friendly."[26]

The Nuär settlement and their resistance against the British government consequently, affected the overall policy in South

26 P.P. Howell, *A Manuel of Nuër Law*, p. 9.

Sudan. According to P.P. Howell, "The 'Nuër problem' was solved by applying those policies of segregation and isolation which were soon applied to the whole of Southern Sudan about the rest of the country." The official rationale of this local policy was that it was forced on the government as a response to Nuär truculence and aggression. It is stated that though they were not the first to resist, yet they were the first to be attacked by the colonizers (British government) on their soil.

Such a terrible form of reprisal consisting of strenuous military operations known as the Nuär settlement, was carried out by the 'super world military power' against unarmed men, yet brave men using their local instruments such as spears, and clubs to counteract their opponents. According to Nuär, defending lives can never be underestimated and therefore, the term 'Nuär resistance' in that historical period of colonization deserves a serious sense of pride from the rest of the South Sudanese people who resisted the colonizers.

1.18 Critiques

It is better to conclude this chapter with critiques because some information that was recorded by famous anthropologists such as H. Johnson and, and Evans-Pritchard on Nuär origin are not correct. However, in the first place, we would like to appreciate their efforts in trying to explain the myths of Nuär origin.

The areas of wrong information that we would like to focus on in our critiques are as follows: first, we found out that they attributed to Nuär wrong name such as nuer, which sometimes they write like nueer with double e. In our conceptual analysis, we made a clear distinction between Nuär and Nuer. We asserted that the term 'Nuär' means a particular tribe or ethnic group found in four major areas in South Sudan such as western Nile, Central Fangak, Nasir, and Akobo. We stressed that the term 'Nuer' has nothing to do with the meaning of Nuär as a tribe, but rather it is an expectation of evil. For example, we said that if a person has killed another human, he/she could not taste any product of earth without bi̱er fear of evil revenge. Besides, the two families in which the killing took place cannot eat or drink with the same cup, fearing evil revenge.

Second, the association of nuer with burial is another wrong information. In burring their dear one, the Nuär do not associate any concept of nuer with it but rather consider it as a corporal work of mercy. For example, the washing of their bodies and asperse with wild rice after the burial, have nothing to do with nuer but rather have other spiritual meanings as we explained earlier.

Third, the attribution of the tamarind tree to Ŋɔ̱ɔ̱b tree is not true. The Nuär know the difference between the tamarind tree and the Ŋɔ̱ɔ̱b tree. Fourth, both H. Johnson and Evans-Pritchard wrongly believed that the tamarind tree of Nuär origin was in 1918 due to misinformation they had received from others. For example, Evans-Pritchard said 'I regard Father Crazzolara's version as the closest to Nuär tradition.' Nevertheless, we rather affirmed that the Ŋɔ̱ɔ̱b tree, not the tamarind tree still exists today in Ko̱ch County. Sixth, H; Johnson claimed that some Nuär either fall directly from the tree or the sky near it. I have never heard some Nuär clans claiming to have fallen from the sky.

All Nuër groups, except Jikäny, claim to have originated

beneath that tree. Seventh, H. Johnson had made a very great mistake by saying that all Nuër groups, except the Jikäny, claim to have originated beneath that tree. Furthermore, H. Johnson was wrong when he negated Jikäny Kiir (Jikäny dɔar) not to be part of the migration to the eastern Nile while Latjɔr who led Jikäny dɔar was from Jikäny ciëŋ. The testimony we gave about Mr. Peter Charleman Shawach is contrary to this negation of H. Johnson. Finally, according to Nuär, the claim to originate beneath that tree permits no exception.

Conclusion

Chapter one has broadly discussed the conceptual analysis of terminologies such as Nuër and ciën as an irrelevance to traditional burial, the matrix of the term Nuër and term Nuär as an exclusion of non-Nuär. In addition, it has explained the following terms ran-human beings, naath-people, the similarities between Nuär and other tribes, and the various opinions of Nuär topography and ecology. Furthermore, the chapter has discussed different theories about Nuär origin such as H. Johnson's version of Nuär origin, Evans-Pritchard's version of Nuär origin, the contemporary Nuär's version of their origin, and the genealogical version of the ancestral line tree

In addition, the chapter has presented mythological and genealogical origins of major Nuär Clans such as the origin of Jikäny ciëŋ and Jikäny dɔar, the mythological origin of Gaatwär Nuär, Nuɔŋ and Dɔk Nuär, Gɛ̈ɛk clans, the origin of Laak and Leek Nuär, and the origin of Thiaŋ Nuär. Finally, it has explained clearly the causes of Nuär resistance and settlement and, the causes of a series of strenuous military operations in addition, it offers critiques on anthropologists.

CHAPTER TWO

THE NUÄR MIGRATION TO THE EASTERN WHITE NILE

Introduction

Chapter two discusses the keynotes on colonization for selfish interest, the background of Nuär Migration which includes two hypotheses related to immigration, the waves of Nuär migration such as five theories of Lɔu Nuär migration to the Eastern White Nile that include the search for better living condition, the challenges they faced, and their confrontation with Murle.

In addition, the chapter presents J̱ikäny migration to the eastern White Nile, the first version of migration, Latjɔ̱r's decision to marry Nyaguɛi, the crossing of the White Nile, the adventure to various destinations, and the second version of their migration. It broadly discusses Gaatwär Nuär's migration to the Eastern White Nile, the dramatic clash between Buok Käpiɛl and Puɔ̱l Buɔyian, their testimony on their migration, and finally, the confrontation between Nuär Mɛr and Dɛg Leekä

Furthermore, the chapter treats Thi̲a̲ŋ Nuär migration to the Eastern White Nile, Laak Nuär migration to the Eastern White Nile, the challenges that all the Nuär migrants faced, and various opinions about Dɔr Komkan. In addition, it explains two gateways to the North of Sudan, the disappearance of Taŋ Kuany to Däpäny, the legend about his Adventure to the neighbouring countries, Taŋ final words: blessing-puɔ̱th and curse-bit, his success and failure, the fulfilment of his prophecies and finally, the attractiveness of Däpäny-Khartoum.

2. Keynotes on Colonization for Selfish Interest

Our assessment of the migration of some Nuär clans from the western to the Eastern Nile will be myopic view without including the wider understanding of human instincts that crave gratification. For example, it is said that when one touches one thread, he touches every thread. In this regard, whether this human instinct and craving for gratification are done through colonization by World Super Power or through migration by a tribe to territories of others, the instinct and craving for gratification remain the same.

This instinct and craving for encroaching into land can take place in a situation where there are no international, national, or tribal boundaries were not clearly defined. Consequently, when boundaries are not clearly defined, and consequently, humankind applies the law of irrationality. In this sense, humankind thinks that the chapters of the world are richer somewhere rather than his actual place. Therefore, because of no clearly defined boundaries, he uses policies of colonization and migration to legally occupy certain parts of the land to be his own. He does this through exploration of the world both from within and from outside. His exploration has reached its climax at the level of scientific discovery by exploring even other planets.

However, if humankind is wise, he ought to make those parts of the world, which he has already occupied become paradises before he explores others. He can do this by practising law and justice otherwise Aristotle was right when he said "For man, when perfected, is the best animal, but, when separated from law and justice, he is the worst of all; since armed injustice is the more dangerous, and he is equipped at birth with arms, meant to be used by intelligence and virtue, which he may use for the worst ends."

Therefore, due to the lack of clearly defined boundaries, both continentally, nationally and tribally, humankind was governed by selfish interest (since he/she is by nature selfish), in the absence of law and justice. Regarding this, colonization carries with it selfish interest, as does an encroachment of certain tribes to others' territory without the exercise of law and justice.

For example, from 1948-1994, the white minority government in a system called Apartheid (Afrikaans: "apartness the name attributed to racial segregation for the exercise of selfish interest. 1880s-1920, the East African Protectorate (also known as British East Africa) was an area in the African Great Lakes occupying roughly the same terrain as present-day Kenya from the Indian Ocean inland to the border with Uganda in the west. This was controlled by Britain in the late 19th century due to commercial interests. 1895-1958, the French colonized West Africa, which included Senegal, French Sudan (present-day Mali) Guinea, Ivory Coast, Dahomey (present-day Benin) Upper Volta (present-day

Burkina Faso), Niger, and Mauritania, for selfish interest. In 11858-1947, Britain colonized India, which started in the 16th century, when the British first set company in India to bring silk, spices, tea, and salt from India to Europe. Therefore, migration of some Nuär clans from the west to the east may have similar elements or it could be for any other tribes in South Sudan.

2.1 Background of Nuär Migration

We would like to have a clear understanding of certain terms called 'Eastern White Nile.' When the Nuär uses the word 'Eastern White Nile', they rather use the term 'kui Kiir' instead of Eastern White Nile. By the word Kiir, they mean a 'deepest river' with strong waves caused by strong current. According to them, the Kiir River is a unique one, which they cannot temper with easily, because to cross it, one ought to think twice. The Lou Nuär call Kiir River-Kiir of the rising Sun-Kiir Käny cäŋ, while the rest of the Nuär who live on both sides of Kiir River, call each other 'citizens 'of the other side of Kiir River-ji̱ Kue̱ Kiir.

However, about migration to the Eastern White Nile, the term 'migration also requires conceptual analysis from the Nuär perspective. According to them, the word migration can mean höth. Generally, the word höth-migration is used when cows are taken to the grazing land during the dry season. In this sense, its use is limited to höth ɣɔ̱ɔ̱k-migration of cows near Kiir River. This höth ɣɔ̱ɔ̱k-migration of cows does not involve elderly people including women, but only young people with some few elderly persons.

It is called höth, due to the fact, it involves movement from place one to another, for almost three months. During these three months, the destination is determined by the availability of grass and water. During this period, young people stay in cows-camps consisting of different groups. Each camp is named after an important person who will always remain as a point of reference. Furthermore, the term höth-migration can also mean venturing to a new place, which is related to the höth-migration of some Nuär clans to the eastern Nile that we shall discuss below.

In chapter one, we emphasized the Nuär origin to the western Nuär land. We can even assert that all the Nuär in all the four major areas like Western Nile, Central Fangak Nasir and Akobo, claimed that they were created under the Ŋɔ̱ɔ̱b Tree (Thar Jiath Li̱ec) in Ko̱ch County, the Centre of the House (Däär ciëŋ) Thus, they all upheld and believed to be their mythological origin.

However, about their migration to the eastern Nile, Nuär believed that such clans are: Gawäär, Thi̱a̱ŋ, Lou consists of Da̱a̱k kä dɔ̱ɔ̱k (three major Dak clans: Bo̱r Da̱a̱k, kɛ Yo̱l Da̱a̱k, kɛ Jack Da̱a̱k, thus includes Gabaal, Mor and Go̱n. In this regard, the migration of Nuär to the eastern Nile deserves the above-mentioned clans. Therefore, this is the reason why we ought to treat this chapter two separately due to its peculiarity about migration to the Eastern Nile in the form of waves or sequences. In this sense, whoever knows Latjɔ̱r Duäc about the Nuär migration to the eastern Nile is mistaken and ought to open his eyes to have a wider perspective.

2.1.1 Hypotheses about Migration

Above, we have discussed issues related to colonization for selfish interest to have a wider understanding of human nature that craves riches. After the independence of South Sudan on July 9, 2011, a census was carried out to identify the number of tribes in South Sudan. The outcome was that South Sudan had sixty-four tribes. However, these tribes are scattered throughout the whole country. Nevertheless, each tribe has its own story of migration and each tribe ought to tell others how they are spread to some parts of the country. These stories are to be told by the tribes themselves and are to be respected without any political motive. Based on this simple logic, I will not attempt to talk about the migration of other tribes in South Sudan but rather about my tribe, the Nuär, nɛy tin naath.

Regarding historical facts of Nuär migration to the eastern Nile, we shall use only hypotheses because whatever assumption we make about the dates or years of migration, will not be exact. In this sense, making hypotheses will save us from making a wrong assumption and wrong conclusion about certain dates or years of migration. The nature of the hypothesis is that it can be proved true or false. We are dealing with both oral and written information on Nuär migration. On the one hand, some anthropologists who were only active observers documented this written information and on the other hand, oral tradition is always conditioned by events of life. Again, using hypothesis can put us to probability or less probability either of the dates or years of Nuär migration.

About hypotheses of Nuär origin, we agree with P. Howell who said that a tribe would, in numbers, be approximately similar to a tribal segment today. This means, that the Nuär as a tribe, were fewer in terms of numbers. First, P. Howell stated that tribal boundaries were less clearly defined. Consequently, the concept of jungle law was the rule of migration. Second, it is said that the periods of initial invasion when they moved eastwards in waves that began with cattle raids and ended in permanent occupation. Third, they migrated in waves; therefore, it is very difficult to determine the exact periods and years of their migration. Fourth, if all the clans of eastern Nuär clans trace their origin back to all the major seven Nuär clans of Western Nuär, then, it is very difficult to believe that Latjɔr was the only leader of Nuär migration to the eastern Nile, as we shall see later.

2.1.2 Hypotheses Related to Reasons of Migration

First, the general phenomenon of migration at the time, as we have above-mentioned, was a lack of clearly defined boundaries between people. Second, among the Nuär, when killing takes place, either between individuals or between clans, due to fear of revenge, migration can happen. Third, sometimes, migration can happen due to individual initiative by creating a new village or fourth, it can occur due to the discovery of large grazing land with an availability of water. Fifth, migration can happen due to the discovery of an Island where fist is plenty. For example, sometimes, among some Nuär clans, fishing is a part of life, as such, if an Island is discovered to have plenty of fish, this can be a good reason for migration to that Island.

Sixth, migration can be a result of raiding other tribes or seventh, it can also happen due to fighting between tribes.

Eighth, it can occur due to human adventure to explore and to discover another suitable place for the sustainability of life. Ninth, migration can happen due to the discovery of valuable natural resources somewhere, rather than the present occupied geographical territory or eleventh, it can occur due to increased numbers of people in one place. Twelfth, migration can happen due to relations such as intermarriages between tribes or even friendship or it can also occur due to the hospitality of some tribes or people, it can happen due to natural disasters such as diseases, and some natural environmental hostility. Nevertheless, the bottom line is that migration aims to discover a place for a better life.

2.2 The Waves of Nuär Migration

We use the term 'waves or sequences' about Nuär migration to the eastern Nile for a good reason. It is generally believed that the höth Nuäri-migration of Nuär to the eastern Nile was gradual. It went through a series of stages, clan by clan and not all at a go. Unfortunately, the majority of people in South Sudan including some Nuär believed that Latjɔ̱r Duäc led migration to the eastern Nile.

However, in reality, if we believe that such migration took place in the form of waves or sequences, then, Latjɔ̱r was not the only one who led the migration to the eastern Nile. Therefore, it will be better for us to use hypotheses to prioritize the first clan that migrated to the eastern side of Kiir River. The first clans that migrated to the eastern side of the Kiir River depended on the oral beliefs of the Nuär people.

2.3 Lɔu Nuär Migration

About Lɔu migration to the Eastern White Nile, there are different legends and versions. We believe that those legends and different versions of their migration may all be correct. Some can be very close to reality and fact, others can be fabrications. However, amidst these divergent ideas about Lɔu migration, one ought to read these legends between the lines. This is because various writers such as anthropologists and other oral sources, have contributed to these legends.

2.3.1 First Theory of Migration

When Lou Nuär talks about their origin in western White Nile-Kiir of the Rising Sun, -Kiir Käny cäŋ. They passed through Waath Yɔ̱ɔ̱kä. The narrative said that after they arrived on the other side of the Kiir River, which they always refer to as Kiir käny cäŋ, they settled at Atar and Korfulus. However, after some time, they fought among themselves, which resulted in many deaths. Due to that incident, they tried to reconcile themselves, but due to the lack of cows, they could not make the compensation possible.

Nevertheless, they said to themselves that we must reconcile before we proceed to the further east of Kiir käny cäŋ-Kirr of the Rising Sun. The narrative said that to resolve the problem of both compensation and reconciliation, the Lou (Lɔu) Nuär decided to raid Luäc Dinka (Jieng). After a successful raiding, they were able to reconcile and finally, they paid the compensations as required by both sides. After that, they proceeded forward to the far east of Kiir käny cäŋ-Kirr of the Rising Sun.

There was another version that said after that the Lou Nuär arrived between Gawäär and Laak Nuär, they stayed there in central Fangak almost for 40 years. We assume that those 40 years, were meant for a preparation to a new destination towards the far south of Central Fangak. According to reliable sources, the Dinäy community stayed with Lak for a long time. However, Dinäy Nuär heard that the community had arrived at Akobo; they expressed the desire to join Lɔu Nuär in Akobo.

However, the Lak Nuär refused them to go. Due to this disagreement, they fought and finally, Lɔu Nuär were defeated because they were fewer in number. After they were defeated, they said to Lak, if you attack us where we are going, my nephews, all of you will finish, and if we attack you in your place, we shall finish. According to reliable sources, from the time of that incident, and up to the present time, there is no fight between Lɔu and Lak Nuär.

2.3.2 Second Theory of Immigration

As to the period of migration of Lou (Lɔu) Nuär to the eastern White Nile, the majority of Nuär believed that they migrated before Gawäär and Laak, Thi̱a̱ŋ Nuär. According to Douglas H. Johnson, "Ŋundɛŋ Böŋ [Ŋundɛŋ Can] was born into a family of Gaaleak Earth-Masters living in Ji̱käny at the end of the 1830s."[27] H. Johnson further said that Ŋundɛŋ was initiated in 1855 (sic) in which the correct year of Ŋundɛŋ initiation should be 1845, and he died in 1906. This information documented by Douglas H. Johnson, can help us to

27 Cf. J. Tab Charoa, *The Nuär Origin, Culture and Moral Evaluation*, Juba, Rafiki for Printing and Publishing, 2021, p.192.

assume the probable period of Lou Nuär migration to the eastern Nile. In this sense, the probable period of Lou Nuär's migration to the eastern Nile could be between the 14th-15th centuries. Thus, in the 18th century, the Lou Nuär had already settled in the east and there were intermarriages between Ji̱käny and Lou Nuär in the Eastern White Nile.

The Lou Nuär consist of three Da̱k-Da̱k kä diɔ̱ɔ̱k (three major Da̱): Bo̱r Däk, kɛ Yo̱l, kɛ Jaak Däk, they include other three clans such as Gabaal, Go̱n and Mor. It is stated that Yien Denäy the son of Gɛ̈ɛ̈k led the Lou Nuär. It is said that Yien Denäy was born from his mother 'Nyego̱n Duol' while his father was Gɛ̈ɛ̈ from Jagɛi Nuär, from the Central House. The wife of Yien Denäy was Nyemour Gai who gave birth him two daughters that is, Ba̱a̱ny Denäy and Nyebil and his son by name Patuay.

2.3.3 Third Theory of Migration

According to Lɔu Nuär, they divided their migrations into the Eastern White Nile into two separate periods of migrations. They believe that Dinäy Gɛkä led the first migration into the eastern White Nile while a certain man called Kuok Gill after Latjɔr Duäc (Latjɔr Diyian) led the second migration into the Eastern White Nile. According to reliable sources, the two groups went at different periods of migration to the Eastern White Nile.

About the legend of Lɔu Nuär of migration that was led by Di̱näy Gɛka to the Eastern White Nile, two myths are to be taken into consideration. On the one hand, there was Lɔu Bull that belonged to Dinäy Gɛka and on the other hand, there was a Rɛ̈ɛ̈ŋ-yian, that belonged to (Dit) Ŋɔ̱r (Thiaŋ) Gɛkä.

The Lɔu Nuär narrate that the two sons Gɛ̈ɛ̈k, each had a bull of a different colour referred to as Lɔu Bull and Rɛ̈ɛ̈ŋ-yian.

According to reliable sources, those two bulls used to fight every day. It is said that every time they fight, the Lɔu Bull used be honed by Rɛ̈ɛ̈ŋ-yian Bull and finally, defeated it. Nevertheless, on the following morning of the day, they used to resume fighting. According to the legend, the supporter of Lɔu Bull was Lak and the supporters of Rɛ̈ɛ̈ŋ-yian Bull were Leek. According to the myth, the two brothers that are, Lak and Leek, sons of Kɛɛr Gɛkä used to support each uncle's bull. However, the myth said that there was never any attempt to quarrel or provoke due to the fighting of two bulls.

According to the legend, after Dinäy realized that his bull was suffering from Dit (Jidiɛt) (Thiaŋ)'s Rɛ̈ɛ̈ŋ-yian Bull, he proposed to his brother Dit (Jidiɛt) Ŋɔ̱r (Thiaŋ) that they could separate their cows to graze in different directions. On the one hand, Dit (Jidiɛt) Ŋɔ̱r (Thiaŋ) replied, my brother Dinäy, we have only one direction to allow our cows to pass through White Nile on the other hand, Dinäy said that unless your Rɛ̈ɛ̈ŋ-yian bull will kill you my Lɔu bull. In this case, I have decided to go somewhere, where my Lɔu bull will survive. The myth said that this was the origin of Lɔu Nuär migration to the Eastern White Nile led by Dinäy Gɛkä.

According to a reliable source, the fighting between the two bulls took place in the western Nuär land specifically in Koch County, "the Centre of the House of Gɛ̈ɛ̈k, near the Ŋɔ̱p Tree at li̱i̱c village. It was said that the sons of Kɛ̈ɛ̈r, leek, and Lak, discussed the dispute between their uncles taking into consideration the decision that was taken by their uncle Dinäy. To solve the problem, (Lak proposed to Leek that I would go with our uncle Dinäy Gɛkä and you Leek, must remain with our uncle Ŋɔ̱r (Thiaŋ).

According to legend, before, could Dinäy depart with his family and his nephew Lak to the Eastern White Nile-'Kiir Käny cäŋ, (Dit) Ŋɔ̱r asked his brother Dinäy, my brother have you decided to go somewhere because your Lɔu bull is suffering from mine? Dinäy answered him, yes, my brother that was the reason, and above all, I did not want to conflict with you. The two brothers concluded their dialogues with lasting words of memorial.

On the one hand, (Dit) (Ŋɔ̱r) said to Dinäy, if the reason to depart from me is your Lɔu bull suffering from mine, from now on, wherever you go, your name shall be always Lɔu. Dinäy on his part said to (Dit) Ŋɔ̱r, also my brother, whether you remain here in Koch Jagɛi or you choose to go somewhere, your name should be always Rɛ̈ɛ̈ŋ-yian. According to reliable sources, this was how the two brothers departed from each other. One remained in the western White Nile and the other, decided to go with his family including his son Yien Dinäy and his nephew Lak, to the eastern White Nile.

2.3.4 Fourth Theory of Migration

Kuok Gil led this second group of Lɔu Nuär. According to a reliable source, Dinäy families were divided into two when they left for the Eastern White Nile. Dinäy himself through Waath Yɔ̱kä took some. Some came later followed Latjɔr and they passed through Waath Ŋök. Collo Shilluk resisted those second groups of Lɔu Nuär).

To resolve this problem, a certain man by the name of Kuok Gil offered his son by the name Lok Kuok to Collo (Shilluk) men. Consequently, they were allowed to pass through Waath Ŋök. According to a reliable source, this group went through Malakal along the Sobat River until they arrived in Yom Ding and Dhore Ding. It was asserted they settled there for some months.

According to a reliable source, after Lou was defeated by Fangak, they crossed River Zeraf; this group went through along the river Nile until they reached Kor-Fulus. They settled there for some days. The Lou was resisted by Colo (Shilluk) or (Tɛ̈ɛ̈t). To resolve this problem, a man by the name Kuok Gil offered his son the name Lök Kuok to the Dinka of Kor-Fulus. Consequently, they were allowed to pass through the Sobat River until they arrived at Yɔm-diŋ and Dhuɔ̱rɛ-diŋ. It is along the White Nile River (at Maluth county), in the North of Malakal).

Unfortunately, Lök Kuok escaped from Collo (men and arrived at Yom Ding and Dhore Ding at night after some months. Kuok recognized the specific place of his father and consequently, went directly to his father. The following morning, the community slaughtered an ox nicknamed 'rum Jök'). According to a reliable source, fearing to be followed by Collo (Shilluk) men because Lök had escaped from them, they decided to proceed along the Sobat River and finally, they crossed the river to the territory of Aynuak. Unfortunately, they fought with Anyuak; however, they defeated them with the help of a young Cäŋ Duɔ̱p Kiir (also nicknamed Cäŋ Buok Kuok, his grandfather).

Due to his bravery, his grandfather Buok Kuok married Cäŋ Duɔ̱p Kiir a wife in a village called Buoŋjak. According to a reliable source, the wife was Nyuot Larɔa. Unfortunately, the young man was told not to sleep with his wife until the settlement at various territories was achieved. This was due to the fact that he may not be exhausted while the search for a suitable place to live has not yet materialized. According to the legend, Cäŋ Duɔ̱p Kiir was a brave young man. He was able to engage Anyuak in fighting in the following territories: Jikmiir, Bur Bëëy, Jöör, and Tilnam. It was said Buok Gill, finally, returned the Lɔu Nuär that led to Buogjak.

However, legend said that there was a dispute between those who would like to come back from the Kirr River. On the one hand, Bɛ̈ɛ̈i Cuol was not in favour of leaving Kiir River while on the other hand, Yuon Nyako̱a̱l, Kuok Gill and Larod Paul, were in favour of crossing to the present territories of Lɔu Nuär. When the majority decided to cross the river back, Beay Cuol told the people to carry him while his head pointed towards the Kiir River. Consequently, the people carried him as he instructed them.

Finally, they arrived in Lɔu Nuär land. When they settled there, they divided the territories according to their choices. For example, Beay Cuol who refused to come but was forced to come occupied the territory of Pan Athiag, Dɔk Kuok occupied Daak Riaŋ, Cäŋ Dup occupied Motɔt, Larod Puɔ̱l occupied Jueet, and Lom Lamb Juc occupied Modiit. These are prominent places in Lou Nuär. Therefore, in present territories, we have Three Däk: Böör Däk, Yo̱o̱l Dak and Jak Däk. Jak was the first-born, followed by, Yo̱o̱l and finally, followed by Bo̱o̱r. these clans are called Cïëŋ Man Jaak.

After the Lɔu Nuär arrived at their present territories above-mentioned, the young man Cäŋ Duɔ̱p Kiir was allowed to sleep with his wife Nyuot Larɔa at Motɔt. They gave birth to the following children: Nyadɛng Cäŋ, Tong Cäŋ, Ruɔ̱t Cäŋ, Pur Cäŋ, and finally, their born daughter by the name Nyalo̱k Cäŋ.

Cäŋ Duo̱p Kiir was not allowed to sleep with his Nyuot Larɔa, because the Lɔu Nuär were still searching for a suitable place of settlement. This means that at one point in life, great sacrifice takes priority over individual needs. For example, on February 2, 2022, in Juba, at St. Stephen Centre which belongs to Kizito's Parish, a young man by the name of Simon Ran was elected head of the development committee. Consequently, he suspended his initial engagement to a certain girl due to two reasons.

First, to focus on the building of the centre for prayer. Second, he did not want to allow the Christian community at the centre to assume that he had used the money for the development of the centre for his marriage. In this sense, the priority for building the centre for prayer took priority over Mr Simon's initial engagement. The priority to finish the building of the centre for prayer took the lead.

The connection between Rɛ̈ɛ̈ŋ-yian of western Nuär and Rɛ̈ɛ̈ŋ-yian of eastern Nuär. The legend said that Kuɛ Duol and his sister by name Nyago̱n Duol were the mothers of Baal and Da̱k. It was said every time Baal and Da̱k were teased by someone that has no uncle. Due this to challenge, both Baal and Dak decided to go back to the Western Nile to bring their uncle by Kuɛ Duol. After they brought their uncle to the eastern Nile, he married many wives who then gave birth to many children. This is why Rɛ̈ɛ̈ŋ-yian were present both in the West and in the East.

2.3.5 FifthTheory of First Generation of Lɔu Nuär

The version of Lɔu Nuär stated that the Wei-Biɛl region is a hill situated in the southwest confluence of the Piboor and

Sobat Rivers, which is a cavernous swampy area. According to the Lɔu-Nuär version, the region had numerous historical phases that influenced its residents' way of life. In this sense, it is associated with the name Wei-Biɛl, Bukteeŋ, and Makak Island or Swampy. According to Lɔu Nuär folklore, We̱i-Biɛl has three significant memories: first, it was the Lɔu people's first meeting place after they fled the Zeraf Valley. Second, Lɔu and Jikäny Nuär had their first encounter there after being split up in Cieŋ-Taaŋ. Third, from there, they began their journey to Buoŋjak.

The reliable source claims that one of the Biliu Yol led by Nyäl Biliu, also known by the moniker Nyäl Cɔ̱t-Wɛ̈ɛ̈, met a strangely attractive female with long hair while the Lɔu was established in Buktee and fishing in the Makak marshes. When no one is looking, the girl dives into the swamps instead of emerging from the water and sitting on the bank like she used to do. Nyäl and his crew made a plan to capture her alive as a result, but they were unable to do so until she emerged one day while they were in hiding. They chose to spear her after failing to catch her. Despite being hurt, she still pulled out the spears, hurled them behind them, and dove into the sea once again. Later on, the three men noticed a brown cow nearby grazing with a white spot on its forehead. They attempted to gather it but they were unable, therefore, they also decided to kill it.

However, an identical incident involving the girl occurred with the cow throwing back the spear while having high blood pressure and entering the river once more. Later on, it became clear that the cow and the girl were the same spirits manifesting as different visions. The family of Biliu Yol died because of the sicknesses brought on by this spirit later on. As a result, rites and sacrifices were made, and the spirit eventually evolved into the god they refer to as 'Biɛl Ju̠ɔ̠ɔt' (the spirit of the virgin).

In Makak wetlands, it is occasionally and yearly worshipped. The youngsters were given names as part of the spiritual devotion. The girls are referred to as Nyabiɛl, while the boys are referred to as Biɛl. Toc Nyäl Biliu, also known as (Nyäl Cɔ̠t-Wɛ̈ɛ̈), gained the name of the region. The marshes were also known as the "virgin's swamps" or "Toc Kueilitä" because of the Makak incident.

2.3.6 Search for Better Living Conditions

The Lɔu-Nuär people encountered numerous climate difficulties when they settled in the Sobat-Piboor regions. The low swampy areas frequently overflowed during the wet seasons, which reduced the number of viable dwelling spaces. So, the search for a better location continues. "The explorers chose a Buɔŋjak region northeast of the Buma plateau as a promising location from 1845-1850 based on three assumptions". First, the whole eastern Nuär combination of Lɔu and Ji̠käny from Bukteeŋ pursued their path until they arrived at the holy rock of Abula and remained together until they returned to Piboor and Sobat."

According to the second viewpoint, only Lɔu was among those who migrated to Buɔjak from 1840-1845. They travelled as far as Abula's sacred rock and slept there for a while before the Lɔu-Nuär encountered fierce resistance from the Openo-Anyuak. As a result, the Ji̠käny assisted the task force following the Lɔu in approximately 1850."[28] According to

28 Evans Prichard, pp.132-3

the third opinion, the Ji̲käny did not simply go as an aiding task force; rather, they similarly followed the Lɔu, hunting for better ground, and engaging in combat with the Anyuak alongside with Lɔu.

The Padaŋ-Jieŋ initially lived in the area where the Lɔu-Nuär now resides, which was formerly called Mun-Lɔ̱a̱l (Lol-Land), before leaving due to climatic conditions. Therefore, getting to the Mun-Lɔ̱a̱l was also risky for the same reasons. The Lɔu-Nuär returned from Buɔjak and settled in Bie̱lKɛi (now known as Akobo Town), as well as the neighbourhoods along the Piboor River and Kor Gɛini.

2.3.7 Challenges Faced by Lɔu Nuär

During this period, the exploration towards the South of Central Fangak beyond Gawäär Nuär was met with serious resistance from Anyuak and Murle. These also included encountering various types of diseases as they continued to sojourn. Douglas H. Johnson in his book entitled 'Nuer Prophets' has discussed these difficulties which the Lou Nuär faced in length. However, most importantly, the Lou Nuär consist of various amalgamations of many elements of other clans from western Nuär.

Due to the hostile environmental conditions above-mentioned, the Lɔu-Nuär departed from the Piboor region once more. In Piboor, they were attacked by smallpox, which claimed many lives. First, to this day, Wudh-Piny is the name given to the region to the northwest of Kor Gɛini's mouth. In other words, the ground had gaped open and sucked the inhabitants inside. Second, The Lɔu Nuär are pastoralists, thus Piboor was not a good place for them to reside. Third, during the rainy season, the land there was too muddy, which was bad for their livestock. Fourth, during the dry season, the ground develops numerous deadly holes that break the legs of people's cows and children as well. Fifth, there were numerous crocodiles and hippos in the river, which attacked and ate many people.

Eventually, a young man by the name Kuoth Both led an expedition from Bie̱lkɛi in Piboor to the west in the quest for a better colony until he arrived at a specific pool that he eventually named Padɔɔi. Kuoth was in awe of the stunning sandy terrain with rich soil and plenty of water. A few men from the Dinka-Padaŋ tribe, most likely from Duk or Abuo̱ŋ, met Kuoth and his entourage there. Due to this interaction between Dinka-Padaŋ (mostly from Duk or Abuo̱ŋ), tribe and Lɔu Nuär led by Kuoth Both, there were still many similarities in the communicative language among them. Another problem was the presence of a large poisonous serpent that lives in the water, which emerges once every seven days was described to Both.

The local people had shown the route by which the snake travelled and returned to Kuoth Both. Usually, the serpent emanated from a smell and was visible only from a very great distance. After an independent verification, Kuoth carried out some protective rituals, gathered a large amount of firewood, and stacked it on the snake's road. Both dismissed them on the appointed day when the snake was about to go. In this sense, the serpent could not dodge the fire because it was unusual to it. As a result, it was burned and eventually died. To this day, that region is known as Co̱w-tho̱a̱l (Co̱w-lɔa kiɛ tho̱l in cɔal ɣä, Lɔw) which means "the bones of the snake."So Padɔɔi was dedicated and consequently, was given the name Pul-Kuoth, which is translated as "the Pool of God."

The majority of Lɔu Nuär, especially the youth in Biel: kɛi, found the report above-mentioned to be favourable. Some elders, however, opposed the move since they believed that the river was the source of all life. An influential figure in the Lɔu community, Bɛ̈ɛ̈i Cuol, often known by his shortened name Bɛ̈ɛ̈i Cɔ̱t-Liɛth, resisted the idea of leaving Piboor. The youth majority, however, overruled the assembly in favour of the migration.

The little marshes you are moving to dry up just a few years from now, Cɔ̱t-Liɛth informed them. They carried Bɛ̈ɛ̈i, who had grown elderly, along on their new voyage and asked that his head be turned toward the east when they reached the Piboör River. Furthermore, Bɛ̈ɛ̈i advised them to be buried with his head to the east for the same reason in case he passed away. This counsel became a part of their culture and burial customs, signifying that they would return to the river.

People started to suffer from guinea worm disease, which replaced the Padaaŋ problem and then turned into the Lɔu problem. Because there was no centralized authority to uphold the law, several powerful clans came to control the water spots. Therefore, the Lɔu Nuär had no alternative but to return to the Piboor and Sobat Rivers, which cover a distance of around 100 kilometres, for grazing and fishing opportunities during the dry season.

Due to that journey, the Lɔu Nuär encountered the Jieŋ of Duk, Tuic, and Bor in the southwest, Gaatwäär in the west, and other food sources like fishing. Upon their return from Buɔŋjak, they parted ways with the Jikäny, as well as the Luäc and Dinka in the north. Even after the Turks around the Sobat River drove them out in the 1870s, communication with the Ciro-Anyuak people along the Piboor River persisted. Since returning from Bujak, the connections with the Murle along the Piboor, Kɔŋkɔŋ, and B<u>ie</u>m swamps have not been severed.

After roughly 30 years, the population quickly grew and their herd of cattle quadrupled. During the dry season, the water in the tiny streams started to diminish until there was not enough for humans and animals. Fish, a secondary source of sustenance, were no longer present.

2.3.8 Confrontation Between Lɔu Nuär and Murle

The Lɔu Nuär met the Murle, who were moving from the highlands under siege from Jiyɛ, Topötha, and Turkana, in addition to their prior encounter with Anyuak in Buɔŋjak. The Anyuak were pushed northward by the Murle along the basins of the rivers Abara, Kɔŋkɔŋ, Aguɛi, Kɛŋɛn, Piboor, and Akobo. According to the Lɔu Nuär oral histories, they encountered the Murle on a mountain near the Kɔŋkɔŋ River.

On the one hand, the Lɔu Nuär nicknamed the Murle "Jäbɛ", which translates to "a person who is short with a strong body built," while on the other hand, the Murle nicknamed Lɔu Nuär 'Jɔŋkɔth; that signifies tall, slim or hot temperature. Unfortunately, both could not listen to each other in terms of conversion (communication).

The drama was that they did not want to hear or be called the name offered by either party because the other side perceived it negatively. In several places, especially near the Piboor River, contact with the Murle persisted over time. The Murle also succeeded in taking control of Nyaadit, a tiny lake situated along the river between Burma̱th and Lekuaŋalɛ. On the one hand, the Murle legend claimed that they absorbed the energy and turned it into their god while other hand, the Lɔu Nuär termed Pul Kuoth, which means “the pool of God.” The interactions between the tribes persisted yearly at the Bie̱m/ Nanam marshes on Kor-Gɛini throughout the dry season.

The internal conflicts between the two fraternal clans of Jinai Gɛkä were thought to have been the historical cause of the Lɔu-Nuär people’s exodus. Conflicts compelled Lɔu Nuär to avoid situations that would result in their deaths. Thus, out of desperation, they fled and moved to the eastern White Nile, where they eventually settled and were known as the Lɔu-Nuär. Migration was the best course of action for Lɔu-Nuär to address that specific issue, even though it is not always the final answer to all communal disputes. They were able to acquire more territories and absorbed other nations into their clans.

2.4 Ji̱käny Migration

Dealing with the migration of Ji̱käny Nuär to Eastern White Nile requires consideration of the mythological origin of their Great Grandfather. According to the myths of the birth of Ki̱i̱r Kak Kër, there are two types. Apart from the two types of myth, Ji̱käny is divided into Western and Eastern Ji̱käny. In this regard, one should expect various versions of the origin of myths of their Great Grandfather.

The myths about the birth of their Great-grandfather contain similarities and dissimilarities at the same time. The convergent and divergent ideas about the myths of the origin of Ki̱i̱r Kak Kër, present opportunities for surprises and admiration for both Ji̱käny Nuär in the West and in the East. However, how Western and Eastern Ji̱käny, present an amazing narrative as it is discussed below in the two versions of mythologies, narrate the myths of the birth of K̲i̲i̲r Kak Kër.

2.4.1 First Version of Jikäny Migration to the East

First, the theory said that the cause of Jikäny migration to the Eastern White Nile was due to the mistreatment of a certain well-known man called Cöl Gɛ̱ɛ̱k. It is said that he possessed a mysterious power, which he used to intimidate people as an Earth-Master/Leopard Skin. For example, Cöl used to command people not to untie the cows and sometimes, not even to milk them. Everybody respects whatever he says even if it is wrong due to fear of death from his mysterious power.

Due to this unbearable situation, a well-known man called Latjɔ̱r (Diŋian) Duäc Puɔ̱t Yɔl, decided to search for another mysterious power that would counteract the one of Cöl. To start with, he put his small axe in his tallest hair. Latjɔ̱r began to consult various magicians to discover the place of his axe. All the magicians that he consulted failed to tell him that his axe was in his hair.

Finally, when all the magicians, failed to discover the place of his axe. Then, Latjɔ̱r went to a certain woman from Nyuɔŋ Nuär by the name Nyaguɛii Muɔŋ who was a powerful ti̲e̲t. He told her that his axe got lost and that he consulted many magicians however, none of them was able to tell him where it was. Madam Nyaguɛi responded to him "Why are searching for an axe which is in your hair"? She added, check your hair. When he checked his hair, then, the axe fell in front of him. Consequently, Latjɔ̱r realized that Madam Nyaguɛi had a mysterious power that could counteract the one of Cöl Gɛ̱ɛ̱k.

2.4.2 Latjɔ̱r's Decision to Marry Nyaguɛi

As Latjɔ̱r was convinced about the mysterious power possessed by Nyaguɛi, he decided to marry her and went back home. After his arrival, he collected many cows and brought them to Kuei Muɔŋ the husband of Nyaguɛi. He told him that I had come with these cows to marry his wife Nyaguɛi while knowing that Nyaguɛi was in her old age. The husband of Nyaguɛi knowing that his wife would produce no children took the opportunity to take the cows from Latjɔ̱r.

Consequently, her husband consulted Nyaguɛi about the matter. She accepted it but asked her husband whether it was possible to give her one child to go with her to her new home, however, her husband categorically refused. Nyaguɛi informed her brothers from Nyuɔŋ Nuär about the refusal of her husband to give her a child to accompany her to her new home. Her brothers said, your husband took the cows from Latjɔ̱r who had remarried you but unfortunately, he has refused to give you a child to accompany you.

Finally, her brothers gave her a boy by the name of Gaany to accompany her to her new home. Then, Latjɔ̱r, and Nyaguɛi with Gaany came back home. When they arrived, at night, Latjɔ̱r asked Nyaguɛi to establish a system of mysterious power, which would counteract the one of Cöl Gɛ̱ɛ̱k. Nyaguɛi did it. The following morning, Latjɔ̱r commanded the people to mild the cows and untie them without any permission from Cöl Gɛ̱ɛ̱k. When Cöl heard this, he asked who was saying that the cows were to be milked and untied. Everybody kept out of fear.

The, Latjɔr replied, I am Latjɔ̱r. Then, Latjɔ̱r started to command his family to milk his cows and untie them. When everyone saw it, they all milked their cows and untied them for the first day. People continued to milk cows and untie them for three days, which means that the mysterious power of Cöl was completely paralyzed by the one of Nyaguɛi and Latjɔ̱r. Cöl realized his mysterious power was incapacitated.

After three days, Latjɔr said to the people, we could longer stay together with Cöl Gɛ̱ɛ̱k due to his dictatorship and brutal attitude. Therefore, Latjɔr to said the people, whoever would like to go with me must come and whoever would like to remain with Cöl must remain. Consequently, those who chose to go with him followed him and those who chose to remain with Cöl, remained. Those who went with Latjɔr became Ji̱käny Kiir Käny cäŋ/ Ji̱käny of Eastern White Nile, and those who remained with Cöl, became Ji̱käny West.

2.4.3 Crossing to the Eastern White Nile

The people who led the migration to the Eastern White Nile apart from Latjɔr and Nyaguɛi were first, Yo̱y Bi̱ni̱, second, Yuɔ̱t Caam Jo̱k the paternal father of Latjɔr, third, Ciɛk Juc Wuɔk Bɛc, and fourth, Böth Lo̱ny. It is said that this group led the people through the periphery of the Nuba Mountains. For example, Yo̱y Bi̱ni̱, used to say, "Biɛl Jökni̱ Nyaguol të rɛ̈ɛ̈dä nä pääm bä däk, mɔ̱a̱c diin kɛl cät kɛ thok bith." However, due to many challenges, which the people faced, many of them tried to return. Nevertheless, it was said that there was a lɛɛt/beast which threatened the life of the people who would like to return to Bentiu under the command of Madam Nyaguɛi. For example, a certain woman by the name Gua̱c Lo̱ny, her one buttock was eaten by lɛɛt/beast. She was recused by the people and remained in Bentiu. Her brother

Böth Lo̱ny went back to Koch and brought her with her four children, Cɔk Thi̱a̱ŋ, Ruec, and their sister Nyakuol.

However, when the people arrived at the periphery of Kiir Käny Cäŋ/the Kiir of the Rising Sun, it was for the first time to say to themselves, "Latjɔr has brought us to a homeless place/ Latjɔr cɛ naath nöŋ dɔr." They realized that they were between lɛɛt and Kiir River. Consequently, they applied the term "Ji̱käny dɔar" to themselves. Latjɔr replied I did not bring you to a homeless place; we must cross the river because, on the other side of the river, there is plenty of food and enough space. However, at night Latjɔr consulted Madam Nyaguɛi on how to cross the river with strong currents and waves, which frightened the people. Madam Nyaguɛi replied we should see tomorrow morning. The following morning, they saw a certain called Ŋo̱k/ngok crossing the river while picking small fish to eat towards them. The bird is called Ŋo̱k with grew feathers which always eats snakes.

Then, they realized that the river became shallow at night under the mysterious power of Madam Nyaguɛi. Consequently, Latjɔr was the first to cross the river followed by the rest of the people to the side of Maluth. However, then, they turned to Puɔ̱d löc/Palo̱c). After they crossed the river, Latjɔr sacrificed two beasts, one for the river to return to its normal level, and one for the forgiveness of sins that were committed when they were in Bentiu. Consequently, they called the cross point to the eastern side of the Kiir River, Waath Ŋo̱k/ Päm Kun Thar.

2.4.4 The Adventure to Various Destinations

The people settled at Palloc after they killed a beast/lɛɛt, which disturbed and threatened the life of the local people. However, after some time, they left Palo̱c under the command of Latjɔr who told them to proceed to Guɛl Guk and settle there. When they were at Guɛl Guk, Latjɔr divided the people to go to three directions: he said Mathia̱ŋ/Thi̱a̱ŋ must go ahead followed by Kun to the left hand, Nyaŋ Ki̱i̱r must go through the middle, and Jo̱k must go to the right side. Latjɔr himself went with the Clan of Jo̱k. Gaajok went to Soba; they found Bäär/Anyuak and Dinka (Jieŋ/ Padang). Dinka was on the west and Bäär/Anuak was on the east side.

Upon their arrival in different directions, Mathia̱ŋ/Thi̱a̱ŋ settled at Larɛ, Kun settled at Thɔ̱ɔ̱y/ May Wud, Oriŋ/Jokɔw, the territory of Ciëŋ Cany. Baar Ciëŋ Kan settled at Guɛl Guk. Nyaŋ Ki̱i̱r settled at Tho̱ro̱, Jo̱k settled at Kie̱c. Jo̱k Ciëŋ Dhol settled at Kuac Lual Tha̱a̱n, Bol Jo̱k settled at Wul Laŋ. Dhol, Yɔ̱al, their mother was called Nyajuak, Bol Biɛl Jök and his sister Kuan Jök, their mother was called Cuol Wuod Jaam Jök, they were joined to Yuɔ̱l Jök.

Latjɔr had four brothers such as Lök Duäc, Puɔ̱t Duäc, Cany Cɔk Duäc, and Lɔu Duäc. Consequently, they are called "Ciëŋ Duäc." All his brothers were married, except Latjɔr who chose to remain with his old wife Nyaguɛi whom he married from her husband in the Western White Nile. He dedicated his entire life to leading the community to their final destination. Fortunately, his adopted Gany married a wife who bore him a son by the name Tɔ̱r Gany. Finally, Latjɔr died and was buried in a village called "Thilɛ Yian."

2.4.5 Second Version of Jikäny Migration

There is another version that is claimed by K. Bichiok and P. R. Kor about the date of the birth of Latjɔ̱r, in which they said he ..." was born to mother Nyaborä and was brought up in a place called Ma̱a̱r near Kɔat Li̱i̱c in Jagɛi, western Nuär-Koch County..."[29] K. Bichiok and R. Kor further affirmed that Latjɔr age-mates from Jikäny were initiated into an age set named Chot-born in Bentiu-Bitim in 1780.

Furthermore, the Nuär themselves believed that Latjɔr claimed to have seen a vision that invited him to move from the Western Nile to the eastern Nile. The aim was to lead Jikäny Dɔar to a new land to form a new community (Dɔr Komkan). It was also believed that before he started his journey to the new land, he consulted many diviners. One common explanation among the Nuär is that Latjɔr fed up with the mistreatment and dictatorship of Cöl Gɛ̱ɛ̱h. However, it is said that the circumstances and the reasons that made him take some Jikäny Nuär from the west to the east are diverse.

Another version according to Dr. Francis Ayul Yuar about the period of migration of Latjɔr was that…"Latjɔ̱r (Eastern Jikany Nuer) migration was convinced at around (1629 AD). This was believed to be the last migration in the sequence of Upper Nile tribal settlers that passed the Shilluk (Collo) land on the western bank of the White Nile but crossed to the eastern bank of the White Nile (15 km) North of the current Melut (Maluth town in a place called Wath-ngok."[30]

29 Duoth Kulang Bichiok and Paul Ruot Kor, *The Nuër Kiir People*, Juba, Rafiki for Printing & Publishing, 2017, p. 89.

30 Dr. Francis Ayul Yuar can be reached via:francisnyok@yahoo.com as from 13/03/2023.

The mention of the passing of Nuär migrants to Collo land is very interesting. This is because, in as1825-1835, the Collo King, Akwot Wad Yor Nyakwac welcomed Latjɔ̱r and his migrants to his kingdom. Due to this hospitality, consequently, Latjɔ̱r gave him his daughter. As a confirmation of this incident, in 2012, the Collo King Kwong Dak, during the formation of the Upper Nile Tradition Authority, made a testimony that the former Governor of Upper Nile Dak Duk Bishok was his relative.

Furthermore, it is asserted that since he belongs to the clan of the Queen of Collo Reth. King Kwong Dak testified that the Queen was a daughter of Latjɔ̱r Duäc (Latjɔ̱r Diŋyiam) but he intended to give her to the Collo King as a wife. However, the Collo King asked Latjɔ̱r that his daughter should take care of the Queen of Reth. This happened when the Nuär led by Latjɔ̱r were crossing the Collo Kingdom before they arrived at their intended destination.

Recaps about the periods of migration, first, Latjɔr's migration from the western Nile, probably took place in the 17th century because, in 1830, Ŋundɛŋ Bööŋ was born. Second, the definitive conquest of Lou Nuär in 1929-30 by British colonial forces of the Anglo-Egyptian Condominium Regime (1898-1956), ended the rapid nineteenth century. If the Anglo-Egyptian Condominium Regime begun in 1898, the Nuär have already settled in the Eastern Nile. Third, it ought to be asserted that the probable periods of migration to the Eastern White Nile, should have begun roughly between 15th-16 centuries.

2.5 Gaatwär Nuär Migration

In dealing with Nuär migration to the eastern White Nile, the majority of them believed that the first clan that migrated from the western to the eastern White Nile were Gawäär Nuär. However, this might not be the case. First, the lack of clearly defined boundaries and thirst for an exploration of vast land to find another suitable place for living in good condition could be the driving force behind this migration. The discovery of a land with an availability of plenty of fish in the eastern White Nile could also be a good reason for Gawäär Nuär migration. Consequently, the fact that Gawäär Nuär persisted in surviving there from the time of first generation to the present generations in the eastern White Nile, means that they are satisfied with their settlement there otherwise.

We ought to point out that within two Gawäär-Gawäär kä rɛw that is, a certain man called Buok Käpiɛl led Nyaŋ and Baar, with their sub-clans, to the Eastern White Nile. These two clans from Gaatwär Nuär such as Nyaŋ and Baar, who left the western Nuär Nile to the eastern White Nile with their sub-clans, are part and partial of the other seven major Nuär clans in the west. If Gawäär Nuär were the first to leave from the western to the eastern White Nile, then, we may say, probably, they might have migrated earlier as from the 16th-17th centuries. However, apart from the period of their migration, we ought to point out that there are various hypotheses about different gates through which a certain clan passed to the other side of the Kiir River. According to Nuär, they believed that Gawäär Nuär passed through the Kiir River by a specific gate called 'Waath-Pawar Jaak.'

Earlier, we mentioned the lack of defined boundaries and

the thirst for exploration for good living conditions; we must not assume that every portion of land in South Sudan was full of people, even now. It might be true that when Gawäär Nuär passed through Waath-Pawarjaak, to the eastern side of Kiir River, it could be possible that the land was empty. In addition, it could be possible that they might have found hospitable local people or they might have found certain resistance, which they might have overcome. Furthermore, the survival of Gaatwär Nuär on the eastern side of the Kiir River depends on what sustains their daily lives. We must assume that what sustains their lives today, ought to be what convinced the first Gaatwär Nuär who arrived at the eastern White Nile.

Furthermore, according to Gaatwär Nuär, the different leaderships, they went through during their journey from the Western White Nile to the Eastern White Nile. The adventure was not easy at all. Apart from travelling through unknown places, there were different types of brutal leadership, they went through. Some of those images that happened to their ancestors during their journey are still vivid even to the present contemporary Gaatwär Nuär. They can narrate their ancestral history orally without any difficulty at all. Those will read about their migration, will know that there is still yet more to be known about Gaatwär Nuär.

The information presented requires confirmation from the contemporary Gaatwär Nuär. According to oral reliable sources, every Gaatwär Nuär in the eastern White Nile can testify that Buok käpiɛl was the one who led them as we have mentioned earlier. According to a reliable source, Buok Käpiɛl took them to the eastern White Nile due to the mistreatment from Duɔ̱ŋ Ca̱a̱t Gua̱r (a dictator from Ɣaak Nuär of the western Nile).

2.5.1 Clash between Buok Käpiɛl & Pu̱ɔl Buɔyian

The Gatwäär Nuär had crossed from the Western White Nile to the Eastern White Nile under the leadership of Buok. When they arrived at Po̱w, at the Eastern White Nile, they said, Buok who claimed that he had a mysterious power mistreated their ancestors. Consequently, with this mysterious power, he was able to eliminate anyone who tried to oppose him. According to a reliable source from the contemporary Gawäär Nuär, the mistreatment of Buok Käpiɛl reached its climax, and consequently, everyone became afraid of him.

Buok used to play his drum in an area covered with tall thistles- (Buok la pa̱a̱t kɛ bulɛ geeth mä tee thillual), and after the area was cleaned up, he would be moved to different locations. Buok would begin to tell a tale as people gathered around him. He used to say, he would do it Gawäär! When I ate food (Kuän mi köp kɛ cak ti piw) food mixed with milk, something strange happened to me; I swallowed the food first, leaving the milk behind. Fear made everyone shout, including me-ɛmä nä ɣän bä. He used to say that to find out who would disagree with him.

One day, Buok was asserting the same claim above-mentioned, when Puɔl was present. Puɔl said to him, this was incorrect. No one could consume food with milk while also ingesting the food first. Buɔk Käpɛl was dissatisfied with Puɔl in this way. Dad, son! He exclaimed. The first rainfall would not occur while the two of us were still alive because of your opposition to me. Before the first rain fell, they would both pass away-either Puɔl or him. Unfortunately, the eight beasts arrived on the same day and devoured Pu̱ɔl's large ox. For this reason, Pu̱ɔl chose to look for power as a result.

It is stated that an opportunity came when eight beasts (lëët bä däk ca thäk Pu̱ɔl Bi̱diid (also nicknamed Buɔyian cam) - ate the big yellow ox of Pu̱ɔl. An ox had a big bell on its neck. When the ox fell, the people at the cattle camp heard the sound of the bell. They said to themselves, the sound of that bell we have just heard, must be the one of the yellow ox of Pu̱ɔl Buɔyian. Immediately, everybody ran towards the cows. Unfortunately, they found out that it was the ox of Pu̱ɔl. They saw eight beasts-lëët bä däk eating the ox. The people said we must wait for Pu̱ɔl because the ox belongs to him.

When Pu̱ɔl arrived, he saw eight beasts-lëët bä däk eating his ox. Those who were waiting for him said, we are waiting for you to be the first to spear them. Pu̱ɔl asked them, why did the beasts-lëët choose to eat my big yellow ox among all other bulls, oxen, and cows? The people could not answer him. Pu̱ɔl told them, the fact these beasts-lëët ti̱ti̱ have chosen to eat my big yellow ox, means that they must be hungry otherwise. Finally, he commanded the people not to kill them, and said, they let them eat it. When Pu̱ɔl was advising the people, all the beasts-lëët were looking at him including the pregnant one that was among them.

Pu̱ɔl had gone through difficult experiences such as the mistreatment of people from Buok Käpiɛl that continued plus the fact that his big ox was eaten by the beasts-lëët. He decided to go to another place searching for a means to counteract the brutality of Buok Käpiɛl.

In his adventure, he happened to find himself in the territory of those beasts lëëtni̱ that ate his ox. After he arrived in the territory of beasts, Pu̱ɔl was taken into the house by one of the beasts, who then informed the other beasts that they might also visit and tidy up his garden. Pu̱ɔl was the calling goat while he was ignorant of that. The beasts said to the owner of the garden, “They wanted to see the goat,” the beast went home and brought a goat named Puɔ̱l. the beasts recognized him. They exclaim! In addition, asked him, “Are you Puɔ̱l Buɔyian?” He replied, I am. Immediately, all the beasts-lëët ran to inform the rest. When the other beasts heard the news, they all ran towards Puɔ̱l and said to him, Puɔ̱l Buɔyian! (Mayian Ker Tun, Bär nä ciaŋ), that means, ‘when we do a good thing to others, the memory lasts forever.’

Their immediate question to Puɔ̱l was, what are you searching for? They added, Puɔ̱l, whatever you ask will be given to you. As you saved our lives in your territory, it is also our turn to save your life and to solve your problem in our territory too. Puɔ̱l told them, we have a big problem at home. I am roaming around searching for a solution to the mistreatment caused to us Buok Käpiɛl. After they heard his problem, the beasts-lëët decided to give him an axe that had a mysterious power, plus its instructions for its usage. Fortunately, before Puɔ̱l could come back home, he was invited by the beasts-lëët to a village called ‘Buk’ where they used to dance during the occasion of drum-cuɔ cɔal geeth ëë la pua̱t kɛ buliɛn thin kiɛ ga̱a̱th ëë la dɔany kɛ buliɛn thin kɛn lëët.

After spending two years at the territory of the beasts-lëët, Puɔ̱l brought the axe with him to the territory of Gaatwär Nuär, where Buok governed. Upon his arrival, the people warmly welcomed him. After three days, he made up his mind to prepare a new place for a drum. After he finished the preparation, he went to Buok Käpiɛl at his house. He said to him, paternal father, there is something I would like to share with you. I have prepared a drum for you.

I suggested that you should have two drums in separate

places because the old one does not accommodate the people. I came purposely to ask you to dig the place for a wooden holder drum. The book accepted the request. The following morning, he came to dig the place for the wooden holder drum. Before he arrived, Puɔ̱l had already dug the place at a specification location and buried the axe there, as he was instructed to do.

Being aware of the location of the axe and instructions given to him by the beasts, he directed Buok Käpiɛl to that specific place where he buried the axe. When Buok Käpiɛl started to dig the place three times, he knocked the axe that was buried there. Immediately, he felt the pain in his heart and his hands. Buok said to Puɔ̱l, paternal son, I am experiencing terrible pain both in my heart and my hands. Puɔ̱l replied, paternal father, please, you can go home and I will finish the rest.

According to a reliable source from the contemporary Gawäär Nuär, in the evening, Buok Käpiɛl started vomiting blood. He sent people to Puɔ̱l to come to him while Puɔ̱l on his part, was also pretending to be sick vomiting blood too. Finally, Buok Käpiɛl died and consequently, Puɔ̱l Buɔyian became the leader of Gawäär Nuär due to that mysterious power from the axe given to him by the beasts. The reliable source asserts that this was the end of the brutal leadership of Buok Käpiɛl upon the Gaatwär Nuär at Po̱w. Consequently, Puɔ̱l Buɔyian took the leadership of Gaatwär Nuär.

2.5.2 Testimony on their Migration

The contemporary Gaatwär Nuär said that when they crossed the White Nile, they settled on an Island called at 'Po̱w.

There, they divided themselves at Pow into two sections such as Nyaŋ and Baar. Consequently, the Nyaŋ section of Gawäär occupied the territory of Moy Gow (Mogok), while the Baar section of Gawäär followed afterwards. At present, the sub-clan of Baar called Baaŋ occupied Ayod while the sub-clan of Baar called Ciëŋ Thööny, settled at Wau. According to reliable sources, until today, the major two clans of Gawäär Nuär with their sub-clans are found there. This division was due to a lack of enough space on that Island.

As to their mysterious distinctive powers, on the one hand, the Nyaŋ section possesses the power of Earth-master (Leopard skin) while on the other hand, within the Baar section, some do have the power of (wud ɣɔɔk)-having power over the cows. In this sense, we have two sections of Gaatwär Nuär, possessing different powers. These two powers also are common to some clans at the Western White Nile. It is common among the Nuär, some do have such powers while the majority of them are 'duɛak or duɛk' meaning having no power at all.

It is stated that Nuär Mɛr, to Moy Gow (Mogok), led the Nyaŋ clan. It is believed that Nuär Mɛr was a Dinka boy found by Mɛr Tɛny Kapiel at the bank of the river, as Douglas H. Johnson also documented in his book entitled "The Nuer Prophets". Consequently, Mɛr adopted him as his son and gave him the name Nuär Mɛr. As for the meaning of Mogok, originally, it meant "Moy gow" which referred to an open gourd for drawing water from the well. The reliable source from the contemporary Gaatwär Nuär asserts that Nuär Mɛr himself dug the well. Consequently, every contemporary Gawäär Nuär can testify that Moy Gow (Mogok) was the house of Nuär Mɛr.

2.5.3 Class between Nuär Mɛr & Dɛg Leekä

After Nuär Mɛr (kuee jöök or Jo̱o̱k kuei)" had led the Nyaŋ Gawäär section to Moy Go̱w (Mogok), he began to call himself prophet. He added that his leadership based was on a mysterious power that seized him with an unknown name. The Nuär will say 'ci̱ kuär muo̱ndɛ rɔ ciɛ-his Earth master (Leopard Skin) has intensified. According to a reliable source from contemporary Gawäär Nuär, he began to mistreat people with that mysterious power that possessed him. The following are some hostile powers he exercised upon the Gawäär Nuär at the present-day Moy Go̱w (Mogok).

First, every day, he is to be given a fatten calf as his food by anyone. Second, everyone who passes by Moy Go̱w (Mogok), and the members of his council will say, 'What kind of food he/she has eaten?"ɛ köp kiɛ ɛ pi̱ec ɛni cɛ cam? To get an answer for themselves, they will say to each other, let us cut his/her stomach to find out the kind of food he/she has eaten, to prove among us whose guess is right. Third, he eliminated all those who opposed him. Nuär Mɛr and the members of his council used to do these things to travellers. As a consequence, many Gawäär Nuär died under his brutal leadership.

According to a reliable source from contemporary Gawäär Nuär, one day, a young boy by the name of Dɛg Leekä and his mother happened to pass through Moy Go̱w)Mogok). When Nuär Mɛr and his team saw them, he called the young boy and his mother. Dɛg Leekä was confirmed by a reliable source from Gawäär Nuär to be the father of Machar Dɛɛŋ Leekä, sometimes, known as (Machar Di̱u refers to his seizure). When the boy and his mother arrived, he said to the boy, you have two options: one, either to sleep with your mother or two, to eat faeces.

In response to these two difficult options, Dɛg chose to eat faeces. Consequently, his mother persuaded him to sleep with him rather than to eat faeces. Nevertheless, he persisted in eating faeces instead of sleeping with his mother, and asserted that 'I cannot go back to the place where I was born.' Consequently, they collected faeces, put them on plate-tɔɔ, and poured milk on them. Finally, he was commanded to eat them. After that, he was allowed to go with his mother to their intended destination.

During the years of growing to the age of maturity, the young boy was disturbed by that inhuman act. Consequently, he became mad. In the process of madness, a spirit called 'Di̱u seized him. After some years, Nuär Mɛr prophesied that the boy called Dɛg Leekä (this Dinka boy would one day come to biɛ. His prophecy became true. Finally, after some years, the Baar section led Dɛg Leekä launched an attack against the Nyaŋ section, which finally, led to the killing of Nuär Mɛr. A song was composed after Nuär Mɛr was defeated and killed, saying "juɔyä Nuär Mɛr ci̱ nɛy tuac kɛ dial mat (when we defeated him, we took his leopard skin). Consequently, Dɛg Leekä the father of Machar Dɛɛŋ (Machar Di̱u) became the leader of the Nyaŋ Gawäär section.

In conclusion, we can say that from the time of migration from the western White Nile and to the time of settlement at the eastern White Nile, Gawäär Nuär were led by Buok Käpiɛl, Puɔ̱l Bi̱diid (Buɔyian), Nuär Mɛr, Dɛg Leekä, and finally, by Machar Dɛɛŋ (Di̱u) the son of Dɛg Leekä. Concerning the period of Gawäär Nuär migration to the eastern White Nile, it should also start between the 16th and 17th centuries.

2.6 Thi̱a̱ŋ Nuär Migration

It was said that as the population of Gëëk villages grew bigger, consequently, the land shrunk and internal disputes began to escalate into actual fights among villagers. It is stated that other factors such as searching for better living conditions also involved. Others said that there was a power struggle between leaders of the community in Ko̱ch. In light of these burning issues listed above, it was determined that migration to the Eastern White Nile could be the best option for Thi̱a̱ŋ Nuär to avoid internal conflict.

In addition to environmental concerns and the lack of availability of enough land that could accommodate all at Ko̱ch, the 'Centre of the House' as they call it, the Thi̱a̱ŋ, Bol families, and other Jagɛy Nuär needed to relocate themselves to another place that could take them all as well as their animals too. Based this on conviction, the Thi̱a̱ŋ began their annual transhumance journey, where they used to go to cattle camps at Toc of Riir, Barjaak, as part of their preparatory migration.

As usual, they returned to their home village of Ko̱ch during the beginning of the rainy season. The Thi̱a̱ŋ Nuär decided to visit Zaraf Island and dispatched a group of young men to assess the area. They went, surveyed, and assessed it. The young men found out that Zaraf Island was on the eastern bank of the Nile, close to where they used to go for cattle camps. The young men brought their findings back to the community about Zaraf Island. When Thi̱a̱ŋ sub-clan heard this news, they believed that the place was suitable for accommodation for both people and their livestock as well.

As for Thi̱a̱ŋ Nuär migration to the Eastern White Nile,

a certain man called Thɔ̱a̱r Kuacjien as we have mentioned earlier led them. As we have stated before, the causes of Thi̱a̱ŋ Nuär migration were based on power struggles and environmental difficulties. According to reliable sources, they passed to the eastern White Nile through a particular gate known as Waath Die̱ŋ. The Thi̱a̱ŋ Nuär settled on the southern end of Fangak Island. When they arrived there, they found out that already Lou Nuär had occupied the land of the Fangak area on the Island. The source also said that they already occupied the land of Laak Nuär on the other side of the Zeraf River.

However, since both Lou and Thi̱a̱ŋ Nuär descended from the same father by the name Gɛ̈ɛ̈k, they were able to co-exist peacefully with each other. This is due to the fact Lou Nuär are the sons of Denäy Gɛkä and Thi̱a̱ŋ Nuär also the sons of Ŋɔ̱r Gɛkä. Therefore, Thi̱a̱ŋ and Lou Nuär are paternal brothers. Based on these blood relationships between the two clans, they were able to maintain good diplomacy among themselves.

As every Nuär, clan has a Faah-a common name for all of them. For example, a single Thi̱a̱ŋ Nuär man can be called Gatkuɔŋ, a girl nyakuɔŋ or in the plural, Gaattkuɔŋ for men, for girls or women, Nyeekuɔŋ. Therefore, due to the commonality of this name among them, marriage is impossible. In this sense, the totem is separated from it. The meaning of Gatkuɔŋ. The possible hypothesis for Thiaŋ Nuär should be the 17th century. (Waath).

2.7 Laak Nuär Migration

The Laak Nuär inhabit the highland between the Bahr-el-Jebel and the Zeraf River. They consist of three groups, with different origins, but linked to the same group. For example, the people of Pulita are the real Laak who descended directly from the son of Laak whose father was Jue̱ny Däre̱l and whose mother was Kɛ̈ɛ̈r Gɛɛkä. The ox of Laak Nuär is named Kuac Böör, and the people of Paguir belong to the Ke̱r clan. Consequently, they joined Laak Nuär, and they are now called Kuac böör (Cieŋ kuacböör). These clans are found today in central Fangak neighbouring Gaatwär Nuär on that Island. It is believed both Thiaŋ, ciënŋ Kuac Böör and Jɔnyaŋ are amalgamations of some elements of western Nuär.

Furthermore, the version said that the man called Laak married a girl by the name of Nyakuɔth Ro̱lduar who bore him two sons, one by the name of Ga̱ŋ and the other, Kuol. The second wife was Nyawär Jiu, who bore him three sons: Ŋo̱l (Ngol), Rial, Yi̱el, and Ro̱l. Nyajihoth bore Yak and Lep. The narrative said that when Laak left Western White Nile for Eastern White Nile, his son Ŋɔ̱l remained there. It is said that Gaatwär passed through Waath Bi̱em Gaaŋ.

Nyakuɔth Ro̱lduar had a sister by the name Muooth Ro̱lduar who was married to a man called Nyaŋ Bul. Unfortunately, the sons of Le̱e̱k were not on good terms with the sons of Laak, although they were paternal brothers. The narrative states that when the conflict between the two paternal brothers intensified, the sons of Nyakuɔ̱th asked the sons of their aunt to join them in fighting their paternal brothers the sons of Le̱e̱k. Finally, the cousins joined against the sons of Le̱e̱k and even engaged in three hostile activities as listed below:

First, the sons of Nyakuɔth called the sons of their aunt to defend them against the sons of Le̱e̱k, consequently, they attacked them. Second, when the cows of Le̱e̱k were taken to grazing land, the sons of Nyakuoth used to follow them and cut off the humps of their oxen and ate them-gɔ̱r kɛ ɣɔ̱ɔ̱k gaani̱ kä ba bööm thiäkni̱ kiɛn tëëm. Every day, the oxen used to come back without any humps-la luny thiäkkiɛn jɔw a this kɛ bööm. Third, one day, the sons of Laak found some goats of the sons of Le̱e̱k, grazing on their territory, unfortunately, the goats ate their sorghum. They caught all the goats and brought them to their huts. They incurred a punishment upon them, by removing their teeth including their premolars-cuɔ car ɛ kɛn ɛn ɣöö ba kɛ naŋ, kä cuɔ nyiimkiɛn and kɛnɛ ro̱o̱kiɛn naak.

However, due to the severe mistreatment of the sons of Le̱e̱k, they decided to launch a merciless attack against the sons of Laak. When the sons of Laak heard that they were going to be attacked by the sons of Le̱e̱k, they decided to meet them to resolve the problem. When the sons of Laak discovered that their paternal brothers were not ready for reconciliation due to the degree of gravity being done to them, they decided to go somewhere else rather than wait for that catastrophic situation.

Consequently, the sons of Laak realized that the situation had become unbearable and that the attack was imminent, so they decided to leave the western White Nile. They immediately called their youth for a meeting and decided to leave at midnight when the sons of Le̱e̱k fell asleep. However, before they could leave, one of the elders by name Kuany Jäŋ called two young men and sent them to look for a mysterious power. Finally, they sent Kuɔ̱ny Ki̱e̱c (Kuony Rɛl) and Kui̱ny Da̱k. The two walked for a long distance until they found a traditional medicine man called Muaŋ Dhiɔak.

When Muaŋ Dhiɔak saw them, he asked "What do you want here?" They replied things are not going in the right direction on our side. What is not going right with you? They said, we want to leave our homeland due to serious problems between our communities, but we have no power, please, we need your hand (your power to protect us on our way)." Muaŋ Dhiɔak told them to make a fireplace and said to them, the fire that will remain burning until tomorrow morning, will be the one you will take and use for your protection. They did as the man told them. In the morning, their bonfire remained burning. Consequently, he commanded them to carry the bonfire with them freely without fear of obstacles on their migration to the eastern Nile.

When the two men returned to their community, another meeting was convened in which all the people agreed to leave at midnight. They decided that few youths should remain behind with few cows. First, the elderly people left the place, while a few youths remained behind as they had agreed upon. As a technique, the few youths who agreed to remain behind started to dance throughout the night until sunrise.

The other sons of Le̱e̱k thought that the sons of Laak were still around. They did not realize that they left at midnight. When they discovered that the sons of Laak had gone, the sons of Le̱e̱k went after them but could not find them. According to reliable sources, the Laak were led to the eastern White Nile by Kuany Jäŋ assisted by Kuɔ̱ny Ki̱e̱c (Kuony Rɛl) and Kui̱ny Da̱k. The bonfire was a guide and a protector on their migration to the eastern Nile. When they arrived at the Eastern White Nile, they also encountered many problems as documented below.

2.7.1 Challenges Faced by Laak

First: it is said that there were waves due to the strong current of the River White Nile. Consequently, the current was too strong to resist and they could not cross it. To resolve this dilemma of strong waves that could not allow them to cross to the eastern side, a man by the name Nyɔɔt Tɔ̱tdäär Kual, sacrificed his daughter called Bie̱mgany to the river as a gift so that the wind could stop. Consequently, the waves stopped. Up to this day, the place is still called Bie̱mgany the place in which she sacrificed.

Second: even though the wind stopped, there were no canoes (dingy). At that time, the Nuär had not yet learned how to make canoes, (dingy) like Collo (Shilluk) who were used to the river. The version said that while they were trying to cross the river, immediately, some Collo (Shilluk) men appeared with their canoes. The Laak asked them to ferry their people and cows to the eastern side of the river, which at the beginning, they refused. However, an elderly man called Duɔth Köör Biddit decided to give them his favour youngest daughter called Nyaköör Duɔth Biddit. The Collo (Shilluk) men accepted the offer.

Consequently, they were provided with canoes and finally, they were able to cross to the eastern White Nile. Till today, the Nuär of Fangak call the Collo (Shilluk) of Tonga in Papwoch village "sons of Nyaköör Duɔth Köör Bi̱diit" or Nuär language 'Gaat Nyaköör, (cɔal kɛ i, Cieŋ Mailiɛɛth ɛn tämɛ-Tɛ̈ɛ̱t Nyaköör Bidiit).

Third: After they had crossed the main River White Nile, they found themselves crossing many streams full of crocodiles, which ate many of them, and their cows too. However, to resolve the problem of crocodiles, another man called Najɔk Kaaŋ offered his daughter called Kiu to crocodiles. Finally, they crossed various streams peacefully. Fourth: once they settled in the eastern White Nile, they found the people of Lou clans, descendants from Na̲i Gɛɛkä who had settled there for many years in the Eastern White Nile. Their number was greater than the one of Laak.

The version said that the Lou Nuär resisted Laak, and consequently, they could not allow them to occupy the land. The war continued with no sign of success. It was said that a man called Kuɔ̲ny from Laak Nuär decided to go to a man called Thɔ̲a̲r Kuajiɛn from Thi̲a̲ŋ Nuär to join the battle. Therefore, to motivate Thi̲a̲ŋ Nuär, Kuɔ̲ny gave Nyadan his daughter to Thɔ̲a̲r Kuajiɛn and Ŋundɛng Kuac an ox and a cow. Now, the war intensified and finally, Laak and Thi̲a̲ŋ pushed the Lou Nuär back.

It was said that when Laak youth reached the cattle camp after they were defeated, one woman stood up and called the warriors by their nicknames (oxen names), e.g, Rɛɛt Duɔth, Puɔ̲t Jakɔ̲a̲k, Jaak Thilwuɔ̲ɔ̲t, and slapped her mons veneris, and she said, this mons veneris would be touched by Lou's youth. She called her ox's name by saying (Cä wär nyaŋä pi̲e̲t kɛ jɔajɔak). When the youth heard this, they all stopped and returned to battle. Based on this moral support from that girl to the youth of Laak, coupled with the alliances between Laak and Thi̲a̲ŋ clans, they managed to push Lou Nuär to the further eastern White Nile.

When Laak and Thi̲a̲ŋ Nuär defeated Lou Nuär, they left behind their elderly people. Laak and Thi̲a̲ŋ said that their elderly people remained behind and they said, they would get other elders. One version said that Laak buried alive one of the old women by the name of Nyachiliɛny, who was witchcraft. After Lou Nuär crossed the Zeraf River, an oath was made between Lou and Laak Nuär. "From now, onwards, we will not fight again against each other. The Lou Nuär said to Laak Nuär, we will not come back to Fangak to fight you, and you will not come to our land to fight us. Any side that will violate this oath will surely die."

Consequently, Laak Nuär remained there alone. Laws were enacted, and a lame girl who a daughter to Najɔk Kaaŋ was named Näknɛɛ was sacrificed instead of a bull. It is said that before she died, she said, "I shed my blood on this land, no one will leave it again, and if fighting happens, stand firm; it would not take two days for it to stop." Consequently, she was killed and buried in Kue̱rdiu (Cieŋ Kar) in Pulita Payam.

The Laak Nuär occupied the southern part of Central Fangak. This would mean, probably, the proximate period of Laak Nuär migration to the eastern side of the Kiir River, could be between the 17th century. In this sense, we are talking about the geographical location that they occupy today. Therefore, the fact that they remained there from the time of migration up to today, means that they are satisfied with what sustained their lives, which includes livestock. In this sense, any migration to another place requires goals and particular objectives otherwise.

2.8 The Challenges Faced by Eastern Nuär

The various clans of Nuär who migrated to the eastern Nile side of the Kiir River as we have discussed earlier, require assessments about the challenges they might have faced on their journey. The emphasis we made about the different gates, as points of departure to the eastern side of Kiir River, is essential in our assessments. The different geographical locations, in which the eastern Nuär migrated, can help to understand the common challenges that they might have faced during their waves of migration.

However, among the most common challenges that all of them might have faced, was the resistance from other tribes at the eastern Nile. For example, Douglas H. Johnson discussed in length, the resistance to migration of Nuär from Anuak, Murle and Dinka. The difficulty in understanding local languages, the difficulty of adjusting to the new environment, the lack of shelters, the various types of diseases, the difficulty of different types of beasts which might have tempered with their lives, including crocodiles and hippopotami in the rivers Nile, while crossing to the eastern side.

According to Francis Ayul Yuar, "Oral sources confirmed authentically that Jikany migrants found one of the Ageer subsection/clan, known as Kill in the area of current geographical Melut. They had serious violent confrontations but could not stop Latjor migrant's determination to pass through the territory."[31] Furthermore, Francis said, it is believed that migrants managed to repulse Kill attackers and temporarily subdued their presence around Thaapio and Ayalnhial villages as they nursed their wounded. It is argued that thereafter they continued to match toward the southeast of Melut (Maluth) along the Yal River to their present home.

Their waves of migration, of different generations of Nuär to the eastern side of the Kiir River might have raised bitter complaints against their leaders. The example of complaints

31 Dr. Francis Ayul Yuar can be reached via:francisnyok@yahoo.com as from 13/03/2023.

against Moses and Aaron by the people is fitting which the sacred Scripture said:

> *Then the whole congregation of the children of Israel complained against Moses and Aaron in the wilderness. And the children of Israel said to them, „Oh, that we had died by the hand of the Lord in the land of Egypt when we sat by the pots of meat and when we ate bread to the full! For you have brought us out into this wilderness to kill this whole assembly with hunger" (Ex 16:2-3).*

There is a common belief among the Nuär that says, the majority of waves of migrations, when they found difficulties such as those above-mentioned, would like to return to the western Nile. However, it was said that their leaders threatened them by saying that 'anyone who would like to go back, will be eaten by a certain type of beast called 'lɛt or lëët.' Consequently, each leader who led the clan (clans), stressed the presence of lëët behind as a strategy for the success of migration. This threat worked perfectly, because if there is anything, which the Nuär are afraid of, it, is this beast called 'lɛt.' For example, when they hear that such a beast has eaten someone in one of the villages, they will choose to sleep before sunset.

In conclusion, about these sections about the challenges that the Nuär encountered during their migration to the eastern Nile, we ought to re-assert that the migrants went in waves according to Douglas H. Johnson or in sequences according to Dr. Francis Ayul Yuar. These periods of waves or sequences of migration indicate that each leader led the big clans with their subclans. Our conclusion will depend on the geographical local which certain migrants occupied characterized their cohesiveness in that territorial integrity.

Furthermore, the various gates that led to the eastern are another important testimony that they never went at one time, under one leader. About the resistance they faced, no oral sources proved that some clans chose to remain behind due to violent confrontations or even families. Logically, in clans fighting or a tribe fighting another one, it would be very stupid for anyone to remain behind due to fear of revenge in those days. In the case of hospitality, such as that of Collo King who warmly welcomed, Latjɔ̱r, someone who would like to remain can make a decision.

However, one can never totally negate the presence of places where different tribes in the eastern Nile are incorporated such as 'Galachel.' It is a territory shared by Dinka Baliet and Nuer currently but it used to be habited by the Anuak. The in-consistory periods that are documented cannot be resolved but must be taken as hypotheses because they originated from different sources both oral and written. Nevertheless, their authenticity and occupancy will always remain questionable.

2.9 Various Opinions about Dɔr Komkan

One should never doubt that the expansion to the eastern Nile by eastern Nuär clans had led to the occupation of the lands of others. For example, this migration led to the invasion of many villages of other tribes. The famous village called, 'Dɔr Komkan' was or lands occupied by Lou Nuär at the far south of central Fangak.

The name of the village 'Dɔr Komkan' requires a clear explanation to avoid confusion with other ideas. 1. One of them is that everybody in the western Nuär believes that 'Dɔr Komkan' means the whole territories occupied by the Jikäny Dɔar or Jikäny Kiir and Lou Nuär. 3. Others believe that Dɔr Komkan' is generally referred to as kaal kiɛ rɛk-a town or a city such as Malakal. According to K. Bichiok and R. Kor, Latjɔr Duäc had..." a vision to move out from Bentiu [Bitim] and to go to a new land with a new community (Doar Komkan)..."[32] 4. According to this version, 'Dɔr Komkan' means a new land with a new community in the eastern Nile that was occupied by eastern Nuär.

My curiosity as an academician has led me to investigate the meaning of the term 'Dɔr Komkan.' Therefore, I contacted one of the heads of Congregations of the Presbyterian Church in Juba, Rev. Pastor Paul. He humbly explained his version of the word Dɔr Komkan 5. According to Rev. Pastor Paul, "The word ''dɔr Konkan referred to one of the villages which the Nuär Latjɔr had occupied in the eastern Nile. He affirms that the word 'dɔr' in the Nuär language means a place without people and 'komkan' means a beast which was known to Nuär by the name lɛt-a beast which eats human beings in both western and eastern Nuärland" as we have above-mentioned.

Rev. Pastor Paul stated that historically, people chose four young people who 'were good runners' to engage the beast-lɛt. Those four young people engaged the beast-lɛt for the whole day in a style of running until evening. According to that version, towards evening time, the beast-lɛt died because of exhaustion. Finally, the people occupied the portion of that

32 Duoth Kulang Bichiok and Paul Ruot Kor, *The Nuër Kiir People*, p. 92.

land which has become known to this day as 'Dɔr Komkan', a village, as Rev. Paul testifies.

6. According to Simon Bol, Pastor Michael Kiir from the Reformed Church and Elder James Mutyul Thɔ̱r from the Presbyterian Church, the word 'dɔr komkan' is referred to the following places: Uröör, Nyirɔl, Akobo, Ayod, Fangak, ManyWud, Wulang, and Loŋɛcuk." Therefore, 'Dɔr Komkan referred to a new land with a new community in eastern Nuärland as we have mentioned earlier.

2.10 Two Gate Ways to the North of Sudan

The western Nuär as 'däpäny' knows the place, where Taŋ used to take young people from Bul Cöl Gɛ̱ɛ̱. The term däpäny is referred to an Island of Mahdi (Mahdi was an Islamic figure in the north of the Sudan). In western Nuär, there are two options to go to the north of Sudan. On the one hand, some do go to the north through the land. They pass through the Nuba Mountains to däpäny (an Island of Mahdi), and finally, to Khartoum-Kathum. On the other hand, some pass through the gate of the Dɔk River known as the White Nile or Adɔk el Ba̱a̱r. These are the two main gateways that lead the western Nuär to Khartoum. Consequently, as the eastern Nuär passed through various gates, also, the western Nuär went to the north through the two gates above-mentioned.

Generally, going to northern Sudan referred to as Khartoum, is done individually mostly by young people for various reasons. For example, young people used to go to the north to find work to get money to buy cows, and clothes for relatives. Alternatively, someone can go to the north due to health problems. Alternatively, some young people used to go to the north to buy necessary things for dance such as tuac-thɔ̱ɔ̱nä and various beds in the case of Jagɛi, Ha̱a̱k, Dɔk, and Nyuɔŋ Nuär as well.

2.11 The Disappearance of Taŋ Kuany to Däpäny

Earlier, we stressed Latjɔ̱r Duäc as the one who led Ji̱käny Dɔar to the eastern side of the Kiir River. We also re-emphasized that everyone in the western, central and eastern Nile knows him. However, apart from Latjɔ̱r, also, there was another man who was known to everyone in the western, central and eastern Nile. His name is called Taŋ Kuany. He was the one who led the first group of young people from Bul Cöl Gɛ̱ɛ̱ to'Däpäny.' By contrast, Latjɔ̱r Duäc was purely from Ji̱käny while Taŋ Kuany was purely from Bul Cöl Gɛ̱ɛ̱ of the western Nile. His full name was Taŋ Kuany Kunnur Juer. As to the period in which he lived, he was a man of the 19th century, roughly born in 1920 A.D).

However, nobody took note of an individual who decided to go to the North. For example, among those who used to go to däpäny, none of them became known to all the Nuär in the western, central and eastern Nile like Taŋ Kuany. Therefore, in the case of Taŋ Kuany, he became known because twice, he took two groups of young people to däpäny only from Bul Cöl Gɛ̱ɛ̱. In my comprehensive interviews with three persons from Bul Cöl Gɛ̱ɛ̱, such as James Mut Kong, Peter Yak and Fr. Abraham Dak, it is believed that Taŋ Kuany Kunur Juer was possessed by heavenly power.

However, this heavenly powerful source had no name, as is the case for other Nuär prophets. Furthermore, there was no traditional ritual or recognition done to him. In addition, there was no recognition from others. However, due to this ambiguity of his seizure, consequently, he was regarded as a crazy person or a mad person. Suddenly, he disappeared and consequently, his relatives and friends thought that he was dead.

2.11.1 Adventure of Taŋ to the Neighbouring Countries

Probably, Taŋ might have left Bul in 1939 for Kordofan. It is believed that from there, he proceeded to Däpäny (an Island of Mahdi) as we said earlier. Some people also believe after he left Däpäny, he went to Khartoum (Kathum). In his long journey, he even went to Ethiopia as well as to Uganda. Finally, some people said that he appeared in Port Sudan and came to Khartoum-Omdurman. He was received in the family of Mahdi. He entered an Islamic school (known as Khalwas) and learned the Quran and consequently, he became a Muslim.

According to J. Mut, Taŋ came back to Bul via Däjul. On his way, someone called Yiel Nyɔay saw him. However, some people believed that the people who had rejected him before he left for Däpäny-Khartoum would not see him. Taŋ told Yiel that he was going to Nyidɛŋ (Kuac) to Kulaŋ Koaŋjäŋ who believed in him before he left for 'Däpäny-Khartoum, When Yiel reported to some people that he has seen Taŋ Kuany, nobody could believe him because he was considered a liar. He said, 'okay, ba jakä thok Yiel Nyɔay or bia luny nɛ thok Yiel Nyɔay. This saying of Yiel Nyɔay has become a famous citation among many Bul Cöl Gɛ̱ɛ̱. According to J. Mut,

Taŋ arrived in Kuac and was highly welcomed by the

people. They organized for him a very big banquet. Many cattle were slaughtered which marked a turning point. People believed in him and mobilization for Däpäny-Khartoum (Kathum) was organized.

The Bul Nuär of Däjul heard about him and consequently, changed their minds and began to believe what Yiel Nyɔay had told them. Taŋ came to Däjul, Thok cɔat ciëŋ Thiey. In addition, he was highly welcomed by the people there. Consequently, they organized for him the same banquet as was done in Kuac. People began to believe in him as someone who had power. Immediately, Taŋ organized his mobilization for Däpäny-Khartoum.

Amidst this mobilization, his family and relatives asked him to build for him a luak-byer. The aim was to marry for him a girl to be his wife. He accepted it and people built for him a very big luak-big byre with two huts on both sides possibly for his wives. After people finished the buildings, he told them to burn them. They burned them and they were also surprised by such an act. This meant that Taŋ had no intention to stay there but rather planned for adventure.

Consequently, Taŋ adventured to take a group of young people to the north. According to J. Mut, Taŋ took his first group to Däpäny-Khartoum-Kathum in 1957. This mission was very successful. Upon his arrival in Däpäny-Khartoum with his disciples, the Prime Minister of Sudan Abdullah Khalil and Mr. Böth Diu received him. Both Prime Minister Khalil and Mr Böth agreed that all those who were mature enough should be recruited into military service. The rest were taken to an Islamic school called 'Khalwas.' Some young people chose to become Christians and consequently, received Christian education such as catechesis. J. Mut asserts that the aim of Taŋ to take young people to Däpäny-Khartoum was for three reasons: education, town life and contemporary city civilization.

In 1959, it is stated that Taŋ returned to Bul Nuär and started his second mobilization for young people to go to the north. In this second mobilization, consequently, he convinced many disciples who were too ready to go with him to Däpäny-Khartoum-Kathum. In this second mobilization, some people including some chiefs became unhappy. They became worried about the disappearance of young people to the north through Taŋ. This was because the first group whom he took Däpäny-Khartoum did not come back to Bul Nuär. Based on this uncertainty and worry, while they were on their way with his second group, he was attacked by Dɛŋ Jaak (Luitluit Dup) the chief of Leek, at Kaljack. There was speculation that the order might have come from Däpäny-Khartoum, which was also questionable to some.

2.11.2 Taŋ Final Words: Blessing-Pu̱ɔth and Curse-Biit

After Dɛŋ Jaak (Luitluit Dup) at Kaljaak in Leek Nuär territory attacked Taŋ and his second group, it became clear that the order did not come from the Khartoum but rather it was from the local chiefs primarily from Monytuil Wicja̱ŋ and Dɛŋ Jaak. Taŋ was arrested, judged and sentenced to life imprisonment in 1959.

However, during the trial before the local chief of Bul, Monytuil Wicja̱ŋ and the local chief of Leek, Dɛŋ Jaak (Luitluit Dup) could pass judgment upon him, he asked all the chiefs including those who refused to pass judgment upon him to say something. 1. He said to Malual Wun, "There is a 'government which is coming that will get you a life, and you will die peacefully on your chair.' The word ruɔm means types of flies which sting people and cows painfully.'

2. He said to Liyliy Gɔa̱h "You will have numerous descendants." He said to Dɛŋ Jaak (Luitluit Dup) "You will see the government which is coming but only for a short time." 3. He said to Monytuil Wicja̱ŋ Wuɔ̱r, "What you want to know alone, you will get it, but it will always fail." Taŋ said to his paternal brother by name Rɔk Daaŋ Nyaŋ, who always criticized him, "You! With your stubborn mind, you will never give birth to a boy; you will always sit like a boy-bi̱ la nyuuri̱ cuelä cet kɛ dhɔl." For example, according to eyewitnesses, his paternal brother, Rɔk Daaŋ Nyaŋ who is still alive, is still sitting like a boy-nyuurɛ cuelä cä dhɔl.

After he finished his speech of blessings upon those who declined to judge him and curse-bit upon those who judged him unjustly, he told them to pass their judgment. The two head chiefs who passed judgment on him were: Monytuil Wija̱ŋ Wuɔr from Bul Cöl Gɛ̱ɛ̱, his chief, and Dɛŋ Jaak (Luitluit Dup) from Leek. Both Monytuil and Dɛŋ Jaak (Luitluit Dup) judged him as a madman. Finally, Taŋ was taken to Malakal and died in 1961. Kiir Tur Kɔŋ and Kuetey Ŋuɔ̱r, went to Däpäny-Khartoum to inform the people about what Taŋ told them before his death. He said those whom he took to Däpäny-Khartoum should come back and it seemed, some went back to Bul.

After these comprehensive interviews with a few people from Bul Cöl Gɛ̱ɛ̱, we can assert beyond no doubt that Taŋ and the people whom he took to Däpäny-Khartoum came back to Nuär land. At least, we have arrived at clarification and verification of some general misconceptions of 'people of Taŋ as if they disappeared for good'.

2.11.3 Success & Failure of Taŋ Kuany

Taŋ opposed traditional initiation (ga̱r) but was broken by gatmanlendɛ-broken by his cousin by name Baŋɔ̱aŋ Kuany. The bottom is, that Taŋ was not contended with village life after he discovered city life in Khartoum. His objective was to take young people to Khartoum to receive education and to accustom themselves to city life. However, his ideas were good but he did enlighten the elders of the community such as chiefs to understand his plan. Consequently, the chiefs and the elders of the community treated him with suspicion due to the ambiguity of his plan.

As we have mentioned earlier, the adventure of Taŋ in western, central and eastern Nuär-land seems to be known to everybody. In comparison with the adventure of Latjɔr Duäc (Latjɔr Diŋyian), generally, it seems everybody thought that the adventure of Taŋ to Däpäny-Khartoum contributed nothing to his or her history but a great loss. However, from various interviews we have conducted, we came to know that Taŋ has contributed a lot to Bul Chöl Gɛ̱ɛ̱. From the list of people whom he took to Däpäny'-Khartoum, we are made aware that some of them became Christians.

Among the group who became Christians, was our late prominent Catholic catechist by the name of Samuel Luke who spent a lot of time in Unity State. Within the Bul Chöl Gɛ̱ɛ̱, Taŋ is considered as a great man. About his success, for example, the majority of people whom he took to Däpäny'-Khartoum, were well-educated including their children. Some worked in the army of Sudan and even at present, in the army of South Sudan. Some held big positions in the government.

Taŋ was a man of adventure and hope though his

contemporary Nuär chiefs, especially his chief Monytuil Wicjaŋ and Dɛŋ Jaak, did not understand him. As a sign of hope for the future of his people, there is a tree at Mapɛɛr or Thok cɔt called 'Thar Thɔaak Gatä Kuany Kunnur Juɛr.' Some contemporary Nuär from Bul Cöl assert that sometimes, people are going there to offer animal sacrifices under that tree. Taŋ had speared the ground with the fish spear and had said, 'Between Mayɔm and Däpäny-Khartoum nothing will block the movement of the people.' As a man of people, Taŋ had a drum for young people to express their joy during the autumn season.

One true thing is that Däpäny-Khartoum as a city is both very complicated and at the same time attractive place for newcomers as it was for the groups of Taŋ. Therefore, was a certain Nuär man who composed a famous song about the unknown direction of Taŋ Kuany and his spectators (the groups whom he took to Khartoum), that says: ci nëën kɔ gaar cet nä nɛy Taŋ ɛ wiɛ̈ɛ̈ mä thil dhol mä ciɛ kɛt jiath ëë te nɛy thin.

The song can be translated as follows: 'Our spectators are confused like the spectators (people) of Taŋ. This song is fitting because the majority of Nuär both in the western, central and eastern Nile are unaware of where Taŋ and his groups had ended. However, through this book, many Nuär people in four major areas of Nuär land such as Bentiu-Bitim, Central Fangak, Nasir and Akobo will get enough information.

Taŋ opposed traditional initiation (gar) but was broken by gatmanlendɛ-broken by his cousin by name Baŋɔaŋ Kuany. The bottom is, that Taŋ was not contended with village life after he discovered a city life in Khartoum. His objective was to take young people to Khartoum to receive education and to accustom themselves to city life. However, his ideas were good but he did enlighten the elders of the community such as chiefs to understand his plan. Consequently, the chiefs and the elders of the community treated him with suspicion due to the ambiguity of his plan.

As we have mentioned earlier, the adventure of Taŋ in western, central and eastern Nuär-land seems to be known to everybody. In comparison with the adventure of Latjɔr Duäc (Latjɔr Diŋyian), generally, it seems everybody thought that the adventure of Taŋ to Däpäny-Khartoum contributed nothing to his or her history but a great loss. However, from various interviews we have conducted, we came to know that Taŋ has contributed a lot to Bul Chöl Gɛ̱ɛ̱. From the list of people whom he took to Däpäny'-Khartoum, we are made aware that some of them became Christians.

Among the group who became Christians, was our late prominent Catholic catechist by the name of Samuel Luke who spent a lot of time in Unity State. Within the Bul Chöl Gɛ̱ɛ̱, Taŋ is considered as a great man. About his success, for example, the majority of people whom he took to Däpäny'-Khartoum, were well-educated including their children. Some worked in the army of Sudan and even at present, in the army of South Sudan. Some held big positions in the government.

Taŋ was a man of adventure and hope though his contemporary Nuär chiefs, especially his chief Monytuil Wicja̱ŋ and Dɛŋ Jaak, did not understand him. As a sign of hope for the future of his people, there is a tree at Mapɛɛr or Thok cɔ̱t called 'Thar Thɔa̱a̱k Gatä Kuany Kunnur Juɛr.' Some contemporary Nuär from Bul Cöl assert that sometimes, people are going there to offer animal sacrifices under that tree. Taŋ had speared the ground with the fish spear and had said, 'Between Mayɔm and Däpäny-Khartoum nothing will block the movement of the people.' As a man of people, Taŋ had a drum for young people to express their joy during the autumn season.

One true thing is that Däpäny-Khartoum as a city is both very complicated and at the same time attractive place for newcomers as it was for the groups of Taŋ. Therefore, was a certain Nuär man who composed a famous song about the unknown direction of Taŋ Kuany and his spectators (the groups whom he took to Khartoum), that says: ci̱ nëën kɔ ga̱a̱r cet nä nɛy Taŋ ɛ wiɛ̈ɛ̈ mä thil dhol mä ciɛ kɛt jiath ëë te nɛy thin.

The song can be translated as follows: 'Our spectators are confused like the spectators (people) of Taŋ. This song is fitting because the majority of Nuär both in the western, central and eastern Nile are unaware of where Taŋ and his groups had ended. However, through this book, many Nuär people in four major areas of Nuär land such as Bentiu-Bitim, Central Fangak, Nasir and Akobo will get enough information.

2.11.4 Taŋ as a Prophet & the Fulfillment of His Prophecies

On the one hand, our reading of the life of Taŋ Kuany should leave us with no doubt about the impact it had on the majority of Bul people. On the other hand, other Nuär considered his disappearance as a loss due to lack of information. For example, for the rest of Nuär, nobody knows anything about Taŋ, except his disappearance for good with his group. Even, though I was not aware that Taŋ and his group had returned to

Nuär land, however, my misconception about him has been clarified by such credible eyewitnesses.

According to the majority of Bul Cöl Gɛ̱ɛ̱, Taŋ is considered a prophet, god and a spirit. Therefore, many of him or her are still expecting his return or the spirit, which seized him, may one day seize another person among Bul Nuär. According to H. Johnson, the Bul Nuär named Tang Kuainy (or Tong Kuie) visited the Mahdi's son, Sayyid Abd al-Raham, in the 1950s and returned home to recruit Nuär labour for the Sayyid's estates in the north. Though circumcised, and said to advocate conversion to Islam, he behaved like a Nuär prophet and attracted large crowds, whom he exhorted to confess their evil deeds. H. Johnson asserts that he went to Nyaruac around 1956 to take her to the real Mahdi, but she ignored him and invoked the duties owed for the government road work and taxes as a substitute for exodus to the north.

As a prophet, his prophecies had become true. He prophesied about the ruɔ̱m-government which was coming and which came. South Sudan through various rebel fighters gained its independence in 2011. Taŋ definition of government as 'ruɔ̱m' requires serious observation. We may not arrive at certainty about his concept of the word 'ruɔm.' Nevertheless, a sensible person can draw the meaning of the term 'ruɔ̱m' from the activity of the 'ruɔm' itself. Therefore, any activity of a brutal government against its citizens or subjects in the world at large could be compared to the biting of ruɔ̱m by a human person or other animals.

His blessing upon Liyliy Gɔa̱h, the head chief of Jagɛi Nuär, had come to fulfilment. Taŋ had promised Liyliy Gɔa̱h numerous children, which happened. There is a famous story about Liyliy among the Jagɛi Nuär that one day, he met a girl whom he admired. He asked that girl to be married to him. Unfortunately, when the girl introduced herself, he realized she was his daughter.

Concerning Malual Wun, he enjoyed the blessing of Taŋ and died peacefully last year, 2018. His paternal brother Rɔk Daaŋ Nyaŋ who always, criticized him, finally, cursed-bit, him to have no male child and, consequently, has never given birth to a boy. Until now, in his old age, he uses to sit like a boy-bi̱ la nyuuri̱ cuelä ca̱t kɛ dhɔl dhɔal. Today, eyewitnesses say that Rɔk Daaŋ Nyaŋ has a big problem sitting on a chair with his buttocks, due to the consequence of a curse from Taŋ.

2.11.5 Attractiveness of Däpäny-Khartoum

Our investigation of the drama of Taŋ and his group will not overshadow the side effects of the disappearance of some young Nuär youths to Däpäny-Khartoum. Our experience with Däpäny'-north Sudan proves beyond no doubt. As we have discussed earlier, many young Nuär men used to go to Khartoum for various reasons. For example, the disappearance of young Nuär men to Däpäny both in the west, central and in the east, from the generation of Taŋ to our generation is undeniable. Consequently, the Däpäny-Khartoum is considered a place of early paradise.

Mr Gatkuoth Pual revealed all the reasons in his song why some people would like to remain in Däpäny'-Khartoum for good. For example, Gatkuoth Pual was never taken by Taŋ Kuany to Däpäny'-Khartoum, but he remained there for good. In this sense, both Gatkuoth and, other thousands of Nuär men and women never came back from Däpäny'-Khartoum. Therefore, today, the Däpäny'-Khartoum of Taŋ

Kuany could be any place where life seems to be enjoyable but with many challenges.

Gatkuoth Pual from Lak, kä Cïëŋ Kuac Böör from Laak composed a song at a place of drinking in Däpäny'-Khartoum-Kathum: Kɔn juɔr Khartoum-Kathum math nɛykɔaŋ mä leny wec ruel, kɛ thokär mä leny duäc, dɔɔm, kɛ dhët bathɔal mä ca kɛl kɛ dhɔn nyatëër, kuɛ̈ l̲ar j̲i cieŋ i̲ c̲i nɛy gua̲ath dɔŋä jek, lab nɛ jɔɔk tä ba kuën män. Ɣän bä wä cieŋ nä Babur kɔaŋ bim kɛnɛ Gatɔr, ɣän Nuär nä cïëŋda piith kɛ pul.

Therefore, the song of Gatkuoth Pual can be: first, wine is far better than summer camps of cattle, second, where there is sugar far better than dancing with girls at the place of drum in our village, third, where there is roasted chicken with oil. Fourth, just inform the people we have found a place for us to become old. Fifth, I will never come home unless the steamer and train will brew wine. Sixth, we are already old people, marry for us wives.

Conclusion

Chapter two has discussed thoroughly the keynotes on colonization for selfish interest, the background of Nuär migration, which includes two hypotheses related to immigration, the waves of Nuär migration such as five theories of Lɔu Nuär migration to the Eastern White Nile that include the search for better living condition, the challenges they faced, and their confrontation with Murle.

In addition, the chapter has presented J̲ikäny migration to the eastern White Nile, the first version of migration, Latjɔ̲r's decision to marry Nyaguɛi, the crossing of the White Nile, the adventure to various destinations and a second version about their migration. It has explained broadly discusses Gaatwär Nuär's migration to the Eastern White Nile, the dramatic clash between Buok Käpiɛl and Pu̱ɔl Buɔyian, their testimony on their migration and finally, the confrontation between Nuär Mɛr and Dɛg Leekä

Furthermore, the chapter has treated Thi̱a̱ŋ Nuär migration to the Eastern White Nile, Laak Nuär migration to the Eastern White Nile, the challenges which all the Nuär faced migration faced, and various opinions about Dɔr Komkan. In addition, it explains broadly two gateways to the North of Sudan, the disappearance of Taŋ Kuany to Däpäny, the legend about his Adventure to the neighbouring countries, Taŋ final words: blessing-pu̱ɔth and curse-bit, his success and failure, the fulfilment of his prophecies and finally, the attractiveness of Däpäny-Khartoum.

CHAPTER THREE

GOD'S ATTRIBUTES AND OTHER VARIOUS POWERS

Introduction

Chapter three discusses the conceptual analysis of God's attributes according to Nuär. It also presents the name of God-Koth and other attributes ascribed to God such as Tutgaär kiɛ Tha̲nya̲ny-God-Unlimited and with Omnipotent Power. The chapter illustrates God as cääk-Creator, ta̲th-to make and Gua̲ndɔŋ-Grandfather (Gua̲ndi̲t-or Big Father). Finally, it discusses the differences between God and other spirits and God's greatness over His created world.

Furthermore, the chapter discusses unprecedented issues related to mysterious powers among the Nuär. Although the Nuär believe in God and his attributes, nevertheless, there exist other mysterious powers, which always cause confusion and even conflict. Some individual persons own these mysterious powers, while others can have access to them by buying from the owners.

Furthermore, the chapter also presents types of traditional

powers such as Kuär Muɔ̱ɔn/Earth-Master/Leopard Skin, consecration & installation of Kuär Mɔ̱ɔ̱n/Earth-Master, intrinsic character of Kuär Mɔ̱ɔ̱n/Earth-Master, Wud Ɣɔ̱ɔ̱k/Gua̱n Puɔ̱dä/Cow-Master, the function of Wud Ɣɔ̱ɔ̱k/Gua̱n Puɔ̱dä/Cow-Master, the myth of ye̱c/broom, Tut Wi̱e̱c and finally, Mut Wiu Ɣä/Wiu Spear & wizard, and Cuol Wi̱c

3. Conceptual Analysis of God's Attributes

In chapter one, we discussed the Nuär origin in the western White Nile. We found out that all the Nuär trace their origin back to a big tree called ŋɔ̱ɔ̱b in their language located at the centre of the House-Däär Ciëŋ at Koch County, at a village called li̱i̱c in Jagiɛ Nuär. In chapter two, we focused on four major Nuär clans such as Gaatwär Nuär, Laak Nuär, Lou Nuär, and Ji̱käny Nuär (dɔar) who went from the western White to the eastern White Nile. We asserted that these four major clans were through different leaders, through different gates, and at different periods. Nevertheless, we stressed their linkages and commonalities to the western White Nile communities.

As we shall discuss below in chapter three, we will also know that both Nuär in the west, in the centre, and the east, all do believe in God. They believe that someone more powerful than everybody else once created the world in which human beings live. Consequently, they attribute to him some names that cannot be attributed to anyone else except to God. Therefore, all the Nuär know these attributes. They use them when they address God on various occasions in life. Below, we shall analyze them one by one.

3.1 The Name of God-Koth

Among the highest and omnipotent beings, which the Nuär people other indigenous Africans, and other people in the world at large believe, is God. His existence and His presence everywhere in Nuär land and everywhere in the world are beyond dispute for those who believe in Him. According to Nuär, the concept of God has prompted the usage of various attributes as it does among other indigenous people in the African continent. These illustrations are related to the concept of God in the Nuär religion.

First, the Nuär do perceive God as Koth Ca̱a̱k. according to them, the concept of the word ‘Koth’ points to the common name for God, a name that is common to all the Nuär. It refers to the Creator of all things both biotic and abiotic-Cäh ŋɔaani̱ diaal tin tëk kɛnɛ tin ci̱ / tëk. Furthermore, the term ‘Koth’ also refers to the ‘Supreme Being’ who has no substitute and who is eternal-Tutga̱ar mä ca / wäny kä mä do̱o̱rar.

The word ‘Koth’ is referred to the ‘Supreme Being’ who has no beginning and no ending-Tutga̱a̱r mi̱ thil jio̱l kä thil pek. He was present, He is present and He will be present thin, jɛn ɛ thin, ka̱ bɛ te thin bä. The tern Koth in the Nuär language is also referred to the Supreme Being who is the Spirit-Tutga̱a̱r mä Yieh. Furthermore, the word Koth has a spiritual connotation. In the Nuär language, the term Koth means to blow. Koth-God then is associated with the concept of the book of Genesis which says, “Then the Lord God formed the man out of the dust of the ground and blew into his nostrils the breath of life, and the man became a living being” (Gen 2:7).

The emphasis is on the “blew into his nostrils the breath

of life, and the man became a living being." For example, a grandfather or a grandmother can pray over his/her grandsons/granddaughters saying, 'My grandsons/granddaughters, May God blow upon you his cool spirit-Gaat gatdä/gaat nyadä bi Koth yɛ kuɔth jiɔm mä kɔ̱c.

3.1.2 Tutgaär-God- with Unlimited Omnipotent Power

The word 'Tutga̱a̱r' refers to the freedom of God which allows him to govern the world without interference from anyone. When the Nuär uses the term Tutga̱a̱r, it refers to his 'absolute freedom' by which he is present everywhere in the world both in heaven and on earth. Furthermore, the term tutga̱a̱r is also associated with his omnipotence. For example, no police officer can command Him to stop; no other powers on earth can surpass His Power, and all sovereignty is under Him. According to L. Magesa, viewed in African religion, the understanding of God should involve, "The understanding of the good that sustains life and the bad that destroys it. They establish both the context and the content of African morality and ethics."

The book of the prophet Isaiah presents beautiful descriptions of the meaning of the word 'tutga̱a̱r as follows: ..."They name him Wonderful-Counsellor, God-Hero, Father-forever, Prince of Peace, His dominion is vast and forever peaceful..."(Isa 9:5-6). The famous British anthropologist Evans-Pritchard who wrote on Nuär religion had encountered such attributes as tutga̱a̱r. According to Evans-Pritchard, another poetic epithet by which God may be referred to is tutgaa̱r. This is an ox name, taken from an ox of the kind Nuär call 'wer', which has widespread horns and is the most majestic of their beasts.

Evans-Pritchard asserts that "The name is the combination of two words: tut, which has the sense of 'strength' or 'greatness', and gar, which has the sense of 'omnipresent', as another one for God's titles, with mi gargar-Kuoth mi̱ gärgär), the omnipresent God (gärgär can be translated as 'limitless')." Such poetic language when applied to the concept of God's existence brings with it a clear understanding of God. By using our dialect words and terms, which we are used to, we influence our way of believing in God and our ways of looking at the whole creation as well.

3.1.3 Cääk-Creator

The Nuär concept of God requires a specific terminology such as the term 'Cääk'-Creator. The concept of the word cääk (cäh) ' can be associated with the Elohistic Tradition which says, "God created mankind in his image; in the image of God, he created them, male and female" (Gen 1:27). In this specific reference to Elohistic Tradition, we have a clear concept about the creation of man and woman. Both man and woman were created out of nothing; there is no specific substance about their creation.

The passage from the Sacred Scripture simply says that God created humankind in his image; in the image of God, he created them; male and female. In this passage from the Holy Scripture of the book of Gn 1: 27, there is no reference to any material in which Adam and Eve were made. The outcome of the creation of Adam and Eve both finds its origin in God's power and God's command.

The Nuär call God-Koth cääk nath-Creator of the people, and cääk ɣɔaa-Creator of the Universe. When they use such words as cääk for God, they simply mean that God created humankind out of nothing; and He has created the whole universe out of nothing. Sometimes, they call God-cääk nhial kɛnɛ piiny- Creator of the heaven and the earth. According to J. Mbiti, "God is the origin and sustenance of all things. He is outside and beyond His creation." He argues that He is involved in His creation, so it is not outside of Him or His reach. In the view of J. Mbiti, God is thus simultaneously transcendent and immanent. J. Mbiti added that a balanced understanding of these two extremes is necessary in our discussion of the African conceptions of God.

According to Evans-Pritchard, "However, the word can be used by men for imaginative constructions, such as the thinking of a name to give a child, inventing a tale, or composing a poem, in the same figurative sense as when we say that an actor creates a part." He argues that the word means not only creation from nothing but also creation by thought or imagination, so that 'God created the universe' has the sense of 'God thought of the universe' or 'God imagined the universe. The Nuär thinking of God as cääk-Creator is based on the reflection of the marvellous universe, which came out as his thought, his imagination and his divine plan.

J. Mbiti argues that "Several societies consider God to be omniscient, that is, to know all things, to be simultaneously everywhere (i.e. omnipresent), and to be almighty (omnipotent)."[33]

33 John Mbiti, African *Religion & Philosophy*, p. 29.

3.1.4 Ta̲th-to Make

The word 'tath'-to make in Nuär language means to make something out of something. According to J. Tab, this is also demonstrated in the "Yahwistic (Priestly) creation narratives that have very different cosmologies and define different roles for humans within the creation."[34] " So the LORD God cast a deep sleep on the man, and while he was asleep, he took out one of his ribs and closed up its place with flesh. The LORD God then built the rib that he had taken from the man into a woman. When he brought her to the man, the man said; this one, at last, is bone of my bones and flesh of my flesh, this one shall be called woman,' for out man this one has been taken." (Gen 2: 21-23).

According to Evans-Pritchard, "'täth' means to make something out of something else already materially existing, as when a child moulds clay into the shape of an ox or a smith man beats a spear out of iron."[35] He further states that the sentence would therefore be better translated as, 'When God created people then he made (or fashioned) man'. Evans-Pritchard affirms that the distinction is similar to that between 'created and made' in the first chapter of the book of Genesis as we have cited before.

Nuär rarely uses the word 'tath' to make, for God but they can use it implicitly. However, when they call God täh-Maker, they deduce this from a physical world. It is by looking at the material universe, which includes every living organism, sometimes, they implicitly use the word täth-to

34 Cf. J. Tab Charoa, *Ethics of Human Sexuality: A Call for Chastity in Christian Families*, Nairobi, CUEA Press, 2007, p. 129.

35 E.E. Evans-Pritchard, *Nuër Religion*, p. 5.

make, applying it to God. According to Nuär, when they apply the word täth-to make, to God, they have in mind the concept of God who cannot be limited to particular words. For God, any word that suits his plan, he can choose it as he wishes for his purpose.

According to them, God has both powers to create something out of nothing and to täth-to make something out of something, however, with an amazing splendour. According to L. Magesa, God is the Great Ancestor, the first Founder and Progenitor, the Giver of life, the Power behind everything that is, God is the first Initiator of a people's way of life, its tradition.[36]

3.1.5 Gua̱ndɔŋ-Grandfather (Gua̱ndi̱t-or Great Father)

Nuär are very good at using social status and applying them to God. The status such as grandfather-Gua̱ndɔŋ, (Gua̱ndi̱t-or Great Father), Gua̱ra (Gua̱nda)-our Father, or Koth while kɛnɛ piny-God of heaven and earth. When the Nuär applies those social statuses to God, they have in mind two dimensions: according to Evans-Pritchard, He is their creator and he is their protector. He asserts that God is addressed in prayers as 'kwoth me cak gwadong', God who created my ancestor. Evans-Pritchard argues that sometimes, God is given a genealogical position about man. This can be expressed by Nuär when they refer themselves to God as 'gaatku' your children, or when they name a child 'Gat Kwoth'-son of God. However, according to Evans-Pritchard, "Nuär does

36 Laurenti Magesa, *African Religion, the Moral Traditions of the Abundant Life,* p. 42.

not think of God as the begetter of man but as his creator."[37]

J. Mbiti asserts that "To the Zulu and Banyarwanda, God is known as 'the wise One' and to the Akan as 'He Who knows or sees all."[38] He states that it is a common saying among the Yoruba that 'Only God is wise' and they believe that God is 'the Discerner of the heart' who 'sees both the inside and outside of man'. For example, prophet Ŋundɛŋ of Nuär describes himself as the greatest witchcraft of all the witchcrafts by claiming to see everything everywhere even when he is in the darkness. H. Johnson states of him ...bi̱ kuäär waŋdɛ [nyiɛnkɛ] böl luaak-And the master's eyes lit up in the byre."[39] If the chosen instrument of God describes himself as the greatest witchcraft of all the witchcrafts in terms of seeing everything everywhere, how great is the greatness of God in seeing everything everywhere?

According to Nuär, social status is usually applied to God during prayer as an official address to God and a sign of respect for him. According to Evans-Pritchard, the frequent use in prayers of the word 'rom' about the lives, or souls, of men indicates the same feeling about God, for it has the sense of the care and protection parents give to a child and especially the carrying of a helpful infant.

Furthermore, it is asserted that the Nuär habit of God outside formal and ritual occasions also suggests an answer to a protective presence, as does the affirmation one hears every day among the Nuär, 'Kwoth-Kuoth a thin', 'God is present. Nuär usually employs this expression when faced with difficulty to be overcome or some problems to be solved.

37 E.E. Evans-Pritchard, *Nuër Religion*, p. 8.

38 John Mbiti, African *Religion & Philosophy*, p. 29.

39 Douglas H. Johnson, Nuër Prophets, p. 86.

'Kwoth-Kuoth a thin' God monotheism according to Nuär belief. Such monotheistic doctrine finds its expression usually in a situation of complete helplessness.

Evans-Pritchard who lived among the Nuär for several years and who wrote a book on Nuär religion, states that a favourite Nuär expression is 'yie wicdä or (cɛ wicdä yiic kiɛ cɛ wic naath yiic kiɛ cɛ wicda yiic kiɛ cɛ widiɛn yiic), my head goes round' or 'I am bewildered' or our heads go round, or our heads are bewildered' or 'the heads of the people go round' or 'their heads go round'. When the Nuär uses such expressions, it means, they are at a loss because they are just foolish people who do not understand the why and the wherefore.

In such a situation of bewilderment and helplessness, the Nuär will console themselves by saying 'Kwoth-Kuoth a thin'. However, they say that God cannot be forced to respond to such a situation. They will simply express their famous saying 'God cannot be forced Kuoth cok.' According to Nuär, as bewilderment and helplessness require hope-Kwoth-Kuoth a thin', hope requires patience-'ca / Kuoth cok.

The Nuär do call God 'Guandɔŋ-grandfather, referring to the physical biological grandfather whose duty is to bless and embrace his grandsons and granddaughters. The role of the guandɔŋ-grandfather and mandɔŋ-grandmother in Nuär custom is to shower blessings upon their grandsons and granddaughters. God is 'Guandɔŋ-grandfather in the sense that he created the cosmos for the subsistence of his creatures. According to J. Tab, "The cosmos itself manifests the highest form of life, that is, God who has power over death."[40]

---

40 J. Tab Charoa, Ecology, *Principle of Stewardship of Creation: The Basic Principle of the Social Teach of the Church, Its Relevance to the African*

Traditionally, grandsons and granddaughters feel more protected in the presence of guandɔdiɛn-their grandfather and mandɔdiɛn-their grandmother. Based on this assumption, the Nuär do believe that guandɔŋ-grandfather and mandɔŋ-grandmother, wish their grandsons or granddaughters to live for eternity. This has great implications for their belief in God.

According to Evans-Pritchard, Nuär seldom attributes death in such cases as death by lightening or following the breach of divinely sanctioned interdictions to the direct intervention of God, but rather to natural circumstances or the action of a lesser spirit, but they nevertheless regard the natural circumstances or the spirit as instruments or agents of God. The final appeal in sickness is made to him. According to L. Magesa, God, the ancestors, and the spirits are all powers or forces that impinge on humans they are all moral agents[41] but not at an equal level.

3.1.6 God's Greatness Over the Created World

When Nuär speaks of the relationship between God and his creatures, they have in mind the created things such as ɣɔɔw-universe, which consists of nhial-heaven and piny-earth. According to them, nhial-heaven and piny-earth both belong to God as the Creator. When the Nuär says to God ɛ 'ɣɔɔwdu-it is your universe or ɛ pinydu-it is your earth, they simply mean that everything that exists both in heaven and on earth belongs to God.

According to Evans-Pritchard, Ghau-ɣɔɔwdu has many

Context, Juba, Printers Company Ltd, 2018, p. 69.

41 Laurenti Magesa, *African Religion, the Moral Traditions of the Abundant Life,* pp. 41-42.

meanings- world, sky, earth, and atmosphere, time and weather-which taken together, as they should be in prayer, mean the universe. Everything, which is created by God, reflects his image and likeness. In his argument, J. Tab asserts that "The African concept of cosmos demonstrates the sacramental aspect for the African human…"[42]

When God manifests Himself through rain, lightning thunder and the rainbow as the necklace of him, the Nuär people ask God not to allow them to inflict violence on people. For example, when rain manifests violence through floods, lightning, thunder and other means, who should be approached? When human life is in danger, the only person whom the Nuär can approach is God.

The Nuär believed that if he created them, he should also be able to control them. A famous example among the Nuär goes like this: an old woman when it was raining, lightning and thundering said to God, Gua̱ndɔŋ ɛ ku ben kɛ nyuɛ̈ɛ̈k kɛ ŋɔ̱a̱a̱r kɛ ŋa? Ɛ ɣɔwdu lö päät. J. Mbiti argues that "African concepts of God are strongly coloured and influenced by the historical, geographical, social and cultural background or environment of each people."[43]

3.1.7 God and Other Spirits

Who is God for the Nuär people? For the Nuär, God is called Kuoth/Kwoth, etymologically from the meaning of the word 'breath or spirit.' God is a Spirit that breathes life into human

---

42 Tab Charoa, Ecology, *Principle of Stewardship of Creation: The Basic Principle of the Social Teach of the Church, Its Relevance to the African Context,* p. 68.

43 John Mbiti, African *Religion & Philosophy*, p. 28

beings. The Nuär believe that God is a Spirit of the sky or the Spirit in the sky. He manifests Himself through rain, lightning and thunder; and they believe that the rainbow is a necklace of God (tik Kuoth/Kwoth).

The Nuär believe in the God of creation who is overall. However, they also believe in the role of mediation of lesser gods or spirits. The lesser spirits, which hold the position of mediation between the God of creation and people, are spirits of which some are above in the air, and others are on the earth. The spirits above the air are believed to be more powerful than those on the earth.

The spirits in the air are normally believed to be the spirits of dead persons who become 'gods.' One example of the spirits in the air is colwi̱c. Col (colwi̱c) is the spirit of a person who dies because of lightning. As the Nuär believe that God manifests himself through rain, when someone dies because of lightning during rain, they believe that God takes him or her; and so, he or she becomes 'god. According to Nuär, the spirit of that person is powerful and it influences his or her relationship with the living. J. Tab and Placide Tempels affirm on Bantu philosophy of life, "Calling upon God, the spirit, or the ancestral spirits, the heathen above all, give me force."[44]

The spirits on the earth possess and work in and through them for good or for bad according to the way, those spirits are directed or used by the possessed. An example of a spirit on the earth is Wiu. In the Eastern Gajaak Nuär, Wiu is called a god to rescue someone during war. According to Fr. Jacob Nhial, it is inherited, which means, its spirit possesses the one

44 Tab Charoa, Ecology, *Principle of Stewardship of Creation: The Basic Principle of the Social Teach of the Church, Its Relevance to the African Context,* p. 68.

he chooses from a family in the sub-clan of Cieŋwiew (the family of Wiu). The spirit of Wiu lives in a spear called Mut Wiu (The spear of Wiu). Sometimes, it is called 'Nyinlony,' which means, 'that whose eyes bleed.'

It is believed that when Wiu is angry, its eyes bleed with blood, and when he does not agree to be taken somewhere, no one carries the spear it indwells. All these small gods or spirits mediate between the God of creation and people. Sometimes, they intervene to resolve the problems such as bringing good things like rain. Sometimes, they kill and destroy human life when someone commits sins, crimes and mistakes.

3.2 Types of Mysterious Powers beside God

According to Nuär, gök is made up of three groups of people such as prophets, medium prophets, and magicians. The people respect Gök Kuoth (prophets). People believe that they can foresee events. Furthermore, they can identify who did what in front of the public. For example, Ngundeng was the first and most popular of all the Nuär prophets.

3.2.1 Medium Prophets and Jɔɔk (Jɔakni̱)

About medium prophets, even though their roots are not well known, it is accepted that this medium soul is the god of the predecessor of all the Nuär. Sometimes, they were called ji̱ Duäŋni̱ or Kuoth duäŋä, the spirit of breath (wind). Nuär considers the possessor of Duäŋ not a genuine prophet.

The owner of Duäŋ uses a certain technique such as the calabash containing pebbles, shaken to call the spirits of the dead. Raan gɛɛrɛ jɔakɛ kɛ jɔɔk, the man shakes (calls up) the spirit with the calabash. According to Nuär, it is as if someone seeking a doctor, when he/she arrives at the house of this middle prophet, presents him/her and his problem. The possessor of this spirit performs the ritual rite by shaking the gourd while heaping the Jɔɔk with a style of prayer of calling and singing. After a few minutes, he/she will present the results.

Apart from the owner of Jɔɔk, there exists also the owner of Mabiɛk. The owner of Mabiɛk uses the same style as the owner of Jɔɔk. For example, he uses the calabash containing pebbles, he shakes it to call the spirits of the dead or shakes (calls up) the spirit with the calabash. These two types of mysterious powers were present among individual persons in Nuär communities. The owners pretend to solve specific problems of a person.

3.2.2 Dɛŋ

About medium prophets, even though their roots are not well known, it is accepted that this medium soul is the god of the predecessor of all the Nuär. Sometimes, they were called ji̱ Duäŋni̱ or Kuoth duäŋä, the spirit of breath (wind). Nuär considers the possessor of Duäŋ not a genuine prophet.

The owner of Duäŋ uses a certain technique such as the calabash containing pebbles, shaken to call the spirits of the dead. Raan gɛɛrɛ jɔakɛ kɛ jɔɔk, the man shakes (calls up) the spirit with the calabash. According to Nuär, it is as if someone seeking a doctor, when he/she arrives at the house of this middle prophet, presents him/her and his problem. The possessor of this spirit performs the ritual rite by shaking the gourd while heaping the Jɔɔk with a style of prayer of calling and singing. After a few minutes, he/she will present the results.

Apart from the owner of Jɔɔk, there exists also the owner of Mabiɛk. The owner of Mabiɛk uses the same style as the owner of Jɔɔk. For example, he uses the calabash containing pebbles, he shakes it to call the spirits of the dead or shakes (calls up) the spirit with the calabash. These two types of mysterious powers were present among individual persons in Nuär communities. The owners pretend to solve specific problems of a person.

3.2.3 Buk and Dayim

Buk is a special female spirit that the Nuär people believe. She is connected to rivers and streams. She helps and protects the people who live near rivers and streams. She is very important to the people in Nuärland. Consequently, they call her by different names such as Buk, Dɛŋ, and Abuŋdit. She is like a mother to a special air spirit called Dɛŋ. It is believed to be powerful and great. For example, it has a healing spirit and protection in war.

By contrast, the Dayiɛmni̲ were often resented because they were the ones who demanded cattle based on their lies. They were frequently accused of living off the prophet's reputation. In the same way, the fetish owner is resented for pestering people for demanding goats from the people for his kulaŋ. The owners of Dayiɛmni̲ were suspected of enriching themselves with their mysterious powers, rather than enforcing moral order. The owner of Dayim is always a master of confusion among the people.

However, the owner of Dayim sometimes puts himself

at risk due to a naked big lie. For example, a certain man by the name Riek Lunylɔj Ruei from Laak Nuär at a village called Paguir was known for his Dayim, which he nicknamed Gatci̱ruei (Tut in Bör). Once Riek was approached by, a man called Ga̱i Däpɛɛr whose children died one after another. Gai told him, my children died one after another, and I have come to you to know the cause of their death. After puffing his pipe puff, for a few minutes, and then, he replied "Your mother was not happy when she died.'

The man went back to his village and came back to him the following morning with his mother. They met Riek, and the man said to him, 'This is my mother whom you said 'She died unhappy with me and that is why my children died one after another. After puffing his pipe for a while, Riek said to them, "You house of this woman, you are looking at me with blinking eyes, we shall not tell each other truth-yɛn ciëŋ ciëk ɛmɛ guɛ ɣä ɛ nyop ɣä nɛ, kɔn canɛ rɔ̱ bi̱ la̱t thuɔ̱k, kiɛ guɛ ɣä kɛ nyin tä cuɔl, canɛ rɔ̱ bi̱ la̱t thuɔ̱k. Sometimes, when our big lies are discovered, we become sleepless as Nhial Ruɛ̈k Thööŋ Dia̱ŋ put it.

When Nhial Ruai Thööŋ Dia̱ŋ from the Läŋ Nuär clan, weaned his child as is required by Nuär culture, he gave his cow that was newly delivered to his father-in-law to feed his weaned baby. Culturally, such a cow is supposed to be brought back to him because it has nothing to do with marriage. Unfortunately, when he asked his father-in-law to bring back the cow, he kept silent. He used to go to him, urging him to bring back his cow. However, his father-in-law person paid no attention to his persistent request. One day, Nhial opened a court against him. He was told next morning would be given a police officer with a gun to take back his cow from his father-in-law. Overtaken by joy, instead of going home, he went to inform his father-in-law that tomorrow morning; I will come with a police officer to take back my cow from you. Then, he left.

Upon hearing this, his father-in-law decided to evacuate all his cows and went to Adok. When Nhial and the police officer arrived the following morning, unfortunately, they found out that his father-in-law had gone away with his cattle. They went back. At night, Nhial could not sleep, realizing that he was the cause of his failure. In the following morning, he uttered a famous statement known to all Nuär "mɔ pe̱n ji̱ ni̱e̱nɔ tok tharɛ ji̱n-sometimes, you are the cause of sleeplessness. In this sense, we need to learn from Riek Lunylɔj Ruei and Nhial Ruai Thööŋ Diaŋ.

In both cases of Riek Lunylɔj Ruei and Nhial Ruɛ̈k Thööŋ Dia̱ŋ, we are confronted with the truth. On the one hand, Riek was caught up when he told a big lie but then, rationalized his big lie while on the other hand, the person to whom Nhial Ruɛ̈k owed something, instead of paying back his debt, decided to run away from the truth. In this sense, truth is only found in God and not in other mysterious powers that we sometimes, trust more than God. We ought to admit the truth and not run away from it. Jesus said, say, "Then you will know the truth, and the truth will set you free" (Jn 8:32).

3.2.4 Ji̱ Wual (Magicians) and Pajɔk

Ji̱ Wual (magicians) is an underclass that threatens people. They are believed to have a guardian spirit. If someone dares to take or damage his property, he can bring about death. There are many different spirits. For example, spirits manifest themselves in many different ways in Nuärland, however, currently; there is no consensus on their status. Nevertheless, Pajɔk as a spirit is viewed with scepticism.

It is one of the ancestors of Dɛŋ, and Dɛŋ's maternal uncle. Nevertheless, in Dinka culture, it is a power spirit, which is associated with a red beaver. It is stated that Dɛŋ Le̱kä included Pajɔk in his sanctuary along with other deities. Pajɔk also adopted one Ŋundɛŋ Dayiɛmni̱ and is the patron deity of the Dɛŋ Le̱kä family. Although the Nuär were aware of a magical connection to Pajɔk, however, some believed that it was god-like and divine worship.

3.2.5 Murjɔk (Nyanjɔk) and Mawum Juoth

The persecution of magic and sorcerers often led to the persecution of certain chieftains. A special form of Dinka magic known as Murjɔk, had first appeared in a major Nuär conflict. Murjɔk is to be classified as a "foreigner" in many ways. About its ritual and mysterious power, ashes collected from a clump of palms where the Dinka once had a shrine represented Murjɔk. The various chiefs or elderly men were accused of buying and using magic to kill their opponents.

For example, owners sell both Murjɔk and Mawum Juoth to people who are enemies to each other specifically, if this enmity involves the killing of a person. In this sense, enemies to counteract each other use both Murjɔk and Mawum Juoth as tools. The Nuär believe that Mawum Juoth is the most dangerous mysterious power, which kills instantly when it is released to attack one's enemy-mä ca luɔ̱ny gua̱n tɛr. Therefore, both Murjɔk and Mawum Juoth are common mysterious powers that are exercised by some men among the Nuär.

The Dinka family, who owned Murjɔk and Mawum Juoth, were among the first settlers in Nuärland. If something happens to you and your children and you look for the one who has a Murjɔk for help, he will tell you that this happened because you opposed the magician. Consequently, he can even mention the name of your opponent. For that, you have to go to him and apologize.

It is believed that an apology is not done the way we normally do in our daily lives. One must offer a bull as an excuse because the owner of Murjɔk has no mercy. The owner of Murjɔk likes to kill (the sorcerer). For example, even after receiving a bull and performs his ritual rite called 'witchcraft' to do away with his enemy and his family too.

It is believed that because of this, the man who became a friend to someone who has a Murjɔk will take it with him at home. Consequently, he will use it to intimidate and even kill others with it. Some men used to buy it from the owner. After buying the Murjɔk, he gives a few days for the ritual performance. On the last day, he plans to call his wife to accompany him. This time, he will erect a stake for ceremonial reasons, which means that Murjɔk will be incarnated at his home permanently.

When the owner comes back with a cow or two, but that is not the end of the scenario. He takes more cows, even the man's daughter who is married, and the magician himself. For example, Murjɔk will claim to have a cow, the so-called magic cow (Yaŋ Kuɔth). For instance, children will not drink the milk of Yaŋ kuɔth except the elderly women. Murjɔk had a deadly habit of killing even his owner's children.

Also, Nyanjɔk and Pajɔk. Magicians (especially Gua̱ndɛ, the owner of the object) imitated the prophet in appearance, but not necessarily in their concern about the moral life of the community. Since there were no doctors; there was a need for healing and protective powers. Consequently, the owners of such mysterious powers made offerings in imitation of the doctors and the prophets. However, fetishes (kulaaŋni̲) are rarely harmless. They were best known for eating food. Rather than imitate prophets, fetish owners parody prophecies, and the fetish itself, is a parody of the God of Liberty. For fetish owners, the prophet's spiritual dangers and lust for livestock are imitated without offering any benefit in return.

3.2.6 Biɛl

Biɛl, according to Nuar, Biɛl was also counted among kuth piɛny. It is a telluric spirit, certain nature spirits called biɛli̲. Furthermore, it is explained as a certain fetish and medicinal spirit. However, it is better to give a brief and condensed description of these ideas, so that they can become sufficiently clear. The Nuär saw it as a manifestation of an almost disparate mind, the same as their fortune-teller and leech practices.

Nevertheless, we need to refer to them again here, because they are spoken of as kuth, spirits. Nature spirits are also spoken of and treated in some respects as being similar to air spirits, but inferior to them about the things and substances they appear to belong, so to speak. Bound; however, it must be emphasized that it is not the thing itself that is considered a spirit. This is evidenced by the fact that the spirits are believed to attach and detach from them. Their presence in the objects and processes ion is detected by luminosity or phosphorescence.

We see here again an implicit metaphor that runs through Nuär religion, light, and darkness combined with heaven and earth; and the word Biɛl probably means the same 'colour', which is not absolute for Nuär abstraction, but the relationship between light and dark tones. One of these sprites is Biɛl pant, a meteorite spirit called Biɛl pukä, an ash sprite.

It is the same as what is called biɛl nhial, heaven-spirit, and biɛl maac, fire-spirit. Like all nature spirits, it can be bought by the owner [Guaṉ bilä)-first for one or two goats. He does not deliver the meteorite itself, but a small gourd containing dung ashes; hence, the name is ash spirit. The purchaser hangs this from the porch of his byre. This pole on the porch and sacrifices the goat to the passion, saying that one day, he will get a cow for it and ask it to fall.

If ash stays in the lane until the meteorite falls, the man anoints it with butter and sacrifices it, then spreads it on the floor behind his hut. One day 'bɛ macdɛ dɔp wi̱c pa̱a̱m, bɛ cu pɛ̈t', 'it (the sprite) lights its fire on the surface of the meteorite and then burns (glows)' When a man sees this light, he sacrifices a goat and brews beer and holds feasts where the assembled people clap their hands and sing hymns.

Furthermore, similar spirits are biɛli̱ yiëër the river spirits. They are found as biɛl rɔa, hippopotamus, on some hippopotami and certain fishes, re̱c. The Nuär report that "cikɛ mat", or "they gathered", is on a certain hippopotamus. It is said that when a man kills one of these animals, he sees a light in his head, and then the spirit takes possession of him. He is expected to perform ritual ceremonies such as breaking the animal's skull with an axe, taking out the brain and boiling it, rubbing some of the boiled brains on his forehead and right arm, and eating the rest.

Shortly, afterwards, he falls ill, and when the prophet or the possessor of this or some other spirit confirms his supposition that the spirit has made him ill, a ceremony of clapping and singing takes place, during which the sick man departs, and the spirit speaks. Through his lips, he says what it is and what he wants. After that, the victim is sacrificed and the bones of the victim are placed near the entrance to the men's hut and a pile of ashes is piled on them, forming a shrine [yi̱k bilä) topped by a branch of a tree which is blocked.

The spirit then departs from the man, but he attends to it from time to time, dedicates an animal to it, and makes sacrifices. Consequently, his children may continue to do so after his death. Other biɛl include biɛl jiath, the tree spirit, and biɛl. Sometimes, the Nuär called it kuoth juaacni̱, the spirit of grasses. The Nuär also speak biɛl rir, cobra sprite and biɛl lööc.

3.2.7 Pɛ̈th (Wiard) and Types of Tie̱t

The word pɛ̈th (wizard) according to Nuär is described as a person with an evil eye that suspends the milk of a cow or holds it back. Pɛ̈th (wizard) näk ɛ naath kɛ waŋdɛ, a person with evil eyes kills people with his eye. Pɛ̈th känɛ cak ɣɔ̱ɔ̱k. The evil eye takes the milk of a cow. According to Nuär's opinion, the evil eye is an act of covetousness.

The most famous type of Tiet is the Tiet Guikä (snail). He throws the conch shell onto the convex surface of the gourd and sees how it falls. This is how a person answers a question such as finding a lost cow, whether his journey succeeds, whether he kills the victim of a blood feud, and whether everything is fine at home while travelling. While he is busy throwing cannonballs, he speaks to his familiar spirit, which is connected to the ground.

Another sort of master in this arrangement is Tiet Däälä. Among their parts, are performing customs to occupy the shepherd and making a difference in recovering the cattle, helping him in recovering his runaway spouse, picking up the favour of a lady, and taking blood. This incorporation takes exact retribution in a battle and evades lances in combat. Another sort of him is "Tiet mi ŋue̱e̱t". All we have heard of women are evacuating objects from the bodies of wiped-out individuals set there by leeches, witches, or holders of the fiendish eye. Another kind of remedy is desolate women, defenceless men, and debilitated calves. It may too, target men with less capacity.

3.3 Types of Traditional Power

Apart from believing in God as a Creator, there exist various types of traditional powers among the Nuär. The most prominent ones such as Earth-Master (Leopard Skin-Kuär Mɔ̱ɔn) and Wud Ɣɔ̱ɔ̱k-Cow Master, Tut Wie̱c, Thuc, Mut/Holy Spears within some clans. However, these are not possessed by everyone. Those who possess these powers are respected (feared) by Duɛk (Duɛ̈ɛ̈k). Furthermore, Duɛk in singular means someone who possesses no power at all, or in plural, Duɛ̈ɛ̈k, mean people who people possess no power at all among the Nuär. It ought to be pointed out that those other mysterious powers; we have discussed above, have a foreign origin, unlike those traditional powers that we shall discuss below.

3.3.1 Kuär Muɔ̱ɔ̱n/Earth-Master/Leopard Skin

According to Nuär, during the antiquity or Stone Age, specifically when they were nomads at Koch, the presumable place of their origin of creation, there were traditional powers possessed by a certain man by the name Daar Kuok Gaw. These powers are as follows: first, there was a Kuär Muɔ̱ɔ̱n/ Leopard Skin/Easter-Master, second, there was a Wud Ɣɔ̱ɔ̱k/ Cow-Master, third, there was a Tut, and fourth, there was a Duɛk (duɛ̈ɛ̈k), refers to ordinary person. All three traditional powers above-mentioned were possessed by Daar Kuok Gaw. However, due to various services, he discharged them to some persons, as we shall discuss later.

In chapter one, we discussed the functional role of Kuär Mɔ̱ɔ̱n /Earth-Master/Leopard Skin. His functional role is well known to every Nuär person due to its importance. In this regard, we take Bul Nuär in the Western White Nile who were the descendants of the last-born son of Gɛ̈ɛ̈k by the name Bol, about Kuär Muɔ̱ɔ̱n /Earth-Master/Leopard Skin.

However, it is believed that on the one hand, Bol Gɛ̈kä had two children that is, Rëm Bol and Lɛk Bol while on the other hand, Rëm had two children as Barpuɔ̱ Rëm and Gaa Rëm. Furthermore, Lɛ̈k had four children such as Bul Lɛ̈k, Lɔu Lɛ̈k, Yo̱t Lɛ̈k, and their sister by name, Duany Lɛ̈k. The list of descendants of Bol Gɛ̈kä will lead us to the consecration and Installation of Kuär Mɔ̱ɔ̱n (Earth-Master), as we shall present below.

3.3.1.1 Consecration & Installation of Kuär Mɔ̱ɔ̱n/Earth-Master

For example, Dhin Lɔu Lɛ̈k was consecrated and installed as Kuär Mɔ̱ɔ̱n/Earth-Master among the descendants of Bul Nuär. The consecration and installation of Kuär Mɔ̱ɔ̱n/Earth-Master were very dramatic events. Some clans among the Nuär people only knew them. The consecration and installation of Kuär Mɔ̱ɔ̱n/Earth-Master require the following items such as an open new gourd/Tuɔk mäka̱ kɔ cam kuän. This ritual ceremonial performance was done at the Kraal in front of the byre with the presence of all the clans and the Senior Elder of the community.

The prospect Kuär Mɔ̱ɔ̱n/Earth-Master/Leopard Skin stood in front of the kraal/thok na̱l, while the members of the clans stood in front of the door of the byre. The members of the clans faced the prospect Kuär Mɔ̱ɔ̱n/Earth-Master/Leopard Skin. According to the ritual ceremonial rite, each member of these clans was commanded by the Senior Elder of the community to spit (send liquid (salvia) out from his mouth to the new gourd/Tuɔk. Each did this in turn. When the ritual rite of spit finished, the Senior Elder of the community asked each member of the clans to cut his skin to allow his blood to fall into the new gourd/Tuɔk. In addition, each did this in turn.

After the ritual rite, the Senior Elder of the community will pray and then spear an ox (with a colour known as rɔ̱l provided by a man called Deng Ja̱a̱ŋ, which was put between the prospect Kuär Mɔ̱ɔ̱n/Earth-Master/Leopard Skin and the people. Consequently, the god became known as Kuoth rɔ̱l). The senior elder of the community will ask the prospect Kuär Mɔ̱ɔ̱n/Earth-Master/Leopard Skin to jump over the sacrificial beast to the side of the people, while the people also jump over the sacrificial beast. After they all jumped over the sacrificial beasts, they left it to the birds.

When the ritual of jumping over the sacrificial beast finished, then, the Senior Elder of the community asked Dhin Lɔu to drink the spit (salvia) and the blood of the people contained in the gourd/ Tuɔk. On the one hand, the spit (salvia) signifies peace and blessings while on the other hand, the blood of the people symbolizes the power of the person consecrated and installed over clans. Consequently, his blood has become his power over the clans. Nevertheless, he is advised strongly not to abuse his power over the people. Anyone, who will attack him, even if he only points his figure towards that person,/will die.

Whoever will tempter with the life of someone, will report himself to him for both refuge and ritual purification. This power is manifested in the area of reconciliation between clans, and individuals. The Kuär Mɔ̱ɔ̱n/Earth-Master among the Nuär plays greater during the reconciliation process. During the reconciliation and compensation processes, the fatal/cuut ran kiɛ yëth thööŋä, the Kuär Mɔ̱ɔ̱n/Earth-Master is the one to spear the sacrificial beast he can choose among the Cows present untie.

Furthermore, when a person kills another in a fight, he must report himself to the Kuär Mɔ̱ɔ̱n/Earth-Master for ritual purification. Otherwise, he cannot taste any products of the earth before bi̱e̱r-cutting the upper part of his arm for his blood to fall as he poured down the blood of the innocent person. After this ritual purification, then, he can eat and drink. Apart from his role as a peacemaker and reconciler, the Kuär Mɔ̱ɔ̱n/Earth-Master is also a refuge for a murderer.

For example, in 1825, among the Age Set called Nyan, a certain man called Rialthin Dua̱l Dɔŋ Nëën was a police officer. He was sent by the chief to the house of a certain man to raid a cow by law. When he arrived at the cattle camp, he tried to unite the cow but unfortunately, the owner of the cow killed him by name Wuɔ̱r Wial Tut.

Consequently, the murderer unknowingly ran to the house of Tëkjiäk Dua̱l Dɔŋ, the brother of Rialthin Dua̱l Dɔŋ whom he killed. Tëkjiäk was informed the people who chased the murderer had killed your brother. He commanded the people that "Nobody should lay a hand against him." Tëkjiäk as a Kuär Mɔ̱ɔ̱n/Earth-Master could do no harm against Wuɔ̱r Wial Tut who killed his brother. He performed his moral and spiritual purification such as cutting the upper arm/ bi̱e̱r or spitting in the mouth of the murderer as required by his office. Consequently, he took Wuɔ̱r Wial Tut to the territory of his clan.

3.3.1.2 Intrinsic Character of Kuär Mɔ̱ɔ̱n/Earth-Master

The exercise of the office of Kuär Mɔ̱ɔ̱n/Earth-Master has an intrinsic character. The consecration and the installation are done once and for all. The exercise of power of Kuär Mɔ̱ɔ̱n/Earth-Master automatically goes to the descendants of Kuär Mɔ̱ɔ̱n/Earth-Master. The power such as cutting the upper arm/ bi̱e̱r of the murderer or spitting in his mouth in case when the murderer is not his subject, is done by males and even by females who are not yet married.

The exercise of the office of Kuär Mɔ̱ɔ̱n/Earth-Master demands the highest moral integrity from the person who exercises it. Any abuse of this sacred office by any Kuär

Mɔ̱ɔ̱n/Earth-Master can lead to the suspension of the ritual powers of that person. The Nuär both in the Western White Nile and Eastern White Nile, show due respect to the person who exercises this office. Neither can any duɛk person abuse him, nor can the Kuär Mɔ̱ɔ̱n/Earth-Master himself abuse this sacred. The example of Tëkjiäk Dua̱l Dɔŋ who focused on his moral duty rather than harming someone who murdered his biological brother, is par excellent model to be followed by everyone.

3.3.2 Wud Ɣɔ̱ɔ̱k/Gua̱n Puɔ̱dä/Cow-Master

Among the Nuär, there is another power, which is exercised by Guän Puɔ̱dä/Cow-Master. This power is one of the traditional offices, which is exercised by some clans apart from the office of Kuär Muɔ̱ɔ̱n/Easter-Master. Originally, Daar Kuok Gaw gave the exercise of the power of Puɔ̱d to Laul Yut Lɛ̈k. On the one hand, Laul Yut Lɛ̈k was given both tuac thɔ̱ɔ̱nä and Puɔ̱d as instruments for the exercise of his office over the cattle among the Nuär people.

However, there was a condition for thɔ̱ɔ̱nä/skin of wild cats. On the one hand, if thɔ̱a̱n/wild cat is killed when the cows are tied down, the skin will be given to the Kuär Muɔ̱ɔ̱n/Easter-Master, and on the other hand, when it is killed when the cows are untied, the Gua̱n Puɔ̱dä will be entitled to take its skin. In this regard, both Kuär Muɔ̱ɔ̱n/Leopard Skin and Gua̱n Puɔ̱dä wear tuac thɔ̱a̱nä for different functions.

3.3.2.1 The Functions of Wud Ɣɔ̱ɔ̱k/ Gua̱n Puɔ̱dä/Cow-Master

In the first place, there are certain instruments, which are used by Gua̱n Puɔ̱dä to exercise his power. These instruments are as follows: first, Puɔ̱d/wooden hammer, second, yie̱c/traditional broom, third, Tuac-Thɔ̱ɔ̱n/Leopard Skin, fourth, Mut/ Holy Spear, and fifth, butter.

First, when a girl has delayed marriage, the Gua̱n Puɔ̱dä will be invited by the father of the girl to perform ritual purification on her while wearing Tuac-Thɔ̱ɔ̱n. When he arrives, he smears the body of the girl with butter to dispel the misfortune that has caused her to delay her marriage. Second, if the cows of someone died due to disease, or due to other misfortune, the Gua̱n Puɔ̱dä is invited by that person to perform a ritual ceremony such as smearing one cow among others with dung ashes at the kraal of the byer. After that, he pulls the piece of wooden hammer to tie the cow down to signify the removal of the misfortune upon the cow. Then, he hammers it again in the same place.

Then, the Gua̱n Puɔ̱dä pours in the butter at the spot of the piece of wooden hammer, which signifies the future productivity of the cows. Finally, he cuts the hock/dhur of a cow and puts it on the spot of a wooden stick to symbolize the future continuity of the cow. Furthermore, if someone has no cows at all, then, he invites the Guan Puɔ̱dä to perform a ritual ceremony such as mixing the dung of cow with milk, steering them, and finally, he commands the man to drink them. Then, he smears his right foot and gives him dung ashes to be put in a container in his house, which symbolizes the imminent expectation of cows.

By performing all these different services, the Gua̱n Puɔ̱dä is always given a calf after successful productivity about those services that he offered to the individual persons. Another function, which is performed by the Gua̱n Puɔ̱dä, is the naming of "Age Set" (initiated Age Set). However, in some Nuär clans, a prophet can do the naming of Age Set.

To do this, either by Gua̱n Puɔ̱dä or by a prophet, two calves with different colours are provided. Then, one of them is killed and the other one is left. Therefore, the one, which remains, its colour will determine the name of Age Set (initiated Age Set). Furthermore, it is said that if the Gua̱n Puɔ̱dä steps on dung, he does not rub it off from his foot fearing that it may bring misfortune to the owner of the cows. Finally, if the Gua̱n Puɔ̱dä dies, he is buried in a heap of dung while milk is poured on the dung. However, it is said some Gua̱n Puɔ̱dä can be very stubborn. Among the Bul Nuär, this office of Gua̱n Puɔ̱dä is exercised by Ciëŋnyaŋ/Chiengnayng.

3.3.2.2 The Myth of Ye̱c/Broom

According to Nuär, when those powers above-mentioned earlier were distributed by Daar Kuok Gaw, there was a certain woman by the name Me̱e̱r Lual Yo̱th whose duty was to serve the people. When the powers were distributed, she was given nothing; someone asked a question, "What shall be given to this lady called Me̱e̱r Lual Yo̱th? Some people, replied, that she would get her portion at home. One day, during the rainy season, there was thunder, and lightning, consequently, a ye̱c/ broom fell from heaven on her shoulder. When the people saw it, they wondered because they had never seen anything like this before. Consequently, people came and they removed the broom from her shoulder. Finally, they put it at the kraal of the byer and it remained there.

After some time, someone called Bol from Adɔk Nuär impregnated Me̱e̱r Lual. However, due to a lack of cows, Bol ran away. After some time, Me̱e̱r gave birth to a boy named Guäl Bol. Then, Me̱e̱r asked her brother Kuon Lual to bring the yi̱e̱c/ broom from the byre because she could use it to sweep her house. Mr. Kuon brought the ye̱c/ broom from the byre and gave it to her.

3.3.3 Tut Wi̱e̱c

Among the powers that were distributed by Daar Kuok Gaw was Tut Wi̱e̱c. The term Tut in Nuär is referred to a bull. However, in the context of the power, it is referred to someone who exercises this power over the Kuär Muɔ̱ɔ̱n/Easter-Master (Leopard Skin). Previously, we pointed out that when someone kills another person, he/she reports himself/herself to the Kuär Muɔ̱ɔ̱n/Easter-Master for ritual purification such as bi̱e̱r/ the cutting off the upper arm of the murderer for his blood to fall as he killed an innocent person.

In this regard, no one is exempted from accountability in terms of killing an innocent person. The Kuär Muɔ̱ɔ̱n/Easter-Master (Leopard Skin) cannot exercise this sacred office when he kills another person; he takes refuge at the house of Tut. Consequently, Tut Wi̱e̱c will exercise his moral duty upon the Kuär Muɔ̱ɔ̱n/Easter-Master (Leopard Skin) should he kill anyone. Furthermore, Tut W̱i̱e̱c has another power, which he also exercises. For example, during the beginning of the harvest season, he prays at midnight and dawn, for the blessing of the earthly products and he also blesses the people. For example, Tut W̱i̱e̱c from Bul Cöl Gɛ̱ɛ̱k is Ciën Gil Bul Lɛk Bol.

3.3.4 Mut Wiu Ɣä/Wiu Spear & Wizard

According to the myth, Ki̱i̱r Kak Kër from the beginning of birth, had a dramatic event. The myth said that he was not born from a human being but rather, Gɛ̈ɛ̈k Gaw at the farm of Yuel Kuot cut him out from the gourd. From the time of his birth, he was a wizard (his eyes were bleeding with blood). Later on, he became a blacksmith, which allowed him to make "Mut Wiu/the spear of Wiu." In this regard, Ki̱i̱r Kak Kër was known to have two powers Wiu and Mut Wiu/the spear of Wiu.

The power of Mut Wiu/the spear of Wiu is possessed by the descendants of Ki̱i̱r Kak Kër called Ji̱käny/Jiaka̱a̱ny. Among the Nuär, two clans have famous yo̱ rɛw/two spears that is, Ji̱käny and Thi̱a̱ŋ Nuär that possess Mutbaak. For example, prophet Ŋundɛŋ Böŋ/Can mentioned them in one of his songs. However, the Mut Wiu/ Wiu spear seems to have a mysterious power, which is exercised by Ji̱käny, both in the Western and Eastern White Nile.

The mystery of Mut Wiu/ Wiu Spear, which was given to Thi̱a̱ŋ by Gɛ̈ɛ̈k. At present, Ciëŋ Diid at Wie̱c Luak, Wiu at Dɔrɔk, at Thi̱a̱ŋ Ciëŋ Ta̱a̱r, own Wiu Mut. For example, Mut Wiu/Wiu/ spear is put in a stick puts it inside fats and rolls in a leopard skin. When people would like to migrate to another place, if refuse to go, no one can remove it from where it is put. However, if responses are positive, then, they can be put in the cradle and carried ahead of the people. For example, Thi̱a̱ŋ clan say, when they fighting with other people, "Mut Wiu/Wui Spear give me a human person, Wiu Mut with bleeding eyes, give me a human person.

3.3.5 The Power of Guän Bööthni/Paternal Brother

We have used the term "guän böothni" several times in the first edition and this present second edition. First, the word guän böothni refers to the intrinsic relation of blood between paternal brothers. Furthermore, the Nuär people refer to one testicle, that is, the paternal brothers descended from one father as their grandfather. In this regard, the paternal brothers we will say that the testicles of their grandfather were divided into two, which gave birth to their fathers. In this sense, the guän böothni" is referred to as tut/bull. Consequently, they call themselves "paternal brothers" which have automatic bilateral roles.

According to Nuär, an outsider cannot exercise the bilateral roles, which the paternal brothers play. Furthermore, they refer to this bilateral role in the word 'guän böothni/ person who has a right to exercise over cunyni/rights within the family. For example, if a daughter of a paternal brother is married, the other paternal brother will be the one to spread yɛk to in-laws on the left inside of the byre while the prospective kinsmen and kinswomen sit on the right side during the negotiation of the bride-wealth. However, before the negotiation begins, his calf will be paid to him first and then, the negotiation of the bride-wealth will continue.

Furthermore, the guän böothni is the one to hammer the cow as a sacrificial beast during the buɔr nyal/during the wedding ceremony. Then, the prospective bride's father will spread the sacrificial beast. Another role that the guän böothni plays is to give the prospective bride to the family of the prospective bridegroom during the last wedding celebration. Furthermore, if twins are born by the paternal brother's wife, he is the one to slaughter a sour fruit called kuɔl or a goat. Then, he squeezes the liquid of kuɔl on the breasts of the mother of twins. Consequently, he commands her by saying "Mother of the twins, you can suckle them now.

Furthermore, if a child of a paternal brother died, the guän böötthni̱ would be the first to dig the grave for a burial. When a deceased person is buried, he is the one to cut branches of a tree called 'ŋue̱r' and put them on wi̱c muɔ̱n ran/grave of the deceased person. According to Nuär, for one month of mourning, the deceased family suspends all joyful activities. After one full month of mourning, the family of the deceased person will terminate the period of mourning by making what is called wuɔ̱c jiäkni̱ kiɛ wuɔ̱c cuɔlni̱/taking away the mourning to resume normal activities of human life. The guän bööthni̱ is the one to remove those branches of the tree above-mentioned and clean the wi̱c muɔ̱n ran/clean the grave of the deceased person.

Furthermore, the guän bööthni̱ is the one to spear the sacrificial beast prepared for the muɔ̱t/ritual ceremony of the prospective bride to womanhood. Finally, he distributes the minor private properties of the deceased person to the rest of the family. During the initiation rite (rite of passage), the wife of the paternal father is the one to shave the hair of the paternal son while leaving very little hair on the middle of his head to be removed before the initiation rite the next day. After one month of seclusion, the initiates are discharged and are consequently, chased to a river very early in the morning. This is followed by a big celebration. When the initiates return home, the paternal father is the first to give a spear to the paternal son and then, followed by the rest.

3.3.6 Two Powers among Nyuɔŋ Nuär

When Tha̱a̱k became a mature man, Liath warned Leek not to put the tribal mark or ritual initiation (Ga̱r) without his knowledge. Leek did not listen to him. Then, Liath called Leek and Tha̱a̱k and said to Leek, your descendent will be smaller than Tha̱a̱k. It is like a curse (bit) up to date, Tha̱a̱k is bigger than Leek as a result of his stubbornness. Consequently, Liath divided the powers among them. Tha̱a̱k became the Easter-master/Kuär Muɔ̱ɔ̱n, Luac and Leek, were given a Thuc/ buddle of grass. The power of Thuc/ buddle of grass is believed to be strong. It can be used by the owner to threaten of the life others. For example, the person who possesses the power of Thuc/buddle of grass can say, if I can remove the Thuc, what about you?

1-The Nyuɔŋ Nuär clan is comprised of two subtribes-Nyääl and Nyawäär with six major sections with their subsections, clans, and sub-clans excluded. The sub-tribes. Nyääl. Nyawäär: Liath, Tiɛl, and Mök Cieŋ Nyawär. Nyääl's subscribe major sections: Tha̱a̱k, Leek, and Luac. For example, call themselves, Gaatliɛth, Gaatmök, and Gaattiɛl.

3.3.7 Three Powers of Gaatwär

The legend says that once there was someone by the name of Wua̱r who used to live on land while Thiliɛy used to live underwater. It was said that Thiliɛy used to beat his drum under water and Wua̱r used to hear the sound of his drum.

Furthermore, Wua̱r used to beat his drum while living on land. The legend said that Wua̱r took the initiative to go to a river and asked Thiliɛy who are you living underwater? Further, Wua̱r said to him, come out because I want to see if you are a human being. Then, Thiliɛy came out with his small drum. When he came out, Wua̱r asked him, why do you live underwater while you are a human being? Then, Thiliɛy answered him, I am staying underwater with Nyiwuär/a kind of fish which Gaatwär do not eat because they consider it as their god.

Finally, Wua̱r invited Thiliɛy to go with him inside a room. Then, they sat down, and Wua̱r showed Thiliɛy his small drum. Fortunately, they discovered that their drums were similar to each other. Then, they decided to agree. However, Wua̱r said to Thiliɛy, we cannot agree with us, because there is another human being called Ba̱r (originated from Dinka Jieŋ). Then, they both went to him and finally, found him. After they met at home, they agreed about the division of their roles.

First, Wua̱r possess the power of nyɔ̱a̱t (a kind of tree that signifies god for exercising his power), second, Thiliɛy possess the power of Taŋ/spear thrower (signifies the exercise of his power especially when he intends to break it to bring misfortunate upon an enemy or enemies. Juɔ̱ŋ possess the power of wud ɣɔ̱ɔ̱k (and has a rope on his neck). He exercises this power over cows by controlling them.

3.3.8 Cuol Wi̱c

Among the Nuär people, another power is called 'Cuol Wi̱c. the term Cuol Wi̱c/black head signifies the concept and belief of Nuär indigenous saints. Many people may people including anthropologists who write about the Nuär religion, were unable to discover the concept and existence of a patron saint among the Nuär people. The term Cuol Wiec/black head exists in all the Nuär tribe.

First, the word "Cuol Wiec/black head" refers to someone who got burned because of thunder/lightning, or second, it refers to someone who was struck by thunder/lightning. Some clans can extend the meaning to someone who got lost in a bush or someone who drowned in a river. Third, if someone dies on those occasions above-mentioned, he/she is considered to be taken by God. In this case, if such an incident occurs, the family of the late will immediately offer sacrifices, considering the late as a patron saint of the family and of the clan at large.

After some time, the family and the clan will prepare a ritual ceremony by planting a tree called "nyɔat" which in the future, will serve as a "riak shrine" for ritual sacrifices, prayer and intercession. As a rule, the family of the late and the clan at large will sacrifice animals during the dark period of the moon. That is why, it is called Cuol Wic/black head, due to the fact the sacrifice is offered during the darkness of the night. When they died, there was no funeral rite to be conducted, not even morning.

Consequently, the ritual celebrations will continue through singing, eating, and drinking wine/kɔaŋ, which will continue until the early morning before the sunrise of the following day. After the spiritual ceremony, the late can become the patron saint of the family and clan. For example, if there is a danger, which threatens the life of the people, they can call his/her name for intervention and protection. Furthermore, even when fighting another clan (clans), his/her name is always called.

Among Gaatwär Nuär, there is a famous Cuol Wi̱c/black head, called Ga̱h Kän who died because of thunder/lightning. For example, the wife of Gil Pakur by name Nyagɔɔ was eaten by a beast known as lɛɛt/nicknamed Gat Bɛl. Gil prayed that "Ga̱h, the beast/lɛɛt which has eaten my wife, show it to us, let it rain, but not too much, to trace the footprints of the beast/lɛɛt.

Gil promised to offer a beast as a sacrifice to Cuol Wi̱c/black head/Ga̱h Ga̱h Kän. God has responded to his request. In the following morning, women got up and cried/co män we̱e̱ kɛ we̱e̱ köör. People came and went to follow the beast/lɛɛt. Finally, they followed its footprints, and consequently, found it and killed it. People believed that it was the power of Ga̱h Ga̱h Kän/ Cuol Wi̱c/black head that led to the killing of the beast/lɛɛt. Consequently, Gil Pakur offered a sacrificial beast/lɛɛt, to fulfil his promise.

Another example is when Kuolaŋ Tɔa̱t heard that Mr. Tut Kuac Diu from Thi̱a̱ŋ Nuär was struck by lightning, people gathered and asked to pray/lam. Instead of mourning, Kuolaŋ said, it is good that you Tut Kuac Diu have gone to heaven ahead of me. It is as if I have gone to heaven. Added, Tut, We suffered from Cuol Wi̱e̱c/black head of Laak by name Kuok Laak; meet him at the top of wi̱c Këk/dyke. From now on, if they call him, we shall call you. Kuolaŋ said this during prayer/lam during the day of the ritual ceremony of Tut Kuac Diu.

Another well-known Cuol Wi̱c/black head is from Jikäny West by the name Riak Lo̱ŋ. Another well-known Cuol Wi̱c/black head from Bul Nuär is Ga̱h Ga̱h Cuɔ̱ŋ Lɔu Lɛk was struck by thunder/lightning. Riak Lo̱ŋ and Ga̱h Ga̱h Cuɔ̱ŋ Lɔu Lɛk are powerful patron saints. It is said that after some time, the Gah Gah Cuɔŋ Lɔu descended upon his two brothers, Dädör Gatdɛni Lɔaŋ Buɔr Daf Cuɔŋ Lɔu. When he died, the spirit descended upon his grandson by name Gatluak Wec Dädör. These mentioned Cuol Wuɔth/black heads are well known among the Nuär people. However, there are many of them among the Nuär and they are considered patron saints of the family and the clans at large as we have mentioned earlier.

Conclusion

Chapter six has discussed broadly the conceptual analysis of God's attributes according to Nuär. It has also represented the name of God-Koth and other attributes of God such as Tutgaär kiɛ Thanyany-God-Unlimited and with Omnipotent Power. The chapter has illustrated God as cääk-Creator, tath-to make and Guandɔŋ-Grandfather (Guandit-or Big Father). Finally, it has discussed the difference between God and other spirits and God's greatness over his created world.

The chapter has discussed thoroughly some mysterious powers that always act as the sources of conflict. Some are pointed out to be deadly. They contradict the loyalty and faithfulness of the human person to God. The good news is that they are disappearing with rapid speed among the Nuär.

Furthermore, the chapter also has presented types of traditional powers such as Kuär Muɔɔn/Earth-Master/Leopard Skin, consecration & installation of Kuär Mɔɔn/Earth-Master, intrinsic character of Kuär Mɔɔn/Earth-Master, Wud Ɣɔɔk/Guan Puɔdä/Cow-Master, the function of Wud Ɣɔɔk/Guan Puɔdä/Cow-Master, the myth of yec/broom, Tut Wiec and finally, Mut Wiu Ɣä/Wiu Spear & wizard.

CHAPTER FOUR

DOUGLAS H. JOHNSON ON THE LIFE OF PROPHET ŊUNDƐŊ

Introduction

Chapter seven presents the compendium of the life of three prophets. First, it presents the life of prophet Ŋundɛŋ Bong-Ŋundɛŋ Böŋ (Ŋundɛŋ Can) and his background includes his birth. It also discusses Ŋundɛŋ's seizure, his first rejection by his relatives and by others, his second rejection in the middle of divisive tensions at Malou and his third rejection and the physical violence that was inflicted upon him.

Furthermore, the chapter presents Ŋundɛŋ's highest at Juɛ̈t and his marital status, and the prayer meeting at Malual initiated by Ran Pinyien for Ŋundɛŋ's recuperation. It also illustrates Ŋundɛŋ's two offices such as leopard-skin (earth-master) and prophet, the emergence of Ŋundɛŋ as a prophet and his function as a prophet with its greatest gift of divinity. The chapter discusses Ŋundɛŋ' Gigantic Mound and its destruction by the British Administration the contradiction and dilemma about the end of his earthly life, and various songs of Ŋundɛŋ.

4. Prophet Ngundeng Bong-Ŋundɛŋ Böŋ

Among the Nuär prophets, the Nuär alone does not only know prophet Ŋundɛŋ. He is well known among Nuär both in the western and in the eastern White Nile. Furthermore, many people both in Sudan and in South Sudan know the prophet Ŋundɛŋ as well. His fame is about his prophecies. For example, the prophet Ŋundɛŋ had prophesized many things about wars between Sudanese and South Sudanese. In addition, his fame was spread across due to the fact Douglas H. Johnson has written about his life in his book entitled "Nuer Prophets." This added more information to be known by people who read the book about H. Johnson.

4. 1 The Background of Ngundeng Bong (Ŋundɛŋ Böŋ)

H. Johnson confirms that his father, Bong Can, came from the Bul area in Bahr el-Ghazal western White Nile. When can arrived at the eastern White Nile, he settled near his sister who had married into a Maleak family among the Gaajok Nuär. Bong (Böŋ) was accommodated as an earth master after his brother-in-law's death. It was asserted that Bong's nephew handed his father's leopard skin over to Bong.

According to H. Johnson, Jikäny East was mixed with foreigners. Consequently, it seems, they have no Earth-Master lineages of their own. However, the predominant clan such as Gaatgankii̱r, do have the protection of the clan spear called 'Wiu.' It is stated that the Earth-Masters (leopard Skin) of the eastern Jikäny, are all Gaaleak, who are originally from Bul Nuär. Nevertheless, must point out that not all the Bul Nuär Earth-Masters. Cöl Geah (gɛ̱ɛ̱h) was believed to be the 'greatest Earth-Master' among the western Bul Nuär.

On the one hand, the Jikäny Nuär of the east owned only the mysterious power of the spear of Wiu plus Jikäny ciëŋ, while on the other hand, Bul Nuär that descended from Cöl Geah (gɛ̱ɛ̱h) in the western Nuär do have the mysterious power of Earth-Masters (Leopard Skin). However, we ought to point out that Wiu, the mysterious power of the spear, belongs to Jikäny ciëŋ and Jikäny dɔar. However, apart from Wiu and Earth-Masters, there is another mysterious power called 'Wud ɣɔ̱ɔ̱h' which we said belongs to Gawäär Nuär, the clan of Baar. This mysterious power is also possessed by some individuals both in the western and eastern White Nile. All the Nuär believe in the existence of these three mysterious powers. Ŋundɛŋ was both the prophet and earth master.

4.1.1 The Birth of Ngundeng

According to Douglas H. Johnson, Ŋundɛŋ Böŋ from the side of his mother named Nyayiel Maul Jɔak from the sub-clan called Puɔ̱l which belongs to Gabaal Nuär. In her early years, Nyayiel was engaged to Hoth Can, Bong's half-brother. She married Hoth Bong after Hoth was struck by lightning. According to Nuär culture and custom Nyayiel was the real wife of Hoth while Böŋ was delegated by the family to be gotten for his deceased brother. Therefore, on the one hand, Böŋ was the biological father of Ŋundɛŋ while on the other hand; Hoth was the ghost father of Ŋundɛŋ. According to H. Johnson, Bong had children with other wives, but Ŋundɛŋ was Nyayiel's only child. The story of the birth of Ŋundɛŋ was very mysterious. H. Johnson argued that Nyayiel gave birth to Ŋundɛŋ after her menopause through the intervention of a messenger as cited below:

Something came by night and said to Nyayiel, 'You Nyayiel, you must go back to your home,' Nyayiel told it, 'Why must I return to my home? It said, you go, you will give birth to a child', Nyayiel told it, 'How can I give birth to a child, when I have become old and have no monthly bleeding? It told her, 'Go back. The child you will be given a name from here. When you give birth, he will be called 'Ŋundɛŋ', like the gift [muc] which is given to a person.' 'Truly?' 'It said to her, 'God![45]

According to H. Johnson, Nyayiel returned to Bong and told him what she had heard. They slept together one night only, but Nyayiel conceived. When she became pregnant, people could see a sign of pregnancy but they assumed that it might be an abdomen swelling because of some disease, which could kill her. She carried her baby in her womb for twelve months. When the time for her delivery came, she cried out in her labour pain. People said,

Why does Nyayiel call people? If it is death, let her die.' They did not know it was a child. Those hard-hearted people 'Will go and see her.' They came. The child was born. Other people heard that Nyayiel had given birth to a child. Then people ran saying, 'Nyayiel gave birth! Is that really a child?' When that was over, they saw it was born with all its teeth: the lower teeth and the upper teeth. They said, 'Nyayiel gave birth to a child which has never been seen before', because of

45 Douglas H. Johnson, *Nuër Prophets*, p. 75.

all its teeth, and it was her first time. It surprised people greatly.[46]

According to H. Johnson, "Ŋundɛŋ Böŋ was born into a family of Gaaleak earth-masters living in Jikäny at the end of the 1830s." Historically, Ŋundɛŋ Böŋ died in 1906 and therefore, he lived for 76 years. The menopause of Nyayiel prompted doubts as to whether it resulted from old age or was due to circumstances. Being barren for many years with Bong, she was old with white hair and nobody reclaimed her bride wealth from her bridegroom's kinsmen.

However, she was allowed by Bong to return to her family's home. According to H. Howell though Ŋundɛŋ Böŋ would normally have been known as Ŋundɛŋ Hoth, after the man for whom his mother was married, however, he was always known as Ŋundɛŋ Böŋ, after his genitor. H. Johnson states that using Böŋ's name, rather than Ŋundɛŋ Hoth, drew our attention to his descent from an active earth master of the leopard skin.

4.1.2 God's Miracle Works without Favouritism

The miraculous birth of Ŋundɛŋ after his mother's menopause requires serious observation such that we do not lose focus. From the time of pregnancy, we have noticed something very strange and after his delivery, we have noticed something strange happened too. First, naturally, a woman's pregnancy does not take twelve months but rather nine months.

Nevertheless, about the birth of Ŋundɛŋ, it happened. Second, after delivery, no child is born with the lower and upper teeth; nevertheless, Ŋundɛŋ was born with both lower

46 Ibid, p. 75-76.

teeth and upper teeth. Third, some people said that Ŋundɛŋ spoke to his mother immediately after his birth. Fourth, according to information recorded by H. Johnson, he crawled off into the bush when he was only an infant but then returned on his own.

Are these things which happened at the birth of Ŋundɛŋ miracles or are they fabrication of human whims? Even H. Johnson in his response to such miraculous birth of Ŋundɛŋ has raised gynecological problems. According to him, there are gynaecological problems in the villages of South Sudan where undernourishment is a seasonal unpleasant fact. It is not uncommon for relatively young women to experience an interruption of menstruation period, which may be mistaken for early menopause.

From the viewpoint of H. Johnson, it seems he had ruled out the possibility of God's intervention in the situation of the barren woman Nyayiel Malual Jɔak. The Sacred Scripture proves beyond no doubt God's intervention in the situation of barren women. Why should the intervention of God upon barren Nuär women such as Nyayiel in her old age be related to gynaecological problems?

In the book of Genesis, we hear of the blessing of Abram after he was ninety-nine years old with his wife Sara. "God further said to Abraham: As for Sarai your wife, do not call her Sarai; her name will be Sarah. I will bless her, and I will give you an heir by her. Her also will I bless; she will give rise to nations, and rulers of peoples will issue from her." Abraham fell face down and laughed as he said to himself. Can a child be born to a man who is a hundred years old? Can Sarah give birth at ninety...God replied: Even so, your wife Sarah is to bear you a son and you shall call him Isaac. It is with him that I will maintain my covenant as an everlasting covenant and with his descendants after him" (Cf. Gen 17. 1-18).

Furthermore, we have the same scenario in the Gospel of Luke in which we were told that Zechariah and his wife Elizabeth were advanced in years, nevertheless God had decided to intervene in their lives. God said to Zechariah, "Do not be afraid, Zechariah, because your prayer has been heard. Your wife Elizabeth will bear you a son, and you shall name him John" (Lk 1:13).

In the same Gospel of St. Luke, we have such a marvellous and miraculous intervention of God in which the angel said to the Blessed Virgin Mary, "Behold, you will conceive in your womb and bear a son, and you shall name him Jesus. ...How can this be, since I have no relations with a man? ...the Holy Spirit will come upon you, and the power of the Highest will overshadow you. ...for nothing will be impossible for God.

Mary said, 'Behold, I am the handmaid of the Lord." (Lk 1: 31-38). The phrase that says, 'for nothing will be impossible for God' was said to Nyayiel the mother of Ŋundɛŋ by the messenger, to Sarah the mother of Isaac, and Elizabeth, the mother of John the Baptist but in a very exceptional way to the Blessed Virgin Mary by the angel Gabriel. In this sense, God's intervention in the situation of barren women knows no favouritism, because, for him, all human beings are equal at all times, at any place and for his purpose. The Sacred Scripture asserts," God created mankind in his image; in the image of God, he created them; male and female he created them" (Gen 1:27).

4.1.3 Ŋundɛŋ's Seizure

H. Johnson argues that in dealing with dimensions of spiritual activity and power on which the prophets based their authority, and which acted as precedents for prophetic activity, one needs to avoid the general expressions inherent in the terminology of spirit possession. He advises us to revive Nora Chadwick's use of the term 'mantic' in her thoughtful, but now neglected, book Poetry and Prophecy. Therefore, we ought to avoid the traditional definition of the word 'prophet' in this specific context but we shall use Nora's mantic concept.

According to H. Johnson, this fits in the definition of the Nilotic prophetic idiom in the context of seizure. Furthermore, according to N. Chadwick, the word 'mantic' indicates an "activity that refers to the acquisition, cultivation, and declaration of knowledge; knowledge of the commonly unknown present and past, as well as of the future."[47] Such a definition will be our X-ray test in treating the Nuär prophets.

The period of seizure of Ŋundɛŋ by DENG was close to the period of invasion of Anyuak land led by Beac Colieth and joined by Jikäny as either individuals or groups. During this invasion, the Anyuak retreated further into their territorial regions. This occupation of Anyuak territory bore two disastrous consequences for Nuär.

According to H. Johnson, the Nuär herds were decimated by tsetse flies, and the Nuär themselves were struck by smallpox and died in large numbers. Consequently, they were faced with two options, either to go back home or to remain there in the bush. However, the man called Beac Colieth urged the people not to return home. Nevertheless, H. Johnson states that Colieth said that if they return home, he should be carried with his head pointing to the bush, away from home. While people were carrying him, he was asked what this meant. He said that a divinity would come to their place. According to H. Johnson, the Ŋundɛŋ's seizure is the account

47 Cf. Douglas H. Johnson, The Nuër Prophets, p. 35.

of his family. Beac Colieth had prophesized about Ŋundɛŋ's Seizure. According to his family's account:

> *People were roaming about in the bush. There was no home in which to settle. People went to Gaajak and people went to a place called Buongjak. The divinity caught him while he was walking. The young men, the old men, and other people walking with him said, 'What makes Ŋundɛŋ stupid [dɔ̱a̱r]? Some said it was a divinity, and some that he was a fool. Nobody spoke with him.*[48]

H. Johnson located the period of the Ŋundɛŋ's seizure after the failure of the Buongjak campaign specifically at Thorow and Weibel, both in Gaajak territory. As a man of Earth-Master's science, he should have commanded some respect. His peculiar behaviour and extraordinary statements were unacceptable. People argued that he claimed to be seized by an unnamed divinity and tried to get people to listen to him, but 'when his divinity then spoke, people denied it [saying], 'Divinity is above [Kuoth ɛ nhial]'. According to Evans-Pritchard, after Ŋundɛŋ..." had established himself as a prophet, he seems to have given up in his solitary wanderings, though he still used to shut himself from time to time to undergo long fasts."[49]

48 Cf. Douglas H. Johnson, The Nuër Prophets, p. 78.

49 E.E. Evans-Pritchard, Nuër Religion, p. 305.

4.1.4 Degree of Ŋundɛŋ's Rejection

Those who claim to have a mysterious power and proclaim that they do possess those powers, sometimes; the very community whom they are supposed to serve rejects them. In the case of Ŋundɛŋ, the rejection may be genuine because he demonstrated some abnormal behaviour contrary to the normal way of life. For example, eating faces and tobacco are not normal food for normal people. Furthermore, strange behaviour such as keeping silent for a long and singing certain songs that people are not used to. These and other things not mentioned had led people to consider him as a mad person including his relatives.

4.1.4.1 First Rejection of Ŋundɛŋ

The period of seizure of Ŋundɛŋ had become for him, a period of isolation from his relatives and others. This was due to his peculiar behaviour and extraordinary statements. It is even said that Dinka killed his father and his sister. Consequently, his half-brother had gone to the territory of Lou Nuär. The descriptions of his peculiar behaviour are as follows: first, his infant sojourns to a bush as a prelude to his solitary wanderings as an adult.

Second, avoided fighting with their age-mates which led him to be termed a 'coward.' For example, one of the boys constantly bulled him until one day; he announced mysteriously that if the boy wanted a fight, he would find something that would fight him. According to H. Johnson, that boy died. He concluded that this too, foreshadowed Ŋundeŋ's later condemnation of fighting. For example, he refuses to fight when provoked, however, he can kill with words, when his adversary persists.

According to Evans-Pritchard, Ŋundeŋ..." used to sit in his cattle byre doing the same thing, and when he is in such a mood, he would refuse all food except ash. This was manifested in the life of Ŋundɛŋ, which revealed that the divinity was already active in his life. According to H. Johnson, Tut Jiak Gai, a Mor Lou Nuär, a member of the Daŋ-Go̱nga age-set, met Ŋundeŋ and spoke to him. H. Johnson states that Tut Jiak asked for a blessing from Ŋundeŋ, even when he was not aware of any miraculous birth of him. However, on the one hand, others denied his divinity, while on the other hand, his descendants believe in the divinity of Ŋundɛŋ from the time of his conception. According to H. Johnson, Ŋundeŋ is unlike other prophets due to his miraculous conception and other extraordinary things related to his birth.

4.1.5.2 Second Rejection of Ŋundɛŋ

H. Johnson states that Ŋundɛŋ's childhood was spent among the Jikäny soon after they crossed to the eastern Nile. His father genitor Bong joined Jikäny after the initial migration at Malou, which lasted until about 1845. This period, was characterized by internal tensions between the old campaigners and the newcomers who followed them to Malou, and between the Gaatganḵi̱ir and Lajo̱r. These tensions led to further divisions and further migration, which resulted in the splitting between Gaajak and Gaajok.

H. Johnson affirms that the Wangkeac and Laag sections of Gaajok entered into conflict, the Laag finally, leaving to raid the Dinka and settling south of the Sobat. Based on these tensions and fighting, we can state that "Ŋundɛŋ had gone through a difficult experience and had observed the divisive tendencies then splitting the Nuär society apart by the time he was initiated into the Thut age-set in c. 1855.es, which he had cooked for him."[50]

Those signs manifested in the life of Ŋundɛŋ revealed that the divinity was already active in his life. It is stated that According to Tut Jiak Gai, a Mor Lou Nuär member of the Dang-gonga age-set, who met and spoke to Ŋundeŋ and was blessed by him, was not aware of any miraculous birth. While others denied his divinity, his descendants believe in the divinity of Ŋundɛŋ from the time of his conception, unlike other Nuär prophets.

4.1.4.3 Third Rejection of Ŋundɛŋ

Divisive tensions, Ŋundɛŋ manhood coincided with a time of famine and scarcity along the Sobat. Activities of raids against the Anyuak augmented; however, there were attempts to co-exist peacefully with Anyuak communities. The Laag section respected their nearby Anyuak neighbours but also joined the combined Lou-Jikäny expedition to the Buongjak areas between the Pibor and Agwei rivers in 1860.

Debono witnessed the raiding of Buongjak as early as 1855, but the main invasion probably took place later. Amidst this divisive tension and resistance from Anyuak, Ŋundɛŋ faced a second rejection at Malou. In this regard, the expansion to the territory of Anyuak was real and costly, because they faced many challenges. Apart from the resistance of Anyuak, there were other issues such as shelter and accommodation, and various kinds of diseases.

50 Evans-Pritchard, *Nuër Religion*, p. 305.

4.1.4.4 Fourth Rejection of Ŋundɛŋ

Ŋundɛŋ moved from Thorow to Weilbel (now Weilbeang). There, he built a small mound shrine but abandoned it when he went among the Lou clans. According to H. Johnson, he passed through Kuanylualthoan, near present-day Nasir. Then, he tried to cross the river by canoe, accompanied by his wives, his two children and his cattle into Laag territory. Unfortunately, during that period, there was a serious enmity between Laag and Wangkeac. The Laag «mocked him as ‹the fool of Wangkeac›, called him a liar, beaten him, broke his bead necklace, threw his shrine stick and his leopard-skins into the river, and took off with some of his cattle.»[51]

Unfortunately, Ji̱käny whom Ŋundɛŋ considered as his paternal kin abused him and mistreated him. He expressed shock at this treatment, saying, 'Why did my father's sister's sons treat me like this? Even if I were a fool, should they take my things by force and throw them into the river?' Ŋundeŋ was caught up in the increased feuding between Gaajak and Gaajok. Reflecting on this mistreatment, he went to the Lou clans to seek his maternal uncles typical of many Nuär because the relationship between a man and his mother's brothers is strong and tender compared to others in times of difficulty.

Another claim of his departure was narrated by his descendants as related to his apparent madness (peculiar behaviour) which his grandson asserts was intended by the divinity to attract attention. It is claimed that his divinity believed that if Ŋundeŋ spoke like anyone, nobody would believe in him. His peculiar behaviour had made him appear mad (yɔ̱ŋ) as

51 Cf. Douglas H. Johnson, *The Nuër Prophets*, p. 79.

a result; his seizures alienated those he was supposed to attract. The Laang people ignored both his words (divinity) and Ŋundeŋ himself. Authority as earth-master suffered from the ridicule and his hope for greater recognition was shifted elsewhere, no longer within the Laang section of Jikäny. As a peaceful prophet, he never uttered a word of curse upon the Laang section.

We are told that Ŋundɛŋ did not go directly to his maternal uncles, but to the Ciec section of the Yoal-Gaadbal at Panyaaŋ (now Pul Turuk). His rejection by the Laang section was based upon the fact that already, they accommodated an earth-master, a Dinka man named Ruɛy Kerjiök, whom they feared would return to the Dinka if they let Ŋundɛŋ in. Categorically, they refused to admit him to their cattle camp. According to H. Johnson:

> *The elders of the Ciec section discussed the matter. They said, 'Boys, Ŋundeŋ Bong and Ruɛy Kerjiok: Ruɛy Kerjiok is an earth-master, and Ŋundeŋ Bong is an earth-master. Boys, can we have two earth-masters in our camp, can we keep two earth-masters both in Panyaaŋ? We will not get rain in our camp if we have two earth-masters.' They asked, how will we solve it?*[52]

52 Cf. Douglas H. Johnson, *The Nuër Prophets*, p. 80. They said, 'We will do it this way: Ŋundeŋ must go to his grandmother's people. Puol and Yoal sections are one, they are Gaadbal together. Ngundeŋ will not be sent away, but he must to go his grandmother's people...Now, if we send Rueac Kerjiok away, he is a foreigner and may leave us completely, but Ŋundeŋ will settle with his grandmother's people.

According to H. Johnson, in a specific period, Ŋundɛŋ was left with bad grace and his family, now claimed that he predicted the coming of 'Turuk' to Panyaaŋ and said that though Yoal and Ŋundɛŋ would someday be one, none of his family would ever live with them at Panyaaŋ. He states this narrative and accounts for the hostility, which later grew between the Ciec section leaders and Ŋundeŋ's family, especially between Kerjiok's grandson Guet Thie, and Ŋundɛŋ's son Guɛk. Now Ŋundɛŋ departed for Juɛ̈t, southeast of Muɔt Dit, where his mother's section lived.

4.1.5 Ŋundɛŋ at the Highest Degree of Madness

After settling at the Malual subsection of Puol, Ŋundɛŋ continued normally cultivating and tending cattle for two years. He was seized by the divinity again and went mad as it was before. According to H. Johnson, the seizure was preceded by an illness, which produced partial paralysis. After a short recuperation, he went mad again. He went to a bush, this time; he ceased to eat normal food or drink milk but ate tobacco, grass, and faces. It is said he would collect faces and dry them in the sun like cow dung, make a small fire with them, and then sit facing the wind while they burned. As a result, Ŋundɛŋ became very thin and his hair grew long and matted. Consequently, Jikäny Nuär had started to avoid him.

According to Evans-Pritchard, Ŋundɛŋ..." acquired his powers by prolonged fasts. It is even said that he lived for weeks by himself in a bush, eating animal and human excrements that he used to sit on a cattle peg in his kraal and let it penetrate his anus, which he used to wander about the bush for days mumbling..." [53]

About his marital status, Ŋundɛŋ had at least four wives. He married a Rumjiok woman in Lou, but unfortunately, they discovered his peculiar behaviour. A second wife was Nyatot Kun, the mother of his second son Reath who is remembered to have been exasperated. Ŋundɛŋ used to go to the bush by himself, and then he would come home. He ate only tobacco and water." The first prediction of Ŋundɛŋ during his madness was that of cursing his wife Nyatot Kun, the mother of his son not to give birth again. However, other sources from the family accounts confirm that he had fourteenth wives. According to his grandson General James Lony, "Ŋundɛŋ had married his first wife Nyathak Thiriɛn who had borne from him the first son Riam Ŋundɛŋ." [54]

The footnote gives descriptions of such a curse after Nyatot Kun abused him. Such a curse may have been as much an expression of his fears and of his intentions. The blessing of his son, about whom he said to his wife 'Reath will beget our children', H. Johnson affirms that Reath did become his most prolific son, inheriting Ŋundɛŋ's youngest wives on his death and becoming the genitor of many of Ŋudɛŋ's posthumous children.

---

53 E.E. Evans-Pritchard, *Nuër Religion*, p.305.

54 Interview with General Micheal Lony Ŋundɛŋ, at St. Paul's Major Seminary, Juba-Munuki, 15/06/2019. 2. Nyajäl Luŋ with her first daughter Nyadiɛw Ŋundɛŋ. 3. Nyajuöl Ciɛk with her first born son Bör Ŋundɛŋ. 4. Nyatoɔt Kuɔ̱r, mother of Reath Ŋundɛŋ. 5. Nyadeet Göh of mother of Chan Ŋundɛŋ. 6. Nyaduɔŋ Duɔth, mother of Guɛk Dundɛŋ. 7. Cän Dhiɔk, mother of Gäräŋ Dundɛŋ. 8. Näpän Wiclɔoh, mother of Tuac kɛnɛ Böruɔth Dundɛŋ. 9. Nyaciɛk Wunɔäák, mother of Dei Dundɛŋ. 10. Cäät, mother of Nyathol Dundɛŋ. 11. Thiyäŋ Wuɔ̱r, mother of Puor Dundɛŋ. 12. Nyan Käŋ Cuätwɛɛ, mother of Thichiöt Dundɛŋ. 13. Nyarial Jiec, Mother of Nyawal kɛnɛ Machar Dundɛŋ. 14. Nyalieth Jiec, Mother of Rɛɛt kɛnɛ Pithiɛŋ Dundɛŋ

4.1.6 Prayer-Meeting for Ŋundɛŋ's Recuperation

One day, while Ŋundɛŋ was wandering in the bush around Juɛ̈t, he came into the territory of the Malual section, when they were sacrificing an ox. As we have mentioned earlier Ŋundɛŋ was not eating meat, but that day 'divinity' told him to come and eat meat. While the prayer was said over the sacrificial beast, Ŋundɛŋ rested. According to H. Johnson, people noticed him and said, 'It is Nyayiel's fool' and to him, the ribs were normally thrown in the bush for Wiu. One man from the Ciec section objected to the ribs being given to a fool and he took them from Ŋundɛŋ. Instantly, Ŋundɛŋ looked at the man and watched him carefully."[55]

The proposal of Ran Pinyien to offer a prayer (pal) for Ŋundɛŋ's recuperation was not accepted. Ran stated that the sacrifice of an ox would cure Ŋundɛŋ from his illness, if he were ill, or reveal his divinity if he was seized. Others objected, wondering why they should waste cattle on a foolish man. However, Ran Pinyien offered a white cow to Ŋundɛŋ first, to see what would happen. According to H. Johnson, first, Ŋundɛŋ drank cow's milk for the first time. Then Ran Pinyien sacrificed a reddish-brown patched ox (makol-miköl) and other sections revised their decisions.

They sacrificial oxen at a prayer meeting for Ŋundɛŋ's recovery. Immediately, his peculiar behaviour ceased.

---

55 Cf. Douglas H. Johnson, The Nuër Prophets, p. 81. His maternal cousin (gatnar) rolled the ribs in ashes and put them in the fire. Ŋundɛɛŋ turned away from them. He went away. Ŋundɛŋ went back to the bush, he went back to his usual place. Ŋundɛŋ said, 'This is good.' His maternal cousin took out the meat and ate it. He went to his hut at midday. He took his headrest and slept. In the evening, at the time the cattle dung is gathered up people tried to wake him. They found that the man was finished; he was dead. Yes', [people said], 'Nyayiel's fool has finished something.'

Consequently, he started to eat normal food, and his speech became even more understandable. According to H. Johnson, "It was after this prayer meeting that he announced that he was seized by the divinity Dɛŋ."[56] Ŋundɛŋ›s highest degree of madness and the prayer meeting revealed his divinity (Dɛŋ) which he himself uttered.

If the revelation of divinity is for them, then, they must participate in it as Ran Pinyien did. The revelation of the divinity of 'Dɛŋ' required faith from the people. Ŋundɛŋ's rejection by the people had made it so long. Ŋundɛŋ's highest degrees of madness show that when we are in total confusion and hopelessness, we are close to clarity, which can lead us to God. How far can we still love his image and likeness even when others are at the highest degree of madness such as the one of Ŋundɛŋ? It is only when we still show his love even to those who are at the highest degree of madness then like Ran Pinyien, we ought to show a perfect example to those who are in need.

According to H. Johnson, this prayer meeting is something of an anachronism in the family's accounts. H. Johnson highlights four versions: first, the family asserts that they claimed no divinity had ever spoken through a man, at prayer meetings were unknown (thilɛ pal). They said it was Ŋundɛŋ who taught people how to pray. Second, other Lou Nuär recalled that there were precedents before Ŋundɛŋ's divinity spoke. Third, others said, a power or other spiritual agent might have caused his illness. Fourth, some said that they have seen in Ŋundɛŋ's divinity something very peculiar and unique to their experience.

There might also have been other men in Jikäny who

56 Cf. Douglas H. Johnson, *The Nuër Prophets,* p. 82.

claimed to be seized by a divinity before Ŋundɛŋ. H. Johnson affirms that if so, they were soon eclipsed by Ŋundɛŋ's reputation, and the divinity left them for Ŋundɛŋ because they did not communicate its words correctly. H. Johnson states that once Ŋundɛŋ divinity spoke, and it was immediately named. Consequently, Ŋundɛŋ establishes the character and the attributes of the divinity through his own words and actions.

The expectation of recuperation of Ŋundɛŋ was high among the people. However, his recovery was achieved through a prayer meeting with the sacrifice of the beasts. It was said that later on, Ŋundɛŋ taught people his prayers through songs, which drew attention to both Nuär and Dinka religious imagery. It is stated that Ŋundɛŋ as a prophet was a very unique compared to the rest of other Nuär prophets. Other Nuär prophets allowed others to compose songs for them while Ŋundɛŋ, prepared to compose songs by himself as a means of communication. He used the technique of communicating his words through songs to make sure that they have a lasting memory in the minds of the people. Today, in Lou Nuär, his words are still alive through songs that he himself composed. His technique as a prophet to convey his message through songs has become a genius one.

4.1.7 Two Offices of Ŋundɛŋ & Wuud Ɣɔ̱ɔ̱k-In-Charge of Cows

From the beginning of this chapter, we are informed that Böŋ descendants came from western Nuär specifically from Bul Chöl Geah. Ŋundɛŋ possessed functional roles such as Earth-Master (Leopard-Skin) and a prophet at the same time. He accepted of Bööŋ as his genitor, which shows that both the two offices were very important to him. H. Johnson illustrates the functions of Earth-Master (Leopard-Skin: first the power to mediate in times of feuds. Second, the power to bless the land and to make cultivation abundant. Third, the power to curse. Fourth, the power to perform rituals for a murderer to eat or drink water after killing. Fifth, the power to pray (pal) over the beast and to spear it during the reconciliation processes.

Before Ŋundɛŋ was seized by divinity, he assumed the priestly office of the Earth-Master (Leopard-Skin). He joined the mediation of blessing and cursing and he was a prophet at the same time as we have mentioned earlier. In this case, his power involves the gift of life in his ministry as both Earth-Master (leopard-Skin) and the prophet. Unfortunately, when he arrived among the Lou Nuär, he was still a minor Earth-Master according to H. Johnson. While at the meantime, the most renowned Lou Nuär Earth-Master was a Dinka, Yuot Nyakong [Yuɔ̱t Nyakoŋ].

Apart from the power of Earth-Master, there is another second power. First, wud ɣɔ̱ɔ̱k-is responsible for cattle such as in the example of Beac Colieth who organized the migration to Buoŋjak. Second, wud ɣɔ̱ɔ̱k-responsible for seasonal movements of herds and cattle camps. Third, he also opens and closes the age-set rites of initiation of young men as warriors. Fourth, a cattle camp is always named after him. Fifth, when people arrive at a new cattle camp, he is the first to hammer a piece of wood on the ground for the oxen-ɛ ram min puɔt lọc kɛ nhiam. Sixth, he is responsible for pouring some milk on the Riak shrine for the ancestors of the families or clans.

Therefore, among the Nuär, it is common that such powers

exist for some individuals. However, a conflict can arise between those powers that can even make a permanent settlement difficult as it happened between Ŋundɛŋ and Nyakong [Yuɔt Nyakoŋ] who was so powerful among the Lou Nuär. Ŋundɛŋ has a hidden mysterious power amidst that power of Yuot Nyakong. However, it was said that Ŋundɛŋ became known as a 'man of divinity.' He warned Yuɔt Nyakong not to visit the Dinka dealing that Yuɔt was dealing with the merchants of slaves at Pul, also known as Panyaaŋ which became known to everybody. Yuɔt ignored the warning from Ŋundɛŋ. Unfortunately, he was lured into the Dinka territory of Nyarɛwɛŋ. He was held for ransom, and then humiliately killed even after the ransom cattle were paid in 1874. It was this period of raiding which resulted in Nyarɛwɛŋ defeat in 1874.

4.1.8 Emerging of Ŋundɛŋ as a Prophet

H. Johnson states, "The Lou attacked the Nyarɛwɛŋ separately, but it was Ŋundɛŋ who organized the most successful defence against Dinka aggression, and it was Ŋundɛŋ who is credited with bringing this period of violence to an end."[57] In 1878, the Lou Nuär was attacked by a coalition of both Dinka and Gaawär Nuär under the leadership of a Dinka man named Dɛŋ Cier. He assumed himself a prophet. Dɛŋ Cier was aiming to establish local authorities such as the Luak Dɛŋ shrine master and Nuär Mɛr of Gaawär Nuär.

While Dɛŋ Cier had wanted to become like him and Nuär Mɛr of Gaawär, Ŋundɛŋ, who had declared his seizure by 'Dɛŋ' only a few years. First, he avoided a fight but then

57 Cf. Douglas H. Johnson, *The Nuër Prophets*, pp. 84-85.

arranged an ambush at the Lou cattle camps, around Padiiŋ at Khor Fulluth (Kofulus). According to H. Johnson, lulled into thinking that the Lou herds were undefended. Consequently, the Dinka raiders led by Dɛŋ Cier and Gaawär Nuär led by Nuär Mɛr were attacked by Lou Nuär and were consequently pushed back into the river.

According to H. Johnson, they were speared like many fish incidents with clear resonances of the Aiwel myth. The battle had far-reaching political consequences. "Not only did Ŋundeŋ gain wide acceptance as the prophet of Dɛŋ, but his victory led directly to the rise of Dɛŋ Lekä, the overthrowing of Nuär Mɛr among the Gaawär, and the break-up of many Dinka groups."

The Victory was attributed to Dɛŋ and especially to Ŋundɛŋ's sacrifice of an ox at the beginning of the battle. The Nuär are used to fight clan divinities however, in the case of Dɛŋ of Ŋundɛŋ, it belongs to all including Padiiŋ. According to H. Johnson, Ŋundɛŋ claimed that Dɛŋ was a divinity for all people, and with Padiiŋ he proves this was so. Paradoxically, his victory helped him to establish Ŋundɛŋ's reputation as a peacemaker; for the battle was fought in self-defence and not for gain, and it reinforced (or even introduced) the idea that, through Ŋundɛŋ, Dɛŋ could control both life and death. H. Johnson states it demonstrated the prophet's gift of life and helped to establish Dɛŋ's primacy over all other divinities.

4.1.9 Functions of Nuär Prophets Including Ŋundɛŋ

First, the greatest gift of divinity is the gift of life. Second, the prophets function as creators and protectors. Third, they are the controllers of life by establishing themselves as men of divinity. Fourth, through them, people receive their blessings through their prayers. Fifth, they attempt to cure the sick. Sixth, to ensure the fertility of women and cows. Seven, to secure the abundance of crops. Eighth, as givers of life, they could also be takers of life. Ninth, their curse was supposed to carry the power of death. Tenth, their sacrifices in war could destroy their enemies.

According to H. Johnson, in contrast to kujurs (magicians) and Earth-Master (leopard-skin), the Divinity controls life and death. Men of sanctity or men who work with magic are both deemed able to manipulate life and death through the aid of a divinity or a lower power. Nevertheless, the curse of an Earth-Master or the spell of a magician generally affects individuals, not whole groups. As proof of a stronger ability, one that affects entire communities, the prophets convinced people that their strengths were greater than that of either the Earth Masters or magicians. H. Johnson states that in doing so, the prophets associated themselves with the Divinity above; thus, stressing the difference between their divinities and those tutelary divinities and lower powers invoked by other persons.

4.1.10 Ŋundɛŋ, the Miraculous Prophet

H. Johnson has illustrated the following DIVINITY of DENG through Ŋundɛŋ. First, Ŋundɛŋ demonstrated his divinity by having the power to control life and his capability to kill. Second, at the first sacrifice to DENG, dogs were supposed to have died after eating the meat of the sacrificial victims. For example, the bodies of dogs were left out in the sun to rot all day, and in the cool of the evening, Ŋundɛŋ struck each dog's corpse with a bundle of grass, resurrecting them all. Third, the defeat at the battle of Padiiŋ was accredited to Ŋundɛŋ. Fourth, according to H. Johnson, all successful prophets became known for their abilities to kill by word or thought, and Ŋundɛŋ was especially famous for this.

For instance, the death of a child who bully and the maternal cousin who denied him Wiu's ribs, are often cited as early proofs of Ŋundɛŋ's capability to kill. Fifth, after Ŋundɛŋ became a prophet, the deaths of many enemies were attributed to him even though he never said a word of curse upon them. Sixth, Ŋundɛŋ had the power to suppress other powers such as 'evil eye' or involuntary witchcraft (pɛth), an inherited trait which acts indiscriminately, endowing its owner with the ability to harm or kill merely by looking at a person. H. Johnson confirms that pɛth is associated with Wiu, the clan divinity of the Gaatgankii̱r of Jikäny. For example, to control their powers, Ŋundɛŋ composed a song for them.

Diit Ŋundɛɛŋ kɛ kuic Pɛɛthä

Ŋundɛɛŋ ca pɛɛthdɛ bi̱ luäŋ
Ŋundɛɛŋ Böŋ ca pɛɛthdɛ bi̱ luäŋ
Kuthɛ to̱ny bi̱ wec wuu!
Bi̱ kuäär waŋdɛ bo̱l luak

Song of Ŋundɛɛŋ for Witchcraft

Ŋundɛŋ›s witchcraft will not weaken
Ŋundɛɛŋ Böŋ witchcraft will not weaken
For he blew his pipe, going 'wuu!'
And the master's eyes lit up in the byre.

By comparison with pɛth-witchcraft, Ŋundɛŋ controlled the harm while a person with pɛth-witchcraft does not. Ŋundɛŋ his spiritual strength against specific targets. The Lou Nuär noted that Ŋundɛŋ sacrifices animals merely by shaking his baton-la yɔ̱k ɛ nä daŋ dɛ) or his pipe-kiɛ yɔ̱k ɛ nä to̱ny dɛ at them.

Here are other miracles performed by Ŋundɛŋ: first, the divinity of Dɛŋ was known for improving the qualities of life. Second, Dɛŋ is associated with rain and with its connotations of cool weather. Third, Dɛŋ can revive grass to feed cattle. Fourth, Dɛŋ had the power to prevent the end of the deadly dry season. Fifth, they came to know Dɛŋ through the shrine at Luak Dɛŋ, where the divinity was appealed for grains and the protection of cultivation through the control of rain and floods.

Sixth, Dɛŋ was also known for taking persons into a bush and returning them safely, as it had done with Ŋundɛŋ. Ŋundɛŋ reinforced these life-giving associations of Dɛŋ. Ŋundɛŋ told the Nuär that his divinity came from the direction of the north wind, which brings coolness. According to H. Johnson, the ox name he adopted after his seizure, was Dɛŋkur. It is a white ox with black eyes calling to mind the black and white of the rain clouds, and by this name, Ŋundɛŋ was commonly known throughout the rest of his life as Dɛŋkur.

Seventh, Ŋundɛŋ gained a reputation for making barren women fertile as Dɛŋ is supposed to have made his mother fertile. For example, the supplicants would bring an ox, which Ŋundɛŋ sacrificed to Dɛŋ. In administering this ritual performance for the fertility of the supplicants, he anointed the woman's stomach with either butter or his spittle, both being fluids considered to have life-giving properties. Then he accompanied this with blessings on the child about to be conceived in a prophecy about its character (for example, it would be a good cultivator, it would be talkative, etc.), sometimes, even announcing the unborn child's name. Because of this ability, to restore fertility, he was known as the spiritual father of the children born by his blessing.

Eighth, he was not known only for the restoration of individual women's infertility but also for curing an entire generation of infertile women. For example, the mothers of Daŋ-gongä age-set in both Lou and Jikäny Nuär were supposed to have suffered mass barrenness until they sought Ŋundɛŋ's help. According to H. Johnson, he sacrificed a white ox for all of them. The children who were born and marked in the Daŋ-gongä age-set (c.1895) were known as the children of the white ox. Ŋundeŋ asserts that it was by such widespread supplication of his divinity for individual and personal problems. He established and maintained his claim to spiritual primacy both within and beyond Lou Nuär clans. For example, Ŋundeŋ treated women with infertilities from Lou, Jikäny, Thiang, Laak, Western Nuär, and Gawäär, including the wife of Prophet Dɛŋ Lekä.

As we have above-mentioned, Ŋundeŋ was not using physical violence but rather fights with words. For example, Ŋundeŋ prophesized about the coming of Turuk (Turkey) to Lɔu Nuär Land. When Ŋul Kuɔk Gill heard this, he was angry at Ŋundeŋ and slapped him at Biɛ Ŋundeŋ. Ŋundeŋ replied, "Did you slap because of Turuk (Turkey) or because of God." He continues, if it is because of Turuk (Turkey), it is until at cieŋ Marɔ̱a̱l (Khartoum), but if it is because of God, God can see what is going to happen in future. In this sense, Ŋundeŋ justified himself as innocent and ought not to be slapped at all. Ŋundeŋ told Ŋul, "Your descendants will be very small."

However, Ŋul kept silent but his brother by name Do̱k Kuɔk responded to Ŋundeŋ, "We don't want Turuk (Turkey)." Ŋundeŋ answered him, "It will begin with you here in Lɔu Nuär." When Turuk (Turkey) arrived at Lɔu Nuär Land, the first-born daughter of Do̱k Kuɔk, was married by the commander of Turuk (Turkey) nicknamed Jaak Ŋuan (four oxen with that same colour). Therefore, the prophecy of Ŋundeŋ was fulfilled.

About those prophecies, Ŋundeŋ used to say to Lɔu Nuär, 'Sons of my uncle, it is very bad when something is known to one person-gaat na̱a̱r Wudni̱ jiäk mɔ ŋa̱a̱c kɛ ɛ ram kɛl lɔ. However, he used to conclude that these prophecies and their lies are based on their delay-gaat na̱a̱r, kaac diɛn ɣöö ke kɛ nä tuɔk (kiɛ kaac diɛn ja̱a̱ny).

In comparison, the response of Ŋundeŋ to Ŋul Kuɔk was like the one of Jesus when he was slapped as the gospel of St. John asserts, Jesus replied, "If I have said anything wrong, make a formal statement about the wrong; but if [I spoke] properly, why did you strike me?" (Jn 18: 23). However, in this comparison, we can see that Jesus never cursed the one who slapped him nor did he wish him evil but rather asked reason for slapping him.

However, regarding ritual purification, Ŋundeŋ had established two pools that are, the Evil Pool and the Good Pool. Evil Pool is at the left side of Biɛ and Good Pool is at the right side of Biɛ. Always Ŋundeŋ used to command people with various types of diseases to go to Evil Pool first to take a shower there. After that, he also commanded them to take a shower at the Good Pool. These two pools were used by Ŋundeŋ for healing people with different types of diseases. Furthermore, the two pools of Ŋundeŋ for healing can also be compared to the pool of Jews for healing. For example, a man said to Jesus… "Sir, I have no man, when the water is troubled, to put me into the pool: but while I am coming, another stepped down before me" (Jn 5:7).

4.1.10.1 Ŋundɛŋ's Intervention to Plagues

The restoration of fertility, and his response to the twin epidemics of smallpox and rinderpest, which entered Nuär land from Ethiopia in about 1888, made his power spread. First, in foreseeing these two epidemics, Ŋundɛŋ went to the bush. Second, there he sacrificed dozens of oxen in front of the path of the plagues, leaving them to rot, and untouched. Third, he sacrificed more cattle in his village, where the meat of the sacrificial animals was eaten.

According to H. Johnson, both the Jikäny and Lou Nuär lost many cattle to rinderpest, the older generations dying in the subsequent famine, but smallpox appears to have been halted and did not afflict the Lou again until the early 1920s. These two related epidemics were extraordinary occurrences, and Ŋundɛŋ adopted an extraordinary method of mass sacrifice to meet the two epidemics. Being so a proactive prophet, to prevent a recurrence, he then built his famous Mound, in which all diseases and bad things were buried.

Observers about his successful prevention of these two epidemics made various responses. First, in later years' British administrators attributed his apparent success to the accuracy of his timing, undertaking sacrifices when the epidemic was already waning. Second, still others said, there were some scientific methods in his madness. Third, it was said that one doctor mistakenly attributed these successes to Ŋundɛŋ's son, Guɛk. He praised the prophet as 'no mean epidemiologist' who, observing the direction in which the rinderpest epidemic was spreading created a 'scorched earth' zone between it and the main body of the cattle.

When the smallpox entered, Ŋundɛŋ could ban dances and ordered people to leave their huts and sleep in the open. There was meat available from daily sacrifices, so "the extra food strengthens their resistance and with the avoidance of normally crowded conditions, the smallpox smouldered out." H. Johnson concludes that whether Ŋundɛŋ controlled these two epidemics by chance or by shrewd observation is beside the point. However, we can say that the prophet was able to apply social distancing, as it was done during the COVID-19 pandemic, as it was also done during other times of both epidemic and pandemic diseases in human history. Ten years later, Lou Nuär was observed to have large healthy herds. Ŋundɛŋ is remembered due to this miraculous power, which he always attributed to the spiritual power of Dɛŋ. According to H. Johnson, the memory of his success has grown within a short time. Disease and warfare in modern Lou Nuär society are frequently explained by reference to the demise of Ŋundɛŋ and Guɛk, and the destruction of the Mound shrine they built and maintained.

4.1.11 Ŋundɛŋ's Gigantic Mound and its End

Prophet Ŋundɛŋ had built a gigantic shrine made out of a large earth Mound. He named it his byre-shrine or his pail. Bieh means the tip of a horn. The Bieh took the shape of Nilotic cattle byres and the tombs of the northern Sudanese Muslim saints called 'pyramids'. However, its significance was not investigated; nevertheless, the prophet Ŋundɛŋ built it to continue the tradition of large fixed shrines in the Upper Nile religion. According to Ŋundɛŋ, the Mound shrine symbolized a spiritual centre for prayer, blessing, and confrontation with both visible and invisible enemies. According to H. Johnson, the Mound drew explicitly on the symbolism of Puom Aiwel and Luak Dɛ̈ɛ̈ŋ. Ŋundɛŋ's Mound became the symbol of a political centre of the Nuär immigrants.

H. Johnson states it was here that Ŋundɛŋ built his last and largest Mound- (yik), providing the Eastern Nuär with a spiritual focus of the type they had in the tree at Koat-liech (Koch Liic) and in the myths surrounding it. The sixty-foot-high Mound had become a shrine like Luak Dɛŋ (known as Luak Kuoth among the Nuär). It transcended the political divisions within and around Eastern Nuär society. It was a place where divinity Dɛŋ could become available not just to the Nuär, but to all people. According to H. Johnson, and Evans-Pritchard's less vivid account of the Mound was based on contemporary witnesses with, and perhaps identical to, Coriat:

This mound was a gigantic task. It was constructed of wet ashes mixed with baked and unbaked earth, for the material was excavated from two large vacated cattle camps where ashes and other camp debris had grown from year to year and became sodden and agglutinated by many seasons of rains. The workers who built it stood one above the other in tiers from the base of the pyramid, and each handed up materials to the man above him. A low palisade of elephants' tusks was planted around the base of the pyramid, a pile of tusks was buried in the centre of the mound, and one or two protruded from its summit.[58]

---

58 Douglas H. Johnson, *Nuër Prophets*, P.91. It does not seem that there

Mr. Coriat describes the Bieh-mound..." as a pyramid, a remarkable able feat both of agility, for the pyramid was the most difficult of ascent and endurance." Ŋundɛŋ asked people to come but did not force them. In building it, they came willingly because they believed in his divinity and wanted his blessing too. Workers were fed in part from their provisions, and in part from a large plantation of sorghum and maize which Ŋundɛŋ cultivated for a considerable distance around the site. He maintained this plantation (covering a square mile or more) for the rest of his life, to feed visitors and supplicants.

Evans-Pritchard affirms that. "Ŋundɛŋ's mound was blown up with high explosives by the British Administration during a punitive expedition in 1928 against his son's followers." He states that however, much of it remains, and Dr. Leichardt tells me it is said that sometimes at night a strange light is seen shining from it. When a recent eclipse of the sun occurred, people said that Ŋundeŋ was returning.

4.1.12 Various Songs of Ŋundɛŋ

This song, addressed to Kerdol's children (the Lou), mentions the Ngok Dinka and the flags of Marol (the Turks) and may

---

was any systematic conscription of labour in the building of the mound but people came voluntarily from all over the countryside to assist and often brought bullocks with them for sacrifices. They would spend three or four nights in one of the temporary grass shelters, which others, since they had departed to their homes, had put; and when the food that they had brought with them was finished, they would return to their homes also, and their places would be taken by other pilgrims. The flesh of sacrificed bullocks was divided among the workers and lengthened their supplies. It is said that people brought handfuls of ashes to add to the mound from Gaajok and Gaawang countries as an act of piety.

refer to the brief, but brutal, raids on the Sobat mouth by the Ansar (habitually an army of many flags) during Al-Zaki Tamal's Shilluk's campaign in 1891-2.

Bi piny kɛɛliw mat kɛ töŋ luaak Dɛ̈ɛ̈ŋ, ɛŋa bi ɣä gak
Gaatkerdööl?
A luak wuɔw!
Tɔŋ luak Dɛ̈ɛ̈ŋ ci tuqŋ guqqri kɛ mat ci la rial (bo̱o̱l)
Cia ben tɔaŋ Gaatkerdöl bia rɔ ŋic kamnikun?
(ɛŋa bi ŋa ŋicɔ)
A cäŋɛ ŋɔɔk bikɛ ben tɔaŋ, cia dual kɛ bɛ̈ɛ̈ri rɔal.
Gueth mi de jääny kä ram kɛl, buɔmdɛ riitɛ ɣɔw, Joknyääl
yiɛth tuŋdɛ puaar.

All the land will gather to build my byre who will deny me,
Kerdol's children?
Let the byre shout!
Build the byre of DENG for the elephants' tusks that have
been gathered and become shining.
Kerdol's children, you came to build
will you recognize each other?
Even the Ngok will come to build, you feared Marol's flags.
The strength that can remain in one man. His power is
charging the universe, the Ox Joknyal, who stabs the
clouds with his horn.

In another song, Ŋundeŋ speaks with the voice of DENG, a hairy man, and pronounces his shrine to be a place of life.

Ɣän Yiaanä Wud guɔri bä naŋ ni luaak.
Tɔŋ Dɛŋ luak min mɔ paduil, jɛn ɛ guaath teekä.

Bä jɛ tɔŋ ɛn guaath ɛmɛ mi wä Wud luaakdɛ wä yɔŋ.
Ɣän Yiaanä Wud guɔ̱ri bä naŋ ni luaak.
Tɔŋ Dɛŋ luak min mɔ paduil, jɛn ɛ gua̱a̱th teekä.
Bä jɛ tɔŋ ɛn gua̱a̱th ɛmɛ mi wä Wud luaakdɛ wä yɔŋ.

I bound a hairy man. And I will take him to the byre. DENG is building a byre which is Paduil. It is a place of life; I will build this Paduil when the man of the byre goes mad.

ŊUNDEŊ'S song DENG announces himself as a divinity

A nyuɔɔrä kam ruac gaatkä diaal
Lapä kuoth mi göl
Lapä kuoth gankä dial

Let me sit while all my children talk
I am a different divinity
I am a divinity for all my children.

But he then goes on to declare his affinity with Longor, saying:

Tɔaaŋä Puɔm Loŋqqr
Takɔ kɛ kaar (Ra̱a̱l)
Ŋundeŋ kɛnɛ ɣän Takɔ kɛ kaar

I will build Puom Longor
we are related,
Ŋundeŋ and I are related

DENG warns the people of this song.

Ram mi bar rɔɔdɛ i ci gaak kɛ Dɛŋ
Mi wi wä nhiam bi Dɛŋ jek
Mi wi wä jɔk bi Dɛŋ jek
Kä mi lunyi jɔk bi Dɛŋ jek
Jɛn ram min both Dɛŋ, bi Dɛŋ wä jek nhiam
Bi Dɛŋ nɛn mi wi jɔkdu liɛɛc

Somebody fled for he quarrelled with DENG
If you go ahead, you will find DENG.
And if you go back, you will find DENG.
He who precedes DENG will find DENG in front.
You will see DENG if you look back.

ŊUNDEŊ denounced magicians in his songs and accused pretended prophets of conjuring, using tueth, the Dinka word.

Göök diaal tin tueth kɔ, (tin tuëth kɛ rɔ̰)
kɛnɛ tin görkɛ wal bäkɛ näk kɛn diaal

Prophets who conjure
and those who search for magic I will kill them all

ŊUNDEŊ stressed the difference between his divinity and the secret use of magic.

Ba kɛ yiee mi gɔaa
Kä lökä tɛɛni
Cä cuuc kɛ tɛɛni titi
Ci Dɛŋ ben la Dɛŋ

Mi wa ji näk kuol (Lou)
Ci Dɛŋ ben la Dɛŋ

I came with a good breath
And I reject secret things
I am tired of these secrets
DENG has become DENG
If I kill you Kuol (Lou)
DENG has become DENG

ŊUNDEŊ attacks three of his best-known rivals, who were Nyakong Bar, Reath Yac and Duop Thar. He denounced them all in this song abusing them with Dinka and Arabic words for women (Tiek and mariem).

Kɛn kuar cuukni cikɛ kɔ̱c, (nyuään)
Ci gɔw ni (ŋu;ni tiɛk) män kä kɛ
Cetkɛn kɛ män ti jäl ɛ lek lek
Gaatkä cuɔrɛ ɣä kuɔn
Kapɛ tetkun nhial palɛ Dɛŋ kɛ tok
Ram mi wä kɛ naŋ thääyä bɛ liw /cɛ bi cop gɔcni

The masters of the ants have become weak
women are better than they
They are like women walking and shivering
Do not leave me children
Lift your hands and pray to DENG with laughter
A man who takes them seriously will die and not achieve good things

Another Gaatjak rival sometimes mentioned along with Nyakong Bar was Reath Yac, who claimed to be seized by DENG. Ŋundeŋ dismissed this in a song which began, DENG has become confused on earth and his head was dizzy | DENG was among the prophets. He then ridiculed Reath:

Göök tin jiäk ci mut rɔ luɔckɛ
Ci mut ben luac ɛ luac (kɔ̱a̱c ɛ thei) kɛ riɛm
Mi wa̱a̱ taŋ yiath ba yiɛth ni cäŋ köör
Mi wa̱a̱ taŋ yiɛth bi ciek wiee (wak)
Kuoth Reath Yac ɛ mi dit idi? Jɛn ɛmi kuiy (tɔt) ɛlɔŋ

The bad prophets' spear was turned against them
The spear became soft with blood
If I stab with the spear-shaft I will stab during war
If I stab with the spear-shaft the woman will cry
How big is Reath Yac's divinity? It is small

The following song is now said to have been composed by ŊUNDEŊ before Duop was so seized. In it, he mentions WIU, the clan divinity of the Gaatgankii̱r clan (a divinity associated with the evil eye), and invokes the Thiang spear, the clan spear of Gaatgankii̱r, but also the clan spear of the Bor clan, to which Duop Thar belonged.ŊUNDEŊ'S song DENG announces himself as a divinity.

Ci Got pɛ̈ɛ̈n cɛ naath moc cier
Wiu köör kämni xä raan
Bi Wiu pɛn piny
Jɛn ɛ mut thiaŋdan
Jɛn ram min dony lɛckɛ nhial, cɛ pɛn piny

E ɣän kärɔa mɔ kuothɔ, Cä pɛ̋ɛ̋n
Kuoth Gankir cɛ pɛ̋ɛ̋n
Kuoth pɛɛthä cɛ pɛ̋ɛ̋n

Got fell and gave the people stars
WIU of war gave me a person
WIU will fall down
He is our Thiang spear
The one who grows the upper teeth, I have fallen down
I am the only divinity; I have fallen
The divinity of Kir's children has fallen
The divinity of the evil eye, I have come down

This song is from a late stage of Ŋundeŋ's life, after 1902 when the Anglo-Egyptian army (the gunmen) raided his village:

Ŋundɛŋ!
Wëu (jwä)
Ŋundɛŋ!
Wëu (jwä)
Ka̱mä ji ɣɔ̱k tin tɔ nyin Buɔ̱k
Guää, /cukɛ käm ɣä (ŋun) (ɛ nɛy kɔŋ thuɔ̱k) a kɔ kɔan kɔ thuɔ̱k kɔnɛ rɔ̱lmaac (Jimaac)
Ŋundɛŋ!
Wëu (jwä)
Ŋundɛŋ!
Wëu (jwä)
Kamä ɣɔk ti jithkiɛn pa̱npa̱a̱n
ce̱tkɛ dɔw jiath päkä
Guää, /cukɛ käm ɣä a kɔ kɔan kɔ thuɔ̱k kɔnɛ rɔ̱lmaac

(Jimaac)

Ŋundeŋ!
Yes!
Ŋundeŋ!
Yes!
I give you the cattle which belongs to Buk
Father, do not give them to me,
Let me finish with the gunmen
Ŋundeŋ!
Yes
Ŋundeŋ!
Yes!
I give you the cattle with ears as large as the fruit of paak-tree
Father, do not give Let me finish the gunmen

Ŋundeŋ!
Yes!
Ŋundeŋ!
Yes!
I give you the cattle which belongs to Buk
Father, do not give them to me,
Let me finish with the gunmen
Ŋundeŋ!
Yes
Ŋundeŋ!
Yes!
I give you the cattle with ears as large as the fruit of paak-tree
Father, do not give them, let me finish the gunmen

In this song, he disputed DENG'S assertion of primacy and invokes Tut Gar, the ox with the spreading horns, an old image of Divinity (kuoth) holding the universe between its horns, against the upstart free divinity (DENG).

Ŋundɛŋ Böŋ, ɛ ŋu cɔɔli naath kɛ lɔar (baŋ)?
Dɛŋ ɛŋu mi bi lat?
Mi ɛ cäŋ kɛnɛ pay, bi ram mi pal ben
Lɛp Cotlual yäpɛ (gakɛ) DENG
Bi liaa jek ci jiɛɛn, bä pal kɛ xöö bi tek ben
Bä lar yɛ kɛ nhiam, ɛ Jɛn ɣän Tut Gar, min nooŋ läär (laat)
Dɛŋ Buɔk, thilɛ tɛɛ kɛ piny kɛɛliw

Ŋundeŋ Bong, why do you call people for nothing?
DENG what will you do?
If it is the sun and the moon, he who prays will come
The tongue of the ox Cotlual denies DENG
You will find death has gone, I will pray for life to come
I will tell you first, that it is I, Tur Gar, who bring news
DENG of Buk, I have no secrets from the whole world

As with the song quoted above, it employs well-known images, this time describing DENG as a herd bull leading the other animals safely through the bush, watched over by a careful herder, Ŋundeŋ.

Tut mi diit, Dɛŋ Kuejiöök
Tut mi jäl kɛ gaatkɛ rɛy dɔaar
Cuɔrɛ bath ɣöö (Löö) gaatkä
Wud in yieen guicɛ yɛ (nɛɛnɛ yɛ)
Wud mi pal cäŋ kɛnɛ pay amäni ciɛr.

Tut mi diit, Dɛŋ kuejiöök
Tut mi nɛɛn gaatkɛ rɛy dɔar
Cuɔrɛ gaay bɛ yɛ mat nhial a thil pɛ̈ɛ̈th
Dɛŋ yieenɛ yɛ
Ram mi lok jal kɛ Dɛŋ, /cɛ rɔ bi mat gaat Dɛ̈ɛ̈ŋ, bɛ te kärɔa
Ram mi lok ni jal kuɔth, /cɛ rɔ bi mat gaat Dɛ̈ɛ̈ŋ, bɛ te kärɔa

The great bull, DENG KUEJIOK,
The bull who walks with his children in the bush.
Be not discouraged my children.
A watchful man is herding you.
A man who prays to the sun and moon even to the stars.
The bull who looks after his children in the bush.
Be not surprised, for he will gather you up without hurrying.
DENG guards you.
Someone who refuses to walk with DENG's children but will be alone.
Someone who refuses to walk with Divinity.
Will not gather with DENG's children but will be alone.

In the following song, he criticizes three large sections for refusing to heed him; the Rumjok, the Nyarkuac of the Gaatbal, and the Gaaliek of the Mor. He reminds them that each person is powerless about his Mound, no matter how large or bellicose his section.

Ɣän göörä xöö bä naath gaŋ (ɣɔr)
Duŋdɛ ɣöö tɛkɛ mi tekɛ Lɔu mi nyon ɣä
Jɛn ɛ ŋɛ̈ɛ̈ny yionni (mutni)

/Cä maatni titi bilɛ tɛɛ Gaatnar
Ɣän kɔnɛ yik thilɛ lany
Bɛ ram ɛmɔ jek golädɛ
Rumjiok cɛ päm lath wicdɛ (däärɛ) ci ben la tuŋ
/Cä dee ruac kɛ Gaatliek, ci Nyarkuac ben la duɔr mi jiäk

I wanted to protect the people
But one thing from Lou confused me
It is the anger of iron (spears)
I cannot hide it, these gatherings, my uncle's sons
The shrine and I, there are no refuge
Everyone will be found separately
Rumjok puts a stone on his head and it becomes a horn
I cannot talk of Gaatliek, Nyarkuac has become something worse

Ŋundeŋ sang bitterly of such rejection and reminded those who would refuse him of the symbols and proofs of his spiritual strength: the ox Jokpading who was sacralised at the battle of Pading, his ox- Kur, the leopard-skins which were the symbols of his master's office, and his baton, the curved stick with which he killed so many persons at Pading that the vultures came swooping down.

Mi cä biɛt, bi naath carni ɣöö ɛ ɣän dɔar
Ci ɣän a dɔar, ɣän pɛ̈lä
Ɣän Lökä ruacni ti but
Ci gaat pal yar (ŋarŋar)
Kä mi cä Jɔkpadiŋ kɛk
Bi cor ben nyuur piny
Mi cä Jɔkpadiŋ luɔc nikä diaal
Mi cä Kur kɛk kä bä kuacdä lath piny

E jɛn bä daaŋ tuoth (cuoth) a kɔc (a thil rɔal)

When I am silent, people think me a fool
I am not a fool, I am wise
I reject continuous words
For children spoiled the prayer (with their chattering)
But if I mention Jokpading
The vultures will come and sit down
If I repeat Jokpading many times
If I mention Kur and put down my leopard skins
Then I can clean my baton without interruption

During the mound, Ŋundeŋ called for cattle. A man of the Bul section of Mor refused since no previous divinity had made such demands:

Ram mi pen ɣä yaŋ bakɔ rɔ bit (lam)
Ram mi pen ɣä yaŋ bakɔ rɔ bit (lam)
Ruac tɛ rɛy luaak, ɛn ruac /kenɛ jääny
Te Nyääl kɛ Wiu

Someone who refuses me a cow, we will cure each other
Someone who refuses me a cow we will cure each other
The word is in the byre, the word has not delayed
Nyal is with WIU

He then sang this song:

Ram mi ci rɔ liak / cɛ bi loc cäŋ (Tiic)
Jɛn /cɛ bi la ruac Dɛ̈ɛ̈ŋ
Nac in lual ca (ci) ben ŋun ɛ tiik (ciek)

Ɣän MAR cä ben piny kɛ ruacdä
Mɛmɛ ɛ rolä ɣän Dɛŋ, ɣɛ̈ɛ̈lä xä kä rɔa

He who was proud will not return home
That will not be DENG's word
A red heifer was given by a lady
I, MAR, came down with my word
This is my world, I DENG, which I alone own

Most of ŊUNDEŊ's songs, which mention Rol Mayok, Marol and Rolmaac, come from this time. One which may date after 1902, and which begins the verse quoted on p. 105, reaffirms his position as an earth-master from the Leak clan, his inspiration from above.

Mi ci yɛn ɣä ŋäth, bi ɣän dhil a gurun
Gatbuleak bɛ nhial
A kɛ ruac kɛ kuiy Ŋundɛ̈ɛ̈ŋ
Katum Baari ɛ duŋ rol mayok
Ci nyinkä (wääŋkä) thiaŋ kɛ riɛm
Määthdä cuor, määthdä cuor
You do not believe me but I will be your father
Buleak's son comes from above
Let them talk about Ŋundeŋ
Khartoum Bahri belongs to rolmayok
My eyes are filled with blood
My friend is a vulture, my friend is a vulture

Other songs were less bloody. In the next one, he mentions the carrion-eating birds Kueilit and Nyalaang, the divinities of two dayiemni, Cuol Nyaljok and GöT, the Mor Lou section

Nyabor, and his village at the Mound, wec Carlel, or the cattle camp of the black ox.

Bä tuŋ biikä car piny
Bi jiath kuëël rɔ duany (gɔŋ) ni däär
Kueilit kɛnɛ Nyalang bi cuor pɛ̈ɛ̈n ɛ wuu!
Cieŋ Nyabor, palɛ a gɔa (palɛ a gɔa, cieŋ Nyabor)
Laaŋɛ a gɔa, ricdiɛn (beriɛn) ɛ jɛn kɛlɔ
Ric bɛ piny kɛ Nuär
Tɔaŋä biɛk wec gankur
tɔaaŋä biɛk bi rɔɔl (tëk) nhial
tɔaaŋä yik
tɔaaŋä biɛkdɛ ɛn ŋundɛŋ
ɛ ɣän Dɛŋ, ɛn ram mi tääth
cu ɣä gɔny /ciɛ xän marol
lökä kor (mut) in nööŋɛ
kuoth yɛnɛ Gök /cuɔrɛ gak
biɛ luɔc ni yɛn (kɛ yɛn kɛn tin bia luɔc)
Ram mi lar jɛ i ɛ (gäy) can, bɛ wä ni buɔr ŋundɛ̈ɛ̈ŋ
Bä rɔdä thac rɛy luaak
Bi Lit ruac thiec
Cuol Nyajiök yɛnɛ Göt a cäŋ lökɛ ruac, bi ruac rɔ tuok wic Karlel

I will lay down the point of the mound
The fig tree will bend in the middle
Kueilit and Nyalaang, the vultures, drop-Wuu!
Pray well, Nyabot section,
Supplicate well, their generation is the same
The generation came down with the Nuär
I build the mound of Kur's children's camp

I build the mound which will heal up
I build the shrine
I build Ŋundeŋ's mound
I, DENG, the one who moulds
Do not accuse me, I am not marol
I reject the fight you bring
Divinity and the prophet do not quarrel
Someone who says he is poor will come to Ŋundeŋ's arms
I will curl myself up in the byre
Lit will ask the word
CUOL NYAJOK and Göt even if you refuse the word the word will begin at Carlel's camp

4.1.13 Mysterious End of the Life of Prophet Ŋundɛŋ

Evans-Pritchard states that "The first prophet, or at any rate the first to achieve fame was Ŋundɛŋ son of Bung [Böŋ], of the Lou tribe, a prophet of spirit dɛŋ, who died in 1906." According to H. Johnson, "In January 1906, the Lou Nuär Prophet Ŋundɛŋ Böŋ died." The record of the year of death of Ŋundɛŋ, 1906, contradicted the family account about the end of the earthly life of Prophet Ŋundɛŋ. The interviews conducted by H. Johnson with the family of prophet Ŋundɛŋ did not testify that he died a natural death. H. Johnson recorded the testimony from one of his sons, Garäŋ Ŋundɛŋ, who later, described to H. Johnson his father's final day:

He came and spent a day here, at Wukuel, at the pool of Nyaŋkor Nhial, where his wife's brother Thieŋjiok was. When he talked, he went to the dance of place and said to the people, 'You people, when I go, you will never find my footprints.' A man named Jiek said, 'Ŋundɛŋ, what is wrong?

Why should your footprints not be found? (Ŋundɛŋ) said, 'That is true, my father's brother, you will never find them.' He left the dance and Jiek followed him, saying, 'Please kill a cow [as a sacrifice].[59]

It is said that the news about the illness and the rumours about the death of the prophet Ŋundɛŋ was very consoling to the British administration. According to H. Johnson, when reports of Ŋundɛŋ's final illness reached the province capital Kodok in January, Captain O'Sullivan was sent with a small escort to make 'Dɛŋ Kur declare if he was not dead. If he were dead, taking such steps would prevent the selection of a new head chief.

On his arrival, Captain O'Sullivan found Ŋundɛŋ's family naturally oppressed but also nervous about the threatening actions of Thie Ruea, one of Ŋundɛŋ's rivals. According to H. Johnson, the family of Ŋundɛŋ confirmed his death to Captain O'Sullivan but declined to identify his grave. After an extended tour of Lou territory, Captain O'Sullivan reported to his governor:

> *There is corroborated information that Dɛŋkur died of lung disease...The probable reason for not wishing to disclose the grave, fear of any desecration. That he was much beloved and feared by all. Always helped the poor, never allowing killing; but hated the 'red-man', and was preaching revenge on the Turk (the day he fell ill) this year.* [60]

59 Douglas H. Johnson, *Nuër Prophet,* p.3.

60 Douglas H. Johnson, *Nuër Prophets*, p. 4.

The report of Captain O'Sullivan about the death of prophet Ŋundɛŋ to his governor requires serious analysis to arrive at its authenticity. First, any person would never believe there was truth between him and the bereaved family of the late prophet. Second, he was commissioned by his governor only to confirm the death of the prophet Ŋundɛŋ without a word of 'consolation.' Captain O'Sullivan was sent with a small escort, to make ''Dɛŋkur declared dead. He had all the power in his hand to intimidate the family of the prophet Ŋundɛŋ to show him his grave. Why he did not do that?

Third, generally, the Nuär in the west and the east bury his or her dead either on the left or on the right side of the hut for everybody to see. His family could not bury Prophet Ŋundɛŋ whom Captain O'Sullivan said was much beloved and feared by all, a just man, who always helped the poor, never allowing killing, in a hidden place.

Fourth, Captain O'Sullivan 'corroborated information'- that Dɛŋkur died of lung disease was not correct. How can somebody confirm the disease, which caused the death of another person without desecration or medical test?

Fifth, Captain O'Sullivan 'corroborated information'- that Dɛŋkur died of lung disease was not correct. How can somebody confirm the disease, which caused the death of another person without desecration or medical test? He said that he did not find the grave of the prophet Ŋundɛŋ, how could he conclude that prophet Dɛŋkur died of lung disease?

Evans-Pritchard asserts that Ŋundɛŋ's mound was blown up with high explosives by the British administration during a punitive expedition in 1928 against his son's followers. With such high explosives, why was the British Administration unable to discover the grave of the prophet Dɛŋkur? One can imagine the magnitude of destruction of everything around the huts within the Mound area. The conclusion is, that nothing was discovered about Ŋundɛŋ'sdeath. Therefore, if the prophet Dɛŋkur had been buried, the British Administration would have found his grave.

Therefore, the following information about the year of Prophet Dɛŋkur's death is not true. First, Evans-Pritchard states that "The first prophet, or at any rate the first to achieve fame was Ŋundɛŋ son of Bung [Böŋ], of the Lou tribe, a prophet of spirit dɛŋ, who died in 1906." Second, according to H. Johnson, "In January 1906, the Lou Nuër Prophet Ŋundɛŋ Böŋ died. Third, Captain O'Sullivan reported to his governor: "Corroborated information died of lung disease... Probable reason for not wishing to disclose grave, fear of any desecration."

Nobody is exempted from the miracles of God if He wants to perform one. God does what is impossible for as the Sacred Scriptures affirm through the angel Gabriel who announced to the Blessed Virgin Mary, "for nothing will be impossible for God" (Gen 1.27). The Sacred Scriptures assert such miracles as not allowing Prophet Elijah to die a natural death. "As they walked on still conversing, a fiery chariot and fiery horses came between the two of them, and Elijah went up to heaven in a whirlwind, and Elisha saw it happening." (2 Kgs 2: 11-12).

Therefore, in dealing with issues such as miracles performed by God, we need to go beyond human reasoning to faith. Such human reasoning is as follows: first, the law of identity: 'Whatever is, is.' Second, the law of contradiction:

'Nothing can both be and not be.' Third, the law of excluded middle: 'Everything must either be or not be.'

These three laws are samples of self-evidence of logical principles, but they are not more fundamental or more self-evident than various other similar principles: for instance, the one we considered just now, which states that what follows from a true premise is true. The name 'laws of thought' is also misleading, for what is important is not the fact that we think these laws are, but that things which happen under them; the fact that when we think about them, we think truly. Nevertheless, this is a big question.

The logical principles, enable us to prove from a premise that something is true, other logical principles, enable us to prove, from a premise, that there is a greater or less probability that something is true.

Conclusion

Chapter four has presented the compendium of the life of the prophet Ŋundeŋ Bong-Ŋundɛŋ Böŋ, and his background including his birth. It has also discussed Ŋundɛŋ's seizure, his first rejection by his relatives and by others, his second rejection in the middle of divisive tensions at Malou and his third rejection and physical violence upon him.

The chapter has explained Ŋundɛŋ's highest at Juɛ̈t and his marital status, and the prayer meeting at Malual initiated by Ran Pinyien for Ŋundɛŋ's recuperation. It has also illustrated Ŋundɛŋ's two offices: leopard-skin (earth-master and prophet), the emerging of Ŋundɛŋ as a prophet and his function of the prophet with its greatest gift of divinity. The chapter has discussed Ŋundɛŋ's gigantic Mound and its destruction by the British Administration and the contradiction and dilemma about the end of the earthly life of Ŋundɛŋ and his various songs.

CHAPTER FIVE

PROPHET KUOLAŊ KËT AND PROPHETESS NYARUAC

Introduction

Chapter five presents the life of two prophets of western Nuär, Kuolaŋ Kët and Nyaruac Kuolaŋ. It discusses the background of Kuolaŋ's life, his wives, and his moral life before the seizure. The chapter also illustrates Nuan's dramatic ritual spiritual purification and his blessing upon Kuolaŋ, the incidence of Kuolaŋ's seizure, and his surrender to the British Administration. Finally, it presents Kuolaŋ being buried alive by Ca̱a̱th ƆBaŋ and his resurrection from the dead as a sign of revenge.

Furthermore, the chapter also presents Nyaruac Kuolaŋ, her family background, and her girlhood, her miraculous powers. It discusses her role during the drum, its moral requirements, and her willing acceptance to live a virginal life as a commitment to her religious profession.

5. Background of Prophet Kuolaŋ

Among the western well-known prophets was Kuolaŋ Kët. It is believed that he had his grandfather from Baar (Anyauk). This was before he migrated to western Nuär in the eighteenth century. Upon his arrival in western Nuär, specifically at a village called Limpuot, he was accommodated in Jiath's house. According to J. Riek and R. Pendle, "Kuolaŋ Kët was the first member of his generation to be fully accepted by his maternal uncle as their own and as a member of the Jiath clan."[61]

Although Kuolaŋ later moved from the homeland of Yeth, yet, the Yeth clan still performs ritual rites over his family such as funerals. About his family background, Kuolaŋ had two sisters, Nyanyuot and Nyabo̱ra who were blessed with two sons. He was the only living male adult in his family. Consequently, he was responsible for all the families According to J. Riek and R. Pendle, when a smallpox outbreak (guɔl) killed both his sisters and their sons.

5.1 Prophet Kuolaŋ Kët

Prophet Kuolaŋ Kët was among the well-known people in the western Nuär land. He lived in the 18th century in a village called Limpuɔ̱t in Koch County. Kuolaŋ lived in the Jabäny section in Jagɛi territory. His fame was due to his miraculous powers that allowed him to provide healing and restoration of the health of many persons. He received people from all corners of Nuär land, seeking consultation and provision

61 Jedeit. J. Riek & Naomi R. Pendle, *Speaking Truth to Power in South Sudan, Oral Stories of the Nuër Prophets*, Nairobi, Rift Valley Institute, p. 17.

of tobacco as an instrument for recuperation for those who were sick with various types of diseases. Kuolaŋ's house had become like a hospital for those who were healed.

5.1.1 His Moral and Family Life

According to one reliable source, Kuolaŋ Kët had ten wives: first, Yieh Ruac, second, Nyalen Bol, third, Kaan Wuer, fourth, Nyapiini Wur, fifth, Both Rut, sixth, Both Kuolaŋ, seventh, Nyaja̱l Kai, eighth, Mer Dɛŋ, ninth, Nyatuɔ̱r Wic, and tenth, Nyathay Yɔ̱k. these are the wives of the prophet Kuolaŋ Kët. Some of them belong to his seizure and some belong to him. It is stated that he married them after the spirit of MAANI seized him.

According to J. Riek and R. Pendle, while Kuolaŋ was travelling, he met with a daughter of a powerful western Nuär man, Yeth from Jagɛi Nuär). The daughter of Yeth who was called Nyagaani̱, unfortunately, was impregnated by Kuolaŋ. We are told that the brothers of Nyagaani̱ threatened Kuolaŋ. However, he persuaded them and eventually, he was forgiven. Besides his wives, he married wives on behalf of his sisters, which stripped him of all the cattle he had. Those wives gave birth to sons of which he shouldered the responsibility alone. Consequently, this led him to the worst state of poverty.

Within the Yeth community section, Kuolaŋ had encountered not only poverty but also constant fighting against him. J. Riek and R. Pendle confirm that during the occasions of those fights, Kuolaŋ also killed two men. This also increased his poverty. He had no cattle to pay the compensation demanded by the families of the deceased and the revenge was imminent.

Consequently, Kuolaŋ faced three crucial issues such as poverty, revenge, and compensation. These had forced him to seek refuge from another powerful man from western Nuär called Jiath Kör from the Jabany section of Jagɛi Nuär. It is said, "Jiath's power was cemented by his acquisition of guns. He was one of the only firearms in the western Nuär region at the time."[62] It is stated that Jiath's offered personal protection to Kuolaŋ as the Kuär muɔn (Earth-Master or Leopard Skin).

Based on this safety and protection from Jiath Kör, Kuolaŋ was able to build his luak-byre at a place called Bar among the Jabany section of Jagɛi Nuär. Being stripped of everything, he worked for self-reliance by fishing at Nour Gatked Doup on the Yuarjuathni River to support himself and his family. He was nicknamed an excellent fisherman, in the Jabany section of Jagɛi Nuär.

According to Nuär custom, as it is for the rest of the indigenous Africans, it is a moral obligation for the living to erect the line tree for the deceased ones. It is said that Kuolaŋ had exercised such moral obligation to marry wives for his two deceased sisters. Furthermore, it is stated that Kuolaŋ worked hard to marry many wives to his deceased relatives, as he was able to acquire good numbers of cattle legitimately and justly. It is asserted that there is a clear message about the moral necessity to acquire material through hardship in a short time as in the case of Kuolaŋ.

According to one reliable source, Kuolaŋ lived near a powerful elderly kuär muɔn (Earth-Master) by the name of Nuan Liep. Nuan had a principal spiritual authority over Kuolaŋ. During this period of being together, unfortunately,

---

62 Jedeit. J. Riek & Naomi R. Pendle, *Speaking Truth to Power in South Sudan, Oral Stories of the Nuër Prophet,* p. 18.

the youngest wife of Nuan Liep was attracted to Kuolaŋ. Consequently, he committed adultery with her, which resulted in pregnancy. Consequently, Nuan and his sons became angry. They were planning day and night to kill Kuolaŋ. Every day, he was hiding himself in a bush fearing for his own life.

One day, he decided to go to Nuan's luak-byre carrying with him a big fish, which was the only thing for him to compensate Nuan. When Kuolaŋ arrived at the house of Nuan, he found out that he had gone out for farming. At that time, only his wives were at home. He gave a fish that he brought to the wives of Nuan to cook it for him. When Nuan came back home from farming, he was served by his wife out of the best fish, fresh fish ever cooked for the first time.

The fish was so tasteful and delicious that Nuan enjoyed eating it. He asked his wife, "Who has provided this fish?" His wife answered him, "It was Kuolaŋ Kët." He immediately ordered her to search for Kuolaŋ to be brought to him. He arrived; he then approached Nuan with a sharpened spear in his hand. It is asserted that Kuolaŋ lay down flat in front of Nuan and told Nuan to behead him for committing an act of adultery with his wife. It is said that the act of confession of Kuolaŋ plus the big fish that he brought to Nuan had compelled him to accept reconciliation. Nuan was convinced by the confession of Kuolaŋ and sought no more revenge against him. Both Kuolaŋ and Nuan were reconciled by an act of humility based on sincere confession and true remorse from the heart as it was documented below.

5.1.2 Dramatic Ritual Purification for Kuolaŋ

Nuan knew that Kuolaŋ had to pay the fine but had asked him to bring anything he had as a symbol of reconciliation. According to J. Riek and R. Pendle, Kuolaŋ had only fish oil (thiir) as a leftover from the meal. Pity his situation, Nuan ordered him to find a cum-cöm (snail shell) from the river bank and fill it with oil. It was confirmed that the fish oil, which was cooked, was brought to Nuan by Kuolaŋ. Nuan asked Kuolaŋ to lie down naked in front of him. He pulled back his fore penis and consequently, poured on it the fish oil brought by Kuolaŋ. J. Riek and R. Pendle state that Nuan said, "Kuolaŋ, my nephew, if the God of this country is there for us, then something big is waiting for you."[63] He promised that the suffering of Kuolaŋ would end and that his name would be remembered by begetting many children.

According to J. Riek and R. Pendle, this period was characterized by various factors such as large-scale famine from 1880-1882, and flooding from 1884-1887 in western Nuär. As the dispute between Nuan and Kuolaŋ was settled through reconciliation, the time of harvest came and hunger ended that year.

After this peaceful period, another flood came upon the land, which forced Kuolaŋ to go back to fishing areas. In that following year, another severe flood flashed the land, which resulted in a poor harvest. J. Riek and R. Pendle emphasized that after this period Maani̱ revealed himself to Kuolaŋ. It was confirmed that Kuolaŋ went as usual to the river for fishing, using the technique of ti̱er, whereby small sticks or thick grass

63 Jedeit. J. Riek & Naomi R. Pendle, *Speaking Truth to Power in South Sudan, Oral Stories of the Nuër Prophet,* p. 22.

are fixed in rows in the water to indicate the coming of fish. However, the small sticks did not move. He caught nothing that day. Finally, he came back home completely exhausted.

5.1.3 The Incidence of Kuolaŋ's Seizure

According to J. Riek and R. Pendle, Kuolaŋ's cousin Yɔak had realized his failure. Yɔak decided to take a black and a white goat to a riverbank to make a petition to the divinities for Kuolaŋ to give him a chance to catch more fish. It was said that towards the sunset, something of magnitude moved towards the direction of Kuolaŋ in the riverbank. Being terrified by the movement of water caused by the unusual creature, he both feared but hoped that it might be a big fish.

The creature came within his reach, and he slammed his fishing spear down upon it. J. Riek and R. Pendle state that Kuolaŋ hit it on the back of the head. Instantly, there was an explosion. Unfortunately, it was not a fish but a big snake called 'lou' in the Nuär language. Immediately, Kuolaŋ was pushed away by the water towards the land as if he were dead. He felt unconscious and instantly felt sickly. He could not find his way home and remained there at the riverbank completely paralyzed.

At home, Jiath Kör and the mother of Kuolaŋ did know where he was. They both feared that an animal might have eaten him. They both rushed to the bank of the riverbank calling out in the dark but they could hear no answer. Finally, they heard a whispered answer in reply. According to a reliable source, it was like a miracle that the divinity of DENG had directed both Jiath Kör and his mother to where he was lying down helpless.

It was said that at this time, Maani- *(*spirit of seizure*)* appeared to Kuolaŋ in the image of a hornless black bull (thäk mä cɔ̱t). They argue that upon seeing the bull in a vision, Kuolaŋ collapsed and consequently became powerless. After he came to his senses, he realized that he had seen a vision, which required instant sacrifice. When his mother and Jiath were almost approaching him, he advised them to keep far from him, which they both obeyed. He asked them to throw grass upon him first. Immediately he appeared like a madman. They took him home and burned a fire near him to warm himself. Now, it was understood that Kuolaŋ was seized by the divinity called Maani.

His madness deepened and he could go around holding a shrine stick (riak). This had made many people who were around debate whether this could be attributed to his mother's minor guan kuolani (a form of kuuth piny-earthly-spirits). However, it was said that "Those who called Kuolaŋ Kët mad and who dismissed his authority, started to die one by one." This made many people pose many questions, whether he has more power than his mother's minor guan kulong (form of kuuth piny-earthly-spirits). Those who considered him a madman and died were famous for his songs and are known by everyone in western Nuär. First, Nyadaah Liad (tiet), Dou Kuai, third, Kɔaat Jääl, fourth, Jɔk Baak, and fifth, Caath Ɔbaŋ.

5.1.4 His Surrender to the British Administration

The assassination of Captain Fergusson, commonly known as Wuɔrkuei in western Nuär by Col Weng and Gatkek Jiek-(also known as Kuel Jiak) had brought with it a serious deterioration in terms of relationships between western Nuär British Administration with western Nuär. According to H. Johnson, "Fergusson landed, going out, 'on a carrier, borne on the shoulder of four porters, sitting upright with a notebook and a pencil in his hand.' Once on shore, he was attacked and stabbed to death by Gatkek Jiek and Col Weng."[64] This assassination took place at Lake Jor. According to H. Johnson's version, the most dramatic and best-known murder of a British office in the Sudan, after that of Gordon in Khartoum, was the assassination of Captain V.H. Fergusson by two Nuong (Nyuɔŋ) Nuär on 14 December 1927.

Consequently, the British Administration demanded the handing over of Gatkek Jiek and Col Weng to face justice. Due to this unfortunate incident, the Nyuɔŋ Nuär suffered because of the assassination of Fergusson (Wɔrkuei). The pressure was mounting upon Nyuɔŋ Nuär, specifically on their head chief Gatluak Nyääk. He was commissioned to arrest and hand over Gatkëk Jiëk and Cuɔl Wɛŋ to the British Administration. As a result, Gatluak fled from Nyuɔŋ Nuär to Dɔk Nuär to seek refuge there. The Dɔk Nuär were aware of the negative consequence that would come from the British Commander upon them, they categorically refused to accommodate him. Instead, they asked him to proceed to Jagɛi Nuär, specifically to the house of Kuolaŋ Kët.

Consequently, Gatluak Nyääk and his groups arrived in Jagɛi. Kuolaŋ Kët in his own house (luak Maani) accommodated them. When The British Commander arrived at a village called Kuo bordering Jagɛi and Dɔk Nuär, he requested Kuolaŋ to hand over Gatluak and his criminals. However, Kuolaŋ insisted that it is not normal for a Nuär

64 Douglas H. Johnson, *Nuër Prophets*, p. 270.

to hand someone to his enemy. Kuolaŋ argued that the case should be settled through dialogue and negotiation to arrive at compensation based on traditional practice.

Kuolaŋ persistence not to hand Gatluak Nyääk and his criminals as they were called, was based on Nuär's concept of justice. As Fergusson had put it, "None of my Nuär (the western Nuär) will tolerate injustice in his day life even from a witch doctor (prophet)."[65] The persistence of the British commander in requesting the handing-over of Gatluak Nyääk and his two criminals had brought serious disagreement between Jagɛi Nuär under the leadership of Kuolaŋ and the British Administration. The British Commander insisted that Gatluak and his criminals should be handed over to him while he was at the border at the village called Kuo, near cɔ̱ɔ̱t Jiök stream at the side of Dɔk.

However, the British Commander and his army became adamant. Nevertheless, prophet Kuolaŋ asked Jagɛi Nuär not to attack him and his army. He added that if they want to come, let them come to my house, specifically to the place of my ox called Thääk mä Pɛɛr at the Kraal. A man from Gawäär Nuär who was accommodated by the Jaba̱ny section by the name Ŋuɛn Thööny, (also nicknamed Mur Bil Liɛth), with others, responded by attacking the British Commander and his army at the border of cɔ̱ɔ̱t Jiök stream. He speared one of the soldiers and said "Bil liɛth mä ci̱ murɛ wee dhɔc"-mentioning the colour of his cow.

A man by the name of Thööny Kuɔŋ from ciëŋ Möök while they were preparing themselves to join the fight at cɔ̱ɔ̱t Jiök stream, told women "Look at us with my friends, we shall not come back. When prophet Kuolaŋ was told that Mur

65 Cf. E.E. Evans-Pritchard, *Nuër Religion,* p. 307.

Bil Liɛth had already launched an attack against the British Commander and his army and had speared one of them, he said, ca moy wum ɛ Mur Bil Liɛth-Mur Bil Liɛth has put it an end to it. Such fighting resulted in a bloody war, which led to the burning of the luak-byre of Kuolaŋ and his displacement from his territory in 1929.

To resolve this unfortunate problem, Jiath Kör intervened by offering one of his daughters to the British commander as a sign of peace between Jagɛi Nuär and the British Administration. According to James Ŋuany Kɛt, "Jiath Kör had offered his daughter by name Nyakat Jiath and an ox to the British Administration. The British Administration in return offered him a British flag to be raised in his territory as a sign of peace between them."[66]

After serious consequences of war upon Jagɛi Nuär, prophet Kuolaŋ decided to hand himself to the British Administration in March 1930. Consequently, he was taken to Omdurman to the base of the Mahdiyya. According to J. Riek and R. Pendle, the name 'Maani' itself is commonly assumed to derive from the Mahdi prophetic Islamic Religious leader of the Mahdiyya. Kuolaŋ stayed for three years in Omdurman, from September 1898. Consequently, he became sickly. At last, the British Administration decided to send him back to his home village.

Finally, H. Johnson states that "Col Weng, the first murderer was arrested in April 1929."[67] According to H. Johnson, Wuon sought Gatkek out in a hiding place among the Gawäär and persuaded him to return to Nyuong, assuring

66 Interview with James Ŋuany Kɛt, the maternal son of Nyaruace Kulang Ket, at St. Paul's Major Seminary, Juba-Munuki, (South Sudan), 31/07/2019.

67 Douglas H. Johnson, *Nuër Prophets,* p. 272.

him that 'the Turuk had left'. Once he was back in his village, Wuon arrested Gatkek and handed him over to the government. Another source states that Gatkek Jiek was finally captured in 1930, and he too, implicated Cak Riang and other Dur headmen. Wuon was reinstated as chief of Dur a few days before Gatkek's execution. H. Johnson asserts that through that time Gatluak was imprisoned in Malakal, where the government was convinced of his guilt. Eventually, it was discovered that he was not guilty and he was reinstated.

5.1.5 The Dramatic Burial of Prophet Kuolaŋ

After Kuolaŋ was released, we were above-mentioned by the British Administration in Omdurman. Upon his arrival at Adɔk el Bar-Thok Yiër Kiir, C̲a̲a̲th ƆBaŋ, the government chief, detained him. J. Riek and R. Pendle stated he told Kuolaŋ that he could die anywhere and mocked him about his age. However, before his being buried alive, C̲a̲a̲th warns Kuolaŋ to look at the sun because it would be the last time that he would see it. This took place in a village called Thör near Adɔk. C̲a̲a̲th commanded his team to dig the grave for the burial of Kuolaŋ. According to J. Riek and R. Pendle, there was resistance from Maani̲ three times in the form of an explosion during the trial to bury Kuolaŋ alive in a tomb. The same source quoted above says that Kuolaŋ got out of the grave three times.

According to J. Riek and R. Pendle, the eyewitnesses were Kuolaŋ's wife Biel Deng, and his daughter Nyaruac. Before Kuolaŋ was forced to be buried alive in the grave, he removed his ring, and his leopard skin, took his sleeping rug and pipe, and handed them to his daughter Nyaruac. He warned his daughter that his descendants should never sleep in the village called Thör. Kuolaŋ told Ca̱a̱th that he would come back to seek in the form of an elephant as revenge. After a couple of months, the British Administration for being too tyrannical, oppressive, and authoritarian dismissed Ca̱a̱th.

According to Douglas' source, Caath Obang, the Dok chief responsible for Kolang Ket's death, had been made chief of the northern Nuong in Gaaluak's absence. Although Coriat approved of him, Nyuong, Nyuong as a tyrant and oppressive leader rejected him. H. Johnson confirms his killing by an elephant. "He was killed by an elephant while hunting in August 1930. His death was now attributed to MAANI's revenge. Before Kolang Kët died, as the earth was being shovelled into his grave, he was supposed to have cursed Caath saying, 'The next time you meet me, I come as an elephant.'"[68]

After a couple of months – as above-mentioned, the British Administration for being too authoritative dismissed Ca̱a̱th. J. Riek and R. Pendle state that sometime later, a large elephant appeared from the north and moved south through Jagɛi to Adɔk. Everyone was amazed by its size and magnitude. Eventually, it reached Gul in Thar ciëŋ Dɔk and everybody was frightened. Ca̱a̱th commanded everyone to stop crying believing that his gun would be able to fire the elephant while forgetting the promise of revenge from prophet Kuolaŋ.

J. Riek and R. Pendle confirm that when Ca̱a̱th shot at the elephant, the gun's bullets failed to hit the target. It was asserted that the elephant charged him, caught him, and disappeared with him as if it were in the storm. Nobody saw Ca̱a̱th or his gun again. After Ca̱a̱th's disappearance

68 Douglas H. Johnson, Nuër Prophets, p. 272.

with the elephant, jakɔ̱a̱k (crows) sat in the luaks-byres and sang that an elephant had killed Ca̱a̱th. The jakɔ̱a̱k (crows) repeated this message in many luaks until everyone received the message. Consequently, everyone recalled what prophet Kuolaŋ had told Ca̱a̱th before his burial, that he would come back to seek revenge and that Ca̱a̱th would mistake him for an elephant. Prophet Kuolaŋ could not wait for the final judgment; he fulfilled his promise by coming to attack see Ca̱a̱th in the form of an elephant.

5.2 Prophetess Nyaruac Kuolaŋ Kët

Prophetess Nyaruac was born to the following parents: her father was Kuolaŋ Kët and her mother was by name Yie̱y Ruac. Yie̱y Ruac was the first in the list of the wives of Kuolaŋ Kët. Her father married many wives as we have mentioned earlier. She was from a big family because her father had a lot of cows after the spirit called Maani seized him.

5.1 Her Girlhood and Marital Status

Nyaruac Kulaŋ grew up in her father's village called 'Limpuot' (nicknamed also as Tharuɔ̱b Nyaruac Kuolaŋ). According to her maternal son James Ŋuany Kɛt, "She grew up to the age of maturity and played with her age-mates and danced with her boyfriends during the drum dance at Limpuot."[69] When she reached the age of maturity, a certain man called Go̱lo̱ŋ Kuoth in a village called Patit engaged her. After their wedding, she stayed for some time at her parent's

69 Interview with James Ŋuany Kɛt, the maternal son of Nyaruace Kulang Ket, at St. Paul's Major Seminary, Juba-Munuki, (South Sudan), 19/06/2019.

home as the Nuär customary law required.

However, before she could go to the home of her bridegroom, something happened to her. She had manifested a certain abnormal behaviour characterized by general fatigue and laziness. The family began to monitor her situation but nobody knew exactly the kind of sickness she was going through. During this period, Nyaruac was constantly complaining of bodily fatigue and itching on her hair.

Everybody among her kinsmen and kinswomen was worried about her situation. The family suspected that she might be seized by MAANI (the spirit of her father). Unfortunately, nobody among the members of her family could remember that when her father died, he removed his ring, his leopard skin, and took his sleeping rug and pipe, and handed them to his daughter Nyaruac.

During this period of sickness that was concentrated on itching her hair, she approached her maternal uncle, Dayim Wur to shave her hair. According to Kutai Kɛt, "Dayim was both her maternal uncle and a friend to her father Kuolaŋ."[70] After the serious insistence on asking Dayim, to cut her hair at night, Dayim said to her, "I will shave your hair tomorrow my daughter."

Early in the morning, Dayim rushed to her parent's home and brought with him an ox with the colour that the Nuär usually call 'jack'. While he was bringing the ox, he was singing the songs of *MAANI*. He arrived and said to Nyaruac, 'Come out my daughter to cut your hair.' Nyaruac came out from the hut but instead of approaching Dayim, she ran straight towards the river in front of her father's kraal. She

70 Interview with Kutai Kɛt, the maternal son of Nyaruace Kulang Ket, at St. Paul's Major Seminary, Juba-Munuki, (South Sudan), 19/06/2019.

jumped deep into the pool while her uncle speared the ox. After he had speared the ox, he ran after her and removed her from the river. She slipped from her uncle and ran straight inside the byre-luck. The byre-luak according to Nuär culture, is supposed to be for men but since her seizure by MAANI, Nyaruac stayed in a byre-luak for the rest of her life.

After her seizure by MAANI, many people came in a multitude to offer sacrifices and celebrated the marvellous occasion of MAANI by seizing Nyaruac. From that moment, Nyaruac became prophetess and successor of her father Kuolaŋ who was buried alive by Ca̱a̱th Ɣɔ̱kbaŋ at the village called Thör at Dɔk. Consequently, her kinsmen returned the bride-wealth to Go̱lo̱ŋ Kuoth who had betrothed her before her seizure.

H. Johnson stated that Nyaruac (the daughter of speech) was married at the time of her father's captivity. According to him, she was without children and left her husband to tend her father in detention in Adok. According to H. Johnson, "Nyaruac Kolang, the prophetess of MAANI who, after the death of her father Kuolang Ket, achieved far greater spiritual influence among the Western Nuär than any contemporary male prophet."[71]

5.2 Her Miraculous Powers

First, she Restored peace between Nuär and Dinka. After that, a team from the Dinka community called 'Luäc Dinka' came to visit her in her village. They brought with them a Drum called 'Bul Dinka [Bul Jäŋä] which is still at Limpuot today. According to Ŋuany, "The team explained to her that they

71 Douglas H. Johnson, *Nuër Prophets*, p. 279.

experienced a period of drought for four years. She promised them plenty of rain on their arrival back to their community while she gave them tobacco as a sign of authority."[72] Second, during her time, there was no raiding of cows between Nuär and Dinka. The community of Dinka Luäc attributed to her the name 'Nyamandit'. She was understood as a peaceful prophetess, as H. Johnson confirms, "When the divinity caught her, people at once knew that it was MAANI', her brother Kuol Kolang later recalled, 'so she did as her father did. She said, "I will not go to raid people."[73]

Third, Nyakuolaŋ was a professional rainmaker for all those who sought help from her. Fourth, she was able to treat various diseases, which affected both humans and animals. Nyakuolaŋ discharged her doctrinal authority like any other Nuär prophet through tobacco. Fifth, she banned both brewing local wines in her kingdom and banned fights among the clans. How was she able to do this? It was through her power.

Those women who ignored her authority and continued making local brewing were always faced with the explosion of their barrels-tiny jur. For example, this is due to the stubbornness of some women who could not listen to her decree. Sixth, she banned fighting between clans by demarcating with tobacco the line between the two clans who would like to engage in fighting. However, those who violated her instruction ended up in a disaster of being killed. According to H. Johnson, Nyaruac established her position as prophetess without government surveillance or supervision.

---

72 Interview with Mr. James Ŋuany Kɛt, the maternal son of Nyaruac Kulaŋ Ket, at St. Paul's Major Seminary, Juba-Munuki, (South Sudan),19/06/2019.

73 Douglas H. Johnson, *Nuër Prophets*, p. 279.

H. Johnson states that Nyaruac was a good judge and this had a good influence on the Nuär. They considered her a sensible and pleasant person to talk to. She was known for preventing fighting, a peaceful pursuit. She experienced no opposition and wholly committed herself to her vocation as a prophetess without compromise at all.

5.3 Rules for Drum and Its Sexual Norms

First, during the drum play, she used to sit outside until the end of playing the drum. Second, while people are dancing, nobody is allowed to take a girl to another place. Third, when a man and a girl violate this principle, specifically by moving away from the place of playing the drum to engage in sexual intercourse, they will stick to each other and will never be separated, unless they call people for help.

When they are brought to her, she will bless them and they will separate from each other. For example, her maternal son Juɔ̱l Makur stuck with a girl by the name of Nyathäyä Jual Riak while engaging in sexual intercourse during the playing of a drum. Realizing that they could not separate themselves, they called for help. According to Kutai Kɛt, "A multitude of people came to their rescue by bringing them to the prophetess Nyaruac. Consequently, she prayed over them. Finally, they were separated from each other."[74]

We mentioned the name of Juɔ̱l Makur who got stuck with Nyathäyä Jual Riak while engaging in sexual intercourse during the playing of a drum, which means that the scandal was witnessed by many people. Juɔ̱l Makur was related

74 Kutai Kɛt the maternal son of Nyaruace Kulang Ket, at St. Paul's Major Seminary, Juba-Munuki, (South Sudan), 19/06/2019.

to prophetess Nyaruac but it seems her moral teaching on sexual intercourse during the playing of a drum, has no room for favouritism. After such a scandalous incident, nobody attempted again to engage in sexual intercourse there.

5.4 Her Willing Acceptance to Live a Virginal Life

Earlier when we treated marriage, we emphasized d so much its importance as if nobody could miss it, however, here we are confronted with a woman whose life of virginity suits her call. One can imagine how difficult it was for her kinsmen to return the cows to her bridegroom Go̱lo̱ŋ Kuoth's family. Such incident is very rare in the Nuär society, Nuär Catholic priests should take Prophetess Nyaruac as a par excellent model, and Nuär girls who would like to respond to the vocation to sisterhood in the Catholic Church. Even among the Nuär, a barren woman does not live without a husband. The case of prophetess Nyaruac was so unique.

If you are a Nuär Catholic priest, know that from the cultural perspective, Prophetess Nyaruac has given you an example of excellence. If you are a religious Nuär sister from the Catholic Church, know that Prophetess Nyaruac has given you an example of par excellence. If Prophetess Nyaruac commanded moral authority on sexual matters with radical requirements, nobody should doubt that she lived her virginal life without wavering. She lived it radically and to the full. Nyaruac should be the first woman among the Nuär who professed her religious life and lived it to the full. She died in 1973.

5.5 Critiques on Nuär Prophets

Douglas H. Johnson has written a very good book on Nuär prophets entitled 'Nuër Prophets' both in the West and in the East. He emphasized the emergence of Nuär prophets at the time of colonization that is, the time of British Rule over Sudan then known as the 'Condominium Rule Policy' from 1899-1947. In his treatment of those prophets, he states that the seizure revealed the spirit's specific name to the person he seized and to the people. This happened with all the Nuär prophets and prophetess both in the West and in the East. Therefore, a seizure without a name will be uncommunicable and ineffective to the Nuär community.

H. Johnson's emphasis on the emergence of the Nuär prophets and prophetesses during the period of colonization overshadowed the normal intervention of God in human situations through various means. Nuär prophets and prophetesses both in the West and in the East, never appeared as resistant to foreign invaders but exercised supernatural activities in favor of others. S. Mbiti puts it right by saying that among the Nuär 'prophets may perform sacrifices on behalf of the individuals or of the people of their neighbourhoods in time of sickness, for bareness, and on other occasions when spiritual aid is required.'

Furthermore, St. Augustine used to say that 'God, who created you without you, cannot save you without you.' Therefore, the role of any true prophet is to help people understand their Creator, to believe in him as their Creator for the salvation of all. This requires cooperation from humans through various means provided by God. Even the choice of any true prophet is one way for God to exercise his protection and mercy, and his love to humanity through that prophet.

The unselfish God who created the whole universe cannot allow it to suffer without his aid and intervention. In those primitive periods and times, he provided means for human survival through others such as prophets and prophetesses. However, such marvellous powers given to some Nuär prophets and prophetesses, were misused and those graces of God were employed for self-benefit and enrichment. Such misuse of God's graces generally shows itself through evil activities such as raiding, raiding other tribes, and waging war against each other. Some were very good at eliminating those individuals who opposed them. Some do arrive at the level of marrying wives to their seizures.

Furthermore, a Nuär would never believe in those prophets or prophetesses except through showing supernatural powers and miracles. It is only when they receive strange and unusual lessons from those prophets and prophetesses that they can believe. For instance, by uttering evil words to their opponents. This happened for the majority of Nuär prophets and Kolang Kët, the prophet of MAANI in the West, was an excellent example. He listed in his songs his opponents whom he had eliminated simply by using words.

For instance, Caath Ɔ̱baŋ who buried him alive was the last opponent whom he killed and consequently took him to the air when he appeared to him in the form of an elephant. He could not wait for the final judgment of God. Here, our critiques of Nuär prophets and prophetesses would allow us to point out that the everlasting mercy and the forgiveness of God sometimes were missing in those prophets and prophetesses.

Prophetess Nyaruac, daughter of Prophet Kolang Kët

of the western Nuär, deserves the true name 'prophet'. Nyakuolaŋ dedicated her whole life as a single devoted prophetess. Her uniqueness is demonstrated as follows: first, she was the only prophetess who was never disturbed by the British Administration. Second, she was a peaceful prophetess. Third, she neither married for herself nor her Seizure 'MAANI.' After she died in 1973, till now, nobody among her family members married her a wife which is not normal in Nuär culture. It seems as if her seizure suppressed such moral obligation among the members of her family to marry her a wife. Fourth, this is not a normal practice among the Nuär; nevertheless, with prophetess Nyaruac, it was possible.

The majority of people of South Sudan and foreigners such as anthropologists like Douglas H. Johnson who wrote his book on Nuär prophets entitled 'Nuër Prophets' knew Prophet Ŋundeŋ Böŋ for his prophecies about the war that lasted for many years between Sudan and South Sudan. For example, the civil war that broke out between the Sudanese Army and the Paramilitary Rapid Support Forces (the Militias) in Sudan on Saturday, April 15, 2023, was prophesized by Prophet Ŋundɛŋ when he said in one of his songs: "Katum Baari, ɛ duŋ rol mayok, ci̱ nyikä thia̱ŋ kɛ riɛm, määthdä cuor, määthdä or-Khartoum Bhari belongs to rolmayok my eyes are filled with blood my friend is a vulture, my friend is vulture."[75]

You can further confirm Douglas H. Johnson's book on "The Nuer Prophets. Here, we have a true prophet Ŋundeŋ who lived in the 19th century, nevertheless, he was able to see what was going to happen in the 21st century, the civil war in the Sunda. Prophet Ŋundeŋ did have capacity sight,

75 J. Tab Charoa, *The Nuär, Culture, and Moral Evaluation*, Rafiki for Printing and Publishing, Juba, 2021, P.223.

which surpassed advanced scientific contemporary telescope. As said in one of his songs, ca pɛɛthdɛ bi̱ luäŋ, Ŋundɛŋ ca pɛɛthdɛ bi̱ luäŋ, kuthɛ to̱ny bi̱ wee wuu! Bi̱ kuär waŋdɛ bo̱l luak- Ŋundɛŋ's witchcraft will not weaken, Ŋundɛŋ Böŋ witchcraft will not weaken, for he blew his pipe, going "wuu! In addition, the master's eyes lit up the byre.

By reading the life of prophet Ŋundeŋ, one could see the power of God among the primitive people. In the life of Ŋundeŋ, in all truth, 'from the highest degree of the madness of Ŋundeŋ such as 'living on human faces and tobacco', God can bring good out of evil. From the highest of Ŋundeŋ, everyone including his wives, lost hope in him and rejected him as a madman.

Through the power of God, he turned the mad man Ŋundeŋ into a prophet with a mission. In a situation of hopelessness, God can surprise us by making a U-turn to our hopeless situation, he did it for Ŋundeŋ and he can still do it to anyone. Paradoxically, 'from the highest degree of the madness of Ŋundeŋ such as 'living on human faces and tobacco' there came abundant graces upon prophet Ŋundeŋ and his contemporaries. The might of God is manifested by bringing holiness out of sinfulness, and by bringing the good out of evil with his amazing power.

The rejection of Ŋundeŋ by his contemporary Nuär community highlights the rejection of every prophet who tries to proclaim the 'revealed truth of salvation from God to humanity.' This happened to all the prophets in the Old Testament until Jesus and his followers. Jesus himself articulates this clearly by saying… "A prophet is not without honour except in his native place and among his kin and in his own house" (Mk 6:4). "Woe to you, scribes and Pharisees, you hypocrites. You build the tombs of the prophets and adorn the memorials of the righteous, and you say, 'If we had lived in the days of our ancestors, we would not have joined them in shedding the prophets' blood. Thus, you bear witness against yourselves that you are the children of those who murdered the prophets; now fill up what your ancestors measured out" (Mt 23:19-31).

It is a challenge to proclaim the revealed truth of God for the salvation of humanity when this revealed truth is not clear to the ordinary man but only clear to the prophets. In his famous saying to his contemporary Nuär, Ŋundeŋ used to say, 'Sons of my uncle, it is very painful when the truth is only known to one person.'

5.6 List of other Nuär Prophets

The following magicians-dayiɛmni̱ such as first, Jɔk, pajɔɔk, malual, mathiaŋ, magäywuɔ̱t, colwic, biɛl, wäl (witchcrafts) truth and madut, all these, ought to be abandoned completely. Their owners confuse people in terms of cheating and exercise them. They cause many problems in the communities. Their owners are liars.

First, Ŋundɛŋ Böŋ was seized by the spirit called Deng Kur in the 19th century. He hailed from Lou Nuär Wa̱a̱d-Buordiid. Therefore, after he died in 1906, the spirit passed on to his son Guɛk Ŋundɛŋ Bööŋ who was killed by the British in 1929 during the war between Nuär and the forces of the Anglo-Egyptian condominium. Due respect ought to be shown to him. He prophesied the current civil war in Sudan, which broke out on April 15, 2023.

Second, a spirit called Tɛɛny Dhurgön in the 19th century

seized Puɔ̱t Nyuɔn. After Puɔ̱t Nyuon had perished, the spirit passed on to his son Maca̱a̱r Tɛny and later, to Gatluɔ̱k Maca̱a̱r Tɛny Who died two years ago in 2017.

Third, Kuolaŋ Kët was seized by the divine power called Ma̱a̱ni Wa̱n in 1921. Sultan Ca̱th Hokbang Koop buried Prophet Kuolaŋ Kët alive in 1925. Hence, after his death, the spirit of Ma̱a̱ni Wa̱n passed on to his daughter Nyaruac Kuolaŋ who died in 1973 naturally. Afterwards, the spirit passed on to Kuɔl Kolaŋ Kët who died in 2008. Prophet Kuolaŋ Ket hailed from Jagɛi Nuär in Koch County.

Fourth, Dɛŋ Lekä was seized by the divinity called Diw in the 19th century. Prophet Dɛŋ Lekä hailed from Gawar Nuär of Ayod County. Fifth, Ruei Kuiy was seized by the divine power called Tut Kuɔ̱r in the 19th century. Prophet Ruei Kuiy hailed from Laak Nuär of Fangak County.

Sixth, Nyäwɛi Nhial was seized by the divine power called Dɛŋ Löth Cöm" in the 19th century. After his death, the spirit passed on to his son Turɔaɣ Nyäwɛi, then to Mut Tutrɔaɣ (Gatdɛ̈ɛ̈ŋ) who died this year 2019. Prophet Nyäwɛi hailed from Bul Nuär of Mayom. Now the Spirit is passed on to Garäŋ Mut Turɔaɣ.

Seventh, the spirit called "Tilliŋ Nyin-yar" in the 19th century seized Li̱a̱a̱ Wäl Rɛth. Thereby, after his death, the spirit passed on to his son Manyuɔn Li̱a̱a̱ Wäl Rɛth. Prophet Li̱a̱a̱ Wäl Rɛth hailed from Dok Nuär of Leer County. Eighth, Ki̱i̱r Kaker was seized by the divine power called Wiw. Identical spirit passed on to his offspring Kun Thɔ̱a̱l in Eastern Nuär and most of his descendants of W. Jikany Nuär respectively. Prophet Ki̱i̱r Kaker hailed from W. Jikany Nuär of Guit County.

Ninth, Biliw Wiw was seized by the divine power called

Däpiir in the 19th century. Hence, after his death, the spirit passed on to his son Gatluak Nyäk Gɔ̱k, and then to his grandson Danhier Gatluak Nyak who was killed in 1982. The Leopard Skin Chief Biliw Wiw hailed from Nyuɔŋ Nuär of Panyijiar County.

Tenth, Wuɔ̱n Kuɔth was seized by the divine power called "Diu" in the 19th century. After his death, the spirit passed on to his son Malual Wuɔ̱n Kuɔth who died in 2009. The Leopard Skin Chief Wuɔ̱n Kuɔth hailed from Nyuɔŋ Nuär in the Door area of Panyijiar County.

Eleventh, Gatluak Yiey was seized by the divine power called "Ni̱ëŋ" in the 1970s and died in the 1990s. The Leopard Skin Chief Gatluak Yiey hailed from Nyuɔŋ Nuär in the Door area of Panyijiar County. Twelfth, Wud Nyaaŋ Gatkek was seized by divine power in the 1990s and died in 2006. He was the founder of the "Nuär White Army" instead of "Bunum". His resistance was late Wud Nyaaŋ Gatkek to external enemies like the Sudanese Armed Forces (Malakal Town) in the 1990s. The Leopard Skin Chief Wud Nyaaŋ hailed from Laak Nuär of Fangak County. Thirteenth, the Prophet of modern times is Da̱k Kuëth of Lou Nuär. Prophet Dak Kueth is active and in control of the youth up-to-date.

Conclusion

Chapter five presents the life of two prophets of western Nuär, Kuolaŋ Kët and Nyaruac Kuolaŋ. It also discussed the background of their lives; e.g. Kuolaŋ's wives and his moral life before the seizure. The chapter also illustrates Nuan's dramatic ritual spiritual performance and his blessing upon Kuolaŋ, the incident of Kuolaŋ's seizure, and his surrender to the British Administration. Finally, it discussed Kuolaŋ being buried alive by Ca̱a̱th Ɔ̱Baŋ and his resurrection as a sign of revenge.

The chapter has also presented Nyaruac Kuolaŋ, her family background, her girlhood, and her miraculous power. It has discussed rules for her drum and its moral requirements and her acceptance to live a virginal life.

CHAPTER SIX

TRUE UNION BETWEEN MAN AND WOMAN

Introduction

Chapter six presents E.E. Evans-Pritchard's famous article on Nuär Marriage entitled *"African: Journal of the International African Institute" Vol. 18. No. 1 (Jan. 1948), pp.29-40.* In this famous article, the chapter deals with marriage among the Nuär as presented by such an outstanding anthropologist who spent most of his time living among the Nuär as an active observer. The author documented in his article, the general features of the ceremonies of Nuär marriage, which this chapter presents. The chapter will discuss those general features such as the preliminaries, the betrothal, the wedding, consummation; and the birth of a child. Finally, it will present a critique of the article.

In his own words, Evans-Pritchard states that marriage thus, reaches completion through many stages: betrothal ceremony, wedding ceremony, consummation ceremony, the birth of a child, the bringing of the first-born to his father's byre, and the presentation of the spoon-tuŋ to the wife, is a sign of her domestic separation from her family. She comes to her husband's home not as a wife but as a mother, whose breasts have suckled a child of their lineage.

6. Marriage Among the Nuär

According to Evans-Pritchard, among the Nuär, marriage is brought about by the payment of the bride's wealth and by the performance of certain ceremonial rites. The rites cannot take place without the payments, but even transfers of cattle, do not by themselves bring about the union. He states that both are necessary and they proceed in a connected movement towards the full establishment of marital union. Each enforces and reinforces the other. The bride's people can, by holding up the rites, the bridegroom's people. The latter can, by withholding the cattle, induce the girl's family and kin to advance the ceremonies.

First, one pedal is pressed down and then the other as the marriage is propelled to its appointed end, which is the birth of children at home. It is understood that payment should have reached a certain point before the rite is held. The performance of the rite is the recognition of cattle up to that point. Payment of cattle and marital rites therefore, though there is no fixity about the alternation and no marriage is the same as another in this respect.

Evans-Pritchard states that the new social ties of conjugality and affinity are made stronger by each payment and by each ceremony. So, a marriage that is insecure at the beginning of the negotiation becomes surer with every new payment and rite; both sides, by the giving and receiving of cattle and by joint participation in the rites, become more deeply committed to bringing about the union. According to Evans-Pritchard, "A marriage which has reached the final rites may be regarded as a stable union and will generally prove to be so."[76]

6.1 General Features of Ceremonies

In his assertions, Evans-Pritchard emphasizes that the chief ceremonies are the larcieng-lärcieŋ, and the mut-wedding ceremony: the betrothal, the wedding, and the consummation- [dɔnyni̱ cökni̱]. He states that all these are important public events in Nuär life, though the betrothal rites are not held on so large a scale to the west of the Nile as to the east. In his observation, the preparations for them are made for days; the young people talk even weeks ahead, and about, especially, long before they take place. Those talks about engagement are usually held in the rainy season. This is because there is then plenty of millet for porridge and beer. Consequently, people have the energy of the well-fed and can travel long distances without fatigue and dance and make love with equal vigour.

Evans-Pritchard asserts that the district attends them, young men thinking as nothing of walking over ten miles to in the dancing, the mere coming together of so many people making marriage a memorable event. Neighbours thus, bear witness to the creation of the new social ties and by their presence, they sanction them. Evans-Pritchard observed that

76 E.E. Evans-Pritchard, "Africa: Journal of the International African Institute" Vol. 18, No. 1 (Jan., 1948), pp.29-40, Published by: Cambridge University Press on behalf of the International African Institute Stable.

neighbours from the crowd at marriage feasts, even though they have no direct concern with the union.

Evans-Pritchard states that apart from those people who attended the ceremonies for dancing, flirting, and general sociability and excitement, some attended it for more serious purposes. He confirms that it will be seen from the paper there are always, besides prolonged discussions about bride-wealth, sacrifices, and other rites, which have to be performed, and that interest only some people present families and the kinsmen of the bride and bridegroom.

In his own opinion, Evans-Pritchard stated that these are the rites that express the relations between husband and wife, husband's kin and wife's kin, and between the kin on one side or the other and the ghosts and spirits of their lineage. Furthermore, those who stood outside were only spectators and often paid no attention to the rite at all. Evans-Pritchard states that it is the dance, which gives the ceremonies their popularity and publicity; it is the rites, which express and bring about their purposes.

In his observation about the essential ceremonial rite of the sacrificial beast to both the ghosts and spirits, Evans-Pritchard asserts that an essential rite in the marriage ceremonies is the sacrifice of an animal to the ghosts and spirits by which they are made cognizant, and witnesses of the union in an address delivered to them before the animal is slain. He points out that this part of the rite, concerns only the close kin of the bride or bridegroom, and the address is sometimes spoken in so low a tone almost inaudible amid the general clamor. On this specific occasion, people chat and shout to each other about affairs that have no connection with the marriage or interpolate comments into the address, a long rambling speech that may refer to almost anything that interests, he mentions the object of the rite and puts into it now and again, some traditional phrases related to the occasion of wedding.

Furthermore, it is said that the young people are dancing, the women engaged in household tasks and it is the older men, mostly kinsmen of the bride and bridegroom, who gather round to watch the sacrifice, which to them is just the ceremony, like the bride-wealth talks and the beer-drinking. Evans-Pritchard has pointed out the aspect of confusion by stating that the sacrifice is often a moment of great confusion, with everyone shouting, advice, and instructions to everyone else and arguing good-humoredly about the division of the meat. He states that the specific religious part of a ceremony seems lost amid all the talk and movement, but it is the core of the ceremony, which occasions it and gives it meaning.

It is said that even the kinsmen of the bride or bridegroom, as the case may be, attend the sacrifice largely because it is the prelude to a division of meat, for though the ox is dedicated to the ghosts and spirits. Its material destiny is to be eaten by the kin of one partner in the marriage, who, being guests, have to be provided with meat by the kin of the other partner. The people who sacrificed the animal, usually an ox, eat very little of it and are interested in the religious part of the rite since it is their ancestors and spirits to whom the animal is dedicated. It is stated that "The visitors are not concerned with the ghosts and spirits of the other party but are interested in the meat which is their due, to each kinsman his customary portion."[77] A sacrifice is thus, a distribution of gifts of meat by the kin of one of the spouses to the kin of the other.

77 E.E. Evans-Pritchard "African: Journal of the International African Institute" p. 30.

In his observations, Evans-Pritchard asserts that one notices the same lack of formality in the order of the rites, and the sequence of their parts, as in the performance of them. The place of each movement is determined only by the logic of necessity. An ox has to be prepared before it is speared-jɔl kɛ lam a ŋuondɛ kän jɛk yiɛth. The sacrificial beast has to be skinned before it can be cut and cooked. Otherwise, there is merely a usual time for acts to be done, though it would not matter if they were merely different in time or performed in a different order. For example, it is usual to sacrifice an ox at the betrothal ceremony towards the end of the evening dance, but it can equally well be done the following morning. In his observation on Nuär rituals, Evans-Pritchard he argues that Nuär ritual procedure is generally happy-go-lucky.

6.2 Preliminaries

Generally, there has been a long understanding between the youth and the girl he wishes to marry and who has become his sweetheart (luum). Although, sometimes a youth decks himself as a bridegroom, and the company of another youth, arrayed in the ornaments of a best man and tours the countryside in search of a bride. In either case, the youth will not ask for the hand of the girl without her consent. According to Evans-Pritchard, a maiden consents to marry a youth only if he has cattle. According to George P. Murdock, Arthur Tuden, and Peter B. Hammond, marriage according to Nuär…" entails payment of a substantial bride price, which consists ideally of 40 head of cattle."[78]

78 George P. Murdock, Arthur Tuden, and Peter B. Hammond, "African Negro Art; Anthropology; Archaeology: Ancient Civilization; Muslims" *in the*

Evans-Pritchard argues that the young man and his friends must then ask her family and they will consult their kinsfolk. He affirms about marriage, the youth ought to have cattle and a good reputation. It is stated that everybody is aware of what is going on, long before they are formally asked for her hand. Therefore, when a girl tells menfolk in the byre, there are guests outside who wish to speak to them, the men know what they have come for. The suitor and his friends enter the byre and seat themselves to the right, the girl's people being seated to the left. They say that the girl has accepted them and ask whether the elders will accept them too. Evans-Pritchard affirms that the elders ask them what cattle they have.

According to Evans-Pritchard, this is the ri̱et ghot- [ri̱et ɣɔ̱ɔ̱k], the cattle talk**.** The best man answers for the suitor, who, to create a good impression. Both wear skins to cover their genitals *with*- [tuac thɔ̱ɔ̱nä according to Nuär] before possible future parents-in-law. It is said that the bridegroom's man and two other friends, accompany him through all the trials of marriage. Consequently, they take full advantage of the opportunities for love-making and courtship. The girl's people preliminarily accept the suits and the youths depart to eat at a neighbouring homestead since they cannot eat in the home of the bride at this stage.

Furthermore, there will later be other and more formal and definite discussions about the cattle in the byre of the father of the girl. The suitor has in the meanwhile been able to consult his own family and kinsmen. When he returns with his friends for further talks, the cattle are more precisely specified and earmarked for particular claimants. The girl's

---

Collier's Encyclopedia, Volume 1. of Twenty-Four Volumes, New York, P.F. Collier & Son Limited, (1995), pp. 257-270.

people are satisfied. At this specific juncture, Evans-Pritchard asserts that they say the marriage is finished and tell the bridegroom, as he can now properly be called, and his friends to bring the ghot lipa- [ɣɔ̱ɔ̱k lëp thuɔk], the cattle betrothal, on a certain day.

The discussion is still in an early stage and by 'finished' they mean only that they are prepared to continue negotiations based on the demands already met and to hold the betrothal ceremony. According to Evans-Pritchard, before the visitors rise to go. Consequently, various men who can claim distant cognatic kinship with the bride, too distant for them to receive assigned portions of the bride's wealth, may ask for gifts, ranging from a 'cow' (which means a sheep or a goat) to a spear. Some of their demands are at once satisfied, the spear being handed over there and then, while others are met with promises or evasion.

6.3 The Betrothal

It is said that a betrothal ceremony, larcieng-[lärciëŋ] or bul luom- [bul luɔ̱m], is not necessary. It is a possible step to proceed at once to the full wedding ceremony. This is sometimes done when a bridegroom is a rich man and the bride is just, a girl who has passed the usual age of marriage. Evans-Pritchard states that usually, the betrothal ceremony is held in the rainy season and the wedding ceremony in the following windy season. If there is a long interval, it is generally due to poverty otherwise.

A poor suitor pays two or three cows to a man who is short of stock at the time to obtain a lien on his small daughter, while he collects adequate bride wealth to marry her later on. Were the suitor a rich man, he would seek a bride among older maidens, and were the father a rich man; he would not feel the need to betroth his daughter at so early an age. According to Evans-Pritchard, a nubile maiden would not be betrothed for several years to a poor. Her brothers would not brook the delay; for them, they want to marry with the cattle of her bridewealth.

The holding of *the* larcieng-[lärciëŋ], ceremony means that both sides provisionally agree upon the marriage. The transfer to the bride's family of the ghot lipa- [ɣɔ̱ɔ̱k li̱pä] or ghot luom- [ɣɔ̱ɔ̱k luɔ̱m], the cattle of the betrothal, maybe three or four to ten heads, is a further acknowledgement of this understanding. It is said that before the ceremony takes place, it has been agreed upon how many cattle should eventually be handed over.

The ceremony is held in the bride's home. When the morning work of the kraal is finished, the bridegroom and his party drive before them the cattle of the betrothal led by a fine ox. The pride of the herd, its horns decorated with tassels, for the bride's brother. They advance on the bride's village in war formation and continue their martial exercises in her father's kraal chanting their war songs before the huts and byres, especially before the hut of the bride's mother, who must be shown particular respect. The bridegroom's girl relatives and friends arrive about the same time as the men and they dance in the kraal. The youths of the bride's village then form their dep, village line formation, and start their exercises and the dancing begins.

Towards sunset, the betrothal cattle, which were left outside the village to graze, are brought into the kraal and tethered. Dancing, duelling, singing, and love-making between the youths and maidens continue well until the night. All pay special attention to the bridegroom, resplendent with his ivory armlets and a coil of brass twisted round his arms, and distinguished by the dang-[daŋ], wedding stick. Before midnight, the father of the bride leads forth an ox with a ceremonial rubbing of ashes (buk*)* on its back. The ox is dedicated to the lineage ghosts and spirits in a long address (lam-pal) by the gwan buthni- [gua̲n bööthni̲], of the lineage. He tells the spirits to take their ox and let the people be at peace. Evans-Pritchard confirms that shorter ashes follow his address on the beast's back.

The jicoa-ji̲cɔaor (cieŋ tuac) the bridegroom's people, take no part in these proceedings but the flesh of the sacrifice is, except the head, neck and some of the entrails, their right. If the ox is not to their liking, they insist on a bigger one being sacrificed or, which amounts to the same thing from their point of view, being slaughtered for their dinner. When the addresses are finished, the gwan buthni- [gua̲n bööthni̲] of the bride's lineage, or her father or another of her senior kinsmen, stabs the ox-the yang- [yaŋ luɔ̲m] as it is called to the heart with a single thrust. It stands for a moment and falls to the ground. Those present, watching to see it fall cleanly.

According to the bridegroom's people, often directed by the bridegroom, though he may not himself eat in the home of his father-in-law, amid much shorting and chaffing, divide the meat among themselves. Each kinsman receives his customary due. It is said that the visiting girls take the ribs and part of the back the next day to their parents and elders in the bridegroom's village. The rest is eaten on the spot. The girls of the bride's village who, like its menfolk, receive little or none of the meat, are up, half the night cooking porridge, (kuän nath) preparing beer, and boiling the meat for their guests, for the girls of the bridegroom's party are too busy flirting with the youths to assist them.

According to Evans-Pritchard, in the morning, there is more dancing, and beer is served to the guests before they depart. He states that shortly before they go, the bridegroom, if he has not done so earlier, throws to the threshold of his mother-in-law's hut, if she has not yet reached the menopause, a tethering-cord, as an earnest that the yang pal- [yaŋ pal], a cow to her fertility, will be paid. He has already given her a present of tobacco.

The wedding takes place weeks later. Meanwhile, there are further discussions about bride-wealth not only in the home of the bride's father but also in the home of her senior maternal uncle, who is responsible for the negotiations on the mother's side. According to Evans-Pritchard, his claims are less flexible and there cannot be much dispute about them. Therefore, they are settled provisionally in the father's byre. Therefore, the final discussions with the uncle himself, who may live far away, are left until after the wedding or even after consummation. Cattle will be probably handed over before the wedding.

Between the betrothal and the wedding, the bridegroom is lipe nyaal- [li̲p nyaal] a man to whom a bride is affianced, but he and she, are spoken of as man and wife and the bridegroom acts towards his in-laws with full respect due from a son-in-law. The bridegroom, according to Evans, visits his wife's home with his best man and other friends, and on these occasions, he may try to cohabit with his wife, but it will be difficult for him because he is closely watched and others probably share the hut in which he and she are sleeping. On this specific occasion, Evans-Pritchard argues that he cannot enforce marital rights at this stage and get his best man to persuade his bride to visit him in the gardens.

6.4 The Wedding Ceremony

According to Evans-Pritchard, both sides want to complete the marriage without undue delay. The bridegroom's people want their wife and the bride's people want their cattle. They do not care to use the cattle of the betrothal they are only for the pledge. If negotiations break down, cows at once, are to be returned, or other substituted if they have died. In the interval between betrothal and wedding ceremonies, if an agreement is reached about the cattle, both parties have had time to accommodate themselves to their new interrelationships. According to Evans, neither party would pursue the marriage to the point of holding the wedding ceremony, with its expenses and publicity, unless they were confident of the outcome.

Furthermore, arrangements are made to hold it. In the homestead of the bride, there is a reception, especially the beer being prepared, and in the homestead of the bridegroom, there is much rejoicing, men and women chanting songs or poems throughout the night. They also chant on their way to the wedding ceremony during its celebration. The main features of wedding ceremonies (kwen-[kuen] are discussions about cattle. In the following morning, the invocation over the cattle of the bride-wealth (twoc ghot- [tuɔ̱c ɣɔ̱ɔ̱k], the wedding ceremonial dance, and the wedding sacrifice, are done in the afternoon and evening.

On the other hand, if the two families agreed on a final

number of cattle and their whereabouts were uncovered, both sides would throw the ash of cattle's dung up in the sky and the person who holds the agnatic spear from the groom's side would point the spear up to the sky and call the gods of that clan by saying, 'This is your wife god of—take care of her'. That would be the finalization of the bride-wealth negotiation. It is problematic for a girl if her bride wealth is not fixed, since she would not acquire the status of a married woman. She would still maintain her status as a member of her family. In addition, she would remain under her family abode. If a man takes, his wife before her bride-wealth is fixed and they give birth to a daughter who has reached marriageable age, her bride-wealth is fixed first.

As the wedding ceremony continues, the bridegroom's kin discuss the situation in his father's byre. They know what outstanding claims are likely to be advanced. This is because they know the persons on the other side who stand in those relationships with the bride to which the beast is due by custom. They run over their herds and assign particular beasts to meet probable claims so that no last-moment demand shall be made that they have not allowed for or cannot reject. Similar talks are going on among the bride's kin in her father's byre. They know more or less what animals the bridegroom can muster.

The families of the bride have also to agree on the division of the bride-wealth among themselves. The problem often is not so much the total of beasts to be paid, but to which of the bride's kin they shall be allotted. The bride's father will do his best to protect his son-in-law against too greedy kinsmen. As we have seen, the bridegroom's people have several times discussed the whole question of the agreed bride-wealth, or kept back till the last moment, so they can be exacted under threat of forbidding the wedding ceremonial dance.

Evans-Pritchard states that the older people of the bridegroom's kin go ahead to the bridegroom's party of the youth and maidens to the bride's home to finish the discussion in the late morning and early afternoon. They generally argue when the bridegroom's party arrives. The paternal uncles on both sides talk foremost part, for it is thought impolite of the fathers to take too prominent a part in the discussions, especially if they are younger than the uncles.

The bridegroom and his gwan buthni- [gua̲n bööthni̲] and the bride's father and his gwan buthni- [gua̲n bööthni̲] wear wild-cat skins around their loins to hide their nakedness, and the gwan buthni- [gua̲n bööthni̲] of the bridegroom holds a wedding stick across his knees (occasionally a woman officiates in this capacity). After greetings have been exchanged, they begin the final cattle talk over their pipes, each claim being stated, restated, and discussed in the deliberate Nuär way-puff, puff, puff of tobacco, a few words, then puff, puff, puff again.

While the jicuong-[ji̲cuuŋni] the people with the right to cattle of the bridewealth are developing their claims, first on the father's side, then on the mother's side, the *gwan* buthni [gua̲n bööthni̲] of the bride brings a tray on which there are lumps of tobacco and an equal number of pieces of charcoal and hands these sums to the bridegroom's senior relatives. The cattle talk, even at this stage, is often loud and it looks until one is used to Nuär, as though the agreement would be impossible.

Evans-Pritchard argues that while the discussions are going on in the byre, the youths of the bridegroom's village charge into the homestead, chanting and skirmishing as they come. They rush to the kraal and the bridegroom hurls his spear at his mother's-in-laws buor-[buɔ̱r], while the girls of the bride's village attack the visiting youths in mock combat and try to catch the bridegroom and size his wedding stick. If they succeed, he pays them a calf. The buor-[buɔ̱r], is a mud windscreen, such as every Nuär woman has in front of her fireplace outside her hut; it is the symbol of domesticity and wifely status. Furthermore, it is associated with the spirit of the husband's lineage.

On the marriage of a daughter, the hut of the windscreen is heightened, or a new one is constructed for the bridegroom to spear it. Some of his close kinsmen may spear it also. It is easily repaired. The spear belongs to the mother of the bride, but it is a war spear from her homestead. The bridegroom has given or promised her a pipe, tobacco, and a smaller spear, which she may give to a small son or keep for scraping hides. The bridegroom may also throw a spear into the threshold of the byre. This goes to his father-in-law. Other parties of youths from nearby villages are by this for the wedding. Drums announced the wedding on the previous day. It is difficult for the older people, still talking in the byre, puffing away at their pipes, and drinking beer, to hold up the ceremonial dance any longer. They begin and it continues for the rest of the afternoon and into the night. It is resumed on the following morning.

Evans-Pritchard states that before the ceremonial dance begins, or as soon as it has begun, the skin on both sides signifies their approval of the marriage by calling out the spear names of the lineages of the bride and the bridegroom. They invoke the ghosts of their ancestors to look upon the cattle of the bride-wealth-a rite, which makes them partners to the union, and witnesses of it. The gwan buthni [gua̲n böötheni̲] of the bride–his role is ritual. He has no part in the bride-wealth talks, demands a cow, and receives the promise of a calf or sheep. He then walks up down the byre, brandishing his spear and delivering a long address. He shouts out his ox name and the spear name of his lineage. He calls on the ghosts of the bride's ancestors to witness that she is married openly with 50 cattle (it is conventional to say this number) not with shame and by stealth.

While George P. Murdock, Arthur Tuden, and Peter B. Hammond argue that, "The bride price is provided by the head of the groom's family, with contributions from both paternal and maternal uncles and aunts. They are distributed among the bride's relatives as follows: ten head of cattle to her immediate family, ten head to her more distant patrilineal kinsmen, and twenty head to her maternal relatives."[79]He says that she will bear her husband a male child.

The gua̲n böötheni̲ e addresses also the bridegroom's kin, his kin, and anybody else he feels inclined to bring into his speech, and while talking he pours beer *(*kɔaŋ) and sprinkles a little tobacco *(*Tab) on the floor of the byre, on its threshold, and the hearth in the Centre of it, asking God (Gwan dong- [Gua̲n Dɔɔŋ] to take his 'cow', the tobacco. Then the *gwan buthni- [gua̲n böötheni̲] of* the bridegroom's lineage, whose role is also purely ritual, has his say, or he may speak first. He talks in much the same vein and also pours beer and sprinkles tobacco in a sacrifice as he walks up and down the byre and may be followed by a senior kinsman of the bridegroom. Then people chant poems.

---

79 George P. Murdock, Arthur Tuden, and Peter B. Hammond, "African Negro Art; Anthropology; Archaeology: Ancient Civilization; Muslims, p. *261.*

According to Evans-Pritchard, during the ceremonial dance, another rite, but not of the same importance, takes place. The father of the bride removes a tethering cord from the kraal and throws it into the air between two lines of men drawn up for the purpose, the bride's relatives on one side and the bridegroom's relatives on the other. They try to hook it in the air with their spears and clubs and whoever catches it may demand a calf or a goat from the opposite side, though he cannot be sure of receiving it.

Towards sunset, or on the following morning, the marriage ox provided by the bride's father, is sacrificed by the gwan buthni- [guan bööthni] of her lineage or a senior kinsman. He rubs ashes on its back and speaks, saying: 'We do not kill you for an evil thing; we kill you for a good thing. Fall well. 'It is a wedding ox, not a funeral ox. The meat, except for the dead, neck, and a few other bits, goes to the bridegroom's kin who, as in the betrothal ceremony, divide the carcass, on the principle determining the division of bride-wealth, between the kin kwi gwan [kuic guan], on the father's side, and those, kwi man- [kuic man] on the other side.

The distribution at these ceremonies depends on the number of relationships represented by persons or proxies. The number of persons standing in these relationships, and other circumstances. The bridegroom's people take most of the meat back to their homes for the older people who attend the wedding and those who have remained to look after the herds and milk the cows. The rest is eaten on the spot.

A large part of the night is spent dancing, flirting, and love-making. The bride and the girls of her homestead are cooking while the bridegroom, who is fasting, is seeing that his companions' area is being properly looked after. On the following morning, beer is reserved, pots being distributed to the bridegroom's kin, his father, his father's full-brother, his father's half–brother, his paternal and maternal aunts, and his mother's full-and half-brothers, who share the beer with members of their age-sets. After a meal, the youths resumed dancing while their elders were fortified with beer; probably starting once more on the seemingly endless cattle talks. For there is generally an odd claim or two that are outstanding, the discussion of which was interrupted by the wedding dance, though their settlement was assured before it began.

The ngut-[ŋuɔt] does not conclude the marriage. It is the mut-[muɔ̱t], and the birth of a child, which do this. But the chances are now overwhelming, a successful conclusion, for had the bride's people not been satisfied with the bride's wealth already handed over, or promised, they would not have allowed the dance to proceed. This is because the wedding has also cost them a second ox for which there is no occasional break up between wedding and consummation. Evans-Pritchard states that in my experience, this is rare and is due to the reluctance of the bride rather than to objections or demands from her family and kin.

If the maternal uncle of the bride lives too far away for his people to attend the bride wealth talks and the wedding, talks will be held later in his byre to settle the cattle due to him and his brothers and sisters. He may hold a wedding dance on his account and sacrifice an ox at it. He may even do this when the father and his members of the same large village. The senior paternal uncle occasionally does the same if he lives far away and is the father's half-brother.

6.5 The Consummation-Dɔnyni̱ Cökni̱

The mut-[muɔ̱t], is the third of the three public marriage ceremonies, the one that at any rate among the eastern Nuär, makes the union legally binding. After it, the husband can then be called and can claim compensation for adultery, which he could not have done before. Previously, the bride's brothers did not feel it obligatory to prevent her from attending evening dances in the neighbourhood, though they well knew from their own experience that she was likely to have relations with old sweethearts. Her future husband's people could not then complain if she attended these dances, whereas after the mut-[muɔ̱t], they would make an unpleasant scene were they to find her at one.

Accordingly, this ceremony of consummation-dɔnyni̱ cökni̱ makes man and wife, and the cattle, which have been paid, are no longer regarded as a pledge but as marriage cattle. They now say of the bride Te yang joked- [tëyaŋ jɔkdɛ] ('She has cattle on her back'). Moreover, if the cattle paid to the bride's family and kin die in their kraals before the mut-[muɔ̱t], and they all die in a year of render pest-they have to be replaced by the bridegroom's people. Whereas if they die after the mut-[muɔ̱t], they will still be counted as part of the bride's wealth. Therefore, the husband's people do not have to substitute for them similar beasts.

The distinction above-mentioned does not apply to animals killed by the bride's family and kin or which have been disposed of by them and have died outside their kraals, for these count as bride wealth before, and after, the consummation. On the other hand, any calves the cattle may bear before this ceremony, count as original bridewealth and not as increment. Likewise, if the incomplete union is broken before the mut-[muɔ̱t], the bride's people do not have to return animals, which have died a natural death in their kraals. They have a mark of married status, and the cow of hair, which is shaved off for the bride's head at the consummation.

It is the mut-[muɔ̱t], therefore which makes the union a contract. Occasionally, it happens when people expedite the marriage, and the consummation takes place before the wedding. I heard it suggested that this should be done by a youth who had speared and could not take the bridegroom's usual part in the wedding ceremony. Although, it was decided to hold the wedding first, with the bridegroom as a spectator. No one suggested that in these circumstances, a reversal of the ceremonies would have been improper. Mrs Smith, of the American Mission, told me of a case of an elderly man who, desiring to marry a girl with the approval from her family but against her wishes prevailed on her relatives to rush her through the mut-[muɔ̱t], leaving the wedding to be held later.

The day of consummation has to be fixed in advance because beer has to be brewed for visitors. In the early morning, the bridegroom goes with a company of youths from his village to fetch the bride, his womenfolk remaining behind to prepare for their visitors. They chant on the way, for this is a happy occasion for the village. Sometimes, they find on arrival that the bride's mother has prepared beer for them. They have to ask her permission to take her daughter away. If she asks them for presents before she gives them, such things as a spear, armlets, a pipe, and tobacco. The young men promise to give her what she asks for and depart, escorting the bride and her girl companions, who have oiled and decked themselves with ornaments for the ceremony.

They go chanting to the bridegroom's village, often being a composition of the bride in honour of her future husband, and there is much horseplay between the sexes. When they arrive near the village, the young men go ahead and the girls are met by the youths of the village who bring them into the kraal where they serenade the bridegroom's mother with poems outside her hut. The ceremony is mostly a female affair while the men are watching.

After a while, a kinsman of the bridegroom places a tethering cord across the inner threshold and the bridegroom crawls over it, followed by the bride, the best man, and a special girlfriend of the bride. This action is said to make the marriage fruitful. Then, towards evening, the rite of consummation takes place, though there is no invariable order of events in these ceremonies and no fixed timetable. The bride retires to a hut wearing a special goatskin cap and here the bridegroom joins her. His age-mates seek him out and say to him: Come now, let the people go to bed, come and loosen the bride's girdle.

The bridegroom is bashful and gets the business over quickly. He enters the hut, gives his bride a cut with a switch, and seizes her thigh if she is refusing his advances and crouching by the wall of the hut. He strikes her with a tethering cord, snatches the cap off her head, breaks her girdle, and consummates the marriage. Reluctance is imposed on her by custom and she pretends to resist even when she has known her husband often before in the gardens. In Nuär land, it is most unlikely that a bride will be a virgin. Wedding and consummation ceremonies are held even for a girl who is pregnant or divorced and is being married a second time if she has not born children. They say that 'she has been returned to maidenhood'. It is only divorced women who have led profligate lives who are not remarried with these ceremonies. Maidenhood is a social, not a physical, state.

If he has finished his duty, the bridegroom leaves the hut, sometimes the bride's girlfriends rush at him and beat him with their fists as he emerges. The rest of the evening is given to the favourite pastimes of Nuär youth, muong-[muɔŋ] and lum-[luɔ̱m], flirting with girls and making love with them. There will be many youths present: the people of the bridegroom's homestead, his mother's kin if they live nearby, the local dep, the youths of the village, and a band of youths from villages for miles come around. It is stated that the mut-[muɔ̱t] is a popular ceremony. It is known that many girls will attend it. Then all retire for the night, the bride's companions sleeping in a hut reserved for them.

On the following morning, three rites take place which may on no account be omitted, the sacrifice (which may take place the evening before), the lustration, and the shaving of the bride's head. The sacrificial beast should be an ox, but if the bridegroom's father is poor, and at this stage of marriage, he is likely to be hard up, the yang muot- [yaŋ muɔ̱t] the ox of the consummation, maybe a goat, or even just a beer. The bridegroom's gwan buthni- [gua̱n bööthni̱] rubs ashes on its back and calls out the spear name of his lineage to witness the union and to bless it with sons, so that the lineage may continue.

Gua̱n bööthni̱ says to them, 'Now see your ox; let her be a good wife; let her bear many children, many sons; let her work well in her husband's home, milk the cows, dry the cattle dung; let her be a faithful wife, not a profligate one'; and so forth, asking them to make the union a lasting and happy one. He then spears the ox, the wife's people, and the visitors, cuts it up and divides it among themselves into the customary portions. Only the head, neck, and a few other pieces of meat go to the people of the bridegroom. The visiting maidens at once cook and eat the ribs, kidneys, and stomach, besides filling themselves with (kuän nath) porridge and beer, the bride alone abstaining because she may not eat in the home of her mother-in-law. They take the rest of the carcass back to their homes for their elders.

Generally, it happens when there is a feast, outsiders, persons not of the bridegroom's close kin, hang about the carcass like kites when being cut up, hoping to obtain a piece of meat by bagging, snatching, or persistently getting in the way. There is much shouting, argument, and general confusion. The gwan butthni- [gua̲n bööthni̲] may perform another duty associated with his office in anointing the bride with butter. Her father will already have blessed her in this manner before she sets out to go to her husband's home.

Now, the rite of lustration takes place, lateetnikaciik- [la̲a̲k tetni kɛnɛ ciik] the washing of the hands with bracelets. The visiting maidens, the young wife's companions, sit in a hut and a pot of warm water is passed to them. One of them washes her hands in water and then takes a bracelet off her arm, drops it into the pot, and passes the pot to one of the husband's kinsfolk's sides, who, squatting in front of it, likewise dips his hands in the water, and then fishes out the bracelet. The pot is returned to the hut and a different kinsman repeats the action of the first pair.

All the close kinsfolk of the husband- his father's brothers and sisters, his mother's brothers and sisters, and his brothers and sisters, and so on- are supposed to receive a bracelet, but persons standing in some of these relationships will be absent. Any person who can claim kinship with the husband can demand a bracelet. If a man's dipping into the pot reveals a poor bracelet, he does not hesitate to upbraid the girl who put it there. He may select a better one from those on her arm. The concluding rite of the ceremony is the act from which it derives its name, the wife's head (mutnyier) by a member of her husband's family.

This may take place by companions, for it is a domestic affair of the husband's gol-[gɔl] his home, of which the wife is now a member. The shaving of the head signifies this change in her status. People speak of the rite as wuɔ̱cmiemni̱, the removal of the hair of maidenhood. They said afterwards of the girl ca cek,'(cɛ la ciek) she has become a woman. She is stripped of her ornaments, which are divided among her husband's kin. She is arrayed in new finery provided by her husband. She belongs to his and not to her father's people now. Finally, it is for them to adorn her.

6.6 The Birth of a Child

The mut-[muɔ̱t] is the consummation of marriage as we have mentioned earlier, but not its completion is the birth of a child. The young wife is now called ciek mi kaw- [cɛ la Kaw] a newlywed. George P. Murdock, Arthur Tuden, and Peter B. Hammond argue, "As a rule, a bride does not move to her husband's home until after the birth of her first child."[80] Her parents give her a hut of her own, and a sleeping-hide, a brush, and a couple of gourds for ablutions. When

80 P. Murdock, Arthur Tuden, and Peter B. Hammond argue that "African Negro Art; Anthropology; Archaeology: Ancient Civilization; Muslims, p. *261.*

her husband comes to visit her in her father's homestead, he sleeps with her in that hut. She continues in all other respects to lead the life she led before marriage. After her husband's visits, she hands up the hide and domestic utensils and sleeps with her unmarried sisters.

On these visits, her husband stays at a neighbouring homestead as he cannot be in the home of his parents-in-law and ought not to be seen. When someone tells the wife that her husband has come, so she may prepare for him, she feigns annoyance or lack of interest, though she is at ease when she is alone with her husband. When everyone is asleep, he visits her and spends the night with her. The bridegroom is expected to leave before the bride's people are about to wake up.

Her parents are supposed to know nothing of his visits, though they know all about his movements and his mother-in-law may rise especially early and squint through a crack in the door of her hut to see him depart. Should he over asleep, and his mother-in-law sees his spears outside her daughter's hut, she makes them aware to disappear. It is not until a child has been born that his wife's people as one of himself accept the husband. He is then the father of their daughter's child and through the child; he has a kinship link with them.

Until a child is born, the husband continues to lead the life he lived before marriage, a bachelor life with his younger brothers in their father's byre. His wife visits him only on rare occasions and for a formal purpose. For example, when, at harvest time, she brings him porridge she has made for the grain on the drying platforms, or when she takes him a bundle of well-cooked porridge with the first millet of the year custom known as puth kuon- [puɔ̱th kua̱n], honouring with porridge.

All are equal, a child to be born, the husband and wife because they want a son, and the wife's parents and kin because they cannot, without risking complications, dispose of the cattle of the marriage till a firstborn completes the union. According to Evans-Pritchard, those whose daughters they might wish to marry would not be happy about accepting such cattle as bride-wealth had suddenly to be returned to the husband. When a child is born, the mother remains with her parents until she has weaned it. This is a suitable regulation, because after the bride's wealth has been paid, the husband's father is likely to be short of lactating cows, while the wife's parents will have plenty of milk from their herd.

According to Evans-Pritchard, if the wife goes to live with her husband before the child is weaned, it may not be weaned without the consent of her parents and I have seen a husband pay several cattle to atone for contravention of this rule. A kee-[kẹẹ] first the child, belongs to the home of his maternal grandparents. If he is weaned in his father's home, he returns to live with them, if a boy, until he is initiated and a girl, until she is betrothed. Evans-Pritchard argues this is a rule, though there is variation depending on the ability of the grandparents to support the child and the relations between them and their son-in-law.

Shortly, after the birth of her first-born, the now wife called pay dap- nursing mother. She brings the baby to her husband's home and lays him in the ashes of the hearth in the centre of his grandfather's byre, a rite known as nong puka- [nöŋ pukä], the bringing to the ashes. Beer has been prepared and is drunk by a few senior kinsmen of the husband who live in his hamlet. It is a domestic, and not a public, ceremony. The wife spends a few days in her husband's home and returns with the child to the village of her parents. She has no hut of her own in her husband's homestead.

According to Evans-Pritchard, when his firstborn has been weaned, the husband builds his wife a hut in his father's homestead facing the family kraal. He then goes to ask his parents-in-law for his wife. They do not deny him, even if, as is likely, some of the bride's wealth is still owed. They give her a horn spoon (tuŋ) and a gourd. She takes these with her to her husband's homestead. The Nuär emphasizes the gift of a spoon-tuŋ because it is a recognition that the woman is now in the full sense, a wife who will eat the porridge of her gardens with the milk of her herd.

Evans-Pritchard asserts that she now milks her husband's cows instead of her father's and hoes the gardens of his home and not those of her childhood. Before, she is given a spoon, even if she goes to a garden at her husband's home she takes the harvest back to her father, or she may live at her husband's home and cultivate in her father's village if it is not far. Evans-Pritchard states it is only when a man's bride has born him a child and tends his heart; that she becomes, in the Nuär sense, wife. She then makes a buor-[buɔ̱r], a mud fire screen, and the spirit of his lineage comes to dwell there. Later on, his father tells the husband to build a byre and gives him a few cows to start a herd.

The marriage thus, has reached a completion through many stages: betrothal ceremony, wedding ceremony, consummation ceremony, the birth of a child, the bringing of the first-born to his father's byre, and the presentation to the wife of a spoon as a sign of her domestic separation from her family. She comes to her husband's home not as a wife but as a mother, whose breasts have suckled a child of their lineage.

6.7 Critiques of the Article about Nuär Marriage

It may not be necessary to be too much meticulous on every aspect of the article. However, some major areas of appreciation must be considered Evans-Pritchard correctly acknowledged the stable union that generally requires social approval through social recognition of Nuär marriage. Stable union between a man and a woman reaches its final stage by performing ceremonial rites. Evans-Pritchard deserves credit because of the recognition of the stable union between husband and wife in Nuär marriage but he added also something of the social dimension to it.

One must appreciate him because, in his observation, he said that marriage among the Nuär creates the 'bond of union' through the rites that express the relationship between husband and wife, husband's kin and wife's kin, and between the kin on one side or the other and the ghosts and spirits of their lineages. He should be appreciated because, in his critical observation on the essential ceremonial rite of the sacrificial beast to both the ghosts and spirits, Evans-Pritchard asserts that an essential rite in the marriage ceremonies is the sacrifice of a beast to the ghosts and spirits by which they are made cognizant, and witnesses, of the union in an address delivered to them before the beast is slain. African marriage and Nuär marriage bring the whole two families together, the living and the dead. Such essential ceremonial rites require the recognition of everyone otherwise, they are incomplete.

Some areas of concern: the way Evans-Pritchard tried to write words in the Nuär language can permit us to conclude that he knew the Nuär language orally. Furthermore, his situation even permits us to conclude that he found difficulties in areas of translation from English to Nuär language. Therefore, any contemporary Nuär who knows the Nuär language both written and spoken will feel uncomfortable with his article on Nuär marriage because of the lack of Nuär alphabets in his writing.

His translations from English to Nuär language are not correct. That is possible due to assumption. It would be unfortunate for the Nuär in the west, central, and in the east that during the sacrificial rite of the beast, confusion could happen. If the intention of the sacrifice of the beast is for the ghosts and spirits of both parties, then shouting and confusion at this highest spiritual prayer pal are not allowed. Traditionally, when an elder delivers a speech, no one can interrupt him.

This has reminded me of an occasion of the reconciliation ceremony between Jagɛi and Jikäny in western Nuär under a big tree in a village called Duar led by Chuol Bi̱li̱u Duäc, the Leopard-Chief -kuäär kuac (master of the earth- kuäär muɔn). While Chuol was praying for the reconciliation of the two big clans, everyone was silent including all the chiefs of both big and small in terms of position on both sides. Unfortunately, while praying, he was interrupted by a kite that was passing over by whistling, while he was moving around the beast that awaited to be speared, brandishing his spear and praying. He stopped and asked the kite by pointing to the sky with his spear saying, 'Are you interrupting me or are you competing with me?' Instantly, the kite fell and died in front of everybody. Therefore, in this sense, I doubt whether the confusion pointed out by Evans-Pritchard was in the right place.

Evans-Pritchard pointed out the aspect of confusion by stating that the sacrifice is often a time of great confusion, with everyone shouting advice and instructions to everyone else and arguing good-humoredly about the division of the meat. The specific religious part of a ceremony seems lost amid all the talk and movement, but it is not. It must be pointed out that according to Nuär in the west, central, and east, the sacrifice of the beast during the essential ceremonial rite, is not done during the betrothal but during muɔt which he called mut but in Nuär language, this simply means spear. For example, it is usual to sacrifice an ox at the betrothal ceremony towards the end of the evening dance, but it can equally well be done the following morning. In his observation on the Nuär ritual, he argues that the Nuär ritual procedure is generally happy-go-lucky.

Traditionally, if the young is to marry a girl, he first shares it with his father or other elder person such as the paternal father or any other elder person within the family. Usually, it is not the young man to approaches the prospective bride's father but the father of the prospective bridegroom or another elder person in the family. The Nuär are very strict on social status. Therefore, it is inappropriate for the prospective bride's father to ask the kinsmen of the bridegroom how many cattle they have. Evans-Pritchard asserts that the elders ask them what cattle they have.

The ear of the cows has nothing to do with a particular claimant but it is part of beautifying the cows whether there is marriage or not. Evans-Pritchard argues that the cattle are more precisely specified and earmarked for particular claimants. Betrothal in the west, central, and east has nothing to do with poverty. Sometimes, it is a sign of beauty and for such a girl to be betrothed at an early stage is a sign of prestige for her parents.

When he says a poor suitor pays two or three cows to a man short of stock at the time to obtain a lien on his small daughter while he collects adequate bride wealth to marry her later. Evans-Pritchard found it difficult to identify the specific period in which the consummation-dɔnyni̲ cöökni̲ takes place. According to Nuär in the West, Central, and East, the precise period of consummation-dɔnyni̲ cöökni̲ is after the wedding ceremony-muɔ̲t not in the gardens but in the village of the bride's parents with a special arrangement. Therefore, it is assumed there is no consummation-dɔnyni̲ cöökni̲ before that period.

During his journey to the bride's parent's village, he goes alone not with his best man. Therefore, it is not true what Evans-Pritchard said, he visits his wife's home with his best man and other friends, and on these occasions, he may try to cohabit with his wife, but it will be difficult for him because he is closely watched and others probably share the hut in which he and she are sleeping. On this specific occasion, Evans-Pritchard argues that he cannot enforce marital rights at this stage and get his best man to persuade his bride to visit him in the gardens.

Generally, according to Nuär culture, there is no rigidity but flexibility as to where the first-born child should stay. However, no other person has the right over the first-born child more than his biological father and the bridegroom's kinsmen. The parents-in-law have no right to claim over the first-born child or other children born after him.

In his article on Nuär marriage, there seems to be a presentation of dance almost in every ceremonial stage, however, for the Nuär, the true dancing takes place during the bul nyala-buɔ̲r nyaal-wedding ceremony. The rest of the ceremonial celebrations are full of yelling, yiet kiɛ ra̲a̲w which according to Nuär are not dancing. Nevertheless, these are also limited to some essential ceremonial stages. Evans-Pritchard said that in Nuär land, it is most unlikely that a bride will be a virgin, for me, he has committed a fallacy of generalization. This was too much for him to say, even where he came from, not every bride was a virgin. These are a few critiques and it should be enough because I do not aim to analyze everything in the article.

Conclusion

Chapter Six has presented E.E. Evans-Pritchard's famous article entitled *"African: Journal of the International African Institute" Vol. 18. No. 1 (Jan. 1948), pp.29-40.* In this famous article, the chapter has dealt thoroughly with marriage among the Nuär as presented by such an outstanding anthropologist who spent most of his lifetime among the Nuär as an active observer. In his article, the author has documented general features of the ceremonies of Nuär marriage, which this chapter has presented. The chapter also has elaborated and has explained broadly some preliminaries on Nuär marriage such as the betrothal, followed by a wedding, consummation, and the birth of a child, and finally, the chapter presents contemporary Nuär critique of the article.

Alternatively, in his words, Evans-Pritchard stated that marriage thus reached completion through many stages: betrothal ceremony, wedding ceremony, consummation ceremony, the birth of a child, the bringing of the first-born to his father's byre, and the presentation to the wife of a spoon as a sign of her domestic separation from her family. She comes to her husband's home not as a wife but as a mother, whose breasts have suckled a child of their lineage.

CHAPTER SEVEN

P.P. HOWELL ON TRUE UNION OF NUÄR MARRIAGE

Introduction

Chapter seven deals with the true union in Nuär marriage by P.P. Howell. It highlights the social and ritual processes of marriage among the Nuär. Furthermore, the chapter treats issues related to marriage such as courting and betrothal, luom nyaal [luɔ̱m nyaal] courting a girl, thiec nyaal: asking for the girl, cuei-[cuic] betrothal, *twoc* ghok- [tuɔ̱c ɣɔ̱ɔ̱k]: 'invocation of the cattle' muot Nyaal [muɔ̱t nyaal]: 'the shaving of the bride hair and luony deeb [luɔny deep]: 'losing the rope. It presents other issues such as noong nyaal [nööŋ nyaal]: 'the bringing of the bride muot nyaal [muɔ̱t nyaal]: 'shaving the bride, distribution of cattle among the bride's family, ideal rules for distribution of cattle and critiques.

7. Social and Ritual Processes of Marriage

According to P.P. Howell, cattle as bride-wealth does not constitute marriage, although it is the most significant aspect of marriage from the legal point of view. Nuär marriage is a protracted affair involving many negotiations and ceremonial meetings. Those social and ritual processes described here, apply to the simplest form of legal marriage and the simplest situation possible. According to P.P. Howell, the same principles involve 'Ghost-marriage', that is marriage by a living person on behalf of a deceased relative. Nevertheless, in leviratic marriage, and in what Professor Evans-Pritchard has classified as 'widow-concubinage' there is naturally no repetition of the ceremonies carried out by the widow's husband in his lifetime and too, no further payment of the bride-wealth. P.P. Howell argues that in other unions, which are not legal, no legal ceremonies similar to those of true marriage are possible.

It is said that "The description which follows applies to a normal Nuär youth who wishes to marry a normal Nuär girl and has sufficient cattle to do so, and in such cases, unless the union is prearranged by the parents, the youth has probably met his future bride at the dances held by young people and has danced and 'flirted' with her for some time."[81]Furthermore, only the most important rituals and negotiations are recorded.

In that sense, the form and order of the ceremonies among primitive peoples usually vary considerably on each occasion. In this case, no marriage ceremony is word for word, act for

81 Cf. P.P. Howell, *A Manuel of Nuër Law*, London, Oxford University Press, 1954, pp. 86-87.

act, or an exact repetition of another. It has to be pointed out that there may be local variations of custom. In his view, P.P. Howell states that it does not follow that all the ceremonies described below are performed in all the Nuär marriages, not that they are always performed with the same publicity. For example, older men, especially men with many cattle, who already have other wives, would think it unseemly to court a girl with the same intensity as a younger Nuär man, and they would not be expected to go through all the preliminaries.

7.1 Courting and Betrothal

According to Merriam-Webster, the word 'betrothal' is defined as "a mutual promise or contract for a future marriage."[82] P.P. Howell states that when a girl has accepted a Nuär youth, she will hasten to inform her family, provided that she knows that her lover has sufficient cattle to legalize the union. It may be that her legal representatives in the family, her more important male kinsmen–will ban the marriage for various reasons. First, verification of relations with the prospective bridegroom's family may already be strained. Second, the family of the prospective bride may have no desire to associate with them. Third, there may even be blood between them [the kamdiɛn kɛ riɛm, cɔa̱h kiɛ tɛr]. Fourth, the memory of a blood feud. Fifth, they may also know at once that a marriage is precluded by the rules of exogamy.

Therefore, based on the impediments above-mentioned, P.P. Howell argues that in such circumstances, the girl will be discreetly told to avoid her lover in the future. However,

82 *Merriam-Webster's Collegiate Dictionary* Eleventh Edition, Massachusetts, U.S.A. Merriam-Webster, Incorporated, 2003, p. 117.

if there is no objection, she will be encouraged to continue and will receive their permission, though this is not made public. In this sense, the first ceremony may then take place. It is stated that this does not concern the older members of either family. It is confined to the prospective bride and bridegroom and their friends and coevals. It is no more than a formal recognition among younger people that the couples are courting. It is known in Nuär as lum nyaal- [luɔ̱m nyaal].

7.2 Luom Nyal [Luɔ̱m Nyal] Courting a Girl

The word 'courting or court' according to Merriam-Webster, is defined as "To engage in social activities leading to engagement and marriage."[83] It also means to win a pledge of marriage from someone. According to P.P. Howell, the meeting about courting is held at the home of a person who is related neither to the girl nor to the young man, often the home of the latter's best friend (määth). A few friends of both parties are present. Among them is the prospective bridegroom's official spokesperson, who is known as the gwan tway- [gua̱n tuac] who performs the duties of a 'Best Man' (squealer). The girl also has a friend, known as ngiiy nyaal- [ŋi̱i̱c nyaal], who takes her part in the ceremony, and who leads the conversation in friendly chaff which are characteristic of these occasions. The meeting usually takes place at night, sometimes all night, inside a hut.

During the process of courtship, no elderly people are present, only the youth who spend time in exchange for elaborate compliments which sometimes go on for half an

83 *Merriam-Webster's Collegiate Dictionary* Tenth Edition, Massachusetts, U.S.A. Merriam-Webster, Incorporated, 2000, p. 266.

hour or more without a break. The verb *lum* in Nuär, from which *luom*-[luɔ̱m] is derived, is used to describe any form of courting, even casual flirtation at dances, but its usage here implies a degree of formality not previously recognized. The recognition of the engagement is restricted to the young people who take part in dances together, and not including the adult members of the communities concerned as we have above-mentioned.

7.4 Thiec Nyal: Asking for the Girl

It is stated that after the luom nyaal- [luɔ̱m nyal] which is not considered a serious engagement and more often than not comes to nothing, a meeting takes place known as thieec nyaal, 'asking for the girl.' This again, may lead to nothing, but it is a more formal affair than anything preceding it. For the first time, the girl's parents or guardians are approached by the prospective bridegroom and possibly, by some of his senior kinsmen. In this sense, it amounted to an opening of negotiations between the two families, but it is not binding.

For example, if the members of the girl's family are satisfied and think that by this time the young man is and has his suit–for they have probably made discreet inquiries long before this–they will ask that the first tokens of formal betrothal be paid. In his observations among the Nuär, P.P. Howell says that this requirement, the bride's family hopes to receive at least four head of cattle (though they may be satisfied with less) known as the yang guan nyal- [yaŋ gua̱n nyaal], a cow and a calf which are intended to supply the girl's father with milk, thak deman nyaal- [thäk däman nyaal] a bull or bull-calf for the bride's brother, and a yang

Kuoth- [yaŋ kuoth], a cow which will be dedicated to the spirits of their lineage.

According to P.P. Howell, "The distribution of these cattle is significant. In the first place, the girl's father or, if he is dead, her eldest brother or paternal uncle must receive a guarantee in material form that the prospective bridegroom is in earnest."[84] The ancestral spirits must be called in to bless and assure the future union, and the yang Kuoth- [yaŋ kuoth], is dedicated to them. Finally, the bride's eldest brother, often a coeval of the bridegroom, must be placated, for he expects to benefit mostly by marriage, which will bring in bridewealth, which he will use for his marriage. If the girl's family fixed a day, then is the formal betrothal, in a meeting when the cattle of engagement will be paid over. This is known as cuiy, and the Nuär will say 'ce cueyde-cuiy- [cɛ cuicdɛ cuic] 'he has engaged himself.

7.5 Cuei-[Cuic] Betrothal

The cuei-[cuic] is part of betrothal negotiations, it amounts to a more public acknowledgement by the bridegroom's family in paying for few cattle, and by the bride's family in accepting the cattle considered necessary for that purpose. The cattle are driven straight to the homestead of the girl's father but remain shut in the cattle–byre while the meeting takes place. The prospective bridegroom and his guan tuac are expected to observe rigidly some customary legal restrictions specifically on their moments in the bride's home, which is a sign of respect, and other observances, which characterize the behaviour towards relatives-in-law.

---

84 P.P. Howell, *A Manuel of Nuër Law,* p. 89.

P.P. Howell states that when they enter the houses, they must cover their nakedness with a special cat skin known *as* tuac thoan [tuac thɔ̱ɔ̱nä.]. This reason the principal assistant of the bridegroom is known *as guan tuac,* 'owner of the skin', and a husband is usually expected to wear it in the presence of his wife's mother. Beer has been brewed beforehand. Finally, it is handed around among the senior guests while dancing takes place. A bull calf known as yang kuen- [yaŋ luɔ̱m] (the 'cow of marriage' or 'of courting') is sacrificed and eaten therein.

The adult males of the two families (except the bridegroom) have therefore drunk together and the kinsmen of the bridegroom have partaken of meat provided by the girl's father. The bridegroom's kinsmen have accepted such hospitality and provided the cattle of betrothal to give legal stability to the pledge. This preliminary betrothal feast does not concern the rest of the local community, though many will turn up uninvited because of the beer and the meat, which are available.

The formal gathering concerns only the kinsmen of the girls and the kinsmen of the bridegroom. Negotiations for the composition of homicide, Nuär have a concise terminology for both parties. The bride's family is throughout known as ji̱ nyaal, while those of the bridegroom are known as ji̱ Wudda- (ji̱ Wudä]. P.P. Howell asserts that "These terms mean no more than the 'girl's people' and the 'man people', but they are used expressly in connection with marriage negotiations, and stress the distinction between the two parties."[85]

According to Nuär customary norms, sometimes, girls are betrothed at an early age, and often when they are ten

85 P.P. Howell, *A Manuel of Nuër Law*, p. 90.

to fifteen years old. This does not mean that their families without their knowledge or consent pledge them; for they are usually approached first by the man concerned and are proud to accept. Girls thus engaged appear to have an enhanced attraction for other Nuär youths. Two cows are paid, which are known as dɔw cikä- [dɔw ciikä] the 'cow-calf of the ring or bracelet' (ciek-[ciɛk], and a larger cow-calf called nac pieth- [nac piethä] the 'heifer of upbringing' (referring to the fact that her family continues to care for her and provide her with food for a long time.

These cattle are not included in the bride-wealth, and after the marriage has gone through, unless there is a divorce. Early betrothals of this sort are not common among the Nuär and, even if happened, often come to nothing. The dɔw cika [dɔw cikä] and the nac pieth- [nac piethä] will be quietly returned. They are rarely a subject for dispute in the court because, until they are returned, it would not be seemly to start the negotiations for another engagement. According to Evans-Pritchard, a betrothal ceremony, larcieng-[lärciëŋ] or bul luom- [bul luɔ̱m], is not necessary. He states, "It is possible to proceed at once to the full wedding ceremony, and this is sometimes done when a bridegroom is a rich man with plenty of cattle and the bride is a jut, a girl who has passed the usual age of marriage."[86]

Professor Evans-Pritchard speaks of the betrothal as larcieng or bul luom [bul luɔ̱m]. According to P.P. Howell, this is the same ceremony as that described above, which is sometimes, known as dour in Lou country. Although his description gives the impression of a greater formality and

86 E.E. Evans-Pritchard "African: Journal of the International African Institute" pp. 29-40.

more elaborate ceremonial than I have encountered myself, I do not think there is any difference in principle. The cuei ceremony is usually performed in the rainy season when grain is plentiful, but sometimes, it takes place in the dry season, in which case, it is likely to be less elaborate for there will be little or no beer and the final wedding ceremonies wait until the people return to the cultivations.

7.6 Twoc Ghok- [Tuɔ̱c Ɣɔ̱ɔ̱k]: 'Invocation of the Cattle'

According to P.P. Howell, the betrothal ceremonies described above are followed by the first marriage ceremony, the twoc ghok- [tuɔ̱c ɣɔ̱ɔ̱k] 'invocation of the cattle.' The time that elapses between them is variable and depends largely on the agreement reached during the cue [cuic] ceremony. It is not usually, in the interest to delay matters, though, this sometimes happens if the bridegroom finds difficulty in collecting sufficient cattle and yet retains the goodwill of the girl's family who wishes that the union should take place.

The tuoc [tuɔ̱c] is the crucial ceremony in the process of marriage. It is public in the widest sense, although, the actual negotiations over cattle and the more intimate rituals are restricted to the closer kinsmen of the bride and the bridegroom. Most of the bride's kinsmen who expect to receive a portion of the bride's wealth are present. If they are not, they will usually send someone to represent their interests.

We see therefore that as the processes of betrothal and marriage proceed, increasingly from both kinship groups are concerned. P.P. Howell affirms, "This emphasizes the collective nature of a union and the extent of the social ties and obligations which are involved."[87] Evans-Pritchard points out two important things from both sides of the prospect bride's kinsmen and prospect bridegroom' kinsmen that is, "The bridegroom's people want their wife and the bride's people want their cattle so that they can marry.[88]

Dancing begins early in the morning and the bridegroom, his father, and the gwan tuac- [gua̲n tuay] as well as the senior legal representative of the bridegroom's lineage, appear dressed in cat-skins (twac thoana-tuac thɔ̲ɔ̲nä] as a conventional sign of respect to the bride's mother and her kinsmen and those of her husband.

7.6.1 The Role of Two Chief Negotiators

The bridegroom and the bride have two representatives. At the bridegroom's side is Gwan tuac- [gua̲n tuac] who is his aide. At the tuoc-[tuɔ̲c] ceremony, he is represented also by the gwan bothni- [gua̲n bööthni̲] an agnatic kinsman of a collateral branch of the lineage, whose activities are not so much personal as concerned with interests of the bridegroom's lineage as a whole.

The duties of gua̲n bööthni̲ are both legal and ritual. He is expected to take the lead in arguments that arise about the bride's wealth and see that the claims of all those connected with the marriage are noted. He also must invoke the ancestral spirits of the lineage and seek their blessings, to call out the honorific (paak) and the spear names (mut) of the clan. He states any further distinctions so all possibility of a breach of the rules of exogamy is avoided.

87 P.P. Howell, *A Manuel of Nuër Law*, p. 91

88 E.E. Evans-Pritchard "African: Journal of the International African Institute". p. 33.

Similarly, the bride has her attendant in the ngiy nyaal- [ŋii̱c nyaal] who is a girl of her age, usually from another family and unconnected lineage, while the gwan bothni- [gua̱n bööthni̱] of her lineage represents them in ritual and legal procedures. The gwan tuac and the ŋi̱c nyaal are usually the age-mates of the bridegroom and the bride respectively. They are unrelated to either, and their duties are essentially personal, while the gwan bothni- [gua̱n bööthni̱] usually much older men, represent the kinship interests of their respective sides.

According to P.P. Howell, after preliminary dancing and singing, which go on more or less continuously throughout the day. The people most early concerned in the negotiations, take up their positions in the cattle–byre. He states that the bride's family seats themselves on the left of the entrance facing the bridegroom's party, and her guan bothni sits in the central hearth (gorei-[gɔlrɛy] of the byre. On the right side, mats are laid (yii-[yiɛk], and on these, sit the bridegroom's party with their guan bothni- [gua̱n bööthni̱] nearest the door. The bride herself and her ngiiy nyaal- [ŋii̱c nyaal] do not appear during the negotiations. They are usually closeted inside the mother's hut (duel or hot) nearby. When all are seated, the gwan bothni- [gua̱n bööthni̱] of the bride breaks up some tobacco and hands it to the father, paternal uncles, and other senior relatives of the bridegroom as a symbol of friendship and hospitality.

P.P. Howell argues that it is also calculated to ease the tension, for Nuär regards the whole procedure as a nerve–racking ordeal, and like to smoke when they are nervous. Chief Negotiator -Gua̱n bööthni̱ then rises to his feet and calls out the honorific and spear names of the bride's lineage, and calls upon their ancestors to the proceedings. The gwan bothni [gua̱n bööthni̱] of the bridegroom's family then rises and scatters tobacco at the entrance of and inside the cattle-byre as an offering to the ancestral spirits of the bride. He then calls upon his ancestral spirits, which are those of the bridegroom's lineage, to witness the negotiations. He calls out their honorific and spear-names. If the honorific or spear names of the bridegroom coincide with those called out by the bride's guan bothni [gua̱n bööthni̱] it will be obvious that the rules of exogamy preclude all possibility of union, but the invocation is largely a formality because it is unlikely that negotiations for marriage would be allowed to go far if there were any possibility of incest.

7.6.2 Negotiations about Cattle

Negotiations about the cattle then begin. The number of cattle handed over, those transferred during the final marriage ceremonies, will vary considerably, but persons are standing in certain relationships with the bride who expect to receive their share. They are the ji̱ cuugni– [ji̱ cuuŋni̱] the 'people of rights.' P.P. Howell argues, "In theory, the bridegroom must produce cattle to meet the claims of all these kinsmen of the bride. But in fact, negotiations usually deteriorate into a heated augment, not always in keeping with the supposed solemnity of the occasion, and the main object of the bride's party is to get as many good cattle as possible, and of the bridegroom's family to avoid payment."[89]

It is, however, noticeable that negotiations of this sort are less clamorous than other Nuär affairs. The gwan bothn- [gua̱n

89 P.P. Howell, *A Manuel of Nuër Law*, p. 92.

bööthni̲] is expected to speak for the parties they represent, but most of those present will have their say. The colors, sex, and qualities of the cattle are discussed, and a clear idea about them. As soon as negotiations have started, the immediate kinsmen of the bride will have set to work to as much as they can about these cattle. In the initial stages of the discussion, however, a certain formality is observed; it is opened by the gwan bothni- [gua̲n bööthni̲] of the bride, who will speak in the name of those persons in the bride's family who have a claim on cattle.

As the argument continues in connection with each animal quoted by the bridegroom's family, he will state to which relative it will go. No cattle are handed over on this day, though a cow called yang gorei- [yaŋ gɔalrɛy], the 'cow of the hearth', which is part of the bride's father's portion, is sometimes handed over on the spot. This is a convention not often followed nowadays.

7.6.3 Celebration after Negotiations

P.P. Howell states that when the negotiations are over, the cattle are finished, and the parties go outside for the feasting that follows. There is no prohibition on the two families eating together, but the bridegroom himself and his gwan tuac- [gua̲n tuac] are not expected to eat the meat or drink the beer provided by the bride's people. They join the dancing. The bride and her ngiy nyaal- [ŋi̲i̲ nyaal] appear for the first time on the scene and enter the dance. The bride wears a black skin known as tuac cara- [tuac cärä] usually the skin of a black calf.

After dancing is over, those who are not closely related to

either party, but the legal representatives of the bridegroom and the bride's family and some of their close kinsmen, both male and female, go into a hut specially prepared for them which is known as duel koam [duel kɔam] for the occasion. There, they sit all night joking and conversing with their hosts until dawn. Another hut, known as the *duel* tuacni [duel tuacni̱] or duel kuen, is set aside for the young people of both parties, and the bride and bridegroom, their guan tuac and ngiy nyaal- [ŋi̱i̱c nyaal] sit there with their friends and coevals, singing and exhausting courting badinage all night through. This completes the ceremony known as twoc [tuɔ̱c].

The marriage is not supposed to have been consummated, but it has been acquired by this time. Some Nuär say that the marriage is now legal in the sense that, were there another man to have intercourse with the bride, full compensation for the adultery could be claimed by the bridegroom. P.P. Howell asserts that Laak and Thiang Nuär at any rate say that the significant act, which confirms the status of the bride as a wife and which subsequently, will be recognized in law, is the ceremony known as yier nyaal, which takes place in the evening immediately after the negotiations for the cattle. When the bride, and also her brothers and sisters present, are rubbed with butter by the gwan bothni [gua̱n bööthni̱] of the bridegroom. The legal status of the bride about the bridegroom and his family, at this point, the social and ritual process of marriage (and the bride-wealth have not necessarily been transferred in full to the bride's family). It is a controversial subject and is one, sometimes disputed in legal arguments.

The tuoc [tuɔ̱c] ceremony, at which negotiations over the cattle are completed and the blessing of the ancestral spirits is publicly invoked, does not usually take place before the girl has reached the age of puberty and is ready for marriage. When talking of a girl who has reached marriageable age, the Nuär will say she is ready for the most [muo̱t ('shaving') which is the next ceremony to take place. Muot [muo̱t] amounts to a public recognition of physical consummation [dɔnyni̱ ciökni̱], although, this does not necessarily mean that the girl has had sexual relations with her bridegroom before. The muot muo̱t has no legal right to physical consummation [dɔnyni̱ ciökni̱] and must visit his wife in secret, though her family will usually allow him to do so. Muot nyaal [muo̱t nyaal] therefore follows the tuoc [tuɔc] ceremony almost immediately.

7.7 Muot Nyal [Muo̱t Nyal]: 'The Shaving of the Bride'

According to P.P. Howell, the ceremonies known collectively under this heading have distinct legal significance, as seen later, and they include three important stages. First, the bridegroom with his guan tuac [gua̱n tuac] again suitably dressed in cat-skins- [ca tuac thɔ̱ɔ̱nä yiɛn ni gɔa] for the occasion, accompanied by other youths of his age, goes to the bride's home to ask for her people's official consent for consummation [dɔnyni̱ cööknḭ]. There, they enter a hut specially set aside for them and are joined by the bride, her ngiy nyaal [ŋi̱i̱c nyaal], and other girls of her lineage and neighbourhood.

They spend the day and the whole night in conversation and singing. There is, as usual, a good deal of sexual badinage, but no physical consummation. The next morning, the bridegroom approaches the muot [muo̱t] that is to follow. Before giving her consent, she will expect to receive, or at any rate obtain the promise of special presents, which are known as the nyin dapä. These include a goat or two, a spear, or fish spear, a ring, and other offerings, and if she has any co-wives who stand in the relationship of the mother to the bride, they will expect to benefit too.

According to P.P. Howell, these follow the ritual performance known as loony deeb [luɔ̱ny deeb], 'losing the rope', which symbolizes the bride's release from her father's homestead. The bridegroom and his representatives stand on one side of the cattle-byre, the bride and her friends on the other, while her father casts a cattle rope between them. The bride is then ceremonially dressed in the clothes, which distinguish a married woman from unmarried girls: a leather apron or a skirt of plaited cotton.

7.8 Noong Nyaal [Nööŋ Nyaal]: The Bringing of the Bride'

P.P. Howell affirms that the same evening, representatives of the bridegroom go to inform the bride's relatives that everything is ready for them. The bride is then, conducted to the bridegroom's home by a party of her girlfriends (who are called noong [nööŋ] or 'bringers'). On her arrival, she sits down on a special mat provided for her outside the bridegroom's house by his gwan bothni [gua̱n bööthni̱]. A bull is brought out and sacrificed, while gwan böthni [gua̱n bööthni̱] again calls out the honorific and spear names of the lineage and calls upon the ancestral spirits to bless the union, to accept the bride, and give her male children to uphold the spear-name in posterity and daughters to bring cattle to the kinship group.

The bride then lies on the mat and is covered with skin (tuac carä). Meanwhile, the bridegroom presents his mother-in-law with a goat or sheep to release her, temporarily at any rate, from the taboo of eating at his home. The bride is then assisted into the hut and the bridegroom, whip in hand, and goes after her. After he has given her a thorough beating inside the hut (wuoc dhoori nyaal), the couple spends the night together and the marriage is said to be officially consummated. The beating is said to symbolize the bridegroom's authority over his bride who is now his wife, emphasizing the rights he now has over her.

7.9 Muot Nyal [Muɔ̱t Nyal]: 'Shaving the Bride'

According to P.P. Howell, the next day the most nyal [muɔ̱t nyaal], the actual 'shaving of the bride', takes place. In the morning, the bride is usually taken away to the home of some unrelated person nearby. Nevertheless, she is brought back to the bridegroom's home towards evening. Her head is then ceremonially shaved by one of the senior female relatives of the bridegroom, usually his elder sister, or by a co-wife of his mother, or sometimes, the wife of his gwan bothni [gua̱n bööthin].

At any rate, a married woman of the bridegroom's family should perform the shaving. It signifies the bride's reception into the status of a married woman in that family. She is then taken once more to her own home. They dress her with a special skirt (yiät-yɔak). This is to express the reaching of womanhood. In the end, the same woman who accompanied the girl to the house of her husband will accompany her back to the house of her father. The father will assign a special hut to her, isolated therein around the family.

There, she will receive the visits of the husband starting a couple of days later and consummate the marriage muɔt also refers to handing over the bride to the bridegroom's family and consummation thereafter. [90]It resembles a delivery of goods sold after families agreed on bride-wealth. She would be given a traditional skirt known as (Yɔak) and then; she would be called a married woman. A grandmother would come to bless the bride after the ceremony in the evening. The bride would be seated on a traditional sleeping mat (Yiɛk). Her breasts would be anointed with butter and flour (döh). Before the above process is done, the bride would undertake an oath to make sure that she would abide by the laws of marriage. (Pledge to honour the marriage contract.)

7.10 The Legal Dimension of Consummation

The marriage ceremony has a variety of effects on the husband. The following are some effects of the consummation ceremony: first, the bride would be put under full control of the groom's family. Second, she would be in a loose relationship with her own family. Third, her husband would own everything she acquires after concluding marriage. Fourth, if she killed somebody, her husband would be liable for it. Fifth, if she finds a treasure, it would be her husband's property. Sixth, a wife would acquire the status of a married woman. Seventh, the husband would have a sexual exclusive right to her. Eighth, if she commits adultery, compensation is given to the husband for the infringement of his sexual right. A groom has sexual intercourse with his wife only if the consummation

---

90 Michael Bol Chan. Interviewed on the 29th May 2019, POCs, Juba, South Sudan.

ceremony is performed.[91] For the consummation ceremony to take place, a bride would first come and see the groom's home whether it is a better place to stay. Her sisters and other female relatives would accompany her to the groom's home.

The process is (nööŋ) by the bridesmaids because the bride's sisters escorted their sister while visiting the groom's home. When they reached the groom's home, a rite would be performed, and the bridesmaids would stay for some days with their sister. The number of days depends on the groom's family's wealth. After their visitation, the bride and her sisters would return to their homes, and her husband would be free to visit her any time he felt like. That is called (dɔnyni̱ cöökni̱).

A person who has reached marriageable age but did not marry is usually stereotyped. For example, he cannot ask for food from a family of his peers who got married if he has known to have cattle to pay for bride-wealth but failed to enter marriage. In all aspects, he is discriminated against until he changes his mind and enters into marriage.

P.P. Howell affirms, "After these ceremonies are over the bride rarely takes up residence at her husband's home, but lives for a period in her own home, where her husband has the right to visit her."[92] Often a special hut is set aside for her there. There is no general rule on this matter, but it is regarded by the Nuär as proper that she should remain in her own home until her first child is born and weaned, for until that time, although the marriage has a legal basis, it is not considered confirmed.

Sometimes, however, the husband has no one to assist him

91 Daniel Kai Liah. Interviewed on the 30th May 2019 POCs South Sudan Juba.

92 P.P. Howell, *A Manuel of Nuër Law*, p. 93.

in his home. For example, to cook for him, in which case, he may receive permission from his wife's people for her to live with him permanently as soon as the muot [muɔ̱t] has been performed. When the first child is weaned, the wife's mother can claim the yang doth garda [yaŋ do̱o̱th gatdä] the 'cow of bearing a child', a cow which is considered a fee for assisting the girl to give birth to a child. This is usually followed by a formal change of residence. The yang doth gatda [yaŋ do̱o̱th gatä] is the last cow which needs to be paid by the husband, although his wife's family may beg him to give them other cattle when further children are born and weaned. Nevertheless, he is not bound to do so and claims of this sort, if they ever arise, would not nowadays be upheld in a Nuär court.

7.11 Ideal Rules for Distribution of Cattle

According to the famous anthropologists E.E. Evans-Pritchard and P.P. Howell, the ideal rules for cattle in marriage are as follows: bride-wealth should consist of 40 heads of cattle. Among the Eastern Nuär, 20 are said to go kwi gwan, to the father's side, and the 20-kwi *man,* to the mother's side, of the bride. There is equal division between the bride's paternal kinsmen (including her father) and her maternal kinsmen (including her mother) as the first rule of distribution.

Of the 20 beasts that go to the father's side, 10 remain with the father (or his sons) and 10 are divided among the family (his parents, brothers, sisters); and of the 20 beasts that go to the mother's side, 10 remain with the mother (or her sons) and 10 are divided among her family (her parents and brothers and sisters. The second rule, therefore, is that the cattle are distributed in fixed proportions between three families: the bride's own family, her father's family, and her mother's family.[93]

Paternal side: a cow and its calf (2), an ox to the father of the girl (8). A cow and its calf and an ox to the girl's paternal uncle (the elder brother by the same mother–4). A cow and its calf, another calf, and an ox to the girl's paternal uncle (the elder brother by a different mother–3). A cow and an ox to the father's youngest brother by the same mother (1). A heifer to the father's sister (1).

Maternal side: a cow and its calf and a heifer to the mother (3). An ox, another ox, a cow, another cow and its calf, and another cow (7). A cow and its calf, another cow, and an ox (the mother's elder brother by the same mother–4). A cow and its calf and an ox (mother's brother of a different mother–3). A cow and its calf to the mother's youngest brother by the same mother–2). A heifer to the mother's sister (1).

7.12 Critiques

In the first place, one should appreciate and acknowledge the effort made by Dr. P.P. Howell by observing systematically the Nuär ceremonial process of marriage. It is evident from the sources that he tried his level best to write every detail of Nuär marriage similar to Evans-Pritchard. According to him, the social and ritual processes of marriage consist of first, courting, and betrothal. Second, luom nyal: [lu̲ɔm nyaal] courting the girl. Third, thiec nyal: [thiec nyaal] asking for the girl. Fourth, *Cuei:* [cuic] Betrothal. Fifth, Twoc ghok: [tu̲ɔc ɣɔ̲ɔ̲k] invocation of the cattle. Sixth, muot nyal: [mu̲ɔt

93 Cf. P.P. Howell, *A Manuel of Nuër Law*, p. 98.

nyaal] shaving of the bride. Seventh, luony deb: [luɔ̱ny dëb]' losing the rope. *'eighty,* Noong nyal: [nööŋ nyaal] 'the bringing of the bride.' Ninth, muot nyal: [muɔ̱t nyaal]' shaving the bride. Tenth, distribution of bride-wealth, which consists of 40 cattle to the family of the bride.

By observing such a renumbering of ceremonial processes in Nuär marriage presented by Dr P.P. Howell, the repetitions of such numbers permit us to conclude that such steps of ceremonial Nuär marriage are not placed in the right order. Some ceremonial steps are repeated and this can lead to confusion if not complication. Every Nuär person will say that seven, Loony deb: [luɔ̱ny dëb] losing the rope has not been used in the right place. The word long deb: [luɔ̱ny dëb]' losing the rope, according to Nuär both in the West and in the East, denotes discontinuity of marriage between the prospective bridegroom and the prospective bride. When that happens after paying some cattle by the prospect bridegroom's kinsmen to the prospect bride's kinsmen, the prospect bridegroom accompanied by a team of senior women of his kinsmen will march to the prospect bride's father's home singing and dancing.

They will stand in front of the byre, and then the prospect bride's father will ask his daughter to untie all the cattle of the prospect bridegroom to be taken away by them. This indicates the discontinuity of marriage between the two families. Therefore, the prospective bridegroom and the prospective bride are from now on free to choose any other girl as their future partner. Concerning the number of 40 cattle in Nuär marriage as it appeared in both records of E.E. Evans-Pritchard and Dr. P.P. Howell; such a number is not consistent in Nuär marriage. For example, the Jagɛi and

Dɔk Nuär marry with 35 cattle. The variation comes from the counting system among the Nuär people but it is important to know this difference.

Furthermore, one can realize the repetitions made by Dr. P.P. Howell about Evans-Pritchard on Nuär marriage. The similarities in terms of contents and steps are noticeable. We can even say that Dr. P.P. Howell used the sources documented by Evans-Pritchard on Nuär marriage.

Conclusion

P.P. Howell concludes his treatment of the true union between a man and a woman in Nuär: This concludes a very condensed account of the ritual and social processes of marriage among the Nuär. It is the payment of bride-wealth, that legalizes the union, and that some ceremonies are sometimes not performed at all is not necessarily evidence in Nuär courts today that the marriage is not a legal union. The payment of cattle, however, usually follows the ceremonies described.

As Professor Evans-Pritchard has pointed out, 'payments of cattle and marriage rites, therefore, tend to alternate, though there is no fixity about the alternation and no marriage is the same as another in this respect *is* likely that a ceremony takes place unless the appropriate stage in the negotiations over cattle has been reached, so that in seeking to determine the legality of a union, a Nuär court will first ask what ceremonies have been performed.

The issue in such cases concerns not so much the number of cattle paid, but the liabilities and rights of the husband and his wife. It would be relevant, for example, if a woman committed a wrong. If she killed someone, the payment of compensation would be a liability to her husband if she was legally his wife, but if there were insufficient legal determination in the union, the responsibility would rest with her kinsmen.

Similarly, if a man lies with a woman who is not his wife, he may be charged with adultery (dhuu ciek*)* and compensation will be claimed, but he might with justification plead that she is not a married woman in the legal sense, and therefore the act is not adultery. Proving that the union is not a legal one, he has no liability, but this will not absolve him from responsibility, for in certain circumstances her kinsmen may claim damages on the grounds of seduction of an unmarried girl.

There are many circumstances considered by the court, circumstances discussed later under this heading of wrongs about women. In such cases, the legality or otherwise of the marriage is an issue, and it is sometimes difficult to what constitutes the legality. In most tribes, the ceremony considered to legalize the union is the *muot [mu̱ɔt],* but this, as it will be seen later, is not a universal law among the Nuär.

CHAPTER EIGHT

REASONS FORTYPES OF UNTRUE MARRIAGE

Introduction

Chapter eight defines the terms sexuality and marriage, their social and religious dimensions, the complexity of Nuär marriage, the types of untrue union of marriage such as marriage between two females (not lesbian), examples of marriage between two females, marriage for an impotent person-kuën luc ciek.

It further explains the desire to have an heir, levirate-kuëŋ ciek jɔkä duel, the strict rules to inherit the deceased wife, the legal union of the levirate, a ghost (surrogate) marriage-kuen jɔkä ciek, the characteristics of a ghost-(surrogate) marriage, the categories of persons for the ghost-marriage, the differences between a ghost and levirate marriage, trial marriage-thop ciek lɔrä, theory of polyandry including the chief husband in the polyandrous union, and finally, polygamy and monogamy.

8. Sexuality and Marriage

Since sex, sexuality, and marriage do not belong to specific people but are innate in human nature; therefore, wider definitions of those terms are permissible. A distinction between the words 'sex' and 'sexuality' to clarify their distinctive meanings is required; otherwise, naivety will permit us to confuse the two. First, the word 'sex' comes from medieval Roman Catholic Latin referring to the commandment against adultery. Consequently, it has various meanings. According to M. Vayhinger, sexual means, sexual intercourse, coitus, sex organs of the male and female, sexual intimacy of marital partners, masculinity and femininity, gender description, the conception of reproduction of the species, immoral and unethical sexual relations (i.e., adultery, fornication, rape, etc.), and psychiatrically defined deviate behaviour."[94] Furthermore, sex is more than genetics biology, and learning. M. Vayhinger and Hyder state that:

Sex is a gift from God... It is the most complete way of giving of oneself to another. It is the most personal, intimate, and sacramental outward expression of the inner physical and spiritual love, which God has given. Sexual intercourse within Christian marriage is the highest symbolic act, which our mortal bodies are capable of performing, and as such, represents worship, and thanksgiving to the God of love who created us.[95]

According to Y. Fehlman, the biology of sex is the study of the functioning of the human body in relationship to the

94 J. M. Vayhinger, (ed.), "Sexual Variety, Deviance, and Disorder" in the Dictionary of Pastoral Care and Counseling, Nashville, Abingdon Press, (2005), pp. 1149-1151.

95 Ibid.

physical development of the male and female body and brain. He argues that regardless of the genetic coding, during the first weeks of development male and female embryos are anatomically identical. At fertilization, when the male sperm and female egg unite to form a zygote, the initial programming for sexual differentiation is set in place. Y. Fehlman asserts that the sperm carries an X or a Y sex chromosome, while the egg always has an X chromosome. When the twenty-three chromosomes of the egg combine with the twenty-three chromosomes of the sperm, the zygote has forty-six chromosomes. Generally, a forty-six, XX chromosome pattern is the genetic code for a female and a forty-six, XY pattern creates a pattern for a male.[96]

B. Nelson asserts that sexuality is not limited to genital expressions and procreative capacities. More broadly, it is the human way of being in the world as female or male persons including varied experiences and understandings of sex roles, sexual-affectional orientations, perceptions of one's embeddedness and that of others, and capacities for sensuousness, emotional depth, and interpersonal intimacy. According to him, "Christian ethics and theology of sexuality attempt to interpret the meanings and expressions of sexuality in the light of the Bible, Christian tradition, and contemporary thought. At the same time, it is important to understand how the sexual experience and perception of Christians give shape to their understandings of Scripture, tradition, and the present life of faith."[97]

---

96 F.Y. Fehlman, (ed.), "Sexuality, Biological and Psychological Theory of." in the Dictionary of Pastoral Care and Counseling, Nashville, Abingdon Press, (2005), pp. 1151-1154.

97 J. B. Nelson, (ed.), "Sexuality, Christian Theology and Ethics of." *in the Dictionary of Pastoral Care and Counseling,* Nashville, Abingdon Press,

8.1 Social and Religious Dimensions of Nuär Marriage

Marriage in Nuär culture is very complex because it seems to be done by everyone, for everyone, and with everyone. This may not be unique to Nuär alone, because it is extended to other indigenous Africans. When it comes to Nuär marriage, however, specialized anthropologists such as Sir Edward Evans Pritchard, Dr. P.P Howell, who wrote a book entitled "A Manuel of Nuër Law" that consists of 256 pages, and Dr. Douglas H. Johnson who wrote a book on Nuär entitled "Nuër Prophets" which consists of 407 pages, made many attempts. All these outstanding figures in the academic field of anthropology might have motivated each.

Furthermore, they might have been motivated also by the information they received from colonizers (British Government and Muslim Arabs of the North Sudan). Alternatively, they might have found themselves in Nuär communities for various humanitarian services. No one can deny his or her efforts to understand indigenous culture, as we shall discuss later.

Therefore, any Nuär man/woman who would like to write anything about the Nuär culture such as customs, religion, prophets, marriage, and other crucial issues, should not ignore those prominent anthropologists above-mentioned. Their efforts as specialized anthropologists have contributed to and are living memories of Nuär culture. It is recommended that one should take their materials as primary sources about Nuär culture. Although one may consider himself/herself as the owner of the culture, which might be true to some extent, for academic respect, one should never overlook their efforts.

(2005), pp. 1154-1158.

8.2 Complexity of Nuär Marriage

Having said that their efforts have contributed a lot to preserving the living memories of Nuär culture, however, this does not permit us to conclude that their contributions have covered everything in Nuär culture. We have mentioned earlier the complexity, depth and richness of Nuär culture, especially about marriage. This complexity, depth and richness of Nuär marriage require special attention such that one must include everything and exclude nothing.

The concept of marriage in Nuär culture according to Dr Howell includes the following categories: first, simple legal marriage, second, ghost marriage. Categories of persons on whose behalf 'ghost-marriages are made. Third, ghost marriage and bridewealth. Fourth, the levirate. However, about 'ghost-marriage' and levirate, there is a difference between them. Categories of persons with whom a widow lives.

Fifth, widow-concubines. Sixth, Unmarried-concubines. Accordingly, this list does not cover everything about the Nuär custom of marriage and Nuär culture. Therefore, Dr. P.P. Howell should agree with me on this dissatisfaction. In his table of contents on Nuär marriage, two important types of marriages have escaped his attention not consciously but because of the delicacy and complexity of Nuär marriage. These two types of marriages are as follows: first, marriage for an impotent person. Second, marriage for a female (not lesbian). These two types of marriages will be explained later on to have a comprehensive list of categories of Nuär marriage.

According to Nuär, cows as bride-wealth are an important step, yet they do not signify certainty of marriage. However, they ought to be considered as a legal step to marriage. Marriage in Nuär culture requires serious steps of negotiations and legally recognized ceremonial meetings between the two families. As such, marriage includes social and ritual processes with flexibility depending on the person involved in the marriage and the marriage in question. For, Levirate-Kuëŋ ciek duel by the close relative of the deceased person requires no processes and ritual ceremonies to be repeated as both P.P. Howell and Evans-Pritchard said. Therefore, as a principle, negotiations, ritual ceremonies, and social processes, are not required for untrue unions, which are not legal, but for true union, they must be followed.

For example, social and ritual processes, negotiation, the ceremonial meetings are required for legal marriage which can be applied to a Nuär young man who has reached the age of maturity (initiated incise g̱ar*)*. Another condition is that his father ought to have sufficient cows. The prospective bridegroom is the right person among his brothers to be allowed to marry an elder). According to Dr Howell..." unless the union is prearranged by the parents, the youth has probably met his future bride at the dances held by young people and has danced and 'flirted' with her for some time."[98]

Consideration is given to the most important rituals and negotiations. Dr. Howell argues that the form and order of ceremonial rites, among primitive peoples, usually vary considerably on each occasion, and no marriage ceremony is a word for word, an act for an act, an exact repetition of another. In this sense, local Nuär customs may have variations, and the degree of ceremonialist and publicity, may not necessarily be followed in Nuär customary marriage.

98 P.P. Howell, *A Manual of Nuër Law*, pp. 86-87.

8.3 Types of Untrue Union of Marriage

Earlier, we have said that even though Dr P. P. Howell and Evans-Pritchard had tried their level best to cover everything about Nuär marriage nevertheless, two essential types escaped their attention. The two types of marriage, which they did not touch in their exploration of Nuär marriage, as we shall discuss below are essential and cannot be ignored by Nuär People. This is because they also reflect the philosophy of continuity of life among the Nuär People.

8.3.1 Marriage Between Two Females (Not Lesbian)

Among the Nuär communities, it is a common practice for a woman to marry another female. This practice of marriage between two females exists in all the Nuär communities in the East, central, and west. This practice occurs for two reasons: first when a woman has no male boy in her household. Second, when she is barren. Therefore, the main reason for her to marry another female is to have a bull-*tut* male to guarantee the continuity of her line tree genealogy, for the erection of her house cuɔ̱ŋ duelɛ, (Pët maacdɛ).

This practice among the Nuär People has nothing to do with lesbians in which the two females engage in sexual coitus. Marriage between females, in Nuär communities, requires a third person, who can play the biological functional role in the name of another. For example, a choice for a person such as a male person related to the prospective woman who carried out the marriage. The purpose is to beget children for the continuity of her line tree through that male person who does such a biological job for her. The 'procreative dimension' is necessary for the continuity and the remembrance of the exact copy of herself. The command of God which says, "Be fertile and multiply, and fill the earth...."(Gen 1:28), is not limited to a man in Nuär concept of marriage. In Africa and specifically, in the Nuär system of marriage and philosophy of life, those who are barren or impotent offer their contribution through their kinsmen.

The crucial and disturbing issue of marriage between females among the Nuär communities is about the continuity or future destiny of that barren woman. First, it is about the continuity of her life here on earth and after her death. Second, it is about the desire to leave behind a photocopy of herself and for the family. Third, it is about believing in the continuity of life. It is about the desire to leave behind a living memory. Fourth, it is about the desire to contribute to the family. Fifth, it is about the desire to leave no gap or vacuum for the continuity of life for any person including herself.

Leaving no gap between the past, present, and future, means that justice is done for the continuity of life. Such reasons should never be dismissed or ignored without harming the person and the philosophical system of life of Nuär communities and indigenous Africans at large, Somewhere, people are campaigning for the legalization of the death of innocent children, however, in Nuär communities, the desire to beget children, is a priority which need to be attained by all and even if it means stealing children like the case of Murle of South Sudan which is morally unacceptable.

Therefore, the attitude of 'traffic police' who stop cars on the road should never be applied to human persons and traditional values, which are related to marriage. This is because these are essential realities of vital force. Unfortunately, there are many attempts to knock at our doors. For example, such as gays and lesbians, confuse our true cultural value of marriage between a man and a woman. We said with certainty that the creation and imposition of some cultural values on others are unjust and intimidating. Respect due to cultural values related to marriage is required in Nuär culture and system of marriage as well as in other African traditional systems of marriage. The African concept of marriage leaves no room for the absolutization of individual freedom but it asserts the principle that says 'all for all and each for all.'

8.3.1.1 Examples of Marriage Between Two Females

Marriage between two females in the Nuär system of marriage cannot happen unless there is availability of wealth such as cattle. For example in western, central, and eastern Nuär communities, marriage between two females: a certain woman by the name Nyaboth after realizing that she is barren, but cultivated a lot with a rich harvest. After receiving a rich harvest, her products brought her many cows. With those cows, she married a girl by the name of Cuol of Där. She asked her brother by name Bol to carry out the biological function of begetting children for her. The children were named after her and not after her brother. To confirm this documentation, the bridegroom madam Nyaboth was a grandmother to seminarian Charles Keah from third year *Philosophicum* at St. Paul's Major Seminary Juba-Munuki (South Sudan) from

Rev. Fr. Jacob Nhial Gatluak, an Ethiopian Catholic priest in the Vicariate of Gambella, from the Congregation of Apostolic Life called "Missionary Xaverian of Yarumal in Columbia," incardinated in the diocese of Malakal accepted to share his experience about female marriages. Fr. Jacob is from the Eastern Nuär, from the clan called Gajaak. While talking about marriage between females in Nuär culture, Fr. Nhial without hesitation, offered me information about what happened in their family before he could join the seminary of the Missionary Xaverians of Yarumal, a Pontifical Institute of Apostolic life.

Fr. Nhial told me that his maternal aunt by name Nyayual Puk in 2001 married a girl named Nyapuot Deng. According to him, her maternal aunt intended him to be the one to bring children for her from this new bride called Nyapuot Deng. Nevertheless, as a strong Catholic, he explained to her maternal aunt Nyayual the doctrine of "monogamy" which was finally accepted by his aunt with difficulty. The family then settled the issue by choosing another man within the family to carry out this biological duty for Nyayual.

Rev. Fr. William Bol, the Vice-Rector and Head of the Department of *Philosophicum*, also has shared with me about the same issue of marriage between two females. According to him, his maternal aunt gave birth only to girls without a single boy. Those daughters had become the sources of wealth for her. Consequently, she became very rich, Nyamonkä Kuɔ̱n. Finally, she decided to marry a girl by the name Dia̱a̱ŋ Köt Kek from western Nuär Leer-Lɛr. She was the maternal aunt of Fr. William Bol.

8.3.2 Marriage for an Impotent Person-Kuën Luc Ciek

Earlier we discussed examples of marriage for females in Nuär communities and we asserted this has nothing to do with lesbians. We mentioned two main reasons for marriage for females: first, when a woman has no male boy in her household, and second, when a woman is barren. In both cases, the reason to get married is the same. The only intention is to have a bull (tut male), to erect the family line tree or genealogy for the continuity of life in that specific house as we have mentioned earlier.

Among the family's concerns in the Nuär community, marriage is an instrument for caring for an impotent person within the family as it does for a barren female. This is not a unique or rare phenomenon for Nuär people, but also for the rest of indigenous communities in Africa at large. However, when each community deals with it, it must require serious attention. The command of God says, "Be fertile and multiply and fill the earth... (Gen 1:28), has unfortunately left out some people for reasons which are known to God alone. We do assume that the distribution of 'sex ratios' should be enough for all and nobody should be deprived of it. Nevertheless, to explain this unfortunate phenomenon, we should focus on our biological and physiological functions of original sin.

Our physiological condition requires medical checkups and thanks be to God, for choosing some of us to specialize in medicine to deal with such issues. According to Merriam-Webster's Collegiate Dictionary, "impotence" is defined as being "unable to have sexual intercourse because of erectile dysfunction."[99] This is broadly explained as sterility.

However, our focus on marriage about an impotent person in Nuär philosophy of life, and how to deal with the physical healing of an impotent person in the family is another thing

---

99 Merriam Webster's *Collegiate Dictionary*, Tenth Edition, Massachusetts, U.S.A, Merriam-Webster, Incorporated, 2000, p. 583.

altogether. Previously, some few prophets among the Nuär do have the power to restore male sexual dysfunction. However, our main concern is, when such a thing happens to somebody within the family circle among the Nuär, how does the rest of the family respond to it? Will the rest of the family leave the case of their impotent son and brother behind? Will they not show concern for his continuity of life after his death here on earth?

According to Nuär, love, justice, and generosity will never allow them to ignore the marriage for a deceased person, but rather will compel them to address it responsibly. Love in this community is not a selfish, individualistic, and egoistic project, but rather it requires the highest sacrifices that have a social dimension. In the Nuär community, one must see all the dimensions related to life such as family, community, disease, impotence, barrenness, ancestors, (living dead) and above all God is considered the source of everything.

The same concern of the philosophy of life about female marriage among the Nuär manifests itself towards an impotent person. However, about the concern shown to an impotent person, the situation is complex and delicate unlike the one of a barren female. The barren female among the Nuär, willingly accepts her status and openly searches for whom she can marry, while the impotent male (Wud mäluc), does not want to reveal his impotence to anyone. It is only known to the mother, brothers, and maybe to his few close friends but no one is allowed to talk about it openly. It has to be kept secret within the family circle including his close relatives. Nobody will mention to him by mistake that you are impotent. It is compared to the seal of the confessional box in the Catholic Church.

The philosophy for keeping it secret is to convince the impotent person that he can marry when the family requests him to do so. There are many techniques to be used to convince him. One is the general pretention that nobody knows that he is impotent, and consequently, to uses his close friends to convince him to accept the marriage. With this, the policy and diplomacy of prevention work. In this regard, all the members of the family will encourage him to choose any girl he wants. If his choice has succeeded, other members of the family will push him to marry that girl of his suits.

If all the requirements demanded by normal marital procedures are completed, everybody in the family will assume that everything has finished, including the impotent person. However secretly, the family will choose a trustworthy person without the knowledge of the impotent person, the 'stupid bridegroom' to carry out this biological function for him. Unfortunately, sometimes, the prospective bride, may not be notified about this problem but will find herself sleeping with a different man related to the impotent person, chosen for her by the family of the prospective impotent bridegroom.

The main reason for the family to marry the impotent person a wife, is to make sure that his house is erected that his line tree must continue, and that he must be remembered. It is still a common practice and I contacted many people about this issue but due to respect of their dignity, I cannot disclose their names. It is not normal to give an example of such an issue. This is the uniqueness and particularity of our Nuär philosophy of life. We believe that although someone in Nuär communities, has a sexual dysfunction, this will never reduce his dignity as a person. His dignity remains equal to all in terms of treatment and concern. According to Nuär, sexuality goes beyond the sexual dysfunction of the individual. If unfortunately, sexual dysfunction occurs to someone, others can offer solutions to it. As we shall discuss below, such a desire to have an heir led to the unfortunate schism of the Church of England from the Catholic Church under the request of King Henry VIII of England.

8.3.3 The Desire to Have an Heir

The majority of the Fathers of the Church believed that the marriage bond is indissoluble. The interpretation, which sees the "fornication clause" as exceptional, is also the position of the tradition existing from the earliest time. Some Fathers of the Church considered an exception in difficult cases; e.g., they usually refer to the fornication clause quoted by Matthew including their opinions. The oriental Churches in early Christian history already adopted this second tradition.

The supreme doctrine of the Magisterium on the indissolubility of marriage is characterized by an 'abiding conviction', which considers the marriage bond as indissoluble. According to the Roman Pontiffs and the Councils, the general teaching on indissolubility is persistent, consistent, and practically unanimous: no marriage is possible after divorce. The Magisterium resolutely and without reservation defended the indissolubility of marriage between partners who lawfully entered marriage even at the price of great sacrifices and suffering. Such was the case presented to Pope Clement by King Henry VIII of England to divorce his wife, Catherine.

According to L. Manschreck, of the six children born to him, Catherine had only one daughter, Mary who survived. King Henry VIII was disturbed and increasingly worried and anxious. A woman who had never ruled England was the concern raised by the King. Manschreck asserts that Henry..." began to doubt the legitimacy of his marriage and to feel that his having no male heir might be the judgment of God upon him for marrying his brother's widow."[100] It is said that under these circumstances drawn by the shapely figure of Anne Boleyn, who refused to share his bed without sharing his crown, Henry directed Cardinal Wolsey to ask Pope Clement to grant him a certificate of divorce for the reason above-mentioned.

Taking the example of John the Baptist, Pope Clement resolutely remained faithful to the sexual ethics of the book of Leviticus which says, "If a man takes his brother's wife, it is severe defilement and has disgraced his brother; he shall be childless" (20:21). Instructions on sexual ethics in the book of Leviticus mentioned above, Pope Clement threatened to excommunicate King Henry VIII, which led to schism due to the complexity of the political implications.

According to Manschreck, the capstone came with the Supreme Act in November 1534 which confirmed Henry as 'Supreme Head' of the Church of England with full power 'to visit, repress, reform, order, correct, retain, and amend all such errors, heresies, offences, contempt's, enormities, whatsoever they are for the conservation of the peace, unity, and tranquillity of this realm. It is stated that the Parliament's Act of Succession, 1534, declared Princess Mary, Daughter of Catherine of Aragon, illegitimate, and named the infant daughter of Anne Boleyn, Elizabeth, born September 7, 1533, the heir to the throne."

---

100 Clyde L. Manschreck, *A History of Christianity in the World, From Persecution to Uncertainty*, New Jersey, Prentice-Hall, INC, 1974, p. 245.

Not to accept this or the supremacy of the king constituted treason. Therefore, one should know without doubt that the truth about this matter of indissolubility of marriage as articulated and stipulated in the book of Leviticus is unchangeable and unalterable. Yes, it has led to the death of John the Baptist and the 'great Anglican schism' led by King Henry VIII of England, yet the Church will always remain faithful to this teaching handed down to her by Christ. Therefore, to have an heir, was very important to King Henry VIII, as well as it is important for both barren women of Nuär and impotent men of Nuär.

8.3.4 Levirate-Kuëŋ Ciek Jɔkä duel

According to Merriam-Webster,' the term "levirate" is sometimes explained as a compulsory marriage of a widow to a brother of her deceased husband. According to Nuär, the word levirate has nothing to do with marriage. According to them, if it is applied to the Nuär language, can simply mean 'putting the wife of a deceased person into a hut by one of his brothers'-Kuëŋ Ciek Jɔkä duel. It is a common practice among the Nuär people. The logic of this practice goes back to the marriage concept. In all the ceremonial marital processes, one observes the participation of all the kinsmen of the prospective bridegroom.

The active participation by all the kinsmen of the prospective bridegroom, during the ceremonial marital processes, can permit us to conclude that the new bride belongs to all members of the bridegroom's family The payment of heads of cattle by the kinsmen of the bridegroom to the bride's family, leaves us no doubt that the bride has become a full member of the new family. While the husband is still alive, he does the job of being a husband to his wife specifically sexual coitus. Nobody among his brothers should interfere with this biological function while he is still alive otherwise.

8.3.4.1 Strict Rules to Inherit the Deceased Wife

Should death occur to him, the kinsmen of the deceased person will automatically assume the responsibility. In such a case, strict principles require serious observation. First, no outsider can interfere with the wife of the deceased person. Second, from the side of the maternal uncle, there is no permission to inherit the wife of his maternal son but the maternal son can inherit the wife of his maternal uncle if he dies. Third, the father of the deceased person cannot inherit his son's wife but the son can inherit his father's wife if his father dies. Fourth, the father cannot inherit his son's wife but the son can inherit the paternal wife.

From the explanation of the word 'levirate,' we heard that sometimes, it is described as a compulsory marriage of a widow to a brother of her deceased husband. According to Nuär, compulsory inheritance of a widow to a brother of her deceased husband happens when the wife of a deceased is being forced on him by the kinsmen. It is not compulsory if she chooses freely among the brothers of the deceased.

However, the concept of marriage has no place in levirate among the Nuär because there is no repetition of any marriage in this regard. P.P. Howell affirms that the union of a widow with her husband's kinsman does not constitute a remarriage or a 'ghost-marriage': the marriage is already in existence, and legally, she is still the wife of the dead man. According to him, any children she may bear after his death are legally his. It merely means that a kinsman, or another man, acts as genitor and foster father of her children.

The explanation above coincided with the investigations and observations made by P.P. Howell. According to him, "Bride-wealth cattle are not collected by the individual efforts of one man; certain categories of kinsmen co-operate and assist him to get married. Moreover, many cattle are held in trust by the family, particularly those inherited by brothers."[101] In his observation, P.P. Howell argues that it is not the legal husband alone who benefits from the domestic and economic services of his wife, though the children link themselves directly to his name; they are part of the lineage to which he belongs.

The brothers of the deceased person are equally anxious that his offspring shall swell the members of the patrilineal group. Based on that concern, it is said that if a man dies, his widow is expected to continue bearing children to his name. Theoretically, also she is expected to remain his near kinsmen and to assist them in normal domestic and economic activities. According to P.P. Howell, for both these reasons, she should live with one of his brothers or, in certain circumstances, with other categories of kinsmen.

8.3.4.2 The Legal Union of the Levirate

The legality of the union of the levirate according to P.P. Howell depends on two things: first, the levirate is a legal union, and in certain circumstances, kinsmen may demand the divorce of their dead kinsman's wife. Second, if an outsider has sexual relations with a widow, her dead husband's kin is

101 P.P. Howell, *A Manuel of Nuër Law*, p. 78.

compensated for adultery unless some previous agreement has been reached between them. The Nuär believe that the legal husband of the woman and the legal father of her children is still the man who has died. The children will be linked in the lineage of his family to his name. His heirs guard the legality of marriage. It is believed that in his name, his heir or heirs will continue to represent his interests. Those interests too, are their own as members of his kinship group.

According to P.P. Howell, this point is all-important in the assessment of the rights of a widow in legal disputes which appear before Nuär courts. Sometimes, it happens, that the bride-wealth cattle are returned to the wife's family husband's death, and the dead man's heirs retain no further rights in that woman; but in this case, the legal marriage has been dissolved. Therefore, the situation is not different from normal cases of divorce.

8.3.5 Ghost (Surrogate) Marriage-Kuen jɔkä Ciek

P.P. Howell argues that it is an accepted rule among the Nuär that if a man dies before he is married or dies without male issue one of his kinsmen, often his brother, must marry to him a wife. This is one of the strongest mutual obligations of kinship among the Nuär as we have mentioned earlier. It is considered essential that a man should have an heir who can carry on his name and 'keep it green' to further the interests of the lineage in posterity. According to Nuär, to die without a male amount to oblivion. Female children do not count, since their offspring belong to their husband's lineages, as in any patrilineal society. Such obligation for the ghost-marriage requires from kinship sufficient cattle. Failure to observe the obligation would mean restlessness of the dead man's spirit, which would bring evil-cien-ciën upon his kinsmen. This assertion is related to love, justice and generosity for the deceased person by the members of the family otherwise.

Without marrying to a deceased person who died before marriage according to Nuär, implies expectations of evil. The Nuär do regard the sense of justice in marriage. Therefore, such an obligation to marry the wife of a deceased would first require seniority of age among males within the family. The obligation to have children or heirs' ghost-marriage is equally applied to marriage between females and marriage for the impotent person.

This concern for the heir/heirs is not limited to Nuär alone. The contemporary Nuär do still practice this ghost marriage even in big cities such as Khartoum and Juba. This has reminded me of the occasion of the funeral rite of the late Joseph Riak Malual Turuk. I presided over that funeral in Juba-Tongpiny block 2 on May 11, 2019. Before the final blessing, the father of the late Mr. Kerbino Da̱k Tuɔ̱rɔ̱k was allowed to speak on behalf of the family as usual. He said:

"House of Turuk-cieŋ Tuɔ̱rɔ̱k, we are all united. Several times, I took care of my late son Joseph Riak Malual Tuɔ̱rɔ̱k. I tried my level best to educate him by being close to me. I have never heard any complaints being brought to me against our son late Joseph Riak Malual Tuɔ̱rɔ̱k." Mr. Kerbino concluded his speech by saying, 'House of Turuk-cieŋ Tuɔ̱rɔ̱k' we have a mission to marry to a wife to our deceased son Joseph Riak Malual Tuɔ̱rɔ̱k as a remembrance for him for his goodness."[102]

102 Kerbino Dak Turuk, his Speech during the funeral rite of his late paternal son Joseph Riak Malual Turuk, Juba-Tongping, block 2, May 11, 2019.

8.3.5.1 Characteristics of 'Ghost-(Surrogate)' Marriage

P.P. Howell has identified six characteristics of ghost marriage among the Nuär communities. First, it is the dead man, to whose name the wife is married, and who is considered the legal father of the children. The ritual processes of marriage are performed in his name, and the bride's wealth is paid on his behalf. Therefore, while he is not the biological father of the children, he is their legal father, and from his name, they trace their descent. Second, the man who marries a wife in the name of his dead kinsman is a father in all roles and is in every respect, the husband of the woman except in the strictly legal sense.

Third, the physiological father fulfils all the domestic duties of both husband and father. In this respect, the characteristics are the same as in a normal legal union. Fourth, on enquiry, though not in normal circumstances, the wife will be called ciek jooka- [ciek jɔkä], 'ghost-wife', while the children will be called gaat jooka- [gaat jɔkä], 'children of a ghost.' Fifth, since the husband is a substitute for his dead kinsman and performs all ritual and domestic obligations on his behalf, the features of a simply legal marriage are found in the structure of this form of union.

Sixth, the behaviour and obligations of the pro-husband are indistinguishable from those of a man who is both the legal and physiological husband and father at the same time. Seventh, this marriage occurs when a man is killed in a feud, and compensated by cattle. The blood wealth payments are used to pay the bride wealth for the dead man's marriage. The rationale is to fulfil the duties towards the dead man's lineage.

P.P. Howell's pater and genitor: According to him, the legal father of the children will bthe e pater, and the physiological father is the genitor. It is said that the difference therefore between a simple legal family and a 'ghost family' is that the former consists of a man who is both pater and genitor, a wife, and children born of that wife, while the latter consists of a 'ghostly father' who is the genitor, a wife and the children born by her. Therefore, ghost marriage is common among Nuär due to high mortality among males.

8.3.5.2 Categories of Persons for the Ghost-Marriage

Dr. Howell again has identified six rules for the categories of persons for whose 'ghost-marriages' are performed among the Nuär. First, as a rule, the system is back more than one generation. For example, a man would not marry a wife for his grandfather or grand-uncle. This was considered the duty of his father or uncles. Second, kinsmen for whom a wife may be married are brothers, paternal uncles, maternal uncles, and fathers. Third, only kinsmen are expected to marry a wife in the name of a dead man.

Fourth, in exceptional cases, a wife is married to the name of a female relative, but usually, barren women, who are counted as men and provided a link in the paternal line. Fifth, an old woman, especially if she has no paternal relative living, and she has the cattle required, will marry a woman in the name of one of them to reopen the line. She will invite some unrelated male to act as husband and as genitor of the children. According to P.P. Howell, in this case, the legal husband will be the dead kinsman, whose interests will be guarded by the woman.

Sometimes, a woman will marry a wife in the name of

her husband if she has no children and is herself beyond the age of childbearing. She will do this if she has cattle that are legally the property of her dead husband. If there were no heirs in the paternal line, to whom they would normally pass. Sixth, sometimes an old man, or one who is impotent, will marry a wife to himself and invite another man to act as a genitor. This is not 'ghost-marriage', because the legal husband is still a living person, but the functions of the pater and genitor are similar to those found in 'ghost-marriage'.

8.3.6 Differences between Ghost and Levirate Marriage

According to P.P. Howell, first, a 'ghost-marriage' means that the vicarious husband as legal representative of the dead man marries the wife in the sense that he collects and hands over the bride's wealth for her and performs the marriage ceremonies with her on behalf of the dead man. In the levirate, the kinsman merely enters as a substitute into a marriage already in existence. Second, generally speaking, in the case of the levirate, since the marriage was not actually initiated and negotiated by the pro-husband, he has less control over the wife than he would over a 'ghost-wife.'

Third, the levirate differs from 'ghost-marriage' in that the legal husband (pater) and his widow once lived as husband and wife. Fourth, although the leviratic family, like the 'ghost-family', consists of the dead husband (pater), the dead man may have begotten the pro-husband (genitor) and the children born of the woman, the children, or at least some of them. Therefore, in a 'ghost-marriage' the dead man is the pater but never the genitor of the children; in a leviratic union, the dead man is always the pater and he may have been the genitor of all or some children. The distinction is emphasized in Nuär terminology:"[103] A child begotten by the dead man is known as ret-rɛt, an orphan. A ghost child is known as gat jooka-gat jɔɔkä.

For example, the case of Pa̱är Kuok was one of the rare cases that proves the ghost marriage in Nuär culture, and probably in other African cultures. Ghost marriage is not limited to males alone, but also to females in some special cases. Pa̱a̱r was a girl from Lare in Gambella, Ethiopia. She was from a sub-clan called Nyiengaach in Thiang of Gajaach Nuär. Pa̱a̱r had a boyfriend who became sick. She wanted to visit him; however, she could do it during the daytime.

She decided to go secretly at night. She arrived there safely. When she finished talking with him, she wanted to come back home on the same night. Therefore, her boyfriend wanted to call somebody whom he trusted to take her back to her village. Nevertheless, his cousin said that he would escort her. However, because Paar's boyfriend knew his cousin was a coward man, he refused and told his cousin, "I would rather look for someone else." The cousin of Pa̱a̱r's boyfriend insisted that he would take her back home.

Finally, Pa̱a̱r's boyfriend gave up and he allowed his cowardly cousin to escort her back home. On the way, a beast roared, and immediately, the cousin of Pa̱a̱r's boyfriend ran away leaving her with an animal. Pa̱a̱r tried to run after him pleading and saying, "Ri̱c buɔlä, /cuo ɤä bäny piny. Which can be translated as, 'My age mate in dance, do not leave me behind.' The man did not give heed to her and the beast caught up with her and devoured her.[104]

103 P.P. Howell, *A Manuel of Nuër Law*, p. 79.

104 Interview with Fr. Jacob Nhial, from the Missionary Xaverians of

The following day in the morning, the mother of Paar tried to call her out, thinking that she was still sleeping. Finally, she realized that she was not in the room. Immediately, with intuition, she cried! "Paar must be the one who was devoured by the beast which roared last night." Consequently, many things happened when the beast devoured Paar. The family of the late Paar had wanted to attack the family of her boyfriend. However, the mother Paar intervened and said, I do not want more blood to be shed due to the death of my daughter. A beast ate my daughter Paar, and I prayed that that beast would not eat another person.

In her village, Paar was an important figure. She was a leader of all the girls in her sub-clan. Based on this fact, the family decided to keep her name alive. They married a wife in her name-by-name Tongyik Lare to bear children for her. Consequently, the woman bore children for Paar. Now the children are called after Paar's name. This is one of the rare cases of female ghost marriage in Nuär culture.

The intervention of Madam Nyayaal, the mother of Paar has reminded me of the importance of forgiveness. If Nyayaal were to be a violent woman, she would have encouraged her kinsmen to fight the kinsmen of her daughter's friend. Yet, she chose the rare road, which is less travelled by many, the road of forgiveness. This readiness for forgiveness here has also reminded me of two occasions of forgiveness in the sacred Scriptures. The example of David forgiving Saul in the sacred Scripture. "He said to the men, "The Lord forbid that I should do such a thing to my master, the Lord anointed, to lay a hand on him, for he is the Lord anointed. With these

---

Yarumal, Pontifical Society of Apostolic life, from Gajaak Nuär, St. Paul's Major Seminary Munuki-Juba (South Sudan), April 20, 2019.

words, David restrained his men and would not permit them to attack Saul" 1 Sam 24:7-8). "And behold, one of those who accompanied Jesus put his hand to his sword, drew it, and struck the high priest's servant, cutting off his ear. Then Jesus said to him, "Put your sword back into its sheath, for all who take the sword will perish by the sword" (Mt 26:51-52).

8.3.7 Trial Marriage-Thoꞑ Ciek Lɔrä

The so-called 'trial marriage' does not exist among the Nuär communities for various reasons. Even the term 'trial marriage' may not fit into their vocabulary. According to Nuär, they may use another term rather than trial marriage due to some reasons. First, at least a trial marriage may occur between two to three men based on the accusation of not producing children. Second, she was divorced by different men. Third the reason, which had led to divorce, may be due to laziness and nagging. Here Aristotle is right when he affirms "Silence is a woman's glory."[105]

Fourth, in some rare cases, when a young man is hard-working and responsible in terms of conduct and cultivation, he can be offered a girl. He can pay later on, but this is not a common practice, however, it can happen and it cannot be called a trial marriage. Fifth, such as blindness or any other natural incapability, which can become absolutely an obstacle to domestic services, free cohabitation can happen without asking for cattle, which is not also a trial marriage.

In such cases, according to Nuär, there are two options. First, the kinsmen of that woman will allow her to walk and choose freely the man she can settle with without asking

105 Richard McKeon, *Introduction to Aristotle*, p. 577.

him beforehand for any cattle. There will be no negotiation between the kinsmen of a divorced woman with the kinsmen of her new man. Therefore, a fitting word for trial marriage would be 'cohabitation'. Should there be a good settlement between her and that man, which resulted in the begetting of a child or children, the silence of her kinsmen towards her and her new man will be broken.

Here the concept of trial marriage will implicitly appear first, the father of the divorced woman can ask someone whom he trusts to cohabitate with her without the payment of any cattle until they beget children. These are two ways among the Nuär where cohabitation or trial marriage implicitly exists for various reasons based on divorce. In such a situation, the rigidity of demanding payment of cattle over the woman is loosened by the reasons above mentioned.

8.3.8 Theory of Polyandry

The concern for the family either in a friendly manner or in hostile ideology, is hotly debated with an uncompromising stand which tarnishes the dignity of the family. Different sociologists offer various types of philosophy about the family. According to D. Composta, "Beyond sociology, today a certain philosophy occupies itself with the family, but in a hostile sense: not only sociologists of materialistic and evolutionistic orientation (such as Aldous Huxley, whose motto was "neither family nor children", William Goode, Barrington Moore etc.) but also the neo-illuminists bound to Marxism, such as Herbert Marcuse…the structuralism represented by Marxist-Freudian idea, such as W. Reich, J. Lacan, etc."[106]

106 Dario Composta, *Moral Philosophy and Social Ethics*, p. 135.

With such ha ostile philosophy, it is impossible and even difficult today to find advocators and supporters of the traditional family outside Christian thought and certain non-Christian religious ideas. Consequently, the hotly and hostile debate about the family has left us with two options. This is because it is focused on two crucial properties of marriage: its monogamous unity and its indissolubility.

Contrary to monogamy: the opinions about this hotly and hostile debate on the family, are categorized into distinct divisions that is, those denying 'monogamy' and those denying 'dissolubility.' Consequently, first, contrary to monogamy (one with one) are the advocators of polygyny (many wives) or polygamy (many marriages) and polyandry (many husbands with one wife) that is, those who consider it legitimate, that one man, with more wives (commonly used in Africa, in tribal culture), or that one woman, with more husbands (Tibet).

We should further our knowledge about Tibet in which the concept of the traditional system of the marriage of polyandry is practiced. In this traditional system of polyandry in Tibet, a woman is allowed to marry more than one man. By description, Tibet is the highest religion on earth with an average elevation of 4,380 m (14,000 ft.). For example, the highest elevation mount is Everest, the Earth's highest mount rising 884.86 m (29,032 ft) above sea level. It is geographically located in the Himalayas and to the southwest of China also bordering India, Nepal, Myanmar (Burma) and Bhutan.

Tibet's three original provinces are U-Tsang, Kham and Amdo. It is stated that the people who occupy these regions, consider themselves Tibetan, although each has a strong identity and different dialects. Therefore, it is within these original provinces where polyandry is practised as a traditional system of marriage. Furthermore, Tibet is described as the remote and mainly Buddhist territory known as the 'roof of the world'. About the system of its government, it is an autonomous region of China. Beijing claims a centuries-old sovereignty over the Himalayan region. The Tibetan Empire emerged in the 7th century.

It is asserted that one deviation from the typical form of sexual union, which, however, is also called marriage, as is polyandry, as we have mentioned earlier. It is described as the union of several husbands with one wife. It is argued that the practice of polyandry has been there for various times by a considerable number of peoples or tribes. The anthropological findings of the existence and practice of polyandry, are not limited to Tibet as we used to hear.

For example, according to A. Ryan, polyandry…"Existed among the ancient Britons, the primitive Arabs, the inhabitants of the Canary Islands, the Aborigines of America, the Hottentots, the inhabitants of India, Ceylon...Malabar and New Zealand.[107] It is further argued that in the great majority of these cases, polyandry was the exceptional form of conjugal union. In this regard, polyandry is considered prevalent as a form of conjugal union in some human races.

8.3.8 1 The Chief Husband in Polyandrous Union

It is believed that the greater number of the polyandrous unions, seem to have been of the kind of fraternal; that is, the husbands in each conjugal group, were all brothers. According to A. Ryan, frequently, if not generally, the first

107 John A. Ryan, "Marriage" *The Catholic Encyclopedia,* p. 694.

husband enjoyed conjugal and domestic rights and was superior to the others, in fact, the Chief-husband for that matter. Consequently, the others were husbands only in a secondary sense. It is believed that both circumstances, show that even in the comparatively few cases in which polyandry existed, it was softened in the direction of monogamy; for the wife belonged not to several entirely independent men, but to a group united by the closest ties of blood. She was married to one family rather than to one person. For example, the fact that one of her consorts possessed superior marital privileges, shows that she had only one husband in the full sense of the term.

Some writers such as McLennan have asserted that the levirate, the custom that compelled [assigned] the brother of a deceased husband to marry his wife (inherit) widow, had its genesis in polyandry. However, levirate can be explicated independently from polyandry in the sense that it merely indicates that his nearest heir, i.e., his brother, inherited the wife, as the property of her husband.

In other instances, as among the ancient Hebrew, it was evidently a means of continuing the name of family, and individuality of the deceased husband. A. Ryan argues that if the levirate pointed in all cases to a previous condition of polyandry, the latter practice must have been much more common than it is shown to have been by direct evidence. It is believed that levirate existed among the New Caledonians, the Redskins, the Mongols, Afghans, Hindoos, Hebrew, Abyssinians and tthe majority of ethnic Africans, yet none of these peoples show any trace of polyandry.

Furthermore, the term 'polyandry' means having many husbands. It is the state or practice of having more than one husband or male mate at one time. The complexity and richness of marriage from various cultures and its moral and ethical approaches require humble observance before judgment. The term 'polyandry' does not exist in the vocabulary of Nuär communities. However, one can never conclude hearing but from insertion, observation and direct experience of a particular community where such practice exists.

If such a marriage system exists. It then requires research and academic findings whether in Africa or elsewhere in the world. The existence of polygamy (polygyny) and polyandry in different communities permits us to conclude that humankind approaches marital philosophy from different perspectives. This has reminded me of the incident which I witnessed in South Sudan Unity State near the river beach. I was looking from a distance when my eyes caught sight of two young men laughing at each other. One was an Arab and the other a Nuär. The Arab man was laughing at the Nuär man because he was not circumcised and the Nuär man was also laughing at him because he was circumcised. Consequently, they both forced me to laugh at them, too.

Sometimes, it is difficult to judge issues because they are approached from different points of view including polyandry and polygamy (polygyny). According to E. Hutchinson, "The central obligation of kinsmen to help one another to achieve personal immortality through the birth of children was also undercut by the increasing intolerance demonstrated by local Church leaders towards polygyny, ghost marriage, and widow inheritance."[108]

---

108 Sharon E. Hutchinson, *Nuër Delemas Coping with Money, War and the State*, London, University of California Press, 1996, p. 346.

8.3.9 Polygamy

According to A. Ryan, polygamy (many marriages) or more correctly polygyny (many wives) has been and is still much more common than polyandry. Polygamy has existed among ancient peoples known to history and occurs at present in some civilized nations and the majority of savage tribes. It is stated that about only important peoples of ancient times, that demonstrated little or no traces of it were the Greeks and the Romans. Nevertheless, concubinage, which may be regarded as a higher form of polygamy, or at least as nearer to pure polygamy, was for many centuries recognized by the customs and even by the legislation of these two nations.

Today, the principal peoples who still practice polygamy are those of Mohammedism, as those of Arabia, Turkey, Africa: North, South, East, West and Central, and some of the peoples in India. The Arab Muslims follow the instructions of the Islamic religion which limits the number of polygamies to four only while the rest, especially; the majority of the African tribes have no determining number with regards to polygamy. A. Ryan asserts, "It's chief home among uncivilized races in Africa"[109]

However, widespread polygamy has been territorial, and more than a small minority of people have never practised it. A. Ryan argued that even where it has been sanctioned by custom or civil law, the vast majority of the population has been monogamous. The reasons are obvious: there are not sufficient women to provide every man with several wives, nor are the majority of men able to support more than one.

Furthermore, it is argued that polygamous marriages

109 John A. Ryan, "Marriage" *The Catholic Encyclopedia,* p. 695.

are found for the most part among the kings, chiefs, strong men, and rich men of the community; and its prevailing form seems to have been bigamy. Moreover, polygamous unions are, as a rule, modified in the direction of monogamy, since one of the wives, usually the first married, occupies a higher place in the household than the others or one of them is the favourite, and has exceptional privileges of intercourse with the common husband.

Polygamy is described as a marriage in which a spouse of either sex may have more than one mate. The word polygamy is the state of being polygamous. Polygamy is a common practice in Nuär communities. To marry many wives, depends on the availability of cattle. As long as someone has cows, he can continue marrying even if he reaches 85 or 90 years. My maternal grandfather by name Marol Nyääk married again at the agof e 85. He had big children all married and their children were also married. The village called Kuer Parä in Ji̱käny west, where I grew up was full of his children, granddaughters and grandsons. After he married that girl, he chose one of the young men in another village to carry out for him the biological function.

There are various reasons to marry many wives such as the following: first, the more one has many children, the more the continuity of his life here on earth is assured. Second, having many wives in Nuär communities is about fame and prestige. Third, more children from many women mean self-defence for the family, clan, and society. Fourth, having many children from various wives, means security and protection for the kinsmen. Fifth, more daughters from different wives, bring riches to the kinship. Sixth, having more women, means that thc availability of domestic services is guaranteed specifically to the husband. For example, one does not depend on one wife for basic needs such as food and local wine. Food appears in every direction.

The desire to marry many wives and to have many children is not limited to Nuär people. The Holy Bible recorded the desire of King David to have many wives and many children. "David took more concubines and wives in Jerusalem after he came from Hebron, and more sons and daughters were born to him. These are the names of those who were born to him in Jerusalem: Shammua, Shobab, Nathan, Solomon, Ibhar, Elishua, Nepheg, Japhia, Elishama, Beeliada, and Eliphelet" (2 Sam 5: 13-16). King Solomon had seven hundred wives of royal rank and three hundred concubines (Cf. 1 Kgs 11:3).

In one of the funeral masses, which I celebrated last year for the soul of the late General Kawac Makuei from Aweil, in the tents, where the celebration of the mass was conducted, he had 50 children from 12 wives. Therefore, the desire to have more wives and more children seems to be common in different cultures. In Nuär communities, polygamy can occur in various ways.

The system of polygamy in Islamic Religion is legitimate and Islam as a religion, recommends its followers to marry four wives. For the majority of Africans, the number of wives is determined by the availability of resources with an emphasis on fecundity (procreation).

In the doctrine of polygamy, man is the sower of the seeds in the womb of the woman and the woman must produce the fruits of the seeds. The perception of man as the active principle in sexual coitus coincides with Aristotelian biology unfortunately embraced by the scholasticism of the 13th century. H. Peschke concurs with Aristotle by affirming that..."man is the active, life and form-giving principle in procreation; i.e., he gives the seed. The woman is merely passive and only offers the matter; i.e. the fertile soil."[110]

8.3.10 Monogamy

Among the Nuär communities, both in the West and the East, the doctrine of monogamy is a rare practice. It exists for various reasons such as; first, monogamy may exist due to poverty. For example, a man who has no cows may not marry more than one wife. Second, there are few men among the Nuär communities who because of toughness and stubbornness, which they have experienced from the first wife, chose to remain with one wife.

In our village, I could remember one man by the name of Kɔaŋ Gatluak, who married a woman by the name Ca̱r Bol. Kɔaŋ used to sing a song, "I will never marry again, Ca̱r Bol has frightened me"-cä kuën bi̱ nyɔk. Cä tɔ̱a̱ŋ näkä Ca̱r Bol. It sounds very nice in the Nuär language. I witnessed that he was a monogamous man; he chose to remain with one wife due to the negative experiences he had undergone with that first wife. Third, an impotent man among the Nuär usually remains with one wife because his condition does not permit him to marry more wives.

Fourth, among the Nuär communities, where true love prevails between two married couples, they choose to remain monogamous fifth, in case of physical handicap, such as blindness of a male, if the kinsmen marry him one wife, he remains with that one for life. Sixth, some women within the Nuär communities do demonstrate hate towards

110 Karl H. Peschke, *Christian Ethics*, Moral Theology in the Light of Vatican II, Vol. 1. Alcester, C. Goodlife Neale, 1989, p. 433.

their husbands if they express the intention to marry another woman. Some do succeed and the husband will have no other option but to remain with one wife.

All these reasons, which allow a man to remain with one wife, permit us to conclude that among the Nuär, both monogamy and polygamy exist. In this case, being a monogamous or polygamous, is to some extent, a matter of choice.

Conclusion

Chapter eight has defined the terms sexuality and marriage, their social and religious dimensions, the complexity of Nuär marriage, the types of untrue union of marriage such as marriage between two females (not lesbian), examples of marriage between two females, marriage for an impotent person-kuën luc ciek.

It further has explained broadly the desire to have an heir, levirate-kuëŋ ciek jɔkä duel, the strict rules to inherit the deceased wife, the legal union of the levirate, a ghost (surrogate) marriage-kuen jɔkä ciek, the characteristics of a ghost-(surrogate) marriage, the categories of persons for the ghost-marriage, the differences betweea n ghost and levirate marriage, trial marriage-top ciek Lɔrä, theory of polyandry including the chief husband in polyandrous union, and finally, it treated both polygamy and monogamy.

CHAPTER NINE

NUÄR CEREMONIAL STEPS OF TRUE MARRIAGE

Introduction

Chapter Nine discusses various occasions for courtship such as love-nhök and courtship-luɔ̱m, different types of drums, four rounds of dance, various ornaments for dance, strict required norms for dance, and composition of negative songs-këët.

Furthermore, the chapter also treats the sharing of information about engagement, areas of social concern of Nuär marriage, social dimension of marriage, marriage and crime/ domestic violence. It explains wrong ways to enter into marriage such as impregnation-ruët & other sexual misconducts, forced marriage of a female person, forced marriage for a male person, customary ceremonial stages of true marriage, engagement- luɔ̱m.

The chapter also discusses betrothal-cubic, muɔ̱y nyaal ciɛk, negotiations of the bride-wealth-tuɔ̱c Ɣɔ̱ɔ̱k, distribution of Cows to both the father's side-pek guandɛ and maternal (pëk mandɛ kiɛ näär), transfer of cows-nööŋ Ɣɔ̱ɔ̱k, the wedding ceremony-bul nyaal, wedding ceremonial conclusion-muɔ̱t nyaal, sacrifice, consummation-dɔnyni cöökni̱ (wäka̱l), the first-born child-da̱a̱p gatdä min jiöl and tha̱t kath-the bride first cook.

9. Various Occasions for Courtship

The Nuär youth are provided with various occasions for courtship, which are very colourful and amazing. These occasions, allow the youth to socialize and to interact with others in a very social manner. In these different social events, elderly people participate to some extent on some occasions. These types of events for socialization for the youth provide means to utilize their talents in terms of dance, composition of songs and other,r necessary things, associated with those social activities through interactions with each other. The focal point of this socialization is the exercise of love among the youth themselves.

9.1 Love-Nhök and Courtship-Luɔ̱m

In Nuär culture and tradition, young people are provided with freedom and responsibility in terms of social interaction with each other as we have above-mentioned. They enjoy freedom accorded to them in a very responsible way on various occasions of socialization. For example, they are given different occasions to attend to and to know themselves better in terms of love and courtship through social interaction.

Those social gatherings include various types of celebrations such as: first, a wedding ceremony called bul nyaal kiɛ buo̱r nyaal. Second, playing of the drum during the autumn-to̱t which is called bul thör, or drum of God-bul Kuɔth. Third, playing of drum of a Chieftain-bul Kua̱r. Fourth, dance during the dry season that is called kiɛ do̱o̱ŋ piny kiɛ nyadɛ̈ɛ̈ŋ. Fifth, and special types of celebration for various purposes such as called-päät.

These various social occasions provide opportunities for the Nuär youth-ŋuɛ̈ɛtni̱ and girls-nyier to engage and know themselves better. In this case, knowing themselves better through engagement can easily lead to a lasting relationship, which can finally lead to marriage. The Nuär believe that these various occasions, prepare and motivate youth to become future parents. According to the Nuär, the absence of such precious occasions could mean a lack of social interactions and socialization among the youths- ŋuɛ̈ɛtni kɛnɛ girls-nyier.

9.3 Types of Occasions of Playing of Drum

Types of playing of the drum are performed when all types of grains are ripened during autumn-to̱o̱d which is called bul thör' consist of first, there are two types of drums such as the drum of God-Bul Kuɔth or second of the drum of a Chieftain-Bul Kua̱r. During the playing of these two types of drums, whether God-Bul Kuɔth or Chieftain-Bul Kua̱r the parents are present as active spectators-nëën. The distance where the playing of drum event takes place will also determine the number of parents participating as active spectators-nëën.

In any case, those who participate in the playing of the drum, especially women, gather palm leaves or other dried wood to be burned during the playing of the drum. This is because they ought to see those who can both dance and sing well. The gathering of palm leaves or other dried wood to be burned during the playing of the drum indicated the lack of presence of electricity. Therefore, those burning palm leaves and dried wood provide spectators with energy and light at the same time.

All the lights are burned around the circle of the kraal of the drum, while the young people are dancing in the middle in their rows. While the parents enjoy those social interactions and socialization among the young people through dancing and singing songs. Those who can dance well and sing well, are fortunate ones and are praised by the parents.

Furthermore, there is a special type of celebration for various purposes which is are called-päät as we have mentioned earlier. The number of participants of päät will also be determined by its type. For example, dancing during the dry season among the youth is called-gany *kiɛ* do̱o̱ŋ piny kiɛ nyadɛ̈ɛ̈ŋ. This is only for young people during special seasons of the year such as the dry season. During the dry season, it is only the youth with few adult men, who can take the cows-ɣɔ̱ɔ̱k to various places for grazing by following the routes of enough water. For example, they can spend three months without their parents.

During this specific period of dry season which is called-gany kiɛ do̱o̱ŋ piny kiɛ nyadɛ̈ɛ̈ŋ, dancing is purely for the youths. On this occasion of gany kiɛ do̱o̱ŋ piny kiɛ nyadɛ̈ɛ̈ŋ, it is only those who can sing well have a lot of lovers. In this specific period, each young man composes his song to attract many girls as as possible.

According to Nuär, plagiarism is considered stealing and dishonesty. It has serious consequences for that young person who attempted to steal the song of another man. It brings about lasting shame upon him and scandal. The one who will attract many girls to make them his lovers due to his good songs which he composed and finally, sings them well, is called balaŋ- However, the term balaŋ in the Nuär language has different connotations. In this case, one needs to understand it from the context in which it is used otherwise.

9.3.1 Four Rounds of Dance

The first round of dance: According to Nuär, bul thör there are: first, drum of God-Bul Kuɔth or drum of a Chieftain-Bul Kua̱r. In this case, the dance consists of four stages. In western Nuär, Unity State, especially in Jagɛi and Dɔk Nuär, dancing playing or beating of the drum that is, the drum of God-Bul Kuɔth or drum of a Chieftain-Bul Kua̱r, the first round of dance is for those who are related by blood which they called-yieec maarä. The first round of dance among relations has nothing to do with love. It nevertheless, is considered as an introductory part of other dances that follow.

The second round of dance: the second round of dance among the youth is called yiëc tuacni̱-kuɔ̱ɔ̱t- for prospective bridegrooms. In this second of dance during the playing (beating) of the drum, it is expected that those who are betrothed, are supposed to dance with the bridegroom kinsmen. This is considered a sign of commitment and loyalty to betrothal. Furthermore, it is expected that those girls who are already engaged, ought to dance with their bridegroom and his kinsmen. This second dance is very important for the prospective bridegroom and the prospective bride to test their love and commitment. For example, even if the prospective bridegroom did not turn up during the playing of the drum, the prospective bride and sisters and friends must dance with the prospective bridegroom kinsmen otherwise.

The third round of dance: is called yiec luɔmni̲-for lovers only. This third round of dance, as we said, is only for those lovers. In this round, every lover expects to dance with their lover. In this case, if a young man whom we early called 'balaŋ, has a lot of lovers, he expects them to dance with them in this round. If his lovers turn up in good numbers, this will qualify him to be balaŋ. The spectators will know that this young man knows how to dance and also sing well. His techniques of dancing and his tone of voice, both attract his lovers and spectators as well.

Fourth round of dance: This fourth round of dance is the one called yiec cuowni̲-which simply means urine round which is the last dance. It is called the urine round of dance because everyone has become tired. Furthermore, it is a time in which everyone goes to urinate at the periphery of the kraal dance. The fourth round of dance is not considered valuable. Sometimes, it can be considered an insult if it is not padded back on the next playing drum, especially on the third stage, which is for lovers-yiëc luɔmni̲. In principle, the fourth round of dance is done given expectation in return, otherwise.

9.3.2 Various Ornaments for Dance

One can understand that if those occasions are preparing young people for parental life, then nobody can take them for granted. For the young people ŋuɛtni̲ and girls-nyieeri̲, it requires the highest care of personal presentation such as first, the decoration of the body with ashes of cow dung-biilni̲pua̲ny kɛ puɔ̱k, kiɛ ŋɛth. Second, the wearing of multiple beads both on the waists and the heads. Third, the crossing of both shoulders with beads-kua ŋa̱a̱ni̱. Fourth, the dying of hairs with ashes of cow dung-la̱a̱nykɛ puɔ̱k kiɛ la̱a̱ny miemni̱ kɛ ŋɛ̈ɛ̈th.

Fifth, the wearing of tuac-thɔ̱ɔ̱nä on the waists by young men during the playing of the drum. Sixth, the dɔɔm and tassels-dhuɔɔr worn by girls and different feathers of birds worn by all on their heads such as the ones of cocks and ostriches-moc kɛ wuɔ̱th kiɛn nɔakni̱ kiɛ juäät. Seventh, Evans-Pritchard observes the "Girl's dancing stick."[111] Such descriptions of various ornaments manifest complexities of requirements while playing the drum. One can never finish listing ornaments. All these, are signs and symbols which demonstrate the highest emotional and social interactions between young people among the Nuär.

9.3.3 Strict Required Norms for Dance

The harmony during the dancing with the beating of the drum requires serious observation. E.g. the Drum (Bull Jääŋä-the Drum of Dinka) of Nyaaruac Kuolaŋ Kët, the prophetess of Western Jagɛi Nuär in a village called 'Thar Ruɔ̱p Nyakuolaŋ', also known as Limpuot.[112] It was a common practice that if a young man dances and consequently, creates disharmony with the beating of the drum, all the spectators will first jeer at him and then chase him away from the Kraal-thöör of the drum. The Nuär call it tui̱nyni̱ and when that happens, you

---

111 E.E. Evans-Pritchard, *Nuër Religion*, New York: Oxford University Press, 1956, p. 74.

112 Jedeit J. and Naomi R. Pendle, *Speaking Truth to Power in South Sudan. Oral Histories of the Nuër Prophets,* Nairobi: Rift Valley Institute, 2018, p. 6.

are not allowed to fight anyone, not even your kinsmen can protect you. The jeering and chasing from the kraal of the drum is only applied to males. In such cases incidents of jeering and chasing away, someone was many. However, no incident of violence had ever been recorded in Bul Jääŋä. Why? Because everybody knows the serious consequences, it can bring upon oneself.

However, we must remind ourselves that there is no uniformity among the Nuär both in the West and in the East when it comes to dancing. The comprehensive explanation we have given above may be applied to some sections of Nuär such as Jagɛi and Dɔk. If you attend the playing of drum dance in J̲ikäny, Bul, Leek, and Nyuɔŋ Nuär in the West, the requirements for the ornaments for dancing, may not be so complicated. The way they dance, may not be the same as those of Jagɛi and Dɔk Nuär.

By comparison, Jagɛi and Dɔk Nuär are good dancers while J̲ikäny, Bul, Leek, and Nyuɔŋ Nuär are good composers of songs. In the west, central Fangak and in the east, specifically in three major areas of Nuär land such as Fangak, Nasir and Akobo, dancing events will also have their variations. We limit our judgment only to playing drums during the rainy season of the year. The rest of the dance during the dry season in the west, central and in the east, may not require too much analysis. Their demands are simple but good songs matter.

9.3.4 Composition of Negative Songs-Këët

Whoever is used to Nuär culture specifically about those areas of socialization and social interaction, during the playing of drum events, or any other social occasion, which brings young people together, will always observe rivalry over girls between initiated males. This is the most unfortunate part of those socializations and social interactions between the youth. In the west, central, and the east without exception, many young people have collided with girls, which always results in the composition of negative songs against each other. Unfortunately, sometimes, it is extended to all the members of the families of both sides.

Composing negative songs against each other is a common practice among the youth in Nuär communities. For example, whenever two young people happen to have a rivalry over a girl, they will always resort to the composition of negative songs against each other. The songs are intentionally formulated and composed against the opponent and his family to tarnish them. The two rivals will begin to compose negative songs against each other and if the situation is not resolved, they can extend those songs to each member of the families of both sides as we have above-mentioned.

Those songs can say anything about the person in each family; for example, about adults such as men and women and young people such as children, adolescents and youths. People who have no business in this collision can become victims for nothing. I know of many young people who are being plagued by everlasting scandal because of those faulty songs.

This practice of composing negative songs is also related to the celebration of the 'chasing of the initiates'-duäc gaat raar. When the initiates have spent one month in seclusion, at the end of the month, they will be chased early in the morning to a river nearby. They must run like men and must not allow themselves to be caught by adults. In such an occasion also, bad songs are formulated and composed by both men and women who are the parents of the initiates. Men compose their songs against their wives and likewise, women formulate their songs against their husbands. According to culture and custom, this is an occasion in which every husband and every wife, can say anything to her partner without expectation of any negative reaction. You can call it, a time of revelation of negative conduct against each other. The celebration is always coloured with dancing, local drinks such as local brew, beating of drum and funnies. For example, it can continue for the whole day.

9.4 Sharing of Information about Engagement

If a young man is impressed by a girl during those various occasions of dancing presented above, he, the prospective bridegroom-kuut, must share-cäät it first with his father. If his father is not available, he can share it with the paternal father or other elder person among his kinsmen. The girl can be his lover-luumdɛ or any other girl whom he might have admired to be his future wife. It must be emphasized that this ought to be the first official approach of the prospective bridegroom-kuut with his close elder.

It is within this official sharing of information that the prospective bridegroom-kuut father or any other elder in his kinsmen, will approach the bride's father about the choice of his son to marry their daughter. Nuär believes those who enjoy their love responsibly through good relationships during those social interactions and socializations, will finally, approach their parents to make their relationship public. It is assumed that the prospective bridegroom-kuut and his prospective bride should have adequate information about each other to convince their parents. During this love relationship and courtship period, the future couple should discuss together issues such as self-introduction, their ancestral lineages and their future home and also about any possible impediments to marriage.

After both the prospective bridegroom-kuut and his prospective bride have shared their intentions with their parents, the parents will conduct proper investigations and will discuss with the prospective bridegroom-kuut and the prospective bride any possible impediments that would have negative effects. The Nuär do not take this official exchange of information about marriage for granted. Therefore, both the prospective bridegroom-kuut kinsmen and kinswomen and the prospective bride's kinsmen and kinswomen will launch a comprehensive research period which is not less than six months or one year. They are both concerned about certain issues which are related to impediments and other issues. Below are various impediments-gääl wuk kiɛ ga̱a̱k.

9.4.1 Areas of Social Concern of Nuär Marriage

The Nuär people both in the West and in the East unanimously asserted that previously marriage was defined as a union between a mature man (initiated man-Wud mä ca ga̱r) and a mature female girl-nyamä mä ci̱i̱ kɔ̱ɔ̱y (kiɛ cɛ dep gɔ̱l) legitimized by the payment of the bride-wealth of the bridegroom's kinsmen to the bride's family through various ceremonial and legal stages, recognized and respected by all.[113] At present, Nuär marriage includes both initiated and non-initiated male persons.

The four major regions such as: first, Unity State in the West, second, central Fangak, Nasir, and Akobo in the East. These four major regions consist of sixteen counties which have highlighted marriage. The Nuär from those major regions have identified benefits that marriage brings: first, marriage creates relationships and social networking. Second, it brings two couples to completion and co-responsibility. Third, it brings about the development and continuity of life. Fourth, it brings about population growth in the community and the society. Fifth, it distinguishes humankind from other lower animals. Sixth, it brings about the highest moral and ethical codes of 'relative laws.' Seventh, it guarantees the autobiography and biography of the genealogy of the parents and the clan as well.

9.4.2 Social Dimension of Marriage

According to Nuär, a marriage is the union between a man and a woman. It is not a personal matter and not even a private relationship. Marriage has social dimensions such as public significance and recognition. On the one hand, marriage is good for the couple, because it also provides optimal conditions for bearing and raising children. The Nuär believe that marriage is the common good.

Therefore, according to them, marriage favours good health such as: first, on average, husbands and wives, are healthier, happier and enjoy longer lives than those who are

113 Interview with a group of contemporary Nuër elders in Juba at POC, May 15/ 2019.

not married. Second, men appear to reap the most physical health benefits from their marriage and suffer the greatest health consequences if they divorce. Third, married mothers have lower rates of depression than single or cohabiting mothers do. This is because probably, they are probably more likely to receive practical and emotional support from their child's father and his family.

Marriage and wealth: the Nuär emphasize that first, married couples build more wealth on average than single or cohabiting couples do. Second, married men earn more wealth than do single men with similar education and job histories. Third, married women are economically better off than divorced, cohabiting or never-married women.

Marriage and children: the contemporary Nuär states those children raised by their biological mothers and fathers are first, less likely to be poor or to experience persistent economic insecurity. Second, more likely to stay in school, have fewer behavioural and attendant problems, and perform well in schools. Third, less vulnerable to serious emotional illness, depression and suicide. Fourth, more likely to have positive attitudes towards marriage and greater success in forming lasting marital relationships of marriage.

9.4.3 Marriage and Crime/Domestic Violence

The Nuär believe that: first, married women are at lower risk for domestic violence than women in cohabiting or dating relationships. Second, boys raised in single-parent homes are more likely to engage in criminal and delinquent behaviour than those who are raised by two married biological parents. Third, married women are less likely to be the victims of violent crime than single or divorced women are. Fourth, married men are less likely to perpetrate violent crimes than unmarried men are

On marriage and society: the contemporary Nuär confirm that first, the institution of marriage reliably creates social, economic and affective conditions for effective parenting. Second, being married changes people's lifestyles and habits in ways that are personally and socially beneficial. The Nuär believe that marriage is a "seedbed" of pro-social behaviour. Third, marriage generates social capital. For example, the social bonds created through marriage yield benefits not only for the family in addition, for the larger society.

9.5 Wrong Ways to Enter into Marriage

The need and desire to have access to marriage is very important for everyone. According to Nuärthe customary system of marriage, it is difficult to have one means to marriage. In this sense, marriage can happen through various means, which are not encouraged by everyone, nevertheless, those wrong means, are present in Nuär marriage. The most difficult part is o control the favourable and traditional ceremonial steps of marriage, sometimes challenged by sexual misconduct among the youth. As we shall discuss below, one will know how difficult it is for the majority of cases, in which ceremonial traditional steps of Nuär marriage are violated and surpassed.

9.5.1 Impregnation-Ruët & Other Sexual Misconducts

Ruet is a marriage initiated by an impregnation of a girl by a man. The Nuär consider any marriage that begins with impregnation as a wrong step. It is not encouraged by Nuär customary law. This is because an impregnation of a girl-ruët nyala) is an unlawful act. It is compared to destruction and spoiling of the daughter of someone, without prior marital customary ceremonial steps. Although impregnation-ruët is not encouraged among the Nuär people, nevertheless it happens occasionally among young people. However, when it happens, it requires various options based on different reasons too.

First, the impregnation of a girl can happen, as it does happen in the majority of cases. However, there are certain degrees to be considered when impregnation takes place. If it happens between a boyfriend and a girlfriend, and the young man is the prospective bridegroom among his brothers, this pregnancy can lead to marriage. Second, if impregnation takes place between a young man and a girl, who are not lovers, and worst, if the young man is not the prospective bridegroom among brothers, this impregnation cannot lead to marriage at all.

In this case, the solution is to punish the family of the young man by paying a certain number of cows to the girl's family. The payment of these cows has already reduced the number of cows to be paid by her future husband if she is going to be married. Third, if a girl is impregnated by a poor young man who has no cows, it will be considered a great loss for the family, and consequently, the young man will not be allowed to stay with that girl. The child will be kept by the family, till the young man pays ruok. However, more about this will be discussed in the context of Nuar customary law, chapter ten.

Fourth, among the Nuär there is an elopement. This type

of technique is used by some youth to enter marriage in the majority of cases, due to various reasons. For example, it may be due to the fact, that the young man is facing serious competition with another from the same girl. Or maybe, he knows that his father has enough cows to pay for the family of the girl. In this case, elopement can lead to marriage if the young man is the prospective bridegroom.

Fifth, there is alsthe o practice of abduction-kaap nyal among the Nuär which can lead to marriage. Abduction of a girl by a young man with kinsmen can also happen due to various reasons. For example, maybe the girl is refusing the young man, and she would like to be married to her lover. Sixth, in case of raping, pregnancy can happen. Seventh, a girl can voluntarily choose to come to a house of one's family if she knows that their son is a prospective bride. This can be subject to discussion and investigation that will depend on the readiness of a young whether to accept an offer or not. If the prospective bride accepts it, then, the family of the volunteer prospective bride will be formed. If not, the girl will be told to go back to her father's house. This is a rare case which sometimes happens in Nuär marriage.

As a rule, if a girl is impregnated and was not married by the one who impregnated consequently, her future marital status will not be productive in terms of bride-wealth as we have above-mentioned. For example, she can be forced by her family to marry an old man.

9.5.2 Forced Marriage for a Female Person

Above, we discussed various sexual misconducts which in the majority of cases do not lead to marriage but rather discredit girls' dignity. The consequences of those sexual misconducts can provide girls with fewer options of their freedom to choose their partner, due to prior pregnancy. In those cases, above presented, a family of a girl can have the only option, to force their daughter who was impregnated, to be married by any person, regardless of his social status. In this case, forced marriage among the Nuär is common, due to various reasons as we shall discuss below.

Kuk kuen-forced marriage: refers to compelling a person to enter marriage against his/her will. Women were and are still a vulnerable part of society. They are mostly affected by forced marriage in the Nuär community as well as in other tribes in South Sudan in Africa at large. According to Nuär elders on forced marriage, they can justify the prevalence of marriage and said Nyal ɛ duŋ ko̱kä kä gua̱n.

Here are some conditions of forced marriage for a female: first, when her family is poor and is in dire need of bride-wealth to sustain their life. Second, when her brothers have reached the age of maturity they need to get married. Third, she refuses marriage proposals several times. Fourth, when another man pleases her father, she can offer her as a gift to that person. Fifth, when she attempted an elopement. Sixth, when she betroths a man, whom her family does not like. Seventh, when she was impregnated and refused by the one responsible for the pregnancy, her parents would force her to anyone they wanted.

9.5.3 Forced Marriage for a Male Person

The following are different ways of forced marriage for a male person: first when his parents have enough cattle to pay the bride wealth. Second, when he is the only son of his parents and has reached the age of adult. Third, when he is selected to marry a wife for his deceased brother or uncle. Fourth, when his family wants him to marry a wife for his barren sister. Fifth, when he intends to delay marriage. Sixth when he delays in a town for academic or any other purposes. Seventh, when he is the elder son of the family and other sons want to get married soon after him. Eighth, when he elopes a girl his parents do not like that girl but rather favours another one. Ninth, when he is attracted by the family of the prospective bride. Tenth, when his brother is killed and the cows of compensation are ready.

9.6 Customary Ceremonial Stages of True Marriage

The Nuär people have various ceremonial stages of marriage that are meant to prepare the young couple for the true lasting union of life. Several steps mark each stage. Since marriage is a family and community affair, each stage is made public either at the beginning or at the end. In this regard, there are three major stages in Nuär marriage, namely: first, introductory initial ceremonial stage, which consists of courtship-this nyaal, searching for each other-göör thuɔ̱kni̱ kamni̱kiɛn. Second, engagement-luɔm nyaal or betrothal-luɔmnyal entails paying the bride-wealth, negotiations-tuɔc nyaal. Third, wedding ceremony-muɔt nyal kiɛ buɔ̱r nyaal.

Fourth, the consummation-dɔnyni̱ cökni̱ consists of allowing the bridegroom to legally have sexual intercourse with the bride. According to Nuär, consummation dɔnyni̱ cökni̱ is translated as the journey of the bridegroom from his village to his bride's village for the consummation-dɔnyni̱ cökni̱.

The phrase 'dɔnyni̱ cökni̱' can laterally mean stepping on the legs of his wife. Therefore, for the Nuär, dɔnyni̱ cökni̱ is a euphemism for the consummation of marriage after the ceremonial celebration of the wedding ceremony-muɔt nyaal kiɛ buɔ̱r nyaal has been completed.

9.6.1 Engagement- Luɔ̱m

After serious investigations of all those impediments above-mentioned are made and all the doubts and concerns are verified and clarified, the prospective bridegroom and the prospective bride can be allowed to continue with their engagement-luɔm. According to Nuär, this ceremonial celebration is only attended by young people. The word luɔ̱m in Nuär language also implies sexual intercourse and therefore, its true real meaning should be understood in the context in which it is used otherwise. The bride's father to come and officially meet the prospective bride, her sisters and her friends, in her village and, will give the prospective bridegroom-kuut, his brothers and friends. In this ceremonial engagement, from the side of the prospect bride, only females attend and from the side of the prospect bridegroom-kuut, only males attend.

Such a ceremonial meeting does not take place in the bride's father's house but in the neighbour's house. This ceremonial meeting is organized by the youth with their peers. The ceremonial celebration manifests the desire of both the prospective bride and prospective bridegroom-kuut. Later on, they should pass the information to their parents about their desire for possible future marriage preparation. The purpose of a ceremonial meeting is to demonstrate that the prospective bride and the prospective bridegroom-kuut should make their love and courtship public.

Furthermore, this demonstration of the ceremonial love and courtship between the prospective bride and the prospective bridegroom-kuut signifies and signals to the rest of the youth that these two have shown their desire to be future husbands and wives. Therefore, in this intense emotional ceremonial interaction and socialization, the Nuär believe that this opportunity can motivate the rest of the youth also to make their lovers and courtship clear in public. It is an occasion whereby, those who are in love and courtship should be motivated.

9.6.2 Betrothal-Cuic, Mu̱ɔy Nyaal Ciɛk

After this engagement -lu̱ɔm, if all agree, either the girls from the side of the bride take cattle (known as dɔw lu̱ɔm) with its number ranging from 10–15 in western Nuär or the kinsmen of the bridegroom take the cattle to the bride's father kraal. In eastern Nuär, the number ranges from 4–10. This ceremony is marked with some dances-yi̱ët kiɛ ra̱w and the singing of some songs that mostly involve youth and some close elders from both sides. This engagement -lu̱ɔm is not as big as the wedding ceremony, yet, it is considered an important part of the ceremonial stage according to Nuär communities both in the West and in the East.

After this ceremonial celebration, according to Nuär, the girl is considered betrothed-ca cui̱c ɣä kä kiɛ ca yiël yaŋ). In this ceremonial stage, it is considered that the girl is already in the presence of a few cows. From now on, no one is allowed to engage her. Unless, there is a reason for an impediment, which might have surfaced as the process continues.

The Nuär believe that this is an important stage in marriage. It is where the commitment to marriage is tested to see whether it can continue or not. During this period, some issues may surface which either affect the marriage negatively or positively. Nevertheless, the most difficult part is to meet the minimum requirement of the brideprice (ɣɔ̱ɔ̱k nyaal) set by the family of the bride. This ceremonial stage will determine the level of commitment from the side of the bridegroom-kuut kinsmen, which foretells their future commitment towards their wives and in-laws. What is more challenging here is how the bridegroom will win the trust of his in-laws though he may not reach the minimum requirements set by the bride's kinsmen. This period of betrothal leads to the highest emotional level of negotiation-wä luak kiɛ tuɔ̱c nyaal.

9.6.3 Negotiations of the Bride-Wealth-Tuɔ̱c Ɣɔ̱ɔ̱k

The description of terminology associated with cattle points to the crucial and central place, which plays a greater role in the life of the Nuär people. This includes other pastoralists in South Sudan and elsewhere in the world at large. Where I grew up as a young man in a cattle camp and at home, certain issues, which are related to the importance of cows, are still vivid in my mind such as:

First, the skin of a cow was our best mattress or sponge, if you like. Second, the urine of a cow (këëth yaaŋ) was our best water for showering and medicine for butter. Third, when the dung of cows is collected, dried and burned, they deter mosquitoes while we use the ashes for brushing our teeth. For example, we consider the ashes of cows' dung as an excellent 'signal or Sensodyne toothpaste. Fourth, the urine of the cow (këëth yaaŋ) was used for showering and for washing our hands as we have mentioned earlier. Fifth, the dung of a cow when dried and burned, serves for both smearing the body, decorating the body during a dance at the place of the drum, and for dyeing the hairs.

Sixth, the horn of a cow was our best tool for eating (tuŋ-spoon). Seventh, the last part of the tail of a cow tassels-juäl was used by girls to tight it on their waists during dancing or to put it on the top of a thin tall stick (Taŋ yɔɔkä) and hold it while dancing. Women also made the tassels-juäl yaaŋ (dhur) and put it on their heads (nooh). Eighth, the milk of a cow is an essential food for the Nuär. For example, all, even those who have no cows, enjoy its meat. Ninth, the cow brings to the family (a wife for continuity of life). Tenth, it creates relationships between the two families concerning marriage. Eleventh, the cow is used for offering sacrifice either when somebody is sick or for Thanksgiving. Twelfth, when it rains, somebody can use the skin of a cow as a shelter. Thirteenth, the cow plays an important role in the reconciliation processes such as compensation when someone is killed. Cows are central and focal points in the life of pastoralists.

Therefore, because of the importance attached to cattle, all the anthropologists who wrote on Nuär marriage, agree that the level of negotiations over the bride-wealth between the bride's kinsmen and the bridegroom's kinsmen is the highest emotional moment in Nuär marriage. For the negotiation to take place, specified days are suggested by the prospective bride's kinsmen to the prospective bridegroom-kuut kinsmen.

The families of the prospective bride can appoint a day on which the bridegroom's kinsmen can come to byre-luak of the bride's father. Since this ceremonial level is the most emotional one, it requires serious preparation on both sides. The kinsmen of the bride must prepare themselves to get the number of cows-ɣɔ̱ɔ̱k according to their rights-cuuŋ kiɛn. The prospective bridegroom-kuut kinsmen must also prepare themselves to meet those rights-cuuŋ as required by the prospective bride's kinsmen.

On that specified day, the prospective bridegroom's kinsmen come as a team to the byre of the prospective bride's father. The prospect bridegroom-kuut kinsmen consist of close elders and senior women of the prospect bridegroom's kin; a well-chosen man spokesperson (squealer jak kɔ̱k-crow) on both sides. In these processes of negotiation, the bridegroom-kueen and his groom-gua̱n tuacdɛ are present. Both the bridegroom-kuen and his gua̱n tuacdɛ must both wear tuac thɔ̱nä on their waists, positioning them on their sexual organs as a sign of respect to relatives-in-law, while leaving their buttocks naked.

The nature of tuac-thɔ̱nä is that it only covers half of the waist. When it is used for normal dancing during the playing of the drum, it is tied on the waist positioning on the buttocks. It is only during the negotiation-tuɔ̱ɔ̱c nyaal kiɛ wä luak, that it is used by the prospective bridegroom-kuen and his groom-gua̱n tuacdɛ tying them on their waists adjusting them in front to cover their genital organs as we have mentioned earlier. In 2009, John Puɔ̱t Keah got married with Angelina Nyadɔ̱ŋ Mawic. According to William Kom Keah, "During the negotiation, the prospect bridegroom went to the prospect bride's home without wearing tuac thɔ̱nä with his tuac thɔ̱nä. They were fined to pay one big ox to the prospective bride's kinsmen."[114]

114 Interview William Kom Keah at Protection of Civilians (POC) site,

Should there be any disagreement between the prospect bridegroom's kinsmen and prospect bride's kinsmen during the negotiation, both the bridegroom-kuen and his groom-gua̱n tuacdɛ will turn both their tuac thɔ̱nä behind. Therefore, the instability of tuac thɔ̱nä during the negotiation-tuucä can be very disturbing. Sometimes, it is natural during the negotiation that the prospective bridegroom-kuen, his kinsmen and his kinswomen go out and then are called back again as long as both sides do not agree.

According to Nuär, these are normal techniques to be used during the negotiation. Should the spokesman-jak kɔ̱k of the bride's kinsmen-gua̱n bööthni pollute during this negotiation, the bridegroom's kinsmen and kinswomen must pretend to be deaf as if they heard nothing at all. Should they laugh, they will be fined and should the spokesperson of the prospective bridegroom-kuen pollute during the negotiation, he will be fined, therefore, in this case, the technique is emphasized on one side.

The prospective bride's kinsmen consist of close relatives-people of rights-ji̱ cuuŋni diaal pek nyaal and their spokesman (squealer-jak kɔ̱k-crow) who is called by Nuär 'gua̱n bööthni. His special role is to point out all the rights-cuuŋ as required by the prospective bride's kinsmen and kinswomen. The atmosphere of negotiation-wä luak kiɛ tuɔ̱ɔ̱c nyaal according to Nuär requires a good moral code of conduct. The negotiators are not supposed to call themselves by their names. Each call another by the nickname of his ox. The Nuär are good in euphemisms. The representatives of the prospect bridegroom-kuen and his gua̱n tuacdɛ are to sit on the left of the byre, while the representatives of the prospect

Unity State-Rubkotnä as from 27/06/2019.

bride, and sit on the byre-center-gɔr rɛy. Pipes töönyni̲ are well prepared for both negotiators of both sides.

As both sides begin the negotiations, the spokesperson of the bride's kinsmen breaks pieces of straw like toothpicks-juaac and fixes them in the lines drawn. Then he takes one stick and addresses the spokesperson of the bridegroom: "You know that in the past, there may have been something between you and the father of this girl. These juaac represent the cow to be given to the father of the bride for reconciliation loc marä-cuɔ̱l. Then, he requests the colour of a cow; the witness of the girl will specify for instance, 'bo̲o̲r (white), and bends the straw, leaving it in the same place, as a sign of an agreement.

Many anthropologists, who wrote on Nuär marriage, have documented the number of forty cows-ɣɔ̱ɔ̱kti̲ jɛn ŋuaan. However, the Nuär themselves from the western, central and eastern, which are comprised of four major areas of Nuär land, do manifest inconsistency when it comes to the number of cows-ɣɔ̱ɔ̱k for marriage. In western Nuär, the number of cattle demanded for marriage consists of 33-35 *cows*, specifically in Jagɛi and Dɔk communities.

The following is the description of the ceremonial negotiation that focuses on the settlement of the bride-wealth by both parties. The spokespersons from both sides are the ones responsible for all the discussions about the number of cattle needed as defined by the customary laws. His or her number comes from the customary law due to right-cuɔ̱ɔ̱ŋ raamɔ accorded to each member of the extended family. This number ranges between 33–35 heads of cattle from both sides (maternal-pëk mandɛ and paternal-pëk Gua̱ndɛ).

The paternal side has a maximum number of 25 heads of

cattle, and a maximum of 10 on the maternal side (given to maternal uncle). However, the parents of the bride reserve the right to withhold any customary due from its rightful owner from their daughter's cattle that pleases them. Here, the specific duty of the gua̱a̱n bööthni, as we have pointed out earlier, is therefore practical in Nuär marriage. According to the rights of the people of the prospective bride's kinsmen and kinswomen. The next page specifies those rights from both the prospective bride's father and the maternal side. Once the cows are given, the father asks the girl if she is ready to pass to the family of the bridegroom. After consent, she will leave her group and join the family of the bridegroom, which welcomes her with joy.

Distribution According to Cow-Rights-Ɣɔ̱ɔ̱k Cuuŋni: Father's Side-Pek Guandɛ

Pek Gua̱ndɛ	**Father's side**
1. Yaŋ gua̱ndɛ (yaŋ dhurä) lotdɛ ni̱ gua̱n nyaal kärɔa.	A cow of heart
2. Yaŋ mandɛ	A cow and its calf to the bride's mother
3. Waŋneen gua̱ndɛ	A cow and its calf to the bride's father
4. Waŋneen mandɛ	A cow its calf to the bride's uncle
5. Gua̱nle̱e̱n Kui̱c luaak wɛɛ kä däman gua̱n nyaal min tëkɛ man go̱lä.	A heifer cow to the paternal uncle (the brother to the bride's father by a different mother)

6.Gua̱nle̱en mandɛ wɛɛ kä däman gua̱n nyaal mindiɛn kɛl	A heifer cow to the paternal uncle (the brother to the bride's father by the same mother)
7. Puɔ̱ŋ	A cow to the bride's grandfather
8. Waai wɛɛ kä nyi̱man gua̱n nyaal.	A heifer cow to the sister of the bride's father
9. Manle̱e̱n wɛɛ kä nyi̱man man nyaal.	A heifer cow to the sister of the bride's mother
10. Kethar gua̱ndɛ	A goat or sheep to the maternal
11.Yaŋ gua̱nle̱e̱n manle̱e̱nä	A cow to the elder brother of the bride
12. Waai in di̱i̱t	A heifer cow to the elder sister of the bride's father
13. Yaŋ Döör	A cow the bride's father
14. Dɔɔŋ Tutni	Calf to the grandfather
15.Thäk gua̱nle̱e̱n mandɛ	A big bull to the paternal uncle (the brother to the bride's father by a different mother)
16. Thäk gua̱ndɛ kiɛ thäk dhuɔrä (thäk mi̱ dhöör), wɛɛ kä gua̱n nyaal kärɔa.	A bull to the bride's father
17. Thäk däman nyaal (kiɛ thäk kɛɛtä) wɛɛ kä däman nyaal min di̱t ni̱ jɛn mi̱ kuɛn kɛ ni̱ nyam min di̱t ni̱ jɛn bä.	A Bull to the elder brother of the bride

18. Cup waayä	Maternal spear to the elder sister bride's father
19. Cup manleenä	Calf to the bride's sister's mother
20.Y aŋ Kuɔth guandɛ	A cow and its calf to the God of the bride's father
21. Yaŋ Kuɔth mandɛ	A cow to God of the bride's mother
22. Yaŋ määtha	A heifer cow to the father's friend of the bride
23. Yaŋ buath	A cow to the bride's father
Pek Näärä	Uncle's side
1. Waŋneen guandɛ	A cow to the paternal uncle by the same mother
2. Waŋneen mandɛ	A cow to the uncle to the bride's uncle with the same mother
3. Näär Kuicluaak	A cow to the uncle's bride by a different mother
4. Nä är mandɛ	A Cow to the bride's uncle by the same mother
5.Puɔŋ	Heifer to the bride's grandfather
6.Dɔɔŋ dɛ̈ɛl, wɛɛ kä mandɔɔŋ nyaal (këër thar).	A she-goat or sheep to the maternal
7. Thäk Näärä	A bull to the bride's uncle
8. Cup Näärä	A goat or spear to the bride's uncle
9. Mut näärä (mut mi tëkɛ taŋ kiɛ bith).	Maternal uncle's spear

9.6.4 Transfer of Cows-Nööŋ Ɣɔ̱ɔ̱k

The number of cows agreed upon by both parties is to be transferred by the prospective bridegroom-kuen kinsmen to the people who have the rights on the side of the prospective bride's kinsmen. The process of taking the cows will depend on the negotiatory period in which the parties agreed upon and the minimum number of cows to be paid by the bridegroom's side before setting the date for the wedding ceremony. When this minimum number of cows, is transferred to the paternal side, the prospective bridegroom-kuen side should see to it that the maternal uncles should their cows before the wedding ceremony takes place.

The bridegroom and his delegates will also be given a chance to meet their mother-in-law. The bride-wealth is taken to the bride's home, to the concerned people who fulfil the role of organization and who will finally announce the days of the wedding celebrations. The date of the wedding ceremony will be after 1–4 weeks, depending on the distance of the bridegroom's people and the bride's family.

Since the wedding ceremony is the biggest celebration in Nuär tradition, it takes a solemn form. Consequently, its preparation includes all the members of the extended family from both sides. It is expected that during this period of awaiting wedding celebrations, the bridegroom and his groom-gua̱n tuacdɛ are supposed to circulate the information to the members of his kinsmen and kinswomen through what the Nuär call 'ŋuëŋ kɛ rääw' while they sing and dance with their kinswomen.

Furthermore, the preparatory period of the wedding celebration is characterized by its intensive preparation that is preceded by two weeks and its celebrations continue for a week (octave). It has to be preceded by and dances, singing of newly composed songs intended for the wedding ceremony which bears the names of some family members, the colours of their cows and the spirits of their ancestors. On this occasion, the Nuär custom of the wedding ceremony, the women from both sides, sing-tuar and a few old and young men sing-*waa* including the bridegroom-kuen and his groom-gua̱n tuacdɛ.

The spreading of this great news is by dance -yi̱et kiɛ räw) and songs and by moving from one house to another (whole kraal) which is carried out for three days before the wedding day as we have above-mentioned. The bridegroom-kuen and his groom-guan tuacdɛ from one house to another, wearing wedding clothes-tuac such as tuac thɔ̱ɔ̱nä tied on their waists, positioning them on their buttocks. It is commonly, used in traditional ceremonial wedding clothes made of wild cat skin and they call skin tuac thɔ̱ɔ̱nä. It is also used by the bridegroom-kuen and his gua̱n tuacdɛ to cover their genital organs during the negotiations and the wedding ceremonial days.

9.6.5 Gëŋ/The Chasing of The Bridegroom and His Groom

Among the western major seven clans of Nuär, that is, Bul, Le̱e̱k, Ji̱käny, Jagɛ, Dɔk, Ɣa̱a̱k and Nyuɔŋ Nuär, certain practices are unique. The practice of what the Le̱e̱k Nuär call 'gëŋ' does not exist among the eastern Nuär that is, Laak, Thi̱a̱ŋ, Gaatwär, Ji̱käny dɔar, and Lɔu Nuär. For example, among the western Nuär, the practice of chasing away the prospective bridegroom and his groom by sisters-in-law is very common.

However, there is a variation on specific occasions. Some do it immediately after the negotiation over the bride-wealth, and some do it, during the buɔ̱r nyal/wedding ceremony. Therefore, it is recommended to readers that each should detect those variations and peculiarities while engaging in reading to enjoy and appreciate their taste of them.

9.6.6 Celebration of Wedding Ceremony/ Buɔ̱r Nyal

About buɔ̱r nyal/the-wedding ceremony, the four major clans of southern the area that is, Jagɛ, Dɔk, Ɣa̱a̱k and Nyuɔŋ do have variations with those of the northern part of Unity State (Bentiu). According to those major clans above-mentioned, when the negotiation is ended with an agreement in the byre of the bride's father, in-laws will specify the dateline for the buɔ̱r/wedding ceremony specifically, by guän bööthni̱. When the day of buɔ̱r nyal/the wedding ceremony comes, the prospective bridegroom, his groom, and his brother's wives will come in the after at 3:00 pm or 4:00 pm to join their kinsmen.

While they are coming to the village of in-laws, it is expected that the prospective bridegroom and his groom tie their tuacni̱/leopard skins in front of their sexual organs. The variation of the Southern is that as a rule, the delegates of the prospective bridegroom will bring with them either one big ox or two big oxen with big hocks tied on their horns for the bride's brother while singing and dancing/räw kɛ. This practice of bringing an ox of the brother of the prospective bride is not a common practice in the northern area. In addition, as we above-mentioned, his groom only accompanies the prospective bridegroom, wives of his brothers and his sisters.

When the delegates of the prospective bridegroom approach the kraal, everybody will focus on them specifically, the prospective bride, her sisters, her cousin sisters, and her close friends while standing at both sides of the door of the byre. When the delegates of the bridegroom arrive at the front of the kraal/wi̱c na̱l, a few delegates of the prospective bride will go to receive them while singing and dancing. For example, one strong girl or two strong ones among them will catch the horns of oxen. Then, the brother of the bride will come and take an ox or oxen while singing a song of joy. The reception and catching of the horns of oxen signify acceptance and willingness from the prospective bride's delegates otherwise. This catching of the horns of an ox or oxen by sisters-in and for a brother of the prospective bride to take it or to take them, is not even a common practice in the northern area.

The word "gëŋ' according to Nuär, refers to the declaration of intention and expression of joy between the prospective bridegroom delegates and the prospective bride delegates. The prospect bridegroom and the prospect bride are to declare their intentions through songs intended for a fruitful buɔ̱r nyal/wedding ceremony between the two families. Furthermore, the prospective bride and her delegates refer to the term 'gëŋ' to chase away the prospective bridegroom. It also signifies the expression of love from both sides.

In this sense, the prospective bride will declare her intention of love towards her prospective bridegroom by stating, "If cows were collected like shells (snails), I would have collected forty cows to marry myself to my prospective husband. Second, she will say again, "my prospect bridegroom is the bravest man among Jagɛ Nuär. For example, he always attacks at waŋ dɔar kiɛ waŋ kɛyä. All these expressions are sung by the prospective bride with her sisters to the prospective bridegroom to signify their love towards him.

On the other hand, the wives of the brothers of the prospective bridegroom will sing a song by saying, "When you going to the place of drum, bring for us nyakun/nyayiël, nyakuɔŋ, kiɛ nyaThi̱a̱ŋ/ (prospect bride). The two delegates express their joy towards each other while do̱ny kɛ/dancing of joy together. Finally, when the prospective bridegroom and his delegates arrive at the front door of the byre of the prospective bride's father, they are resisted by the sisters-in-law who are standing at both sides of the door of the byre. However, when the prospective bridegroom spears tut lauk/front door of the byre with a spear.

Immediately, the sisters-in-law on both sides of the door of the byre will start to beat the prospective bridegroom and his groom. The delegates of the prospective bridegroom will try to defend them. However, the sisters-in-law will determine to chase them to wi̱c na̱l/front periphery of the kraal. If they catch them, then they will beat them and can even mishandle them. After the prospective bridegroom and his groom are chased to wi̱c na̱l/front periphery of the kraal, the sisters-in-law will stop.

Furthermore, the prospective bridegroom with his delegates will proceed to a duel/hut where the mothers-in-law are to dance with them. The Nuär call it "ŋuëŋ man thuwni̱. After this ceremony, the prospective bridegroom, and his groom will be directed to a neighbour's house not related to in-laws where the untying of tuac thɔ̱ɔ̱nä of both the bridegroom and his groom will take place. For example, in the southern area, while the bride unties the tuac thɔ̱ɔ̱nä inside the duel/hut for women, she will beaten by her husband.

Furthermore, it is said that the rest of the delegates will be directed to their respective places prepared for them by in-laws. Now, the kinsmen and kinswomen of the prospective bridegroom will be given services which they deserve by the kinsmen and kinswomen of the prospective bride. As a rule, after these services are over, the paternal father/guän bööthni̱ of the prospect bride will hand over her paternal daughter to the kinsmen and kinswomen of the prospect bridegroom.

9.6.7 Celebration of Wedding Ceremony after Negotiation

According to Le̱e̱k and Ji̱käny Nuär, the kinsmen and the kinswomen of the prospect bridegroom are headed by jakɔk/ crow, the chief negotiator/ guän bööthni̱ to the byre of the prospect bride's father for a negotiation over the bride-wealth. During the negotiation, the prospective bride's family are divided into two that is, the father's side and the uncle's side. Both do not sit in the same byer during the negotiation. The delegates of the uncle of the prospective bride sit in a different byre however, after the kinsmen of the prospective bridegroom finish with negotiation from the side, then, they will move to other byre where the delegates of the uncle are located. The negotiation will focus on cows required by the uncle's side.

Always the negotiation is based on the number of cows needed by the prospective bride's kinsmen and kinswomen. In this negotiation, it is expected that the kinsmen of the prospective bridegroom should bargain about the number of cows needed by the kinsmen of prospect the bride. If both parties have reached an agreement, then, the kinsmen of the prospect bride will ask the delegates of the prospect bridegroom to go out to allow them to have a private consultation.

Then, the delegates of the prospective bridegroom plus his groom will go out of the byre and stand in the middle of the kraal (ba rɔ̱ guŋ wi̱e̱c Tɔŋä/stand around unvitriflied dung ashes while singing songs of joy by beating their spear throwers with small sticks call ca wuaat. If the consultation is positive, the senior delegates of the prospect bridegroom headed by jakɔk/crow will be called back to the byre while leaving the young men and girls of the prospect bridegroom and his groom outside singing there.

The guän böötbni̱/ jakɔk/crow will officially communicate to the delegates of the prospective bridegroom kinsmen and kinswomen about an agreement. The mother of the prospective bridegroom with other mothers-in-law will yell/köök and sing/tuar while the father of the prospective bridegroom will mention the name of his ox/bɛ mua̱a̱y. Consequently, the atmosphere of the byre will be filled with emotional joy.

Then, the paternal sisters of the prospective bride and her sisters will come out of the duel/hut. They will bring the prospective bride to the prospective bridegroom and his kinsmen in the middle of the kraal while wearing disguise clothes. The wearing of disguise clothes aims not to recognize the prospective bride by the delegates of the prospective bridegroom. After they arrive at the front of the prospective bridegroom's kinsmen, the sisters-in-law will retreat to the hut/duel leaving the prospective bride alone there with them.

Then, the prospective bride will remove the disguise cloth or veil. After that, she will run back to the duel/hut where she was brought. Then, the sisters of the prospective bride will come out inside the hut/duel to chase away the prospective bridegroom and his groom from the kraal. From there, the prospective bridegroom, and his groom will be put in a separate place while the ceremonial celebration continues. Finally, the kinsmen of the prospective bridegroom will be notified by the guän bööthni̱/ by jakɔk/crow about the possible specific day of buɔ̱r and muɔ̱t/wedding ceremony before they go away.

According to Le̱e̱k and Ji̱käny Nuär, buɔ̱r and muɔ̱t/wedding ceremony are combined together for a good reason. According to them, the term 'buɔ̱r' refers to how the prospective bride is encircled and surrounded by her groom, her sisters, and her paternal sisters and by a few mothers-in-law. Furthermore, the term buɔ̱r also refers to how the above-mentioned sisters and mothers-in-law are to accompany the prospective bride to the house of her husband for muɔ̱t/wedding ceremony for the prospective bride to womanhood. Therefore, the word 'buɔ̱r' according to Nuär, is fitting in this context, otherwise.

However, there can be a high risk for the celebration of the wedding ceremony immediately after negotiation by the northern area. This is because if the family of the prospective bride and the family of the prospective bridegroom do not reach an agreement, then, all the foods and drinks, which are prepared for the celebration, can be wasted or eaten only by the prospective bride's family. In the southern area, they celebrate the wedding ceremony during buɔ̱r nyal/wedding ceremony after a period of negotiation. This is to make sure that all the foodstuff and other necessary things such as koaŋ are prepared and surely be eaten by the prospective bridegroom's kinsmen and kinswomen.

9.7 The Bul Nuär on Muɔ̱t Nyal/Gëŋ/Wedding Ceremony

During the buɔ̱r nyal/wedding ceremony, the delegates of the prospect bridegroom that is, his brother's wives, sisters, and his grooms/gua̱n tuacdɛ will come to the byre of the prospect bride's father. It is expected that all the members of the prospective bride's family will be around. These include her sisters, her cousin sisters, her girlfriends, and her mother-in-law. While the prospective bridegroom and his delegates are coming to towards the kraal, the prospective bride and her sisters above-mentioned will stand on both sides of the door of a byre. However, when the delegates of the prospective bridegroom arrive at the kraal/wi̱c na̱l, the delegates of sisters-in-law will go out to receive them while the rest will remain behind standing on both sides of the door of the byre.

The delegates of the prospect bride will accompany the delegates of the prospect bridegroom to the front door of the byre while each delegate sings his/her songs. When the delegates of the prospective bridegroom arrived at the front door of the byre, while resisted by the sisters-in-law, then, the gua̱n tuac dɛ/his groom will spear the front door of the byre with a spear/bɛ tut luak yɛth kɛ mut. Then, immediately, the sisters-in-law who stand on both sides of the door of the byre will chase away the prospective bridegroom including his groom to the front of the kraal/wic na̱l.

According to the sisters-in-law, the chasing away of the prospective bridegroom and his groom signifies the correction of their bad attitudes. This is because the way they came to the house of the father-in-law, has shown disrespect towards in-laws. Worst, even spearing the front door of the byre of the father-in-law, adds more anger to the sisters-in-law. Therefore, the chasing away of the prospective bridegroom and his groom also means disciplining them so that in the future, should he come to the house of the father-in-law, he will show respect otherwise.

9.7.1 The Wearing of Kara Bracelets

When the prospective bridegroom and his delegates are chased away to the front kraal/wi̱c na̱l, the sisters-in-law will go to bring them to the mothers-in-law. The mothers-in-law are expected to sit down while waiting for the prospective bridegroom at the front door of the duel/hut of the mother-in-law. When the prospective bridegroom and his delegates arrive at the front door of the duel/hut of the mother-in-law, the exchange of Kara bracelets will take place between the prospective bridegroom and his mother-in-law while the rest are watching.

The prospective bridegroom and the mother-in-law ought to put the Kara Bracelets on each other right hand, without the physical context of their hands as a sign of respect. They put Kara bracelets on each other hands in terms of competition. According to Nuär, the exchange of Kara bracelets between the mother-in-law and the prospective bridegroom signifies love and a wish for the new couple to give birth to children. As the mother-in-law gave birth to children, she wished that her daughter would also give birth to children with her new husband. Furthermore, the exchange of Kara bracelets symbolizes the union between the two families.

After the ceremonial stage of exchange of Kara bracelets has finished, the prospective bride will be called by the gua̱n bööthni̱/person of rights to the middle of the kraal. She will come and stands in front of the unvitriflied dung ashes. Then, the gua̱n bööthni̱/person of rights will smear her body with dung ashes as a sign of blessing for a good productive life. All these ceremonial rites are done while the prospect bridegroom, his kinsmen and kinswomen stand there, ready to receive the prospect bride with her delegates. Finally, the gua̱n bööthni̱/person of rights will declare to the prospective bridegroom kinsmen and kinswomen to take their wife.

9.7.2 Muɔ̱t/Ritual Ceremony to Womanhood

After the ritual ceremonies above-mentioned have finished on the evening of the same day, the prospective bride and her sisters, cousin sisters, paternal sisters, and a few mothers-in-law will accompany her to the village of her husband. The two delegates will go together to the house of the father of the prospective bridegroom for a muɔ̱t/ritual ceremony to womanhood. From the side of the prospective bride, only women and girls are allowed to accompany her. Upon their arrival, the mothers-in-law will be put in a separate hut/duel and the prospective bride with her sisters will be put in a different room/duel.

When the prospective bride and her groom enter a room with her sisters, the prospective bridegroom and his groom will enter a room but the prospective bride will immediately throw at them the hocks, which she used to tie on her waist during a drum dance while she was a girl. However, as a principal, the prospective bride and her groom cannot go for a short call or long call, and not eating food or drink water in the prospective bridegroom's house. Then, the prospective bridegroom and his groom will go out of the room.

The throwing of the hocks to the prospective bridegroom by the prospective bride signifies the end of her girlhood. Furthermore, it can also mean that she can never use them again as she enters into the ritual ceremony to womanhood through what the Nuär called “muɔ̱t” as we have above-mentioned. Throughout the night, the young men of prospect bridegroom will seriously joke with their sisters-in-law. For example, a joke that will involve even touching sexual organs except the prospective bride.

Very early in the morning, the senior sister (or any of the sisters) of the prospect bridegroom will come to duel/hut accompanied by a few delegates to the room where the prospect bride and her sisters spent the night. Then, she will tie the animal hides (aprons)/Ya̱a̱t kiɛ yɔak) on her waist which is only worn by women. Such an event also terminates the girlhood of the prospective bride. This is because she will never go naked again.

Afterwards, the prospective bride with her sisters will come outside a room/duel. All will sit down on a traditional instrument called ‘yɛk.’ All the prospective bridegroom sisters especially, the senior sister of the prospective bridegroom are expected to be around with brothers of the prospective bridegroom. Then, the gua̱n bööthni̱ will pray/lam over the sacrificial beast. The gua̱n bööthni̱ will emphasize the blood of the sacrificial beast as a witness to the union between the prospect bridegroom and the prospect bride. He will also say to each of them, anyone of you who will betray this union, will be cursed by the sacrificial blood of this innocent beast. The gua̱n bööthni̱ will stress the importance of loyalty and fidelity between the new couple.

Furthermore, he will say to them that the family wishes

that this union must last for eternity. The gua̲n böötḫni̲ will say to the sisters of the prospect bridegroom, do not disturb this woman, and to the woman, this is your house, take care of it, and respect the members of the family of the prospect bridegroom. After these ritual prayers, the gua̲n böötḫni̲ will spear the sacrificial beast. Then, he will remove the veil from the head of the prospective bride and smear her neck with butter. He then, cuts off the beds on her neck, which signifies the end of her girlhood also.

Afterwards, the gua̲n böötḫni̲ will cut some of her hair on the middle of her head and pour butter on the specific spot where he cut the hair. The cutting of the hair of the prospective bride has great significance. It signifies that the prospective bride will die in her house, as her hair is cut and buried on the plot of her husband, when she dies, her hair will be shaved and buried at her own house and not at the home of her father. Therefore, those few hairs, which are cut on the middle of her head, are an anticipation of her long stay with her husband until death. The gua̲n böötḫni̲ applies the Nuär traditional custom to this ritual ceremony of the prospect bride to send a signal to the prospect bride and the family at large. The wish for a lasting union between the prospective bride and prospective bridegroom is very amazing and rich in this ritual ceremony.

Finally, the gua̲n böötḫni̲ cuts a piece of meat from behind one leg of the sacrificial beast and puts it on the head of the prospective bride. The putting of the piece of meat on the head of the prospective bride by gua̲n böötḫni̲ signifies her future responsibility that she will render to her husband and the whole family at large. However, the prospective bride intentionally throws down the piece of meat from her head.

Then, she will get up and run through the kraal until the wi̲c na̲l/front kraal. Then, she will untie the animal hides (aprons)/Ya̲a̲t and remain with yɔak) from her waist which were tied on her waist by the senior sister of the prospective bridegroom.

This demonstrates the fact that in future, she could be tempted to run away from her home due to the many challenges she will face. However, the brothers of the prospective bridegroom beat her slightly at wi̲c na̲l/ front kraal, which signifies that any attempt for her to run away from the house of her husband will be impossible. Nevertheless, she will not come back to her husband's house but is taken to one of the neighbour's houses with her groom to have something to eat and drink. It is there that her delegates will depart with her to their village. According to Nuär, the beating of the prospective bride by the brothers of the prospective bridegroom means "ca wi̲c dɛ ri̲e̲t cie̲ŋ/they turns her head back to the house. Furthermore, the beating of the prospective bride by the brothers of the prospective bridegroom indicates that she belongs to all the members of the family.

The distribution of parts of sacrificial beasts is very strict about rights/cuŋ. Since from the side of the prospect bride and her groom are represented by females, then, in the distribution of the sacrificial beast, mature sisters of the prospect bride are given hook/ɣo̲o̲y, her adolescent sisters, are given loin/bo̲o̲m, and finally, her paternal mothers, are given 'crops/ jiar. While cuɔt/fats are being put inside the intestine, and kidneys/ruok will be taken to the mother-in-law back home.

9.8. Common Songs for Buɔ̱r Nyal/ for Wedding Ceremony

In the first place, the wives of the brothers of the prospective bridegroom and his sisters will sing the common songs usually fit for the muɔ̱t/wedding ceremony. The song they sing raises, complaints as they sing it, "cä de̱e̱ niin, ca diar yaŋ dä naŋ, cä de̱e̱ bud, ca diar yaŋ dä naŋ. The song can be translated as follows: I will not sleep, the bottle gourd (lagenarai secarai) of my cows has been taken away, I will not spend the day, because the bottle gourd of my cows, has been taken away.

Then, the sisters-in-law of the prospective bridegroom will also sing a common song intended for the muɔ̱t/wedding ceremony. First, it refers to the penis of the prospective bridegroom as follows: I will cut it, I will tie the bell on it, and I will tie it on my neck like a bed. The song can be translated as follows: bä tɛm, bä moc lööth, bä yian nä ŋuäk batik. Furthermore, they will sing another song that refers to the clitoris as follows: tëm ëë ri̱t ɣɔ̱ɔ̱k, cɔ̱t lual nä tem, ri̱t ɣɔ̱ɔ̱k, cɔ̱t rɔ̱a̱l nä tem, ri̱t ɣɔ̱ɔ̱k. This song means: clitoris, turn the cows, clitoris, turn the cows or clitoris bring cows. Furthermore, they will continue with another song as follows: ɛ ga̱a̱y ɛmɛ jek ɣä jɛ, kɛ ji̱k, hay tem, ɛ ga̱a̱y ɛmɛ jek ɣä jɛ, kɛ ji̱k, hay tem. This song can be translated as follows: the suffering I got it because of you, ho! Clitoris.

Then, they will further sing another song by saying "bä rɔdä guic kɛ ne̱e̱n, bä rɔdä lak kɛ thabuny. This song means: I will look at myself in the mirror, I will take a shower with bathing soap. This song demonstrates how a wife can make herself beautiful to her husband. The sisters-in-law will continue singing: Mɛ ci̱ ɣɔ̱ɔ̱ku diaal kuɛnɛ bi̱ dɔth kɛ ŋu? Di̱d culɛ. According to Nuär culture, the brother-in-law and sisters-in-law do have serious jokes by teasing each other. However, the above-said song, can be translated as follows: "You have paid to us all your cows on marriage, what will be left for you? They will answer by singing, "Man of big penis." While the sisters-in-law will yell! It is "a heifer", referring to the prospective bride and the sisters of the prospective bridegroom including the wives of his brothers will say to the sisters-in-law it is "a calf" referring to the prospect bridegroom.

Those songs that are sung by women both in southern and northern areas of western Nuär, prove beyond no doubt about expression of joy at the highest climax. We have said that this happened either during the negotiation of the bride-wealth or during the periods of the wedding ceremony. In a normal situation, it is taboo to mention the clitoris or penis because they are considered as something sacrosanct. During my encounter with some Nuär women, I thought they were going to feel shy to sing those songs, but on the contrary, they sang them with confidence, courage, and joy. However, it ought to be pointed out that anthropologists cannot arrive at this knowledge, except the son of the soil. Therefore, it is only through Nuär women both in the southern and northern areas that one can arrive at such knowledge otherwise.

However, during the period of the wedding ceremony and negotiation, we are surprised to hear Nuär women both in the southern and northern areas sing those songs at the top of their voices without shame. In this regard, one should know that there are no other occasions in which such feelings can be expressed by women, except during marriage celebrations.

By contrast, Nuär men expressed their emotions at the highest emotional level during the negotiation of the bride-wealth by puffing their pipes: puff, puff, puff puff, continuously.

9.9 Consummation-Dɔnyni Cöökni̲ (Wäkal̲)

If the bride goes back to her family, the bridegroom will go to his father-in-law to get permission for the consummation-dɔnyni̲ cökni̲**.** This also has to be approved by the mother-in-law. If there is anything about the bride-wealth that is needed from the bridegroom, he will be asked to bring it first before going to bed with his wife.

Dɔnyni̲ cökn*i̲*-consummation does not take place at the house of the bridegroom-kuen family but at the house of the bride's parents. The word dɔnyni̲ cökni̲ if translated laterally could simply mean 'stepping on the legs of the bride'. According to Nuär, its true meaning refers to the journey of the bridegroom-kuen from his village to his father-in-law's house to have sexual intercourse with his wife after he has been given the green light.

Now, we can speak of true consummation-dɔnyni̲ cökni̲ but not during the muɔ̲t ceremony. Dɔnyni̲ cökni̲ is a euphemism for sexual coitus between the bride and the bridegroom-kuen. Therefore, the word dɔnyni̲ cökni̲-consummation is used for this specific period. The bridegroom-kuen usually goes to the evening to his wife in the village of his father-in-law. He is expected to stand somewhere behind the house. If the people delay there, due to long conversion, he can throw a stone at the house for in-laws to know that the bridegroom is already there waiting. He is expected to get up early in the morning so as not to be seen by anyone as a sign of respect to the parents-in-law. In principle, the bridegroom and the bride usually sleep in the hut chosen by the parents-in-law in their village as we have mentioned earlier.

9.10 The First-Born Child-Da̱a̱p Gatdä Min Jiöl

According to Nuär culture, the new bride should stay in her father's house until she delivers her firstborn child. Unless there is urgency for service in her husband's house, the traditional practice of marriage, allows the bride to stay with her parents before the first child is born. After delivery to her parents' house, she stays for at least one year. During this period, the bride and the bridegroom-kuen prepare themselves for long life commitments.

The bridegroom-kuen prepares a new hut for his wife and a new-byre-luak for himself. All the kinsmen of the bridegroom will help him to build for himself and his wife a suitable shelter for their stay as husband and wife. Such kind of preparation is good for every member of the family and the family of the bride. It is a period of psychological preparation for both the bride-kaw and the bridegroom-kuen and for all the members of both families. After her delivery, there is always an official visit by the bridegroom's relatives and the bridegroom to congratulate their wife on the newborn baby, which requires gifts.

9.11 Tha̱t Kath-The Bride First Cook

After one year of delivery, the bride is expected to come to her house. An arrangement should be made in such a way that her coming to her house is to cook officially for the first time for the age mates of her husband. She, her sisters, and the rest of her close associates, a few women, come with her during this specific period. They will bring all the food items from their village nööŋ kɛ puɔ̱th.

The official food for this specific occasion can be kuän manytapni̱-maize foods usually, with butter is put on it. During that day, all the age mates of her husband are invited to eat there. She is expected to cook as if it were her first time and last time for her to cook in her life. She brings with her the spoon-tuŋ for her husband and her father-in-law. The bride will kneel before the husband when she brings food to him. Bi kaw rɔ ka̱m mua̱l mä läthɛ kuän nhiam cɔadɛ.

When the food is ready, before it is eaten, there is a ritual rite to be performed. The bridegroom's father will be the one to cut some of the food and put it on the ground specifically on riäk shrine for the ancestors. The age mates of the bridegroom and bridegroom after one year or two years can now for the first time eat from the food cooked by his wife.

In 2019, I attended the first official cooking of food by the bride Madam Martha Nyakuoth Chuol at the home of her bridegroom's parents. She was married to Mr. Gabriel Chuil Gielon on July 9, 2016, at the Protection of Civilians site (POC), Unity State. The prayer and the blessing of food were officiated by the Parish Priest of St. Mary's, Fr. Joseph Makuei. At first, I thought that the contemporary Nuär had abandoned such practice, but it is still existing. She joined her bridegroom's family after she gave birth to her first-born child. Therefore, such practice recorded by Evans-Pritchard, H. Howell and I is still effective in contemporary Nuär nations.

According to Nuär, a woman leaves her father and mother

first to join her husband and, second, the husband leaves his father and mother to join his wife and the two become one. According to Aristotle, such preparation for both partners to be united requires "First house and wife, and an ox for the plough."[115] Jesus on his part asserts in reply to the Pharisees who asked him, "Is it lawful for a man to divorce his wife for any cause whatsoever? He said in reply, have you not read that from the beginning the Creator 'made them male and female' and said, 'For this reason, a man shall leave his father and mother and be joined to his wife, and the two shall become one flesh? So, they are no longer two, but one flesh" (Mt 19:3-5).

Conclusion

Chapter nine has discussed various occasions for courtship such as love-nhök and courtship-luɔ̱m, different types of drums, four rounds of dance, various ornaments for dance, and strict required norms for dance and composition of negative songs-këët mä jiäk.

Furthermore, the chapter also has treated the sharing of information about engagement, areas of social concern of Nuär marriage, social dimension of marriage, marriage and crime/domestic violence. It explains wrong ways to enter into marriage such as impregnation-ruët & other sexual misconducts, forced marriage of a female person, forced marriage for a male person, customary ceremonial stages of true marriage, engagement- luɔ̱m.

The chapter has also discussed betrothal-cuic, muɔ̱y nyaal

115 Richard McKeon, (ed.), *Introduction to Aristotle*, New York, The Modern Library, p. 555.

ciɛk, negotiations of the bride-wealth-tuɔ̱c Ɣɔ̱ɔ̱k, distribution of Cows to both the father's side-pek guandɛ and maternal (pëk mandɛ kiɛ näär), transfer of cows-nööŋ Ɣɔ̱ɔ̱k, the wedding ceremony-bul nyaal, wedding ceremonial conclusion-muɔ̱t nyaal, sacrifice, consummation-dɔnyni cöökni̱ (wäka̱l), the first-born child-da̱a̱p gatdä min jiöl and tha̱t kath-the bride first cook.

CHAPTER TEN

THE NUÄR CUSTOMARY LAWS & RITUAL CEREMONY

Introduction

Chapter ten discusses Title I, about various impediments of Nuär marriage, including ten impediments, it further explains Title II, about the ritual ceremony of twins Article III about penalties for sexual misconduct, and Title IV, about various norms that govern an inheritance of a deceased's wife. Furthermore, the chapter also discusses Title V, about rules that govern sexual relations before death, title VI, about norms for levirate and ghost marriages, title VII, about physical harm, title VIII, about the role of Earth-Master-Kuäär Muɔ̱ɔ̱n and finally, title IX, about compensation-cuut

Title I. Various Impediments of Marriage

1. The stresses given to various impediments in Nuär marriage are because they believe in the indissolubility of marriage. To avoid, any possible case that may tempter the processes of

marriage between the prospective bridegroom and prospective bride, the parents have an obligation not to rash into the marriage ceremony.

2. The parents take their time to investigate any possible reason for impediment- g̱a̱ak kiɛ gääl wuk, which may arise, and how best it should be handled based on the moral and customary law of the Nuär people. As such, this period is very important and it determines the validity of marriage according to Nuär Law. Any attempt by any party to bypass this period, most of the time, leads to quarrels and uncertainty about the future of that marriage.

Article 1.1 First Impediment About Age

1. In Nuär tradition, the male who has been initiated-dho̱o̱l mä ca ga̱r after puberty is qualified to be a mature man who can handle family affairs and defend the community. The minimum is above 18-20 years of age for a male person. As is the case, a male person in the Nuär tribe does not marryan at an early age. However, a female person needs to have reached the menstruation period-nya mä ci̱ dëp go̱l (kiɛ nyaal mä ci̱ ko̱ɔay). Usually, the Nuär tribe does not delay the marriage of a girl. The age of maturity for a girl according to them is between 15-16 years. At this age, they assume the girl can handle her husband's affairs well. If the woman is below the expected age, the husband has to wait until the appropriate age for marriage to take place.

2. According to Nuär, age is considered the first impediment -ga̱a̱k. The contemporary Nuär should respect the standard age of the international community which from 18 years and above. However, the lack of schooling may

present many challenges for those girls who have reached the age of menstruation period. This consideration of age seems unanimous for all the Nuär communities although we do permit violations during this period by some individual members in the communities. Nevertheless, the general opinion favours such age of sixteen as appropriate for marriage, which requires reconsideration to meet the contemporary standard.

Article 1.2 Second Impediment about Age Mate

1. This impediment is concerned with fathers of the same age mates and their sons and daughters of the same age mates. The Nuär culturally and morally believe that those couples whose fathers were initiated together kɛ gar kɛɛl, either on the same day or they bear the same name of the age group) are not permitted to marry each other. This is because their fathers by initiation–ca gar kɛɛl, become brothers. In general, the Nuär do observe this impediment with great respect and they do not allow the children of the same age to marry each other. In this regard, any age group that is initiated together-riic kɛ gar or bears the same name of age group cannot marry themselves.

2. The fact that they shed blood on the same day during scarification or bearing the same name of age group, confers unto them a relationship termed as ric. However, if they want to marry, one of the age-mates is 'promoted' to another age set so marriage takes place. A cow for promotion would be sacrificed and a promotion rite commences. Nevertheless, if the proposal for promotion were rejected, no marriage would take place at all and consequently is gääl wuk-difficult to

annul. In this case, the Nuär consider two types of age, those by maturity regardless of age, and those by either initiation or bearing the same name of age group.

3. About this impediment of age mate, I would like to give a practical example, which happened d December 19, 2022, in Juba Maiya Saba (107). I was invited by General Thomas Gatɔt Chio̱k to attend the ceremonial negotiation of the bride-wealth of her prospective bride-daughter, by name Veronica Nyemal Thomas who was engaged by prospect Puɔ̱l Ca̱a̱r Wuan. There, I happened to be the age mate of General Thomas and a spiritual father at the same time. I was asked to open the ceremonial negotiation of the bridewealth with a word of prayer.

4. However, left them due to other commitments. On the following December 20, 2023, someone sent me an envelope, which contained the sum of money equivalent to the price of a cow. The Nuär called it 'yaŋ kɔ̱ɔ̱c ni̱'- cattle of my age mate. For example, when one's age mate dies, and an animal is slaughtered for the funeral rite-wuɔ̱c juɔli̱, the other age mates are not allowed to eat that meat.

Article 1.3 Third Impediment of Incest-Rual

1. By blood relationship, we mean natural relationships for those who want to marry themselves. In the direct lineages, male to male-tuut kɛnɛ tuut, marriage is never allowed. It is good to know the descendants of both the prospect bridegroom and prospect bride otherwise. In the collateral lineages, these are relationships between brothers-dämaani̱ and sisters-nyi̱er and cousins-gaat gua̱n lëën kiɛ gaat man lëën. No one is allowed to marry when the collateral lineages

are related up to the fifth degree for sisters and the sixth degree for brothers.

2. Any relationship with one side on the sixth and the fifth degree for sisters is allowed, and for brothers, one side should be sixth and the other seventh degree. Generally, according to Nuär, such impediment-g<u>aa</u>k has to be observed regarding marriage. The scope of this moral norm is to avoid incest at all costs. Therefore, where it is discovered that there is a blood relationship, there will be no permission for marriage.

3. The great African Theologian Charles Nyamiti contributes a lot to the concept of blood relations based on the ancestral model (exemplar) with its implication for the moral and ethical life of the earthly progeny. According to him, generally, the African traditional concept of ancestor is determined by: first, consanguineous kinship between the ancestor/ancestress with his/her earthly kin. This implies that no one can be an ancestor of an individual who is not consanguineously related to him. C. Nyamiti asserts "It is for this reason that, in traditional customs, the ancestral relationship never extends beyond tribal limits."[116]

4. Second, superhuman sacred status, usually acquired through death. This means that thanks to his proximity to the Supreme Being, the ancestor acquires a superhuman sacred condition with magico-religious powers that can be beneficial to his earthly relatives. Third, exemplarity of behaviour in the human community. In many African traditional societies, no one can attain ancestral status without having led a morally good life according to traditional African moral standards.

116 Charles Nyamiti, *Studies in African Christian Theology*, Vol. 2. Jesus Christ, the Ancestor of Humankind: An Essay on African Christology, Nairobi: CUEA Press, 2006, p. 3.

An ancestor is a model or exemplar of conduct in society and is a source of tribal tradition and its stability.

5. Fourth, mediation (not everywhere indispensable) between the Supreme Being and the ancestor's kin members. C. Nyamiti argues that the ancestor is frequently, although not always, believed to play a mediatory role between the Creator and the ancestor's earthly relatives. Fifth, the ancestor is believed to have a right or title to regulate sacred communication with his earthly kin through regular prayers, and ritual donations (oblations). According to C. Nyamiti, this communication is intended to be a manifestation of love, thanksgiving, confidence, petition, and homage to the ancestor from his kin on earth. Such marvellous explanations of the role of the ancestor towards his earthly progeny contribute to the prohibition of incest in many various indigenous communities.

Article 1.4 Catholic Church on Fourth Impediment-Incest

1. Incest by description is sexual intercourse between persons related by blood or consanguinity. The experts in sexual ethics agree that no known society has it conventional or permissible for father and daughter, mother and son, or brother and sister to have intercourse or to marry. According to H. Peschke, society rejects marriage between close relatives, because inbreeding proves prejudicial to a healthy offspring, biologically psychologically, and socially. However, the immorality of incest is not limited to intercourse between father and daughter, or mother and son, or brother and sister, it is extended to all those who are relatives. In this sense, we

must admit exceptions to this universal prohibition about incest. For example, the Arabs do allow marriage to take place within the relatives depending on their philosophy of marriage.

2. The Old Testament on sexual morality forbids incestuous unions. This is also the norm of sexual ethics in most societies. Prohibition is wedlock between a man and his granddaughter, stepdaughter or stepmother, step-granddaughter, daughter-in-law or mother-law, aunt or niece, sister-in-law or half-sister, and vice versa the wedlock of a woman with the corresponding relations. Each prohibition of the moral nature of the above-mentioned relations requires cultural analysis. The New Testament adopts the same norms especially John the Baptist who reproached Herod's marriage with his sister-in-law during his brother's lifetime as a grave depravity (Cf. Mk 6:17f) and St. Paul excommunicated a man sexually linked to his stepmother (Cf. 1 Cor 5:1-13).

3. The book of Canon Law does not use the term incest but it establishes marriage impediments for various relations between persons related by blood or by affinity on a broader scale than the prohibitions of the Old Testament. According to canon law, impediments exist for the marriage between all ascendants and descendants in the direct line; in the collateral line between brothers and sisters and between first cousins (CIC 1091; cf. 108); between those who are related by affinity in any degree of the direct line; i.e. between a man and his mother or daughter-in-law and between the woman and her father or son-in-law (CIC 1092). However, the prohibition of marriages between first cousins is an impediment from which the Church dispenses, although reluctantly. Rare is the dispensation from affinity in the direct line.

4. The universal prohibitions of incest emerge as a concern first for a healthy offspring, for a sound family, and for the stability of social life. K. Peschke argues these prohibitions function to eliminate sexual competition and ensuing tensions within the nuclear family and restrain sexual abuse of close family relations. They do have the function of forcing the children to leave their next of kin to seek mates; the prohibitions foster the integration of the young in society and prevent the concentration of undesirable familial peculiarities.

5. It has been asserted that concrete incest prohibitions depend on cultural traditions and do have the character of customs rather than moral laws. However, the innermost circle of the family constitutes a moral. For example, any offence of incest committed between grandparents, parents, children, brothers, and sisters is the greatest grave sin.

Article 1.5 Fifth Impediment About Murder-Cɔa̱k kiɛ Tɛr

1. By this impediment, we mean that when any close relatives of the prospective bride's kinsmen or bridegroom's kinsmen, such marriage killed one member of the family cannot be permitted unless the killing had happened years back and the descendant reached the fourth or fifth degree behind the family. The Nuär by large, do generally agree on this impediment -ga̱a̱k. If it is discovered that there is fatal-thööŋ between the relatives of the bridegroom kinsmen and the bride kinsmen, no marriage can take place.

2. In chapter one, we have discussed this issue fatal-thööŋ thoroughly. We stressed the lasting memory it caused to the two families that is the family of the person who was

murdered and the family of the murderer. The Nuär do not take this thing for granted fearing that the blood of the innocent one can bring misfortune if compromises. In this regard, where there is a fatal-thööŋ, the al, aloofness, and reservation are natural towards each other families. Even the discovery of this fatal-thööŋ between the families can recharge their enmity once again especially the family of the person being murdered.

Article 1.6 Sixth Impediment about Bad Conduct

1. Earlier, we discussed the family of the bridegroom and the family of the bride to investigate each other conduct. This impediment of bad moral conduct involves the assessment of the bad characters of both families and their sons/daughters. If there is any story of theft or witchcraft within or other issues related to notorious brutality in that family, such marriage cannot be permitted.

2. The Nuär believes that children learn all good or bad conduct from their parents, so any bad or good conduct from the parents might have been transferred to the children. Furthermore, this impediment requires serious investigations from both sides of the prospective bridegroom's kinsmen and kinswomen and the bride's kinsmen and kinswomen. Therefore, should there be any discovery of theft or witchcraft from either side, no marriage will take place.

Article 1.7 Seventh Impediment about Seniority of Age

1. The Nuär tradition gives much regard to the first male born in the family. The first male born will marry first, followed by

the second one and the list continues. Any shortcut will not permit the marriage to continue. For example, with regard, to females, if the younger sister is married first, due to any reason, the elder daughter will be 'compensated' with a pregnant cow-yaŋ mä liac for that marriage to continue and be fruitful. Among the Nuär, this sometimes may happen but not always.

2. It is strictly observed among males in the family whereby a shortcut is never permitted. The seniority according to age is strictly restricted to male persons. However, if among brothers, some can get cows by working hard, this seniority can be loosened, provided that person will no tempter with cows of the family intended for the marriage of the elder son in the family. In this case, the rigidity of the seniority is sometimes challenged by certain situations.

Article 1.8 Eighth Impediment About In-Laws (Affinity-Tuac)

1. By relationship through marriage, we simply mean relationships such as father-in-law, mother-in-law, and daughter-in-law. In such cases, marriage cannot be permitted in direct line, for instance, a man cannot marry his dead wife's mother (his mother-in-law), or his dead wife's daughter, by a previous marriage, or his dead wife's sister unless he did not sleep with his wife. The relationships of in-laws in Nuär demand the highest morality and strong ethical behaviors. Nevertheless, there are sections of Nuär in which two brothers can marry two cousin sisters.

Article 1.9 Ninth Impediment of Adoption

1. This impediment makes marriage invalid between adopted children and those who brought them up. By adoption, we simply mean the direct line for all relationships, the child (rɛd) is/are adopted when (he/she) becomes (s) adult(s). According to Nuär, no marriage can take place between those who adopted the child and the child. Any attempt to do that will be considered invalid and an abuse.

2. The above-mentioned eight impediments among the Nuär present to us clearly how a true union between a man and a woman can be evaluated based on those first eight impediments. The Nuär believe these are preliminary requirements and assessments for a true marriage. Therefore, should there be any violation of either of them, true marriage must not be considered.

Article 1.10 Tenth Impediments of Friendship

1. Of the most important and valuable in human relationships is friendship. Friendship, as understood a distinctively personal relationship that is grounded in a concern on the part of each friend for the welfare of the other, for the other's sake. It always involves some degree of intimacy. Friendship is central to our lives, in part because the special concern we have for our friends must have a place within a broader set of concerns, including moral concerns, and in part. After all, our friends can help shape who we are as people.

2. Given this centrality, important questions arise concerning the justification of friendship and, in this context, whether it is permissible to "trade up" when someone new comes

along, as well as concerning the possibility of reconciling the demands of friendship with the demands of morality in cases in which the two seem to conflict."[117]

3. However, to link impediment with friendship, one would have no doubt. This is due to three notions, which are related to friendship such as love: *agape, eros,* and *philia.* By description, agape is a kind of love that does not respond to the antecedent value of its object but instead is thought to create value in the beloved; it has come through the Christian tradition to mean the sort of love God has for us persons as well as, by extension, our love for God and our love for mankind in general.

4. It is said that by contrast, *eros* and *philia* are generally understood to be responsive to the merits of their objects-to the beloved's properties, especially his goodness or beauty. Furthermore, the difference is that eros is a kind of passionate desire for an object, typically sexual, whereas *philia* originally meant a kind of affectionate regard to or friendly feeling towards not just one's friends but also possibly towards family members, business partners, and one's own country at large. Given this classification of kinds of love, *philia* seems to be that which is most clearly relevant to friendship.

5. The descriptions of friendship above, amount to the consideration of its degree of level of impediment. Based on those convincing explanations, nobody can doubt about real impediments to marriage. Among the Nuär as it is for other human beings, no marriage is allowed between sons and daughters of friends.

6. Instead, among the Nuär when a daughter of one's friend

---

117 https.//plato. Standford.edu/entries/friendship/standford, Standford Encyclopedia of Philosophy, retrieved as from 04/04/2023.

is married, there is a cow designated to a friend. Furthermore, when the son of a friend is going to marry, there is a cow for a friend to be paid to the bride's father's friend. Therefore, in every marriage among Nuär, there is always a cow for a friend. In this case, the impediment about a friend is real, otherwise.

Title II. Norms about Ritual Ceremony of Twins

1. The Nuär believes that giving birth to twins is something abnormal. They associate it with birds. This is because birds always give birth to twins. In this sense, the Nuär always gives names to twins like birds. For example, gatdiɛd-son of bird or naydiɛn-daughter of bird.

2. Apart from associating the twins with birds, there is strict ritual purification of twins. These strict ritual purifications of twins are common among the Nuär both in the West and in the East. Even about their maturation and funeral, there are also strict rules to be followed.

Article 2.1 After the Delivery of Twins

1. The Nuär believe that immediately, after the delivery of twins, and before their mother suckles them, the gua̲n bööthni̲/ is called to perform ritual purification fits for suckling the twins. The gua̲n bööthni̲/ will come to the house in which the twins are born. He comes and kneels in front of the door, and other siblings including the father of the twins and other relatives are standing in front of Bur/specific place for cooking. For example, the untied ram, not a twin that is brought for scarification stands with the people behind the gua̲n bööthni̲.

2. The gua̱n böötthni̱/ will pray and cut a sour fruit called 'kuɔl'. He will throw up the two halves, the one that will fall with the cutting part upward; he will squeeze its liquids on the breasts of the mother of the twins as a blessing. Then, he blesses the water and sprinkles the twins with their mother with the holy water and the people standing behind him. The gua̱n böötthni̱ will say "The mother of the twins, suckle them. The title "mother of the twins or father of the twins" will be the dominant name throughout their entire lives, even if they have other children. Then, the ram is slaughtered for the celebration.

Article 2.2 Rule of Sleeping for Twins

1. As a rule, the twins are sleeping on their beds by turning their heads in opposite directions as their mother puts them. This precept applies to them during their infancy, until adulthood. For example, even when they become adults, they sleep with heads in opposite directions on the bed, that is, one's head to the position of the legs of each other on the bed.

Article 2.3 After Three-Four Days of Delivery

1. According to customary law, after three or four days of delivery, there is a ritual ceremony to be done by the mother of the twins and the one who is helping her. The ritual purification requires her to boil some grains of wheat. After she finishes boiling them, she calls the Gua̱n Bööthni̱ to bless them, she puts them on traditional stray called lääth. Then, she invites the Gua̱n Bööthni̱ to throw them to birds, while some will be given to children. The throwing of grains to

birds is the symbolic gesture of joy, which manifests her motherhood both for her twins and for birds too.

Article 2.4 About Weaning Ceremony of Twins

1. The Nuär traditional weaning ceremony of twins requires the presence of the Gua̠n Bööthni̠ after two years and a half. This ritual ceremony takes place at the house of the parents of the twins with the presence of other siblings plus relatives. During this ritual performance, the parents of the twins stand in front of the door of the duel/hut holding their hands, while other siblings and relatives stand in front of the Buur/a traditional place for cooking food. The twins also stand in front of Buur with their brothers, sisters, and other relatives. The Gua̠n Bööthni̠ stands between them, however, facing the parents of the twins with water for blessing. First, he blesses the water using prayer fit for the occasion.

3. After the blessing of water, then, he sprinkles the parents of the twins, the twins, and other people standing behind him. Finally, he commands the parents of the twins by saying "Go inside the room/duel/hut" as a symbolic gesture of weaning the twins. Then, they enter the duel/hut without sexual intercourse and come back outside. Finally, the Gua̠n Bööthni̠ will bless the types of food and drink/kɔaŋ prepared for an occasion of weaning the twins. The celebration will continue colored with some entertainment.

Article 2.5 Bööth/Rights after Five-Six Year

1. Traditionally, during their growth to adolescence, the Nuär believed that twins are not supposed to greet people by hand

nor do others greet by hand. This is because they are not puuth/ritual purification. During this period, they can greet people by embracing them otherwise. However, within this period, there is also a ritual performance to be done for them.

2. Given the celebration of these ceremonies/rights, it is expected that all the members of the family cook different types of food, each according to his/her capacity including slaughtering some rams. When everything is prepared, then the gua̱n bööthni̱ will bless the food and distribute it to the people according to their cuuŋni̱/rights, including cuo̱ŋdɛ/his rights. Consequently, after this ritual ceremony, the twins can then greet the people by hand.

Article 2.6 Puuth/Kiɛ Kue̱r Puukä

1. According to Nuär, when the twins have reached the age of puberty, they must be puuth/ritual purification for maturation. First, if the twins are girls, they choose boys for their puuth/ ritual purification and if they are boys, they choose girls for puuth/ritual purification. If they are a boy and a girl, they choose a boy and a girl for their puuth/ritual purification.

2. It is a must for the twins and their parents to inform the parents of those they chose for their Puuth/ritual purification. Consequently, those parents must agree otherwise.

3. If the parents of those whom the twins chose for their puuth/ritual purification agreed, then the twins and their team would go to the house of the boys (boy/girl while they dressed like boys and sat like boys when they arrived. The boys, on the other hand, will dress like girls and sit like girls. In this regard, the ritual purification will require the assumption of playing the opposite role.

Article 2.7 Items Required During Puuth/Kiɛ Kue̱r Puuk kä

1. Certain items are required for kue̱r puuk kä/ the dung ashes, two cradels, ye̱c/broom, yiɛk, kur rɔny da̱a̱ŋ rɛw/two pieces of straw, gourd-diar, spoons-tuɔ̱ŋ, tuɔk/an open gourd, and four rams that were brought by four of them, which are not twins. All these items are put into four cradles by those four players that is, the two twins and the two persons whom they puuth/chose.

2. The puuth/kiɛ kue̱r puuk kä must take place at the house of the parents of the boy chosen by Nyaböth or at the house of the parents of the girl chosen by Böth and not the other way around.

3. When the twins and their team arrive at the house of those whom they puuth/chose, each of them will spread his/her yiɛk/ in front of those they puuth/chose. Those they puuth/chose will spread their yi̱i̱k in front of them too, facing each other. On the one hand, the team of twins stands will behind them, and on the other hand, the team of those they puuth/choose will stand behind their persons.

Article 2.8 The Wearing of Beds and Kue̱r Puuk kä

1. It is expected that each of the twins will tie the beds on the hand of the person he/she puuth/chose, and those whom they puuth/chose, will tie the beds on their hands too. The tying of beds on the hands of those they puuth/chose symbolizes the choice they made for those persons, while the tying of beds on the hands of the twins by those persons, and signifies their willingness and acceptance of the choice offered by the twins to them.

2. At this juncture, the real celebration will start by throwing the dung ashes to each other including cradles. The exchange of four rams takes place immediately as gifts to each team. Then, the twins will be chased away however; they must run faster like boys to prove their maturity. Then, a serious celebration will continue as the abundance of food is prepared for the celebration including drink/kɔaŋ for the elderly people. From now on, the twins are considered mature adults.

Article 2.9 About Marry of Twins

1. In principle, the twins are expected to marry the persons they puuth/chose during their /kue̱r puuk kä. However, if they decided to choose other persons for their marriages, then, they are supposed to pay two cows to those they puuth/chose during their ritual purification. The Nuär believe that if they chose other persons, misfortune can happen to those they puuth/chose.

Article 2.10 The Bride-Wealth for the Twins Girls

1. Nyaböth is always the name given to the first twin during the delivery. When Nyaböth is married, 35 heads of cattle are required. However, if Nyaduɔth who is the second is married first, then, Nyaböth will receive a cow as her right. This rule applies to other girls from the same mother in Nuär culture.

2. In comparison, Nyaduɔth is always married with less bride wealth. For example, 7 heads of cattle are required for the main cuuŋni̱/rights. Today, 10 heads of cattle are demanded. However, Nyaduɔth marriage continues as long as she continues giving birth to children.

Article 2.11 Wedding Ceremony/Muɔ̱ɔt of Nyaböth

1. When the wedding ceremony/muɔ̱ɔ̱t of Nyaböth takes place at the house of the parents of the prospective bridegroom, her twin brother Gatdiɛd/Duɔth, must be present. Usually, the sisters of Nyaböth, her cousin sisters, and other girls in the village including the mothers-in-law are to accompany her.

2. Her brother Gatdiɛd/Duɔth is the bridegroom. When they arrived at the house of the parents of the prospective bridegroom, the bridegroom and his groom including his senior sister in front of the house waiting for them. Upon their arrival, they stand at a specific place called 'wi̱c ke̱k/wi̱c na̱l' by Nuär at the periphery of kraal facing the bridegroom and his team who stand at the front of the byer.

3. Then, the senior sister of the bridegroom will ask the team of the bride, "Where is the twin of the bride? Then, Gatdiɛd/Duɔth will come forward and say, here, I am. Then, the senior sister of the bridegroom will say to him, please, come forward. He comes and stands in front of the team of the prospective bridegroom.

4. Then, the senior sister of the bridegroom will give him a traditional skirt called 'yɔak', which is meant for the newly wedded woman. Furthermore, she will ask the brother of the bride to tie it to his waist. Then, the senior sister of the bridegroom will ask Gatdiɛd/Duɔth again to go inside the room while the two teams are standing outside.

5. Then, the twin brother of the bride will open the door of the duel/hut and enter a room. Then, the senior sister of the prospective bridegroom will command her brother to follow him inside the room. Upon his arrival inside the room, Gatdiɛd/Duɔth will untie the 'yɔak'and throw it to him. Then,

he will come out of the room and everyone will begin to laugh and the prospective bridegroom will promise him an ox, which the Nuär call 'thääk yɔkä. Then, the team of brides will be welcomed inside the room duel/hut while the bridegroom will look for a place in which Gatdiɛd/Duɔth will sleep.

6. In the following morning, Gatdiɛd/Duɔth will come again during the muɔ̱ɔ̱t. Then, the senior sister of the bridegroom with other sisters will ask him to come inside the rthe room of duel/hut. Then, the senior sister of the prospective bridegroom will tie the yɔak on his waist and he will untie it and give it to his sister to tie it on her waist. Then, he will come out of the room. In this sense, the Nuär will say, that the newly wedded bride has become a woman after this last dramatic ceremony.

Article 2.12 Rule about Funeral Rite

2. According to Nuär, when one of the twins died, there was no funeral prayer to be performed. They believe that any funeral rite to be done will be like wishing the other twin to die. Therefore, the funeral rite will be said after the death of the other twin. How long that twin will live, does not count.

Article III: Giving of Rope/De̱e̱b to Mother-in-Law

1. In some areas of Nuär customary law, when a man marries a girl whose mother is still giving birth, it is expected that after the muɔ̱t/wedding ceremony for prospect bride to womanhood, the prospect bridegroom with his prospect bride must give a rope/de̱e̱b to mother-in-law through a window/ wue̱r nyiin. She will catch it while sitting inside the room.

Consequently, the prospect bridegroom and the prospect bride will pull the rope/de̲e̲b from her again.

2. Finally, they will take the rope/de̲e̲b with them back to their home. There, they will choose a doe (buck) dɔw dɛl mä nac or a ewe lamb, and ie it with that rope/de̲e̲b. Then, they will bring it to the mother-in-law. The giving of a doe (buck) dɔw dɛl mä nac or a ewe lamb, signifies the future fruitfulness to the daughter of the mother-in-law and her son-in-law. Furthermore, the bringing of the doe (buck) dɔw dɛl mä nac or a ewe lamb to the mother-in-law has a connection with an exchange of Kara bracelets between mother-in-law and son-in-law as we have mentioned earlier somewhere.

This practice is unique to Bul Nuär in the northern area, however, it can also be found in some clans with variations. In this regard, we that Le̲e̲k, Ji̲käny, and Bul Nuär do use ropes/de̲e̲b for different reasons during the marriage ceremony. These practices show certain peculiarities and richness to the meaning of marriage itself. Therefore, an outsider ought to know this practice too.

Article IV: Throwing of a Rope/Deeb

1. When the time comes for buɔ̲r and muɔ̲t/wedding ceremony, a few delegates of brothers-in-law will come to the house of the father-in-law to accompany the sisters-in-law to their village. When they arrived at the periphery of kraal/wi̲c na̲l, they stopped there, waiting for their sisters-in-law. Then, the sisters-in-law will come towards them accompanied by jakɔk/crow while standing facing each other. The jakɔk/crow will step backwards and will throw a rope/de̲e̲b up while the sisters-in-law and brothers-in-law must doggy it.

2. The reason for dogging the rope/de̱e̱b is that, that it carries with it all the negatives and bad things, which might have been said during marriage. It is believed that the rope/de̱e̱b contains misfortune. Therefore, either each group sisters-in-law or brothers-in-law ought to make sure that the rope/de̱e̱b does not fall upon them. They must struggle to prevent it from falling on anyone but rather fall in the middle of him or her. After this ceremony, the jakɔk/crow will dismiss them to go with his blessing. This practice of throwing a rope/de̱e̱b by jakɔk/crow to sisters-in-law and brothers-in-law is peculiar to Le̱e̱k and Jikäny Nuär in the southern area of Bentiu.

Article V: Rules with Regard in-Laws

1. According to Nuär customary law, there are strict rules that govern the relationships between in-laws. For example, fathers-in-laws on both sides cannot eat either in the prospective bridegroom's father or in the prospective bride's father. This customary law is also applicable to mothers-in-law on both sides. This includes even a son-in-law in the house of the father-in-law. This customary law is not only limited to food alone but even drinking water is not permissible.

2. The customary law demands that there must be an official way in which the in-laws can properly invite themselves. For example, the father-in-law can officially invite his son-in-law to his house to eat and drink water. The son-in-law with his friends can come and eat, and drink water officially in the house of the father-in-law. The father-in-law can also invite other people to participate in that banquet. Furthermore, this customary principle applies the to prospective bridegroom's

father, to the prospective bride's father and to mothers-in-law on both sides.

3. Therefore, any outsider who would like to marry a girl from Nuär ought to know this principle. For example, even sitting place at the home of in-laws requires certain norms to be observed. One ought to be directed to a proper place prepared for him/her otherwise, eating and drinking anyhow is not permissible regard to principles, which govern the relationship of in-laws.

Article VI: Dɛɛl of Gaatwär

1. Among the Le̱e̱k Nuär of the western Nile, there are two clans of Gaatwär. First, there is Cie̱r and Padaŋ clans. These clans have a peculiar practice about the reception of the prospect bride or prospect bridegroom. However, this peculiar practice is common to all the Gaatwär Nuär as well. This specific customary law is applied to a girl who is married by any man from these two clans if she is not from Cie̱r and Padaŋ clans. For example, when another man from another clan of Nuär marries a girl from these two clans, the customary practice of 'dɛɛl' will be applied to her husband.

2. The term 'dɛɛl' refers to the song of the reception of the prospective bride to the home of her husband. When her sisters bring the prospective bride to the home of her husband, the paternal mother of the prospective bridegroom and his brother's wives will receive her at the kraal/wi̱c na̱l. Then, they will sing a special song called 'dɛɛl' to welcome the prospective bride home.

3. The term dɛɛl also referred to the conditions, which Wua̱r, Thiliɛy, and Juɔ̱ŋ agreed among themselves. He said to

Wua̲r and Thiliɛy that when my sons marry your daughters, I will be the one to negotiate.

4. Furthermore, Juɔ̲ŋ said, when your sons marry my daughters, you will be the one to negotiate. Second, when their children have a peak/share the same totem, no marriage among them. Third, gaatkɔn/our sons, and our daughters/ nye̲kɔn bi̲ kɛ te̲k kɛ dɛɛl, which will be, sung during the reception of the prospective bride during the reception of the wife of prospect bridegroom. Then, three of them agreed upon these conditions as we have earlier.

5. The song goes as follows for the prospective bride: dɛɛl lö dɛɛl lö lany, nyaralɔ lany, nyaralɔ lany. For the prospective bridegroom, the song goes like this: dɛɛl lö dɛɛl lö lany, gat ralɔ lany, gat ralɔ lany. This song called dɛɛl is sung by the paternal mother of the prospective bridegroom and his brother's wives as a ritual ceremony of reception at the kraal/ wi̲c na̲l during muɔ̲t/wedding ceremony of the prospective bride to womanhood.

6. They sing this song while moving around the house with the prospective bride before she enters a room, beating their drums. They have to repeat it until they complete going around the house. After that, the prospective bride will enter a room and other activities can follow. This song cannot be translated into other languages, due to its complexity and ambiguity. Therefore, an outsider who would like to marry a girl from Gaatwär clans ought to know this ritual practice and must be ready for it, otherwise.

7. Bilɛ Gaatwär: When a man from Gaatwär sleeps with his wife during rain, the pregnancy of his wife will take only six months. His wife will deliver before nine months and the child will survive. This happens occasionally among the

Gaatwär Nuär. Nobody knows its origin, however; some of them suggest that it might be related to the origin of wua̱r (who like meat so much) who came from the river and their sister nyiwuor that they believe to be in a river.

Title VII. Penalties Concerns Sexual Misconduct

1. As there are rules that govern marital life in Nuär customary law, such as those of impediments, there are also penalties for sexual misconduct. Those rules are many and they are meant to deter people from messing up in sexual relationships.

Article 8.1 Adultery (Dhöm)

1. Adultery is considered by most jurisdictions to be a criminal offence that endangers the marital relationship and communal harmony. In common law, adultery applies only to married women. Adulterers and adulteress are usually subject to some forms of punishment in addition to the compensation that the guilty man must pay to the husband. The Nuär consider adultery as the most exceedingly breaching of marital fidelity. Furthermore, it is considered as infidelity of a spouse.

2. When adultery is committed, a spouse is given six head of cattle (ruɔk dhuɔ̱k ciek) as compensation for the ethical harm caused to him by the philanderer. They would be reestablished into their past conjugal status without the requirement of divorce. In differentiation, the infidelity of a spouse isn't considered a basic ground for separation. A spouse might not request the court to separate for the reason that her spouse has committed such an act of adultery.

3. In some cases, when someone commits an act of

adultery, sometimes, the killing of the adulterer can happen. Always the law will judge the husband of a woman to be right because a third party has entered illegally into a sexual relationship with his wife. However, compensation will be paid to the family of the person being murdered.

4. If a man kidnaps another man's wife and the legal husband does not want to divorce his wife, in this case, it is primarily adultery, the adulterer must pay (6) head of cattle (ruɔk).

Article 8.2 Fornication

1. Fornication is usually consensual sex between two people who are not legally married to each other. In this sense, there is a difference between adultery and fornication. Fornication can be described as sexual intercourse between two unmarried people (to each other or someone else) who engage in consensual intercourse.

Article 8.3 Rape

1. Rape is a felony under common law only. Rape; means forcing someone to have sex when they do not want to, using violence, or engaging in threatening behaviour. For example, when a man rapes a girl, according to Nuär customary law, he pays (ruɔk) a cow (liac) and a female calf (dɔw mi gur kɛl). If the girl's father refuses, the ruɔk, the man is released.

2. When a man rapes another man's wife and succeeded in sleeping with her, the offence is primarily adultery. Compensation (6) head of cattle (ruɔk) is paid. There is room for revenge.

Article 8.4 Elopement (Kuël)

1. Kuël, literally "stealing," is a type of marriage initiated by the two spouses' secret escape (away) from where their families live intending to live together as husband and wife. In other words: (elope with a lover, especially to get married).

2. If a man kidnaps a girl, gets her pregnant, and refuses to marry her, he pays (1) cow (liac) and (1) bull (ruath mi gur kɛl as (ruɔk), and later pays (3) more cattle if he is a boy. That will make (5) cattle. But she is a girl, he pays 2 more and that will make (4) cattle.

3. If a man kidnaps a girl and gets pregnant and the girl's parents reject him, he has to pay ruɔk of (1) cow (liac) and bull (ruath mi gur kɛl).

Title IX. Norms for an Inheritance of a Deceased's Wife

1. According to Nuär customary law, certain principles about article 4, ought to be followed. Accordingly, in Article 3 about the inheritance of a deceased person's wife, certain criteria required serious observation. These criteria or customary laws are operational in the four areas of Nuär land such as Bentiu, Central Fangak, Nasir, and Akobo. In these customary laws, there is no reverse but rather, the principles about inheritance, remain rigid.

2. In those of inheritance, morality, and ethics are only found in the philosophy of family and the communitarian concept of Nuär people. In this sense, if one would like to assess the aspect of morality and ethics of inheritance about a wife of a deceased person, focusing on one thread such as sexuality, will be considered premature. Therefore, one

ought to take into consideration the moral duty and justice between those who are still alive, towards those relatives who are living dead. According to Nuär law, justice ought to exist between the living and the living dead about the inheritance of the deceased wife.

3. Furthermore, responsibility, moral obligation, justice, familial breakdown, psychological impact upon the children that will come as a consequence of separation from their mother, psychological impact upon the mother that will come as a result of separation from her children and communitarian dimensions, all, are counted among other things about divorce and inheritance otherwise. Therefore, in these practices of Nuär customary laws about the inheritance of a deceased person's wife, there is no room for prostitution in Nuär society as it is for other tribes of indigenous Africans.

4. Therefore, there is a lasting bond between the wives of the deceased person with the kinsmen of her husband, and between in-laws. Even death cannot separate it but rather allows the family of the deceased person to continue with it in a lasting bond. In this case, even divorce comes only when the situation becomes intolerable between in-laws.

5. How painful is the divorce? We have three statements from the three understanding figures, one a pious Jewish Rabbi Eleazar who said, 'When a man divorces his first wife, the very altar sheds tears.' Second, another outstanding philosopher Aristotle said, "Divorce is to the family life what civil war is to the state."[118] Third, the Pharisees were quick to respond to Jesus: "Why then," they asked, "did Moses command that a man give his wife a certificate of divorce and send her away?" (Mt 19:7).

118 Cf. Raymond E. Brown, *The New Jerome Biblical Commentary*, p.642.

6. This is a logical response because no one can disallow what God has allowed, that would be abolishing the Torah. Yeshua [Jesus] responds: "Moses permitted you to divorce your wives because your hearts were hard. Nevertheless, it was not this way from the beginning. I tell you that anyone who divorces his wife, except for marital unfaithfulness [unchastity], and marries another woman commits adultery." (Mt 19:8-9)

Article 9.1 No Uncle Can Inherit a Wife of His Nephew

On one hand, this article affirms that in the case of death, no uncle among the Nuär can inherit his nephew's wife. However, on the other hand, a nephew can inherit the wife of his uncle in the case of death.

Article 9.2 No Father Can Inherit the Wife of His Son

This article stipulates that in the case of death, no father can inherit his son's wife. Nevertheless, in the case of the death of a father, his son can inherit his stepmother to get children for his father. This same article applies to the paternal father and his paternal son in which case, it is the paternal son to inherit of wife of his paternal father after his death.

Title X. Rules of Sexual Relations Before Death

1. The norms about inheritance of the wife of the deceased persons according to Nuär have their very strict rules before each category of each person dies.

Article 10.3 No Sexual Intercourse Before Death

1. In those cases discussed about an inheritance, no sexual intercourse is allowed before someone dies. For example, if a son slept with his stepmother while his father was still alive, he would be considered a wizard or ill-willed, wishing him to die. If sexual intercourse happens between a nephew and his uncle's wife or it happens between paternal sons with their paternal wife, while the either uncle or paternal father is still alive, this involves both incest and adultery.

2. Consequently, this will require ritual purification, forgiveness, and reconciliation. However, after the death of any of those categories people above- mentioned, if sexual intercourse happens between stepmotherthe, and her stand epson, between paternal son with her paternal wife, and between uncle's wife and his nephew, there is no conception of incest or adultery.

Title XI. Norms for Levirate and Ghost Marriages

1. According to Nuär, there are strict rules to be observed about both levirate and ghost marriages. Those are binding because they are part and partial of Nuär customary laws. However, to an outsider, their moral integrity may be questionable nevertheless for Nuär themselves, their moral dimensions are to be found in every thread of their own lives, as it does to the rest of other tribes in South Sudan and in the continent at large.

Article 11.1 About Levirate Marriage

1. Levirate marriage is described as a type of marriage in which the brother of a deceased man is obliged to inherit his brother's wife. For example, levirate marriage has been practised by societies with a strong clan structure. According to Nuär, there is no marriage in levirate but rather something, which they call 'kueŋ ciëk duel-putting a woman in a hut. As a customary law, there is no marriage at all about levirate marriage. The family of the deceased person must choose someone among the brothers a deceased person or sometimes, they allow the wife of the deceased person to choose among those brothers.

2. Therefore, anyone who is chosen either by the wife of the deceased person or by his relatives, will take the responsibility to get children for his deceased brother. Also, he takes other responsibilities apart from sexual obligations.

Article 11.2 About Ghost-Marriage

1. By description, a ghost marriage is a legally binding marriage in which one or both parties are deceased. The ghost wedding serves as a form of emotional compensation for bereaved relatives, as finding a dead bride is something they can do for a son who died young while working to support the family. It is said that ghost marriages take place in many parts of the world, including China, Sudan, South Sudan, France, and the US, among others.

2. However, since they occur in such geographically diverse areas, there are various reasons and ceremonies associated with them. According to Nuär customary law,

the reason behind this ghost marriage is to make sure that the deceased person ought to continue his life here on earth with his relatives otherwise, his life will diminish. However, most importantly, if he is the elder son among his brothers, justice will take priority for his brothers to marry him a wife before theirs.

Article 11.3 About Role at Home

In very Nuär culture both in the West and in the East, it is the woman who cooks and sweeps the house otherwise, the opposite will be considered breaking news.

Article 11.4 About Entitlement of Children

1. According to customary law, any undivorced wife always belongs to her husband. She goes away due to some reasons with her husband; she will always remain the wife of that man. She begets children with another man, the children will belong to her husband due to the fact she is not divorced by her husband. She is considered as a concubine.)

2. If she looks for another man when her husband dies, the family of the deceased person will claim the children. This is because the death of each partner is not the end of marriage according to the African indigenous perspective. If the husband dies, the wife belongs to the family of the deceased person including the children.

Title XII. Rules that Govern In-Laws

1. The various we have discussed are related to marriage. However, no person can enter marriage without specific terms such as in-laws. The term in-law refers to the relationship through marriage. In this regard, various words fit for communication between in-laws otherwise.

Article XII.1 Required Word for Communication

1. According to Nuär, it is never permissible for the son-in-law to call his mother-in-law by name or his father-in-law by name. He is expected to call his mother-in-law mandi̠d (mathu) and father-in-law guandi̠d (ga̠thu). Both father-in-law and mother-in-law are expected to call their son-in-law gatŋu. These terms are applicable on both sides unless other suitable nicknames are used such as the colour of one's ox.

Article 12.2 Rule of Eating Together for the In-Laws

1. It is expected after marriage everyone will assume that the two families become in-laws. However, it ought to be pointed out that does not involve eating together, especially with fathers-in-law on both sides and mothers-in-law on both and son-in-law. According to Nuär, there must be an official way in which the fathers-in-law or mothers-in-law and son-in-law can eat in the house of each other otherwise. We use the fathers-in-law and mothers-in-lathe w in the plural for good reason. This is because the word in-laws is inclusive.

Article XIII About Physical Harm

1. Regarding physical harm which can later lead to death, the Nuär customary law provides various degrees of penalty based on each case. This is because in some cases, a human person can be wounded but may not die immediately.

Article 13.1 Thöŋ Nyindiɛt

1. When another person wounds a person, and he survives for two years, and then later on dies, it is called nyindiɛt. In this case, the support of eyewitnesses or pursuit must be provided and the incident must be reported immediately to the nearest chief or elders by then. If the wounded person dies before two years have elapsed, it is a matter of murder. For example, if the wound is practical or visible, there is a fright, even if he dies after two years, it is a murder, and Nyindiɛt is compensated with (25) head of cattle.

2. If a man kidnaps a girl and she dies in hiding before her parents are informed of her whereabouts, the parents will be paid compensation of (15) head of cattle. This is called (thöŋ yikä).

Article 13.2 Physical Injury

1. Under common law only, pulling out a girl's teeth is unacceptable. Therefore, if a girl has someone's teeth removed, that person must pay compensation that depends on the number of teeth removed. In addition, the girl's teeth were pulled out in this incident; it is up to the elders and Kuär Muɔ̱ɔ̱n to solve the problem by summoning the two families to handle the case.

2. Furthermore, whoever removed the girl's teeth should pay compensation. However, the compensation depends on the number of teeth. If it is a tooth, he/she pays a bull (ruath) and the calf dɔw) of one year. For a woman, one calf and bull, but if she is an old woman, one bull only.

Article 13.3 Intentional and Accidental Murder

1. According to Nuär customary law, there is a difference between intentional and accidental killing. The compensation for intentional killing will require compensation of, 50 head of cattle whereas accidental killing will require compensation, of 35 head of cattle.

2. However, murder is described as the unlawful intentional killing of a human being by another. This type of killing a human person in cold blood is considered a crime and not acceptable

Article 13.4 The Role of Women During the Fighting

1. For example, when the men when for fighting the women followed them. Women knew that when their men fought there, killing may occur, and one side may be defeated. Usually, when men are fighting, women also follow them and carry their sticks. Sometimes, few men cannot run faster. In such a situation, if a man is caught, women will run to rescue him and take him inside the house. It is never allowed to kill women who protect the wounded person or someone who is caught and protected by women.

Article 13.5 If a Woman is Killed by Her Husband or If She Kills a Person

1. A man cannot kill a woman. If a man killed his wife, he must pay the remaining dowry first, and after that, the compensation shall be paid to him as well. If she kills a person, her husband shall be responsible for paying the compensation. This article is unique in terms of exempting a woman from the crime she has committed. Always the husband will shoulder the responsibility and not the woman.

Title XIV. The Role of Earth-Master-Kuäär Muɔ̱ɔ̱n

1. According to Nuär, the common law described the Kuäär muɔ̱ɔ̱n's procedure for settling the killing dispute as follows. Once a man kills another person, he rushes to a Kuäär muɔ̱ɔ̱n's house to cleanse himself from the blood he has shed on the ground. He is not allowed to drink or eat until the dead man's blood has been drained from his body. For it is believed that the blood of an innocent man may poison him in some ways. To do this, the Kuäär muɔ̱ɔ̱n makes one or two vertical cuts on his arm by stroking down from the shoulder with a fishing spear. The murderer offers the Kuäär Muɔ̱ɔ̱n an ox, a ram, or a he-goat as a sacrifice. This rite and sign are known as Bi̱e̱r.

2. As soon as the dead person's relatives learn that he has been killed, they try to avenge his death on the killer, for revenge is the most binding obligation of paternal kinship and the epitome of all their obligations. By living with the Kuäär Muɔ̱ɔ̱n as a guest from the moment his arm was cut off, until the final settlement, the murderer has asylum because

the Kuäär Muɔ̱ɔ̱n is sacred and no blood may be spilled on his homestead.

Title XV. Compensation-Cuut

1. According to the Nuär theory, forty to fifty head of cattle are paid, but they are unlikely to be paid all at once. The atonement ceremony is performed when about twenty have been handed over, and then the killer's relatives can walk around without fear of being mugged, at least for the time being. Even if all the cattle are paid, there is always a risk of revenge.

Conclusion

Chapter ten discusses Title I, about various impediments of Nuär marriage, including ten impediments, it further explains Title II, about the ritual ceremony of twins Article III about penalties of sexual misconduct, and Title IV, about various norms that govern inheritance of a deceased's wife. Furthermore, the chapter also has explained Title V, about rules that govern sexual relations before death; Title VI, about norms for levirate and ghost marriages, title VII, about physical harm, title VIII, about the role of Earth-Master-Kuäär Muɔ̱ɔ̱n and finally, title IX, about compensation-cuut.

CHAPTER ELEVEN

RECOMMENDATION

Introduction

Chapter eleven deals with recommendations in areas of the Church, on the promotion of cultural heritages, which are compatible with Gospel virtues and values. It also treats various prophets and magicians-dayiɛmni̱, which ought to be abandoned. The chapter ends with the use of the words ought to and ought not to about those issues above-mentioned.

Furthermore, the chapter also explicates customs that are mere conventions and those that are inherent in human nature. It explains principles like first, the principle of respect for human dignity. Second, the preferential option for the poor and vulnerable. Third, the principle of solidarity. Fourth, the principle of subsidiarity. Fifth, the principle of dignity of work and the rights of workers. Sixth, the principle of common good. Seventh, the principle of promotion of peace. Eighth, the principle of participation. Ninth, the principle of rights and responsibilities. Tenth, the principle of the role of government. Eleventh, is the principle of stewardship of creation (ecology).

The chapter expounds the transcendental morality and horizontal morality as stipulated in the book of Ex. 31: 18 and 34:1–29. All these principles, ought to become part of the practical life of contemporary Nuär communities.

11. For the Promotion of Nuär Cultural Values

Jesus said, "Do not think that I have come to abolish the law or the prophets. I have come not to abolish but to fulfil. Amen, I say to you, until heaven and earth pass away, not the smallest letter or the smallest part of the letter will pass from the law until all things have taken place" (Mt 5:17-18). Referring to the quotation from the Sacred Scripture above does not justify any cultural values to be good as the law or prophets, but rather, Jesus' teaching can purify cultural values. Each Nuär man or woman can never assume every cultural value of Nuär people is perfect. However, our assessment of cultural values, ought to allow us to those that are not compatible with the pulse virtues and values. In this regard, Jesus did not come to abolish good cultural values but rather to enrich them and purify them with the gospels' virtues and values.

Neither does the Church in her teaching, abolish cultural values but rather promotes those good ones that are compatible with the gospels' virtues and values. In fact, in every culture in which Jesus has accepted, that culture of a particular people ought to be ready to allow the gospels' virtues and values to permeate that culture to give it true meaning and perfection. In this regard, the majority of Nuär from different denominations who have accepted his teaching, ought to bring along with them their good customary and cultural values. Jesus confirmed this in the Gospel of Matthew as he says, "Then every scribe who has been instructed in the kingdom of heaven is like the head of a household who brings from his storeroom both the new and the old" (Mt 13: 52). Therefore, it will be unfortunate, for anybody to follow him with empty hands.

According to St. John Paul II, inseparable as they are from people and their history, cultures share the dynamics, which the human experience of life reveals. He asserts that they change and advance because people meet in new ways and share their ways of life. In this, the Church believes that cultures are fed by the communication of values, and they survive and flourish insofar as they remain open to assimilating new experiences. The Nuär ought to know that all people are part of a culture, depend upon it, and shape it. The Nuär must know that human beings are both children and parents of the culture in which they are immersed.

Furthermore, the teaching of the magisterium states that it is only through culture that everything they do, they bring something, which sets them apart from the rest of creation such as their unfailing openness to the mystery and their boundless desire for knowledge. The Nuär ought to know that lies deep in every culture; there appears this impulse towards fulfilment. St. John Paul II says that culture itself has an intrinsic capacity to receive divine revelation as the teaching of the magisterium affirms.

The Nuär ought to agree with the teaching of the magisterium, which states that cultural context permeates the living Christian faith, which contributes in turn little by little, to shaping that particular context of culture. The Nuär must concur with St. John Paul II when he says that to every culture Christians, bring the unchanging truth of God, which he reveals in the history and culture of a people.

11.1 For the Call for Unity in Diversity

Repeatedly, the Church states that in the course of centuries, we have seen repeated events witnessed by the pilgrims in Jerusalem on the day of Pentecost. After the multitude heard about the preaching of the Apostles, they asked one another: "Are not all these who are speaking Galileans? In addition, how is it that we hear, each of us in his native language? Parthians and Meds and Elamites and residents of Mesopotamia, Judea and Cappadocia, Pontus and Asia, Phrygia and Pamphylia, Egypt and parts of Libya belonging to Cyrene, and visitors from Rome, both Jews and proselytes, Cretans and Arabia, we hear them telling in our tongues the mighty works of God" (Acts 2:7-11).

The Nuär ought to know that the celebration of the day of Pentecost is the birth of the Church in Jerusalem in which everybody hears the preaching of the Apostles. The Nuär must know that the descent of the Holy Spirit upon the Apostles had brought understanding in terms of communication, unity in diversity, and readiness to receipt baptism, in contrast to the tower of Babble. (In the Bible) a tower built in an attempt to reach heaven, which God frustrated by making its builders speak different languages so that they could not understand one another (Genesis 11:1–9). In this sense, each Nuär man and woman ought to work for unity in diversity both in the Church and in the society otherwise. After descending the Holy Spirit upon the Apostles, everyone must work for unity in diversity, unless someone, chooses to remain at the tower of babble.

Furthermore, the teaching of the magisterium asserts that "While it demands of all who hear it the adherence of faith, the proclamation of the Gospel in different cultures allows people to preserve their own cultural identity" (*Fides and Ratio* no.*71*). This in no way, creation of division, because the community of the baptized, is marked by a universality which can embrace every culture and help to foster whatever is implicit in them to the point, where it will be fully explicit in the light of truth.

11.2 For the Criteria of Promotion of Nuär Local Culture

St. John Paul II affirms that this means that no one culture can ever become the criterion of judgment, much less the ultimate criterion of truth about God's revelation. The Nuär ought to know this principle of inclusivity. They ought to know that the Gospel is not opposed to any culture. The gospel does not seek to strip it of its native riches and force it to adopt forms, which are alien to it. On the contrary, they ought to know that the message, which believers bring to the world and cultures, is a genuine liberation from all the disorders caused by sin and is, at the same time, a call to the fullness of truth.

The Nuär ought to know that the Church teaches that cultures are not only diminished by this encounter, rather they are prompted to open themselves to the newness of the Gospel's truth and to be stirred by this truth to develop in new ways. According to St. John Paul II, in preaching the Gospel, Christianity first encountered Greek philosophy; but this does not mean at all other approaches are precluded. The Nuär must know that today, as the Gospel gradually comes into contact with cultural worlds, that once lay beyond Christian influence, there are new task of inculturation, which mean that our generation faces problems not unlike those faced by the Church in the first centuries.

St. John Paul II confirms that my thoughts turn immediately to the lands of the East, so rich in religious and philosophical traditions of great antiquity. Among this land, India has a special place. A great spiritual impulse leads Indian thought to seek an experience, which would liberate the spirit from the shackles of time and space and would therefore acquire absolute value. The dynamic of this quest for liberation provides the context for great metaphysical systems.

Nuär must know that it is the duty of Christians now to draw from this rich heritage the elements compatible with their faith, to make their contributions to Christian thought. In this work of discernment, which finds its inspiration in the Council's Declaration *Nostra Aetate*, certain criteria will have to be kept in mind as St. John Paul II stipulates and articulates them as follows: 'The first of these is the universality of the human spirit, whose basic needs are the same in the most desperate cultures.

The second, which derives from the first, is this: in engaging great cultures for the first time, the Church cannot abandon what she has gained from her inculturation in the world of Greco-Latin thought. Third, care will need to be taken lest, contrary to the very nature of the human spirit, the legitimate defence of the uniqueness and originality…of particular cultural tradition should remain closed in its difference and affirm itself by opposing other traditions" (*Fides and Ratio* no.72).

11.3 Monogamy According to the Nuär People

The sacred Scripture speaks of the creation of man and woman as a pair that is, opposite to each other, male and female. The concept of pair fits in the context of monogamy and not in the context of polygamy or polyandry which Nuär ought to know. Neither is it to be understood in the context of gays and lesbians nor the context of various sexual perversions. The term "pair" in the sacred scripture involves the creation of both male and female and of all higher and lower creatures. It is meant by God for the propagation of offspring and the continuity of species. The Nuär people are recommended to enrich themselves with this knowledge regarding marriage

The Elohistic tradition in the sacred Scripture asserts that "God created mankind in his image; in the image of God he created them; male and female he created them. God blessed them and God said to them: Be fertile and multiply; fill the earth and subdue it" (Gen 1:27-28). In this doctrine of monogamy, there is no room for polyandry and polygamy neither for gays nor for lesbians and not even other sexual perversions.

The Yahwistic tradition in the sacred Scripture said, "So the LORD God cast sleep on the man, and while he was asleep, he took out one of his ribs and closed up its place with flesh. The LORD God then built the rib that he had taken from the man into a woman. When he brought her to the man, the man said: This one, at last, is bone of my bones and flesh of my flesh. This one shall be called 'woman', for out of man this one has been taken" (Gen 2: 21- 23).

The doctrine of original paradise about monogamy as presented by the sacred scripture on the creation of Adam and Eve as male and female demonstrates the desire of God for monogamy. Adam confirmed this doctrine when he said 'this one, at last, is bone of my bones and flesh of my flesh. It is believed that men and women were created equal to complement each other as pairs. It is stated that as soon as Adam sees his wife, he realizes that she is completely different from all other creatures; she is flesh from his flesh, bone from his bones. This implies Jewish expression, which means that they are of the same nature and the same dignity.

This solemn celebration of the 'Ever First Union' between Adam and Eve in the original paradise that was instituted by God. He was the cause and origin of it. God brought Eve to Adam in which he could also use other means but he did it by himself to prove that he was the first to administer the Divine solemn celebration of the wedding between Adam and Eve. By his presence, he was the witness and Divine Minister of the first marriage ceremony.

Consequently, God has to hear to the consent of Adam. The consent of Adam in his words that says 'this one, at last, is bone of my bones and flesh of my flesh' demonstrates that he was responding to Eve willingly, freely, consciously, and fairly. The response Adam displays is that he is satisfied with his single wife. He did not complain to God for giving him only one woman in the original paradise nor did he say to God, this woman will not be enough for him please, add more. Adam accepts Eve and endorses monogamy in the original paradise.

Adam's words which read: this one, at last, is bone of my bones and flesh of my flesh' express complete satisfaction. These words in another way demonstrate what the bridegroom and the bride do say to one another during the celebration of the sacrament of matrimony when exchanging their rings in the Church in the presence of a witness or minister. These words go beyond the contemporary expression of love and are sometimes very ambiguous and confusing due to various motives. The words of Adam are clear and distinct. Consequently, Adam knew that one can never lie before God because God reads the hearts and minds of all. In this regard, the teaching of both Elohistic and Yahwistic traditions about monogamy ought to be embraced by Nuär people.

11.4 For Areas of Concern in Family Life

The Nuär ought monogamy ought to know monogamy requires courageous choice in line with God's plan institution of marriage. It is observed that the majority of contemporary Nuär whether living in villages or towns, seem to have engaged in drinking irresponsibly. Consequently, has a great impact on marital life, up to the point of abandoning wife and children. This unhealthy attitude ought to be discarded. It must be recommended married men should to take care of their children and their wives while idleness ought to be avoided completely. In case of sickness, care for each member of the family ought to be considered.

In the towns and megacities, there are manifestations of unhealthy foreign practices such as having a boyfriend or a girlfriend in such a way, that a boy and a girl, behave as if they were already husband and wife. This must be avoided completely. Regarding responsibility at home, each couple ought to be encouraged to carry out his/her duties to contribute to the benefit of the family. Specific reference must direct to both informal and formal education for the children.

In informal education, re-visiting cultural values of shame and respect, ought to be restored. Furthermore, beating wives, ought to be avoided, and love for each other couple, must be prioritized within the family's environment. In this regard, love between couples, ought to be enriched with human virtues and cultural values. This requires true love for the person as she is.

Furthermore, on the one hand, if monogamy is recommended for the Nuär who have embraced Christianity, on the other hand, polygamy, ought to be discouraged. Therefore, for the good of the family, sleeping in hotels and constantly eating in restaurants by men ought to be stopped. This is because such money, which is used in renting hotels and eating constantly in restaurants, must be used for the welfare of the family otherwise.

Nuär women are recommended to shun any unhealthy practices such as magic, witchcraft, and various forms of diviners-dayiɛmni̱. Should there be any case of sickness within the family, first seeking medical diagnoses and prayer are required.

12.4.1 For Bride-Wealth and Dignity of Nuär Women

Some people say marriage, is a sale not the consent of the two spouses in Nuär society, which ought to be avoided. A woman ought not to be treated as a body but as a partner and a human being with full dignity; even cows are not compatible with her own life. Women's rights and dignity ought to be the same as those of men in Nuär. The concept, which says, if you killed your wife, you simply add heads of cattle to the bride's wealth, ought to be stopped. A woman ought to have a right to acquire her property justly through her hard work.

Traditionally, it is believed that anything that a woman acquires would belong to her husband. For example, if she kills or injures somebody, her husband ought to pay the damage or compensation. The Nuär believed that her husband, ought to have full control over her, once he paid all the bride wealth. In this sense, the bride-wealth must not be considered as buying her own life but rather as a traditional system required for customary marriage among the Nuär. It ought to be recommended that this traditional customary system of marriage among the Nuär must be re-visit and analyzed, to eradicate untrue understanding of marriage about bride-wealth.

According to this new approach to marital relationships, a woman ought to maintain a healthy relationship, first with her husband, family, and friends. The same is expected from men too. She must avoid any unhealthy relationships with outsiders which is also true for her husband. Marriage ought to be understood as an investment among the Nuär communities because it is an instrument for procreation that guarantees the continuity of life here on earth.

11.5 For Areas to be Safeguarded in Marital State

The areas that ought to be safeguarded in marital life among the Nuär are as follows: love and respect between the prospect bride and the prospect bridegroom which includes the two sides of kinsmen ought to be maintained. It must be recommended that throughout marital life, the bridal name ought to be valued as a sign of respect. In this sense, the terms bride and bridegroom must have no limit about time, and age as well. Furthermore, couples of Nuär as well as other tribes, ought to know that the terms bride and bridegroom are instruments to be used for martial renewal, in terms of relationships between couples. These two terms are very powerful and essential elements to be used for creating an atmosphere e of joy and happiness between couples.

It ought to be recommended that the marital steps such as various ceremonial steps are to be observed. The functional roles of two representatives of the bride kinsmen and the bridegroom kinsmen such as jackɔk-crow or gua̲n böthni̲ are to be observed and respected. The official traditional way of allowing the bride to give birth at her parents' home ought to be maintained if circumstances require. All the issues related to impediments, are to be observed. Both the prospective bride and the prospective bridegroom must go for medical testing before they marry each other for verification of capability to procreate. It ought to be recommended that marital life, must be renewed within the couples in many various ways as we have emphasized earlier.

11.6 For Areas to be Shunned in Marital Life

We ought to point out that some areas in Nuär marriage are not valuable: the exaggeration of asking too much from the bridegroom kinsmen in megacities and towns has become unaffordable. It is unfortunate to hear that the bride's kinsmen through their spokesman or representative nicknamed jackɔk-crow or gua̲n böthni̲ will ask the bridegroom's kinsmen to pay the money that was used for educating their daughter. It must be recommended that all parents have the right to educate their daughter whether she is going to be married or not. There should be no such a claim from the side of the family of the bride's kinsmen through the spokesman. This is because they have a moral duty towards the education of their daughter regardless of marriage.

It must be recommended that elopement and early marriage in Nuär communities as well as in other tribes in Africa ought to be stopped completely. Forced marriage both for males and females must be shunned by the parents. Marriage for diseased, barren, impotent, polygamy, and marriage without responsibility ought to be stopped. Taking the wife of a deceased as your own ought to be avoided.

It ought to be recommended that superficial response to love such as that of Nyakiir Bol Yɔ̱a̱l who was eloped at a village called Thör from Dok Nuär to Laag Nuär by a beast nicknamed 'Gatluak Maŋuɛl' ought to be avoided. Therefore, any prospective bride and prospective bridegroom who would like to engage themselves ought to have enough time to know themselves well before they enter marriage.

11.7 For the Promotion of Inculturation

According to the assessment I made about various issues practised by Nuär people, such as mysterious powers, traditional powers, and ritual ceremonial stages of twins, it ought to be pointed out that any attempt for inculturation, requires dialogue between the Gospel's values/virtues, and cultural values of the indigenous people. The gap is too big, and the ignorance between the cultural values of the indigenous people and the gospel is great. Furthermore, this requires an identification of categories of people within the Church and outside the Church within our locality.

Therefore, instead of passing judgment on the cultural values of the indigenous people without listening to them through deep dialogue, we ought to pay careful attention to the preservation of the local people. We must discover their concern, and fears and cling to their cultural values to understand them. The local clergy, ought to engage their people, using their local language as a tool to discover the myths, philosophy of life, and certain beliefs about their traditional religion. In this sense, it will be possible for them to assume the role, which was previously exercised by traditional leaders. For example, the ritual ceremony of twins about Nuär people.

11.8 For Careful Evaluation of Mysterious and Traditional Powers

When dealing with chapter three about God's attributes and other mysterious powers, we have discovered that the exercise of those powers overshadowed the true belief in One God. People seem to trust so much those powers, even though they bring more harm to them than good, especially the mysterious powers. The good news is that those mysterious powers are now disappearing among the Nuär people. People who embraced Christianity, shun to exercise them and are even threatened by the rest. Furthermore, if some still exist, people ought to know that they should not practice them anymore.

However, the difficult part is the exercise of traditional powers, which I think, can be problematic to Christianity. We must point out that no clergy can exercise those traditional powers due to their peculiarities and intrinsic characteristics.

However, some need serious evaluation about the benefits or harm they can bring to the local people.

11.9 For Observation of Moral Principles

On the one hand, it must be pointed out that in any culture, there are mere customs such as stable manners, modes of dress, and forms of speech, greetings, dancing, and singing subject to change in different parts of the world. On the other hand, there are customs or supernatural precepts inherent in human nature such as first, the principle of respect for human dignity. Second, the preferential option for the poor and vulnerable.

Third, the principle of solidarity. Fourth, the principle of subsidiarity. Fifth, the principle of dignity of work and the rights of workers. Sixth, the principle of common good. Seventh, the principle of promotion of peace. Eighth, the principle of participation. Ninth, the principle of rights and responsibilities. Tenth, the principle of the role of the government. Eleventh, is the principle of stewardship of creation (ecology). These principles of the Catholic Social doctrine are to be observed by Nuär couples and other couples from other tribes as well.

According to the social doctrine of the Church, there are immutable, unchangeable principles inherent in human nature. Therefore, they are recommended to contemporary Nuär to put them into practice in their daily lives. They observed that transcendental morality (vertical morality) and horizontal morality are articulated and stipulated in the book (Ex. 31: 18 and 34: 1 – 29). Those precepts that ought to be put into practice are as follows: first, you should have no other God before you. Second, you shall not take the name of the Lord your God in vain. Third, remember the Sabbath day, to keep it holy. Fourth, honour your father and mother. Fifth, you shall not kill. Sixth, you shall not commit adultery.

Seventh, you shall not steal. Eighth, you shall not bear false witness. Ninth, you shall not covet your neighbour's wife. Tenth, you shall not covet your neighbour's house, field, or anything that is of your neighbor. This Decalogue is the summary of the two commandments of love: love of God, love of neighbor, and love of oneself. This ought to be practised by the contemporary Nuär community without fails. With these divine precepts, the contemporary Nuär ought to respect natural laws, positive laws, and international laws and to have faith, hope, and love for God.

Love among couples which involves reconciliation and forgiveness within the communities ought to be exercised. Friendship, good relationships, hospitality, and generosity such as sharing as both receiving and giving ought to be practised without abuse. The traditional respect of elders, unity, and togetherness ought to be observed. Other actions such as moral implications that ought not to be exercised are: stealing, lying, robbery, revenge mentality, discrimination, nepotism, adultery, gossip, looting property of others, and raiding cattle both within the Nuär communities and of the Dinka communities ought to be stopped. Corruption, a sense of pride, diffidence, and gluttony ought to be avoided.

Conclusion

Chapter eleven has dealt with moral recommendations on areas where the Church on promotion of cultural heritages that are compatible with the Gospel, in areas of concern in marriage such as negative practices in marriage, areas which ought to be safeguarded in marital life, and areas which ought to be shunned in marital life. It has also treated various prophets and magicians-*dayiɛmni̠* which ought to be abandoned and it has clarified the bits of advice by the use of the words ought to and ought not to.

As we have seen above, the chapter deals with and illustrates customs that are mere conventions and those that are inherent in human nature. It explains principles such as: first, respect for human dignity. Second, the preferential option for the poor and vulnerable. Third, the principle of solidarity. Fourth, the principle of subsidiarity. Fifth, the principle of dignity of work and the rights of workers. Sixth, The principle of common good. Seventh, the principle of promotion of peace. Eighth, the principle of participation. Ninth, the principle of rights and responsibilities. Tenth, the principle of the role of government. Eleventh, is the principle of stewardship of creation (ecology).

The chapter expounds the transcendental morality and horizontal morality as stipulated in the book of Ex. 31: 18 and 34:1–29. All these have to be put into practice in the life of the contemporary Nuär society.

BIBLIOGRAPHY

1. Biblical

The African Bible, Nairobi, Paulines Publication Africa, 1999.

2. Magisterial Documents

Second Vatican Council, Pastoral Constitution on the Church in the Modern World, *Gaudium et Spes, AAS58,* (1965).

3. Books

Charon, J. Tab, Ethics *of Human Sexuality: A Call for Chastity in Christian Families*, Nairobi, CUEA Press, 2007.

___, Ecology, *Principle of Stewardship of Creation: The Basic Principles of the Social Teaching of the Church, Its Relevance to the African Context,* Juba, Printers Company Ltd, 2018.

____, The Nuär Origin, Culture, and Moral Evaluation, Rafiki for Printing and Publishing, Juba, 2021.

Kulang, Duoth, Bichiok and Ruot, Paul Kor, *The Nuër Kiir People*, Juba, Rafiki for Printing & Publishing, 2017.

Howell, P.P. *A Manual of Nuër Law*, New York, Oxford University Press, 1954.

Hutchinson, Sharon E. *Nuër Dilemmas. Coping with Money, War and the State*, London,
University of California Press, 1996.

Johnson, Douglas H. *Nuër Prophets, A History of Prophecy from the Upper Nile in the*
Nineteenth and Twentieth Centuries, New York, Oxford University Press, 1994.

Magesa, Laurenti, *African Religion, the Moral Traditions of the Abundant Life,* Nairobi,
Paulines Publications Africa, 1998.

Manschreck, Clyde L., *A History of Christianity in the World, From Persecution to Uncertaint*
New Jersey, Prentice-Hall, INC, 1974.

McKeon, Richard, (ed.), *Introduction to Aristotle*, New York, The Modern Library,

Mbiti, John, *African Religion & Philosophy,* Kampala, East African Educational Publishers
Ltd, 1969.

Nyamiti, Charles *Studies in African Christian Theology*, Vol. 2. Jesus Christ, the Ancestor of
Humankind: An Essay on African Christology, Nairobi: CUEA Press, 2007.

Peschke, Karl H. *Christian Ethics*, Moral Theology in the Light of Vatican II, Vol. 1. Alcester,
C. Goodlife Neale, 1989.

Pritchard, E.E. Evans, *Nuër Religion,* New York: Oxford University Press, 1956.

Riek, Jedeit. J & Pendle, Naomi R., *Speaking Truth to Power in South Sudan, Oral Stories of*

the Nuër Prophets, Nairobi, Rift Valley Institute, 2018.
Zeller, Edward, *Outline of the History of Greek Philosophy*, New York, The World Publishing
Company, 1795.

4. Dictionaries

Dictionary, Eleventh Edition, Massachusetts, U.S.A. Merriam-Webster, Incorporated, 2003.
Merriam-Webster's Collegiate Dictionary Tenth Edition, Massachusetts, U.S.A. Merriam-
Webster, Incorporated, 2000.

5. Articles

George P. Murdock, Arthur Tuden, and Peter B. Hammond, "African Negro Art;
Anthropology;
Archaeology: Ancient Civilization; Muslims" in the *Collier's Encyclopedia, Volume 1 of*
Twenty-Four Volumes, New York, P.F. Collier & Son Limited, (1995), pp. 257-259.
Fehlman, F.Y. (ed.), "Sexuality, Biological and Psychological Theory of." *in the Dictionary of*
Pastoral Care and Counseling, Nashville, Abingdon Press, (2005), pp. 1151-1154.
MurDock, George P., Tuden, Arthur and Hammond, Peter B., "African Negro Art;
Anthropology; Archaeology; Egypt: Ancient Civilization" in the *Collier's Encyclopedia,* Vol.
I. of Twenty-Four Volumes, New York: (1995), pp. 260-270.
Nelson, J. B. (ed.), "Sexuality, Christian Theology and Ethics of." in the *Dictionary of*

Pastoral Care and Counseling, Nashville, Abingdon Press, (2005), pp. 1154-1158.

Pui, Yak James, *The Nuär Culture*, Rak Media Group for Printing, Juba, 2021.

Pritchard, E.E. Evans, "Africa: Journal of the International African Institute" Vol. 18, No. 1
(Jan., 1948), pp. 29-40, Cambridge University Press on behalf of the International African
Institute Stable.

Vayhinger, J. M. (ed.), "Sexual Variety, Deviance, and Disorder" in the *Dictionary of Pastoral*
Care and Counseling, Nashville, Abingdon Press, (2005), pp. 1149-1151.

6. Internet Source

Dr Francis Ayul Yuar can be reached viafrancisnyok@yahoo.com as of 13/03/2023.

APPENDIX

Guit County Jikäny Clan	
Kuerge̱ŋ Payam	It belongs to Cieŋruɛ̈ɛ̈
Thörkɛ̈ɣni̱ Buma	It belongs to Cieŋge̱ŋ
Dhɔrɛ̈ɛ̈k Buma	It belongs to Cieŋyian
Ci̱liny Buma	It belongs to Cieŋwuɔ̱t
Kuac Payam	It belongs to Thiääŋ
Kue̱rkol Buma	It belongs to Cieŋlɛm/ Cieŋnyaluɔ̱k
Caŋ Buma	It belongs to Cieŋyɔl/ Cieŋkuɔth
Käät Buma	It belongs to cie̱ŋbur/ Cieŋyäär
Nyathɔ̱at Payam	Cieŋwaŋkɛ̈y
Dhɔrbuɔ̱k Buma	It belongs to Cieŋbol
Kue̱rthɔ̱ak Buma	It belongs to Gaatguaŋ
Kogak Buma	It belongs to Cirŋjɔak
Ke̱dët Payam	Cieŋdhulɛ̈ɛ̈k
Wi̱cruɔ̱p Buma	It belongs to Cieŋbön
Lathtaŋ Buma	It belongs to Cieŋcuɔl

Muɔmkuän Buma	It belongs to Cieŋmac
Kue̱rguini̱ Payam	Gaatguaŋ
Thɔa̱r Buma	It belongs to Cieŋwuröm
Dhɔrböör Buma	It belongs to Cieŋpinyiɛn/ Cieŋkɔ̱rɔ̱
Päm Buma	It belongs to Cieŋdup
Cɔ̱tyiël Payam	Thiääŋ Tharcieŋ
Burɛpiny Buma	It belongs to Cieŋjäŋ
Pagɛ̈ny Buma	It belongs to Cieŋta̱a̱r
Kue̱rthɔa̱k Buma	It belongs to Cieŋduäc/Cieŋda̱k
Wathyɔ̱tni̱ Payam	Cieŋyɔl
Mari̱al Buma	It belongs to Cieŋdhuɔŋ
Tho̱rgo̱k Buma	It belongs to Cieŋnyaduŋkär
The̱pcaak Buma	It belongs to Cieŋmalɛ[ɛ̈k
Bil Payam	Cieŋbii
Tharkueer Buma	It belongs to Cieŋnyäk
Kuanyrɔw Buma	It belongs to Cieŋjääŋ
Mayleek Buma	It belongs to Cieŋnyawaath

2. Rupkɔtni County Leek clan	
2.1 No̱r Payam	It belongs to Cieŋcuɔɔl
2.2 Ŋɔ̱p Payam	It belongs to Cieŋlɔkjaak
2.3 Wathjaak Payam	It belongs to Cieŋmatjaak
2.4 Panhia̱ny Payam	It belongs to Ke̱rluaal
2.5 Budaŋ Payam	It belongs to Padaaŋ
2.6 Kaljaak Payam	It belongs to Cie̱r
2.7 Rupkɔtn**i** Payam	It belongs to Cieŋgany
2.8 Dhɔrboo**r** Payam	It belongs to Cieŋlɛɣ

3. Mayɔm County Bul clan	
3.1 Kuerbuɔwni Payam	It belongs to Cieŋdiɛŋ
3.2 Ŋɔp Payam	It belongs to Gaatcaam
3.3 Mankien Payam	It belongs to Cieŋnyawäär
3.4 Waŋkɛ̈y Payam	It belongs to Cieŋparɛ̈ŋ
3.5 Riaak Payam	It belongs to Cieŋnyalɔak
3.6 Ruädhnyibol Payam	It belongs to Cieŋduɔk
3.7 Pup Payam	It belongs to Nyaŋ malɔak
Biɛk Payam	It belongs to Nyaŋgaatgaak
3.9. Kueryiek Payam	It belongs to Cieŋdäär
3.10. Waŋbuɔr Payam	It belongs to Cieŋcuɔɔl
.11. Rialthiaŋ	It belongs to Cieŋ lil

4. Koch County Jagɛy clan	
4.1 Jaak one Payam	It belongs to CieŋNuan
4.2 Jaak two Payam	It belongs to Cieŋyat
4.3 Ŋɔny Payam	It belongs to Padaŋ and Jabany
4.4 Pakur Payam	It belongs to Wuɔt
4.5 Buaw Payam	It belongs to Läärŋ
4.6 Gany Payam	It belongs to Kuey
4.7 Mirmir Payam	It belongs to Cieŋmök
4.8 Nor Payam	It belongs to Cɔndɔk

5.Mayiandit County Ɣaak clan	
5.1 Rupkuay Payam	It belongs to Cieŋkaaŋ
5.2 Tutnyaŋ Payam	It belongs to Cieŋcakuɔk
5.3 Mirnyäl Payam	It belongs to Nyiduät
5.4 Daplual Payam	It belongs to Kuey
5.5 Jakguär Payam	It belongs to Cieŋkuɔɔn

5.6 Luɔɔ̱m Payam	It belongs to Cieŋge̱ŋ/Cieŋyɔam
5.7 Madöl one Payam	It belongs to Cieŋnyäk
5.8 Madöl two Payam	It belongs to Cieŋda̱rnyɔap
5.9 Pabuɔ̱ŋ Payam	It belongs to Gaabaaŋ
5.10 Malkuër Payam	It belongs to Cieŋkui̱c
5.11 Buɔ̱r Payam	It belongs to Cieŋbakrial
5.12 Pullual Payam	It belongs to Ruɔ̱m

6. Leer County Dɔk clan	
6.1 Piliɛny Payam	It belongs to Gaatrɛŋ
6.2 Thɔnyɔɔ̱r Payam	It belongs to Cieŋluuth
6.3 Adɔk Payam	It belongs to Janbɛk one
6.4 Där Payam	It belongs to Janbɛk two
6.5 Bo̱w Payam	It belongs to Duɔɔ̱k
6.6 Payaak Payam	It belongs to Cieŋbaluɔny
6.7 Juɔŋ Payam	It belongs to Cieŋmärnyäl
6.8 Nyaŋdia̱r Payam	It belongs to Cieŋmär
6.9 Paluot Payam	It belongs to Cieŋluɔm
6.10 Kɔat Payam	It belongs to Cieŋba̱ny
6.11 Kayga̱y Payam	It belongs to Cieŋmuɔ̱t one
6.12 Dhɔrgɔcni̱ Payam	It belongs to Cieŋmuɔ̱t two
6.13 Guät Payam	It belongs to Gaakuay
6.14 Rup in ca̱r Payam	It belongs to Cieŋcuɔlguëth
6.15 Nyamirnyäl Payam	It belongs to Cieŋgäl
6.16 Yaŋ Payam	It belongs to Rɔɔ̱l

7. Panyijiar County Nyuɔŋ	
7.1 Mayɔm Payam	It belongs to Cieŋnyawäar one
7.2 Nyääl Payam	It belongs to Cieŋnyawäär two

7.3 Köl Payam	It belongs to Gaakaal
7.4 Tiep Paayam	It belongs to Lok
7.5 Thuanhom Payam	It belongs to Lok
7.6 Ganyliɛl Payam	It belongs to Cieŋtɛny
7.7 Paciɛnjɔk Payam	It belongs to Cieŋtɛny
7.8 Pacak Payam	It belongs to thääk
7.9 Pacar Payam	It belongs to Thääk

8. Fangak County	**It belongs to Lak and Thiaŋ**
Manɛjaaŋ (Juaiboor) Payam	It belongs to Cieŋ Nyapiir
Pakur buma (Taŋnyaŋ) buma	It belongɛ to cieŋ yɔai
Tharliɛɛl buma (Palɛy) buma	It belongs to Cieŋ jiguäk
Kuerwal Buma	It belongs to Cieŋ Duɔk
Kuɛmrɔany buma	It belongs to Cieŋ Nyieny
Barbuɔy Payam	It belongs to Cieŋ Kuduɔɔp
Kuernyaŋ Buma	It belongs to Cieŋ Luŋaai
Biɛi Buma	It belongs to cieŋ Thior
Waŋlɛɛl Buma	It belongs to Cieŋ Lɔk
Panyaaŋ buma	It belongs to cieŋ bath
Nor buma (Kuɛmduɔɔk)	It belongs to Cieŋ Nyabulä
Paguir Payam	**It belongs to ker**
Thokcak Buma	It belongs to Cieŋ Jɔk Däbuɔt
Nyimkuan Buma	It belongs to Cieŋ Cɔar Dhɔɔl
Kuerpön Buma	It belongs to Cieŋ kieec

Känynhial Buma	It belongs tp Cieŋ Man ruɛ̈ɛ̈ini and Cieŋ Wur
Ci̱o̱tbo̱o̱rä	It belongs to Cieŋ Dɔap, Ga̱ŋ, and Cieŋ Nyaköör
Puyai Buma	It belongs to Cieŋ Nyaja̱a̱ŋni
Pulita Payam	Thiääŋ & Cieŋ Kaaŋ
Kɛɛw Buma	It belongs to Cieŋ waŋ
Patai Buma	It belongs to Cieŋ Bol, Cieŋ Duoth, Cieŋ kök, Cieŋ Bum, Cieŋ Yäär and Cieŋ liɛm
Pajuɔŋ Buma	It belongs to Cieŋ cuak
Nyamitɛ (Thi̱a̱ŋɛdi̱a̱a̱r)	It belongs to Cieŋker
Kue̱rBilieu	It belongs to Cieŋ Ge̱m
Marɛ̈ɛ̈ŋ Payam	**It belongs to Thi̱a̱ŋ**
Töc Buma	It belongs to Cieŋ Gin
Dhɔrnöör	It belongs to It belongs to Cieŋ Jaak
Kue̱rdɛ̈ɛ̈ŋ	It belongs to Cieŋ Cuol
Nyadin Buma	It belongs to Cieŋ li̱e̱p yieer
Kue̱rtɛt	It belongs to Cieŋ li̱e̱p raar

9. Ayod County	It belongs to Gaatwäär
Ayod payam (pajiek)	It belongs to Ba̱a̱ŋ Yöl
Gɔrwaai Buma	It belongs to - cieŋ Malɛi Ba̱äŋ and Tɛɛny Ba̱a̱ŋ
Ke̱e̱r Buma	It belongs to cieŋ Bidiit
Yian Buma	It belongs to cieŋ juɔl
Juac Buma	It belongs to cieŋ Ruɔɔl

Welriäth Buma	It belongs to cieŋ Tööt
Kanaal Buma	It belongs to - cieŋ Turuoh/ Ja̱a̱ŋ
Mogo̱k Payam	**It belongs to cieŋ Tɛny**
Ɣa̱a̱t Buma	It belongs to Cieŋ pɛ̈r
Kändäk Buma	It belongs to Cieŋ TɛIny
Thuɔp Buma	It belongs to Cieŋ nyayguak/ kuorwai
Panyaaŋ Buma	It belongs to Cieŋ Tɛny
Pakuɛ̈ɛ̈m Buma	It belongs to Cieŋ käpɛl
Wau Payam buma	**It belongs to cieŋ Thööny**
Gaaguak buma cieŋ lɔŋ	It belongs to Cieŋ lɔ̱ŋ
Cuolmabuay Buma	It belongs to cieŋ dɔ̱ɔ̱l
Tɔŋɛdie̱e̱r Buma	It belongs to Padaaŋ
Pedek Buma	It belongs to Cieŋ Buoy
Paguoŋ Buma	It belongs to Cieŋ Caam
Pagil Payam buma	**It belongs to Ji̱the̱e̱p**
Wecdiɛŋ buma	It belongs to cieŋ Ga̱i
Wecdɛ̈ɛ̈ŋ buma	It belongs to jitheep
Chuilbuoŋ buma	It belongs to Jithe̱e̱p
Mätnimɛ buma	It belongs to Cieŋ Jɔak
Mätnimɛ buma	It belongs to Cieŋ Jɔak

10 Greater Akobo (Bieɣ) Lou clan	
Uror	**Cieŋda̱k**
10.1 Pieri̱ County (Pie̱ri̱)	It belongs to Cieŋ ki̱di̱t
10.2 Padie̱k County (Yuai)	It belongs to Lorjɔk

10.3 Pulcuɔl County (Pathai)	It belongs to Böör
10.4 We̱cko̱l County (Pamai)	It belongs to Maikir
10.5 Yiöl County (Muɔ̱tɔt)	It belongs to Yiöl
11.Nyiro̱l	**Gaatbaal**
11.1 Nyi̱ro̱l east County (Laŋke̱n)	It belongs to Cieŋläŋ
11.2 Nyi̱ro̱l north (Pulturuk)	It belongs to Cieŋthäc and mutcuok
11.3 Nyi̱ro̱l west (Pa̱di̱ŋ)	It belongs to Cieŋmök
11.4 Cuiil (Yakuac)	
12. Akobo	**Mor**
12.1 Akobo East (Akobo	It belongs to Jɔajɔa, Gaatliäɣ and Go̱n
12.2 Akobo west (Walgak)	It belongs to Jimaac and Jagueth
12.3 Akobo central (Buɔ̱ŋ)	It belongs to Jɔajɔa and gaatliäɣ

11. Nasir County (Cieŋ Nyalith)	**Gaat Jio̱o̱k**
Jikmir Payam	It belongs to cieng nyanjaok ka cieng wang
Kɔat Payam	It belongs to cieŋ jäŋ kɛnɛ cieŋ yɔalken
Kieckuon Payam	It belongs to cieŋ yiec kɛnɛ cieŋ yɔalken
Maker Payam	It belongs to nyaŋ kɛnɛ gaatguaŋ

Madiŋ Payam	It belongs to cieŋ nyakier kɛnɛ gaatguaŋ
Wanding Payam	It belongs to cieŋ kuɛk
Gacrieŋ Payam	It belongs to cieŋ caam kɛnɛ cieŋ duäc
Tiŋkaar Payam	It belongs to cieŋ nyathuol
Mandɛ̈ɛ̈ŋ Payam	It belongs to cieŋ buoi kɛnɛ cieŋ waŋ
Kuerɛŋge Payam	It belongs to cieng thiep
Rɔam payam	It belongs to cieŋ malɛ̈ɛ̈k kɛnɛ cieŋ yɔalken
Kier payam	It belongs to cieŋ wan kɛnɛ cieŋ waŋ
Thourdiŋ payam	It belongs to cieŋ nyaguak kɛnɛ cieŋ minyääl
Nasir payam	It belongs to cieŋ jɔak ka cieŋ minyääl
12. Ulang County (Cieng Lang, Gatbulbek)	
Dɔma payam	It belongs to cieŋ kueth
Yiag payam	It belongs to cieŋ duoth
Baarmaac payam	It belongs to cieŋ dɛ̈ɛ̈ŋ
Yomdiŋ payam	It belongs to cieŋ thor
Kuic payam	It belongs to cieŋ ŋuon
Kurmuo̱t payam	It belongs to cieŋ rɛŋ
Kerciot payam	It belongs to cieŋ ŋuon
Nyaŋɔ̱ɔ̱rɛ	It belongs to cieŋ gua̱ndɛ̈ɛ̈ŋ
To̱rbaar payam	It belongs to cieŋ thior
Makak payam	It belongs to Cieng Maac
Ulaŋ town/center payam	It belongs to cieŋ köör

13. Lo̲ŋɛchuk County	**Gajaak**
Udier payam	It belongs to thieng baar
Wajo payam	It belongs to caani
Pacime payam	It belongs to Roma
Jaak payam	It belongs to cieŋ kaaŋ
Cɔ̲tbora payam	It belongs to cieŋ kaaŋ
Pamac payam	It belongs to cieŋ nyaruony
Jaŋok payam	It belongs to cieŋ riadh
Guelguk payam	It belongs to cieŋ ga̲a̲c
Bɛlwaŋ payam	It belongs to cieŋ col
Jongjith payam	It belongs to cieŋ rɔaɣ
Malɔu payam	It belongs to cieŋ nyani
Mathia̲a̲ŋ Administrative center	It belongs to thiääŋ
Warwɛŋ payam	It belongs to cieŋ kueth
Malual payam	It belongs to cieŋ nyaja̲a̲ŋni
Guɛŋ payam	It belongs to cieŋ rie̲ŋ
Maiwut County	**Gaat Guaŋ**
Maiwut centre payam	It belongs to cieŋ waaw kɛnɛ cieŋ cany, Thi̲a̲ŋ
Jotoma payam	It belongs to cieŋ mandit kä cieŋ Ɣo̲th
Wunkir payam	It belongs to cieŋ jigɔal yac ka cieŋ Ɣo̲th
Ulɛŋ payam	It belongs to cieŋ car ka cieŋ kueth
Malɛk payam	It belongs to gaatwaw ka cieŋ kueth

Turɔ̱w payam	It belongs to cieŋ cany kä cieng jo̱krɔ̱a̱l
Jokɔ̱w payam	It belongs to cieng cany ka cieŋ mankuoth
Pagak payam	It belongs to thiääŋ kɛnɛ cieŋ cany
Kigilɛ payam	It belongs to Caayni
Pinythor payam	It belongs to cieŋ thiɛp

INDEX